THE RUSH CHRONOLOGY

The Recording & Release History Of The Band

By Patrick Lemieux

Published by
Across The Board Books™
Toronto, Ontario, Canada

The Rush Chronology. Copyright © 2015 by Patrick Lemieux. All Rights Reserved. This book may not be used or reproduced, in whole or in part, without written permission from the copyright holder except in the case of limited Fair Dealing or Fair Use (or similar with respect to territorial legislation) excerpts for critical articles and reviews. For information address Across The Board Books at: acrosstheboardbooks@outlook.com

The right of Patrick Lemieux to be identified as Author of this Work has been asserted by him in accordance with the Copyright Act of Canada, 1997.

ISBN: 978-1-926462-03-5

First print edition: September, 2015

Cover photograph:
Rush at Copps Coliseum, July 6, 2013 – *Clockwork Angels Tour*
© 2013, Patrick Lemieux
All Rights Reserved

Cover design by Patrick Lemieux

To Tom, Mark, Michael and Scott
Rush Bros.

Table of Contents

THE EARLY DAYS	1
YOU CAN'T FIGHT IT	11
RUSH	14
FLY BY NIGHT & CARESS OF STEEL	26
2112 & ALL THE WORLD'S A STAGE	37
A FAREWELL TO KINGS	46
HEMISPHERES	56
'LIVE IN ENGLAND'	64
PERMANENT WAVES	72
MOVING PICTURES & EXIT...STAGE LEFT	81
SIGNALS	91
COUNTDOWN	97
GRACE UNDER PRESSURE	102
POWER WINDOWS	108
MYSTIC RHYTHMS	114
HOLD YOUR FIRE	119
A SHOW OF HANDS	124
PRESTO	131
CHRONICLES	136
ROLL THE BONES	142
GANGSTER OF BOATS	146
COUNTERPARTS	152
BURNING FOR BUDDY	155
VICTOR	161
TEST FOR ECHO	165
RETROSPECTIVE I + II	170
DIFFERENT STAGES	176
GHOST RIDER	178
MY FAVOURITE HEADACHE	180
GRACE TO GRACE	183
VAPOR TRAILS	186
THE SPIRIT OF RADIO: GREATEST HITS 1974 – 1987 & RUSH IN RIO	192
FEEDBACK & R30	195
CANADA FOR ASIA	201
GOLD	204
SNAKES & ARROWS	209
SNAKES & ARROWS LIVE	216
WORKING MEN	222
CARAVAN + BU2B	225
TIME MACHINE	230
CLOCKWORK ANGELS	238
CLOCKWORK ANGELS TOUR	244
R40	250
R40 TOUR	256

What Is The Rush Chronology?

The Chronology tracks the known recording and release dates of Rush and its members' solo projects, collaborations and guest appearances, with the additional aim to account for every known version of songs the band members worked on and to document known live dates.

What you will find in this book is a chronological list of dates compiled from many sources. These dates range from exact days, to months, to seasons and to years, based on how specific the source material was. It is presented here in the most linear fashion for ease of reference and simplicity. Some entries are marked Date Unknown, because, despite exhaustive research, the date could not be found. These entries are placed where they seemed mostly like to have occurred, given what is known at the time of print.

You will also find descriptions of every known song version, including pre-release performances, edits, remixes and released live versions. Each such description is presented in the following way:

- Demos and Alternate takes appear with the date the sessions were recorded.

- Single Versions, Edits, Remixes, Non-album tracks, etc., appear with their original release dates.

- Live tracks released on singles or otherwise individually are listed with the concert, where they were recorded, with a few exceptions where the performance date isn't known.

The focus of the book being the band's recording and release history, there are inevitably periods of quiet on those fronts. Outside their studio and stage work, the Chronology does not endeavour to cover *every* interview or things like Neil Peart's many trips recounted in his travelogues and books. Some such dates emerged in the course of research and appear accordingly, if only to illustrate examples of their time away from work. Additionally, while major works like Neil's commercially released books are noted, writings for magazines and other publications are generally not noted, as they exceed the scope of the Chronology.

The author did his best to avoid mistakes or inaccuracies, and to be as transparent as possible. Should a mistake be found, it is hoped that the discrepancy is viewed as appearing despite the authors' efforts to the contrary.

Lastly, thanks go out to everyone whose work prior to this release formed the foundation upon which original research for the Chronology could be built. Credit is given where applicable throughout the main body of the text and as complete a list as possible of archival information used in the Chronology appears in the Bibliography section.

Patrick Lemieux
September, 2015

THE EARLY DAYS

1952

(July 23)
John Howard Rutsey is born to Howard and Eva Rutsey, Toronto, Ontario, Canada.

(September 12)
Neil Ellwood Peart is born to Glen and Betty Peart, Hamilton, Ontario, Canada.

1953

(July 29)
Gary Lee Weinrib is born to Morris and Mary Weinrib (nee Manya Rubenstein) in Willowdale, Toronto, Ontario, Canada. He would later be nicknamed **Geddy**, from the strong Polish pronunciation of "Gary" by his mother and would eventually adopt the stage name **Geddy Lee**.

(August 27)
Aleksandar Živojinović is born to Nenad and Melanija Živojinović in Fernie, British Columbia, Canada. At a later date, the family moves to Willowdale, Toronto, Ontario, Canada. He would later adopt the stage name **Alex Lifeson** (from Živojinović, meaning "son of life").

1954

(Date Unknown)
The **Peart** family moves to St. Catharines, Ontario, Canada.

1956

(Date Unknown)
The **Peart** family moves to Port Dalhousie, Ontario, Canada.

1958

(Autumn)
Neil Peart attends Gracefield Public School, Port Dalhousie, Ontario, Canada, starting in Grade 1 and continuing through to Grade 5.

Geddy Lee attends kindergarten with future actor/comedian Rick Moranis (MSN chat December 20, 2000). They are in the same class until grade 6.

1961

(January 1)
Port Dalhousie is amalgamated into St. Catharines, Ontario, Canada.

(September 11)
Hurricane Carla hits Texas, US, causing massive devastation and resulting directly in the deaths of 43 people. It is the most intense tropical cyclone to make landfall in the US. At Galveston, Texas, photographer Flip Schulke photographs the destruction. An altered image he captures at the Galveston Seawall is later used by **Rush** for their *Permanent Waves* album cover.

1962

(August 25)
Bobby "Boris" Pickett And The Crypt-Kickers release their single "Monster Mash."
"Limbo" – in 1997, **Rush** would use samples of this song in their instrumental off *Test For Echo*.

(November)
The Cookies release their single "Chains" in North America. **Neil Peart**, in a 1994 article he writes about his childhood for the *St. Catharines Standard*, says this was an influential song in his interest in the dynamics of music.

1963

(Date Unknown)
Alex Živojinović's cousin lends him a flamenco guitar, which **Alex** teaches himself to play.

(Dates Unknown)
Alex Živojinović and **John Rutsey** meet at St. Paschal Babylon Catholic School, Willowdale, Toronto, Ontario, Canada.

1965

(Date Unknown)
Morris Weinrib, father of **Gary Lee Weinrib**, dies of health complications from his time at the Dachau concentration camp during Word War II. **Weinrib** practices the Jewish mourning customs for 11 months minus 1 day.

(Date Unknown)
John Rutsey becomes a member of the The Guide. The line-up is Wayne Bulger, Leo Smits, Steve Barringer and **John Rutsey**.

(September 12)
Neil Peart is given a pair of drum sticks, a practice drum and lessons for his 13th birthday by his parents, as well as the offer of a full kit for his 14th birthday if **Neil** stays committed to drumming. He begins lessons with Don George, Peninsula Conservatory of Music, St. Catharines, Ontario, Canada.

(December)
Neil Peart performs live for the first time as one of the Royal Bakers in a school Christmas Pageant, drumming to a parody of The Rolling Stones "Get Off Of My Cloud," "Get Off Of My Pizza," at St. John's Anglican Church Hall, Port Dalhousie, St. Catharines, Ontario, Canada.

(December 25)
Alex Živojinović receives a guitar as a Christmas present.

1966

(Date Unknown)
Following his period of mourning, **Gary Weinrib** is once again allowed to listen to Western pop music.

(Summer)
Alex Živojinović visits relatives in Yugoslavia. He discusses the visit in a 2014 interview with *Guitar World* magazine, noting it was the summer he was 12 and that he brought with him the 7" single of "(I Can't Get No) Satisfaction," by The Rolling Stones.

(July 29)
Gary Weinrib celebrates his bar mitzvah at age 13.

(September 12)
Neil Peart is given a full drum kit by his parents for his 14th birthday.

1967

(Date Unknown)
Neil Peart (drums), Don Brunt (piano) and Don Tees (saxophone) form **The Eternal Triangle**. They play mostly covers. "LSD Forever" – an original number written by the band.

(Date Unknown)
The Eternal Triangle performs at a school variety show, Lakeport High School, St. Catharines, Ontario, Canada. The set list includes:

"LSD Forever"
"Drum Solo" – **Neil Peart** notes in 1994 that this was his first live performance of a drum solo.

(Date Unknown)

The Guide changes its name to Summerwind. The line-up is Wayne Bulger, Leo Smits, Peggy Smits, Steve Barringer and **John Rutsey**.

(Date Unknown)
The Eternal Triangle breaks up and **Neil Peart** joins Mumblin' Sumpthin'. Among Mumblin' Sumpthin's live repertoire are the following (according to the *Feedback* liner notes):
"Crossroads" – a cover of "Cross Road Blues," the 1937 song by Robert Johnson, later popularized by Cream.
"Summertime Blues" – a cover of the 1958 song by Eddie Cochran, using the 1968 arrangement by Blue Cheer.

(Summer)
Neil Peart and his family attend Expo '67, the World's Fair, in Montreal, Quebec, Canada.
"The Analog Kid" – During the family's stay at the campground, **Peart** meets and falls in love with a girl from Beach City, Ohio. They exchange letters later for a period of time. **Neil** notes in *Roadshow* that she is the "fawn-eyed girl with sun-browned legs" from this song written for *Signals*.

Gary Weinrib buys his first acoustic guitar.

Neil Peart gets a job at Lakeside Park, Port Dalhousie, St. Catharines, Ontario, Canada.
"Lakeside Park" – this job and his childhood/teen visits to the park inspire him to later write this song.

(Autumn)
Gary Weinrib meets **Alex Živojinović** in their Grade 9 year at Fisherville Junior High School, Willowdale, Toronto, Ontario, Canada. It's reported that **Weinrib**'s nickname **Geddy** starts to appear around this time.

(Date Unknown)
Alex Živojinović and **John Rutsey** form the band **The Lost Cause**, with Gary 'Doc' Cooper and Alan Grandy.

1968

(Spring)
The Lost Cause becomes **The Projection** with the addition of Bill Fitzgerald. Among **The Projection**'s live repertoire are the following (according to the *Feedback* liner notes):
"Crossroads" – a cover of "Cross Road Blues," the 1937 song by Robert Johnson, later popularized by Cream.
"Mr Soul" – a cover of the 1967 Buffalo Springfield song.
"Shape Of Things" – a cover of the 1966 song by The Yardbirds.
According to friend Ian Grady (later their roadie; GuitarInternational.com September 16, 2009), **The Projection** also played the following:
"Louie Louie" – they could play "the lead break" of the 1955 Richard Berry song, later popularized by The Kingsmen.
"For Your Love" – a cover of the 1965 song by The Yardbirds.
"Hungry" – a cover of the 1966 Paul Reverie & The Raiders song.

(April 7)
Neil Peart attends The Who concert, Canadian National Exhibition Coliseum, Toronto, Ontario, Canada. The opening acts are Raja, MC5 and The Troggs.

(Summer)
Neil Peart is fired from his job at Lakeside Park, Port Dalhousie, St. Catharines, Ontario, Canada, for his laidback approach to work.

(August)
Jeff Jones (bass guitar and lead vocals) joins **Alex Živojinović** (lead guitar and backing vocals) and **John Rutsey** (drums), who change their band's name from **The Projection** to *Rush* (the same is suggested by **Rutsey**'s older brother Bill).

(September 18)
Rush performs live at The Coff-In, St. Theodore's of Canterbury Anglican Church, Toronto, Ontario, Canada. In a 2002 interview with Chum TV, **Alex Lifeson** notes this was the date of the first *Rush* performance (he confirms the date in a VH-1 *Hangin' With Rush* interview in 2005).

(September 25)
Rush performs live at The Coff-In, St. Theodore's of Canterbury Anglican Church, Toronto, Ontario, Canada. **Geddy Weinrib** replaces Jeff Jones as bassist and singer. The official biography *Visions* says Jones chose to go to a party that night instead. In the *A Farewell To Kings* tour book, **Geddy** says **Alex** called him on the day because they needed a singer and that they rehearsed for a few hours before the show. **Geddy** says in a *Tylko Rock* interview (November, 1996) that Jones was drunk and that he got the call at 4 PM.

After the show, the band celebrates at Panzer's Deli, Willowdale, Toronto, Ontario, Canada, and **Weinrib** officially replaces Jones.

Note: *Visions* says these shows took place on Friday evenings, whereas the dates indicated are actually Wednesdays.

(Date Unknown)
Rush write the following during rehearsals in their basements:
"Losing Again" – from an idea by **John Rutsey**, who worked it out with **Alex Živojinović**.
"In The Mood" – **John Rutsey** notes in *Visions* that this was mostly written by **Geddy Weinrib**

(Dates Unknown)
Rush would continue to play school dances, drop-in centres, church basements and other local venues. Known dates are noted, though there are certainly many unknown such dates.

Mumblin' Sumpthin' disbands and "a few weeks later," according to **Neil Peart** in his book *Travelling Music*, he joins The Young Generation, who soon change their name to The Majority. The Majority plays high schools and small venues locally and around Ontario for the next few years. The line-up also changes periodically.

(November)
Rush performs live at The Coff-In, St. Theodore's of Canterbury Anglican Church, Toronto, Ontario, Canada. In attendance is Lindy Young, a local musician whose guitar **Alex Živojinović** borrows for the show.

(December 25)
Alex Živojinović asks Lindy Young to join *Rush* as keyboardist. The line-up is now **Alex Živojinović** (lead guitar and backing vocals), **John Rutsey** (drums), **Geddy Weinrib** (bass and lead vocals) and Lindy Young (keyboards and backing vocals)

(Winter)
Rush rehearses through the winter break.

1969

(Early January)
Rush performs live at The Coff-In, St. Theodore's of Canterbury Anglican Church, Toronto, Ontario, Canada.

Around this time Ian Grandy becomes the band's roadie (*GuitarInternational.com* January 23, 2009).

(February to April)
Rush continues to perform regularly around Toronto, Ontario, Canada. Around this time, they meet Ray Danniels, a young promoter and event organizer.

(Spring)
By this time, about a third of *Rush*'s live repertoire is original material (*Total Guitar* November, 2007).

(May)
Geddy Weinrib is kicked out of *Rush*, apparently at the insistence of **John Rutsey**. The remaining members reform as **Hadrian**, adding Joe Perna on bass and lead vocals. They take Ray Danniels on as manager under his promotions company S.R.O. Productions Ltd.

(May 3)
Geddy Weinrib attends **Hadrian**'s concert at The Coff-In, St. Theodore's of Canterbury Anglican Church, Toronto, Ontario, Canada, in order to help Joe Perna with the song lyrics.

Note: In the book *Visions* that **Lee** says he missed Jimi Hendrix' last Toronto performance to help out the band, placing it on this date.

(May 19)
Neil Peart attends The Who concert, The Rockpile, Masonic Temple, Toronto, Ontario, Canada. Leigh Ashford is also on the bill.

(June)
Geddy Weinrib forms the band **Ogilvie** with Sammy Rohr and Xavier "Sam" Dangler, a band which Ray Danniels also manages.

Lindy Young leaves **Hadrian** and is replaced by Bob Vopni.

Hadrian performs live at Northminster United Church, Willowdale, Toronto, Ontario, Canada.

(July)
Ogilvie changes its name to **Judd**.

Lindy Young joins **Judd**.

Hadrian performs its last gig at Willowdale United Church, Willowdale, Toronto, Ontario, Canada, before breaking up.

(July 20)
NASA mission Apollo 11, with Commander Neil Armstrong and Lunar Module Pilot Edwin "Buzz" Armstrong aboard the Lunar Module (Command Module Pilot Michael Collin is aboard the Command Module in orbit), historically lands on the surface of the moon, the first time humanity has done so. The landing is watched by **Neil Peart** with The Majority guitarist Terry Walsh and Terry's wife, Jill.
"Dreamline" – live performances of this song during the 2013 *Clockwork Angels* Tour are dedicated to the then-recently deceased Neil Armstrong.

(Dates Unknown)
The Majority breaks up. **Neil Peart** suggests joining the band JR Flood and they audition him. In order to spare the feelings of the current drummer, JR Flood decides to "break-up" and later reform with **Neil** on drums. Their manager is Brian O'Mara.

In the 'now reformed' **JR Flood** (line-up: Bob Morrison [organ], Paul Dickinson [guitar], Wally Tomczuk [bass], Gary Luciana [vocals] and **Neil Peart** [drums]), **Peart** writes a number of original songs, sharing songwriting duties with Luciani, including:
"The Little Red Fox"
"Gypsy"
"Retribution"
"You Don't Have To Be A Polar Bear To Live In Canada"

(August 18)
Geddy Weinrib attends Led Zeppelin's concert at The Rockpile, Masonic Temple, Toronto, Ontario, Canada, noted in a 2014 interview with *Guitar World* magazine. He is in the 2nd row.

Note: In the *Newcastle Journal Live* October 4, 2007, **Alex Lifeson** says he attended a 'Mighty Monday' rock night Led Zeppelin concert with his bandmates (presumably **Haridan**) on August 30th this year in Toronto, but there is no listing for Zeppelin performing on that date and the 30th was not a Monday (it was a Saturday), whereas the 18th *was* a Monday, so it was likely this concert **Alex Lifeson** and his band went to.

(Date Unknown)
Neil Peart drops out of high school to pursue music full time with **JR Flood**, on the condition with his parents that he gives it a year and goes back to school if full-time music does not work out.

(Date Unknown)
John Rutsey drops out of high school to focus on his music career.

(Date Unknown)
Various members of **Judd** and **Hadrian** form **Wild Woodpecker Revue** for a single show, venue unknown, Toronto, Ontario, Canada. The line-up is **Alex Živojinović**, **Geddy Weinrib**, **John Rutsey**, Sammy Rohr, Ian Grandy and Steve "Stove" Moffat.

(September)
Judd disbands.

John Rutsey contacts **Geddy Weinrib**, and with **Alex Živojinović** they reform *Rush*. Lindy Young is apparently also approached, but declines as he is attending Seneca College, Toronto, Ontario, Canada, and does not want to pursue music as a career (reportedly, he occasionally jams with them during rehearsals).

Note: With the help of Ray Danniel's promotion, *Rush* begins touring nights and weekends around Ontario from this point into 1970.

(Dates Unknown)
Rush writes more original material, including the following:
"Number 1"
"Keep In Line"
"Run Willie Run"
"Mike's Idea"
"Tale"

(October 14)
Neil Peart attends The Who concert, Canadian National Exhibition Coliseum, Toronto, Ontario, Canada.

1970

(Dates Unknown)
Manager Brian O'Mara sets up demo sessions with various Canadian record companies in an attempt to sign **JR Flood**. The first session is at Toronto Sound Studios and the second is at RCA Studios, both in Toronto, Ontario, Canada.

"Retribution (Toronto Sound Studios Demo)" 3:17
Written by Neil Peart
Appears on: Unreleased
This is earliest known proper studio recording of a member of Rush, with the added bonus of having been penned by Neil, as well (as opposed to being a period cover). In his book Travelling Music, Neil describes this as "an up-tempo song [...] about a karmic afterlife" and that pretty much sums this up. It's got that late-'60s groove and Neil's drumming is quite noticeable. Even back then he was not content with simply keeping the beat.

"Gypsy (Toronto Sound Studios Demo)" 4:22
Written by Neil Peart
Appears on: Unreleased
A bit more sophisticated now, this mid-tempo number reflects the more complex experimental sounds of the turn of the decade, such as that of Yes and King Crimson.

"Wake Up (Toronto Sound Studios Demo)" 3:51
Written by Neil Peart or Gary Luciani
Appears on: Unreleased
This track seems influenced by Yes and psychedelic rock of the period, as it's very much in that vein.

"It's Not Hard (Toronto Sound Studios Demo)" 4:04
Written by Neil Peart or Gary Luciani
Appears on: Unreleased
Like with "Wake Up," this piece chugs along nicely, demonstrating just how tight, if not rough around the edges, the musicianship was in this band.

"Lonely Man (Toronto Sound Studios Demo)" 3:49
Written by Neil Peart or Gary Luciani
Appears on: Unreleased
A slower-paced song, which if I had to guess, sounds more like it was written by Luciani, given the more traditional sad lyrics. There's a definite influence of songs like King Crimson's "Epitaph" in this. JR Flood certainly wore their influences on their sleeve.

"Tide Keeps Rolling In (RCA Studios Demo, Take 4)" 5:48
Written by Neil Peart or Gary Luciani
Appears on: Unreleased
It's not clear from Travelling Music how much time passed between the Toronto Sound and RCA Studios sessions, but there is a noticeable polish on the second batch of recordings, both in terms of musicianship and the level of arrangements. The RCA tracks are longer with more complex jams and interludes. The RCA Studios tracks also each start with the engineer noting which take it is.

"Flaming Blackbird (RCA Studios Demo, Take 5)" 4:22
Written by Neil Peart or Gary Luciani
Appears on: Unreleased
After the engineer notes that this is "Take 5," there is a pause and he adds sardonically, "in a minute," because Neil needs his monitor level adjusted, as he's hearing more out of the PA than out of his own feeds. The band tests the new level and starts the song moments later. It's very cool to hear Neil speak during the studio chatter, as he's instantly recognizable and sounds much older than his eighteen years. The song itself is a more straightforward rocker!

"Giant Killer (RCA Studios Demo, Take 6)" 8:51
Written by Neil Peart or Gary Luciani
Appears on: Unreleased
This track starts with the engineer announcing "Flaming Blackbird - Take 6," before some studio chatter and the change to the proper song title. There's more studio chatter and you can again hear Neil amongst his bandmates. The song features short monologues of the melodramatic variety typical of the late '60s and into the '70s (and you'll be forgiven for thinking of Spinal Tap's "Stonehenge," when you hear them). Musically, it's very sombre and serious throughout.

"You Don't Have To Be A Polar Bear To Live In Canada (RCA Studios Demo, Takes 7 & 8)" 9:57
Written by Neil Peart or Gary Luciani
Appears on: Unreleased
Introduced simply as "Polar Bear," Neil notes the full title as above. "Take 7" is a short false start, with the full run done in "Take 8." This piece is mostly an extended jam and showcase for the organ, which dominates

the middle and end with Neil's drumming keeping a typically intense, heavy pace for everyone. There are some dropouts, probably from the age of the original tapes, but not many and the recording suffers very little from it.

"Retribution (RCA Studios Demo)" 4:22
 Written by Neil Peart
Appears on: Unreleased
The leaked copy of the JR Flood recordings had this track repositioned to follow the earlier Toronto Sound Studios take. Honestly, it would have been more considerate to fans to leave the entire thing alone, because it's now impossible to hear what may have gotten lost, such the "Take #" announcement of this recording or any studio chatter heard throughout the rest of the RCA recordings. Also, heard out of order, the full impact of the two different sessions is diminished.
This is a good, follow-up recording of the song, much less raw compared to the Toronto Sound cut.

(Dates Unknown)
Rush reportedly writes the following songs this year:
"Sing Guitar"
"Morning Star"
"Margerie"
"Feel So Good"
"Love Light"
"Garden Road"

(Dates Unknown)
Geddy Weinrib and **Alex Živojinović** drop out of high school to pursue their musical careers.

(September)
Rush performs live at Staynor Collegiate Institute, Staynor, Ontario, Canada.

(September 20)
JR Flood opens for The Guess Who and Mashmakhan at Brock University, St. Catharines, Ontario, Canada.

(October)
Justin Shawn Živojinović is born to **Alex Živojinović** and Charlene McNicol.

Around this time, **Alex Živojinović** auditions for an Allan King documentary titled *Come On Children*, which plans to capture the lives of ten kids for ten weeks. **Alex** gets the job and footage is shot at a rural Canadian farm.

Note: in a *Classic Rock* interview (October, 2004) **Alex** briefly describes the making of the film and his participation. He notes that he was 17 year old and it was shot in 1970. Other indications as to when this documentary was filmed include: the farm footage takes place in winter, **Alex**'s son Justin has already been born and his parents are trying to convince him to finish his Grade 12 year of school (which would start in the late-summer of 1970).

(December 21)
Rush performs live at Y.A. Jackson Secondary School, Willowdale, Toronto, Ontario, Canada.

1971

(January 1)
The Ontario government lowers the legal drinking age from 21 to 18 in the province. This positions the *Rush* band members upon turning 18 this year to play bars and pubs. **Neil Peart** would note that it later allowed him to perform in similar venues.

(February)
Michael "Mitch" Bossi joins *Rush* as a second guitarist. The line-up is now **Geddy Weinrib** (bass and lead vocals), **Alex Živojinović** (lead guitar and backing vocals), **John Rutsey** (drums) and Mitch Bossi (guitar).

(Early 1971)
Neil Peart leaves JR Flood due to their apparent disinterest in reaching beyond their current level, following a lack of interest by record companies.

(Spring)
Rush performs live at the Genosha Hotel, Oshawa, Ontario, Canada.

Rush performs live at The Gasworks, Toronto, Ontario, Canada.

(April)
Rush performs live at Staynor Collegiate Institute, Staynor, Ontario, Canada.

Note: In a 2014 *Radio.com* interview (October 30), **Alex Lifeson** says at the time they'd recorded one of their high school concerts from this year onto a mono reel-to-reel tape. It may not have been Staynor Collegiate, but it demonstrates they were playing lots of high schools and were recording their shows when they could. In a 2014 *Radio.com* interview (November 6), **Geddy Lee** says he and **Alex** recorded a demo tape of songs for copyright purposes and that recording survives, with songs **Geddy** no longer remembers.

(May)
Mitch Bossi is kicked out of *Rush* due to lack of musical ability and lack of interest.

(June)
Neil Peart travels to New Barnet, North London, England, to pursue his music career. He auditions for several bands without success.
"Circumstances" – written later for *Hemispheres*, the first verse seems to refer to **Peart**'s thoughts and feelings about taking the chance to follow his dream and to do so far from home. He discusses this further in his book *Travelling Music*.

During his time in London, **Peart** discovers the book *Fall Of The Towers* by Samuel R. Taylor, which would spark his interest in science fiction literature, later influencing the following:
"2112"
"Cygnus X-1"

(Summer)
Rush reportedly only plays three shows in the summer, but rehearse and write new material:
"Working Man" – apparently dates from this period
"Slaughterhouse" – "a hardrocker" according to **John Rutsey** in *Visions*, about endangered wildlife.
"You Can't Fight It" – written by **Rutsey** and **Geddy Weinrib**. According to **Alex Lifeson** in a 2011 *MusicRadar.com* interview, this song likely dates from this year and became a popular live song for late in their sets.

(July)
Neil Peart runs into a friend from St. Catharines while in London, England, named Sheldon "Stan" Atos. Stan helps **Neil** land a stockroom job at the shop Gear and introduces him to the guitarist of the band English Rose, who is looking for a drummer.
"Nobody's Hero" - among **Neil**'s circle of friends at Gear is a man named Ellis, who is the opening "hero" of the song, as he dies of AIDS in the late '80s.

(August)
Neil Peart's drums and record collection arrive in London from St. Catharines. **English Rose** sets up their rehearsal space in the basement of the Pop Shop, London, England.

Around this time, **Alex Živojinović** starts taking classical guitar lessons, which last about a year (*Total Guitar* November, 2007).

(Late Summer)
English Rose's manager begins setting them up with local London gigs, which later expand to include other parts of England. The manager also arranges a demo recording session.

Note: **Neil Peart** mentions the demo session, but does not note anything else about it in his book *Travelling Music*, so it is unknown what became of those recordings, whether they exist somewhere and even what songs were recorded. **Neil** does say they played some original material.

(September 18)
Neil Peart attends The Who's Goodbye Summer concert at the Oval Cricket Grounds, London England. The Faces are also on the bill.

(October)
Neil Peart quits his stockroom job to focus on **English Rose** full time.

English Rose performs live in Keswick, England.

English Rose performs live in Whitehaven, England.

Note: There were other live dates north of London by **English Rose**, but **Neil** only recalls those locations from memory in *Travelling Music*.

English Rose disbands after a lack gigs and their manager being unable to secure a record deal from the demo recordings.

(November 19 & 20)
Rush performs live at the Abbey Road Club, Toronto, Ontario, Canada.

(Late November)
Neil Peart fills in as drummer for the band **Heaven**, performing live at the University of Salford, Manchester, England. **Neil** recalls in *Travelling Music* only being paid half of the agreed upon fee for his services after this gig.

(December)
Neil Peart returns home to St. Catharines, Ontario, Canada, for the Christmas holidays.

1972

Note: The 40th Anniversary *Rush* ReDISCovery Edition LP boxed set includes a rough timeline and line-up listing for the various groups which lead to the formation of *Rush*. It lists **Alex** and **Geddy** under their stage names (**Alex Lifeson** and **Geddy Lee**) instead of their proper names beginning this year. For simplicity (and because that is an official source), this Chronology will do the same. In a 1996 interview with *Bass Frontiers* magazine, **Lee** says he did eventually change his name legally to "**Geddy**."

(January)
Neil Peart returns to New Barnet, North London, England, and takes a "day job" as manager of The Pop Shop.

(Date Unknown)
Rush performs live at Larry's Hideaway, Toronto, Ontario, Canada.

(Date Unknown)
Neil Peart takes a job as manager of the shop Gear, London, England. During this time, he reads J.R.R. Tolkien's *The Lord Of The Rings*, which would later influence the following songs:
"Rivendell"
"The Necromancer"

(February 20)
Neil Peart attends Pink Floyd's concert at The Rainbow Theatre, London, England.

(Date Unknown)
Rush performs live at The Piccadilly Tube, Toronto, Ontario, Canada.

(Date Unknown)
Rush records various tracks at Rochdale College, Toronto, Ontario, Canada. These recordings are presumed lost.

Note: *Visions* says the band also made recordings in their basements and at some shows, none of which survive.

(Spring)
Neil Peart and his flatmate move to Collier's Wood, London, England.

(April 7)
Rush performs live at T.L. Kennedy High School, Toronto, Ontario, Canada.

(May 3 & 4)
Rush performs live at The Colonial Tavern, Toronto, Ontario, Canada.

(Summer)
Neil Peart is asked to join the band **Music** as it forms. The band performs live at clubs and bars in London, England.

Music performs live at The Marquee, London, England.

Music performs live at the University of Brighton, Brighton, England.

Music disbands.

(Date Unknown)
Rush performs live at 999 Queen Street, Toronto, Ontario, Canada.

(June 16 & 17)
Rush performs live at the Penthouse Motor Inn, Scarborough, Ontario, Canada.

(July 2)
Rush performs live at The Colonial Tavern, Toronto, Ontario, Canada.

(July 3)
Rush performs live at the Abbey Road Club, Toronto, Ontario, Canada.

Neil Peart attends a free concert by Grand Funk Railroad, Humble Pie and Head at Hyde Park, London, England.

(July 4, 5, 6, 7 & 8)
Rush performs live at the Abbey Road Club, Toronto, Ontario, Canada.

(August 21, 22, 23, 24, 25, 26, 27, 28, 29, 30 & 31)
Rush performs live at The Gasworks, Toronto, Ontario, Canada.

(September 1 & 2)
Rush performs live at The Gasworks, Toronto, Ontario, Canada.

(Date Unknown)
Around this time, *Rush*'s live repertoire includes the following (according to **Geddy Lee** and **Alex Lifeson** in a 1998 *SonicNet* fancast):
"For What It's Worth" – a cover of the 1967 Buffalo Springfield song, done as a 20 minute jam (*High Times* June, 2012).
"Spoonful" - a cover of the 1960 Howlin' Wolf song
"Suffragette City" – a cover of the 1972 David Bowie song
"The Tale" – apparently an original piece, noted later by **Geddy** (*Classic Rock* October, 2004)
"Margarite" - apparently an original piece, written by **John Rutsey**, noted later by **Alex Lifeson** (*Classic Rock* October, 2004)
"Fancy Dancer" – this song noted in *Visions* as eventually becoming a popular live number at bars.

Alex notes in the *High Times* interview that they also play Grateful Dead songs as a bar band.

(Late 1972)
Neil Peart comes across Ayn Rand's *The Fountainhead* on his way home from work at the Gear, London, England. This sparks his period of interest in her writing, which would later influence the following songs:
"Anthem" – the song shares its title and themes with an Ayn Rand novella.
"2112" – features a dedication to Ayn Rand.

Neil Peart moves back to St, Catharines, Ontario, Canada.

(December 1)
Rush performs live at Midland Avenue Collegiate Institute, Scarborough, Ontario, Canada. The contract for this gig is dated October 11, 1972, noting **John Rutsey** as the "leader" of the band (likely as a formality).

(December 15)
Rush performs live at L.S. Beattie, Willowdale, Toronto, Ontario, Canada.

YOU CAN'T FIGHT IT

1973

(Date Unknown)
Neil Peart is "set up" with Jacqueline "Jackie" Taylor by her brothers Steve and Keith, **Peart**'s friends.

(March 5)
Rush performs live at the Embassy Hotel, Windsor, Ontario, Canada.

(April)
The day before *Rush* begins their recording sessions, **John Rutsey** reportedly rejects the previous lyrics he wrote for the band's original material, thereby forcing **Geddy Lee** to write new lyrics to those songs (*Classic Rock* December, 2007).

Rush performs live in Ontario, Canada (exact venues unknown).

Rush begins recording their debut album for Moon Records at Eastern Sound, Toronto, Ontario, Canada. **Alex Lifeson**, the book *Success Under Pressure*, is quoted saying he "thinks" the band only spent three days "actually recording" for these sessions. **Lifeson**, in a 1976 *Circus* magazine article, notes the first album session was done in 8 hours following a gig (noted above). **Neil Peart**'s later official description of the recording of the album, written for the *A Farewell To Kings* tour book, notes similarly that some of the sessions took place after gigs. Dave Stock produces these sessions. Tracks worked on include:
"Not Fade Away" – a cover of the 1957 Buddy Holly song.
"You Can't Fight It" - According to **Alex Lifeson** in a 2011 *MusicRadar.com* interview, this track is selected for the single because it's under three minutes and radio friendly.
"In The Mood"
"Take A Friend"
"What You're Doing"
"Before And After"
"Working Man"

In various interviews, **Alex Lifeson** notes that there was another song recorded for the album during these sessions which, along with "Not Fade Away" and "You Can't Fight It," which was left off to make room for later, newer recordings done at Toronto Sound in November. One such interview in 2014 (*Red Hot Rock* May), **Alex** at these sessions they recorded "a couple of other things" in addition to what appeared on the album and the "Not Fade Away" single, but this other material was dropped later during the Terry Brown, November sessions.

Following the recording sessions, manager Ray Danniels shops the tracks around to find a distributor or record company to release the album. His attempts are fruitless for about four months (according to Danniels in *Rush: Beyond The Lighted Stage*).

Note: in a 1989 *East Coast Rocker* magazine interview, **Geddy Lee** says the band did get offers at the time for singles deals, the idea being to record several singles and if they did well, an album deal would follow, but this wasn't the direction in which the band wanted to go.

(Date Unknown)
Alex Lifeson later notes that "for a while" this year, **John Rutsey** was too sick to play in *Rush* and the band employed a substitute drummer named Gerry Fielding (*GuitarInternational.com* January 23, 2009).

(June 4, 5, 6, 7, 8 & 9)
Rush performs live at the Abbey Road Pub, Toronto, Ontario, Canada.

(Summer)
After unsuccessfully trying to find an outlet to release *Rush*'s first single, Ray Danniels does manage to find a company, London Records, to press the band's work on vinyl and distribute it. He decides on an independent release, sells his booking agency (Music Shoppe International) and sets up Moon Records to

handle the production and costs, planning "Not Fade Away" and "You Can't Fight It" as the first single (*Beyond The Lighted Stage* and *Billboard* October, 1996). Asked in 1996, why "Not Fade Away" was the A-side, **Geddy Lee** says he does exactly remember, but suspects it was probably a management idea to have a known song (*Tylko Rock* November, 1996).

Neil Peart forms **Hush** with Paul Luciani (bass), Gary Luciani (vocals) and Brian Collins (guitar), who provides the name as used by an earlier band of his. **Hush** performs around bars and clubs in St Catharines and likely the surrounding area.

(July 9, 10, 11, 12, 13 & 14)
Rush performs live at the Abbey Road Pub, Toronto, Ontario, Canada.

(August 31)
Rush releases their debut single "Not Fade Away" in Canada on Moon Records.

7" single (MN-001):
"Not Fade Away" – a cover of the 1958 Buddy Holly song
"You Can't Fight It"

> "Not Fade Away" 3:18
> Written by Norman Petty & Charles Hardin
> Appears on: 7" single
> Rush's first single is the holy grail for the band's fans and collectors, as it was limited in its original release and neither track appeared on their albums, despite numerous opportunities to re-issue it or include it as a bonus track. Rush's cover of the Buddy Holly song is heavier than the original, of course, but the production seems a bit thin compared to their debut album. It sounds like the band is holding back from really laying on the hard rock. Rush was known for being both loud and heavy live right from the start and as great as the recording is, it doesn't really reflect what the band was at the time, which may explain why they've chosen to never revisit. For fans, though, it deserves to be properly remastered and re-released. Seek out both this and "You Can't Fight It" if you're a fan, it's highly recommended, if just a bit imperfect as a snapshot of their earliest recording days.

> "You Can't Fight It" 2:54
> Written by Geddy Lee & John Rutsey
> Appears on: "Not Fade Away" 7" single
> As rare as the single's A-side, "Not Fade Away," but slightly more valuable as an historical record, as it's the first original Rush song ever released. Like with "Not Fade Away," the production is a bit weaker than the band's live sound was known for at the time, but the song still has a lot of energy as a straightforward rocker. Play it loud!

Note: the date comes from handwritten notation that appears on the label as posted on discogs.com. Other sources simply list the release date as "Summer," so the handwritten date in certainly plausible.

(September 3, 4, 5, 6, 7 & 8)
Rush performs live at the Abbey Road Pub, Toronto, Ontario, Canada.

(October)
Rush performs live at the Thunderbird Motor Inn, Thunder Bay, Ontario, Canada. The arrangement lasts more than a week, according to **Alex Lifeson** in the book *Contents Under Pressure*, after which time the band stopped being paid and was billed for their alcohol consumption.

This month, the OAPEC begins an oil embargo, triggering the 1973 Oil Crisis. Among other effects, this limits production of vinyl records and delays the release of many artists' albums during the period between October 1973 and March 1974.

(October 12)
Rush performs live in the Quadrangle of Waterloo Lutheran University, Waterloo, Ontario, Canada, as part of the Homecoming festivities. A photo of this outdoor, daytime performance exists in the Wilfrid Laurier University Library Archives.

(October 27)

Rush performs live at the Victory Burlesque Theatre, Toronto, Ontario, Canada, opening for New York Dolls (there are two shows, one at 8 PM and the next at 11 PM). The poster advertises them as recording artists under Moon Records. The October 29th review of the show by Peter Goddard for the *Toronto Star* focuses on the New York Dolls, but mentions *Rush* at the end (and not complimentarily).

(November)
Road And Track magazine dated this month publishes the Richard Foster short story "A Nice Morning Drive."
"Red Barchetta" – **Neil Peart** would be inspired to write this song based on Foster's story. It's not clear when **Peart** read the story originally.

Rush continues work on their debut album at Toronto Sound Studios, Toronto, Ontario, Canada (*Rush* sessions). **Alex Lifeson**, in a 1976 *Circus* magazine article, says the band decided they "could do it better and recut the whole thing eight months" after the earlier album sessions done at Eastern Sound. He also is quoted in *Success Under Pressure* saying they spent "a couple [days] re-doing two songs and mixing the whole thing." Producer Terry Brown is enlisted at this point. In a 2014 interview (*Radio.com* March 27), **Alex** says the first version of the record was "really crappy," before the band met Brown, who encouraged the remixing and re-recording of material.

The band adds overdubs to the following April Eastern Sound recordings:
"What You're Doing"
"Before And After"
"Working Man"

The following are newly recorded during these sessions, replacing "Not Fade Away," "You Can't Fight It" and at least one other unidentified song, which were planned for the first album:
"Finding My Way"
"Need Some Love"
"Here Again"

> "Working Man (Vault Edition)" 7:18
> Written by Geddy Lee & Alex Lifeson
> Appears on: Rock Band 2 (Downloadable Track), iTunes
> This version features an alternate guitar solo from Alex, which sounds a bit more off-the-cuff compared to the standard version. The rest of the track appears to be the same recording heard on the album, though mixed much more heavily (by Rich Chychi in 2008). It was first released as a downloadable track for *Rock Band 2*, but by popular demand, the band released it for purchase on iTunes. It's a great alternative, losing none of the power of the standard version and offering fans a glimpse into their early recording sessions.

(November 15)
Terry Brown completes the Album Master tapes for Sides 1 and 2 of the debut album (*Rush* sessions).

(December)
Moon Records plans to release *Rush*'s debut, self-titled album this month, but the 1973 Oil Crisis forces its delay.

RUSH

1974

(February 4, 5, 6 & 7)
Rush performs live at Larry's Hideaway, Toronto, Ontario, Canada.

(March 1)
Rush releases their debut album *Rush* on Moon Records in Canada. Unlike the later Mercury and Anthem Records re-issues, the original sleeve features the "Rush" text in red. Mercury would replace it with pink text, standard to subsequent releases. Track listing as follows:

"Finding My Way"
"Need Some Love"
"Take A Friend"
"Here Again"
"What You're Doing"
"In The Mood"
"Before And After"
"Working Man"

(March 18, 19, 20, 21, 22 & 23)
Rush performs live at Piccadilly Tube, Toronto, Ontario, Canada.

(March 24)
Rush performs live in Arkona, Ontario, Canada.

(Spring)
Rush performs live at Parkside Collegiate Institute, St. Thomas, Ontario, Canada.

(April)
Ray Danniels contacts A&M Records to try to get a record deal for *Rush*. The company doesn't sign the band, but Bob Roeper of A&M sends a copy of the album to Donna Halper, a music director of WMMS 100.7 FM in Cleveland, Ohio, US, feeling the band has potential.

Note: in a 2014 radio interview with the German show *Rock Bottom*, Donna Halper is asked specifically when she first discovered the band and replies that she doesn't remember exactly when, given the nature of her job listening to many new artists, but guesses it was April, 1974.

(April 1)
Rush performs live at Laura Secord Secondary School, St. Catharines, Ontario, Canada. The show is recorded for the TV show *Canadian Bandstand*. Excerpts from the concert are later released on the *Rush: Beyond The Lighted Stage* DVD & Blu-ray, as well as YouTube to promote the R40 boxed set, and the full concert is released on the *R40* DVD and Blu-ray boxed sets. Setlist as follows:

"Need Some Love"
"Before And After"
"Best I Can"
"I've Been Runnin'"
"Bad Boy" – a cover of the 1959 Larry Williams song
"The Loser"
"Working Man"
"In The Mood" – the entire song is not broadcast

> "Need Some Love (Live at Laura Secord Secondary School, 1974)" 3:24
> Written by Geddy Lee & Alex Lifeson
> Appears on: Time Machine 2011: Live In Cleveland DVD & Blu-ray
> This excerpt starts the same as the full concert later released on the R40 boxed set and ends with a fade out after John thanks the audience.

> "Best I Can (Live at Laura Secord Secondary School, 1974)" 3:23
> Written by Geddy Lee
> Appears on: Rush: Beyond The Lighted Stage DVD & Blu-ray
> This excerpt starts with John Rutsey introducing the song as one they wrote just a little while earlier, suggesting it is a fairly recent addition to the repertoire. The most noticeable difference from the Fly By

Night recording is John's drumming, which is much more standard, lacking the flourishes and fills Neil would bring to the song. The clip ends with the announcer leading into a station break.

"I've Been Runnin' (Live at Laura Secord Secondary School, 1974)" 4:54
Written by John Rutsey (words), Geddy Lee & Alex Lifeson (music)
Appears on: Official Rush YouTube release
When the Laura Secord concert was unearth and both this song and "The Loser" were released, fans went into something of a frenzy. This is exactly the sort of treasure they'd had been hoping was in the Rush vault. This show takes place not long before John's departure, making it even more significant a recording. He introduces the song and invites the audience to clap along. The song is an up-tempo rocker similar to "Finding My Way" and "Need Some Love." Note: the writing credits come from Alex in a *Radio.com* (October 30, 2014) interview.

"Bad Boy (Live at Laura Secord Secondary School, 1974)" 4:42
Written by Larry Williams
Appears on: R40 (boxed set)
Introduced by John as a song by The Beatles, this was actually a Larry Williams single from 1959 which The Beatles covered in 1965. Unlike The Beatles' version, Rush's cover has a different arrangement, indicative of the British blues-rock stylings of Led Zeppelin (of course). The song would stay in the band's repertoire through the upcoming 1974 US Rush tour and the 1975 Fly By Night tour before being dropped in favour of newer, original material.

"The Loser (Live at Laura Secord Secondary School, 1974)" 3:23
Written by John Rutsey (possibly)
Appears on: Official Rush YouTube release
With "I've Been Runnin'" from this show, as well as songs like "Fancy Dancer" and "Garden Road," it is clear that in the early days Rush had a respectable number of songs that would never see proper studio releases. It's not known if any of these songs were even recorded for the early albums, which in part makes archive footage like the Laura Secord Secondary School show so valuable. In the *Radio.com* interview, Alex seems to suggest John is the writer.

"Working Man (Live at Laura Secord Secondary School, 1974)" 8:40
Written by Geddy Lee & Alex Lifeson
Appears on: Rush: Beyond The Lighted Stage DVD & Blu-ray
This is pretty tight, blistering version of the song, with pre-Neil Rush at the top of their form as a power trio. There's some fun experimentation in the jam section, already pointing toward where Alex and Geddy wanted to go musically (that is, away from the mainstream). Later live versions this year, during the US tour, would see the introduction of the "7/4 Battle Furor" that would become part of "By-Tor And The Snow Dog," but it doesn't seem to have emerged at this point in their live act.

(April 5 & 6)
Rush performs live in Toronto, Ontario, Canada.

(April 8, 9, 10 & 11)
Rush performs live at Sir Sam's, Niagara Falls, Ontario, Canada.

(April 12)
Rush performs live at Victory Burlesque Theatre, Toronto, Ontario, Canada, opening for Bloodrock.

(April 13)
Rush performs live at Sir Sam's, Niagara Falls, Ontario, Canada.

(April 21)
Rush performs live at Don Mills, Ontario, Canada.

(April 22)
Rush performs live in Toronto, Ontario, Canada.

(Mid Spring)
WMMS 100.7 FM radio (sometimes promoted as 101 FM) begins putting *Rush*'s self-titled debut album into heavy rotation in its market of Cleveland, Ohio, US. WMMS, not being a Top 40 radio station (which focuses on singles) but instead an album rock station, was in a position to play album tracks, so gave particular attention to tracks like "Working Man," which Donna Halper correctly predicted would appeal to the city's working class audience (she also says in the *Rock Bottom* 2014 interview that lots of songs from the album were played after the success of "Working Man," including "Finding My Way" and "Here Again.") This boosts *Rush*'s profile in that US market.

Halper also contacts S.R.O. Productions directly and speaks with Ray Danniels and Vic Wilson (who co-run the company) to inform them that *Rush* is a hit on their radio station. S.R.O. sends a box of copies of the album for Halper to get into a local record store (Record Revolution), which sells out in a day.

ATI, an American booking company, also takes interest in the band. **Neil Peart**'s later official description of these events (as written about in the *A Farewell To Kings* tour book) is vague on exactly how ATI became interested, whether there was a connection to the growing popularity in the Cleveland market, which seems likely.

(May 3 & 4)
Rush performs live at The Colonial Tavern, Toronto, Ontario, Canada.

(May 10)
Rush performs live at Gravenhurst, Ontario, Canada.

(May 15)
Rush performs live at Banting Memorial High School, Alliston, Ontario, Canada.

(May 17)
Rush performs live in North Bay, Ontario, Canada.

(May 18)
Rush performs live at North Side Drive-In, Lansing, Michigan. This is *Rush*'s first US appearance.

(May 19)
Rush performs live in Port Dover, Ontario, Canada.

(May 20, 21, 22, 23, 24 & 25)
Rush performs live in Toronto, Ontario, Canada.

(June 3, 4, 5 & 6)
Rush performs live at Larry's Hideaway, Toronto, Ontario, Canada.

(June 7)
Rush performs live in Petrolia, Ontario, Canada.

(June 8)
Rush performs live in Port Credit, Ontario, Canada.

(June 12)
Rush performs live at Brock District High School, Cannington, Ontario, Canada.

(June 13)
Rush performs live in Toronto, Ontario, Canada.

(June 14)
Rush performs live at Elliot Lake, Ontario, Canada.

(Mid-June)
Cliff Burnstein, a record promoter at Mercury Records, Chicago, Illinois, US, is given a copy of *Rush* with a note (likely from Donna Halper) saying that the band is popular in Cleveland, Ohio, US, and are looking for a US record company. In the 2014 *Rock Bottom* interview, Donna Halper says she spoke to Burnstein during Mercury negotiations, as the two knew each other (Burnstein would promote Mercury releases and artist to stations such as WMMS). Cliff gets approval the same day to sign *Rush* and contacts S.R.O. Productions to work out the finer points.

Note: In *Rush: Beyond The Lighted Stage*, Burnstein says this occurred on a Monday in June. An interview published August 31st, 1974, with **Geddy Lee** also notes that the record deal happened within 24 hours. It also says Mercury "rush released" the album in North America and "within a matter of weeks" had arranged for the band's US tour (with involvement from ATI).

Around this time, **John Rutsey** is asked to leave *Rush* by Vic Wilson of S.R.O Productions primarily due to concerns about his health and the affect continued touring and performing will have on it, given the large, upcoming US tour being scheduled. The decision was made after serious conversations between Vic, Ray Danniels, **Geddy Lee** and **Alex Lifeson**. Secondary reasons, according to interviews such as in *Rush: Beyond The Lighted Stage*, include a difference in musical direction, as **Geddy** and **Alex** prefer performing harder, experimental rock influenced by groups like Pink Floyd and Yes, whereas **John** leans more towards straightforward rock bands like Bad Company. A third reason is also suggested, that **Rutsey** may not have been as keen to follow through with the next level of the band's growing popularity after the release of the first album and their eye towards touring in the US.

Note: **Alex** later says the decision surrounding **John**'s departure came with "a couple of months' worth of club gigs" scheduled which **John** played before leaving, placing the decision close to the time of *Rush*'s signing with Mercury Records (*GuitarInternational.com* January 23, 2009).

Note: Depending on the source, different emphasis is sometimes placed on the circumstances of **John Rutsey**'s departure from the band. Some interviews don't mention his health at all and likewise say it was his decision to leave because of musical differences. *Rush: Beyond The Lighted Stage* seems to be the most balanced and in-depth telling of what happened in that regard, that his health was the key reason, but that the musical differences and level of commit to the direction of the band were very much concerns at the time.

(June 17, 18, 19, 20, 21 & 22)
Rush performs live at Duffy's Tavern, Hamilton, Ontario, Canada.

(June 28)
Rush performs live at Allen Theater, Cleveland, Ohio, US, opening for ZZ Top. Locomotive GT is also on the bill. A 1976 article in *Circus* magazine claims ZZ Top refused to let *Rush* do an encore after their opening set because *Rush* stole the show. Donna Halper is in attendance at this show.

(July 1)
Rush performs live at Minkler Auditorium / Seneca Theatre, Toronto, Ontario, Canada. Nazareth is also on the bill. A report written by Don Shaeffer the following day notes the band played material from their album, as well as "some new things."

(July 2, 3, 4, 5 & 6)
Rush performs live at The Colonial Tavern, Toronto, Ontario, Canada.

(July 12)
Rush performs live at Garden City Arena, St. Catharines, Ontario, Canada. Mahogany Rush and Bull Rush are also on the bill.

(July 13)
Rush performs live in Sarnia, Ontario, Canada.

(July 15)
Rush performs live in Bramalea, Ontario, Canada.

(July 18)
Rush performs live at the Hamilton Forum, Hamilton, Ontario, Canada. Mahogany Rush and Bull Rush are also on the bill.

(July 19)
Rush performs live at Cornwall Arena, Cornwall, Ontario, Canada. Mahogany Rush and Bull Rush are also on the bill.

(July 20)
Rush performs live at M.Z. Bennett Public School, Acton, Ontario, Canada.

Note: Some sources list this concert on this date, whereas other tour archives state the M.Z. Bennet Public School show takes place on July 26th. I'm inclined to think this show, about which there is very little information, took place here (if it took place at all). A look through the *Acton Free Press* newspaper online archives turned up no mention of the band on or around either date, nor of any event where they might have appeared.

(July 21, 22 & 23)
Rush performs live in Port Dover, Ontario, Canada.

(Mid-July)
Vic Wilson, at the suggestion of John Trojan (a local drummer) approaches **Neil Peart** at Dalziel Equipment Ltd, St. Catherines, Ontario, Canada, where he works as Parts Manager and offers him an audition for drummer in *Rush*.

Note: **Neil** says in *Travelling Music* the invitation was made a few days before the audition.

(July 25)
Rush performs live at Centennial Hall, London, Ontario, Canada, opening for KISS. Ronny Legg is also on the bill.

Note: both a promo ad for this show and a backstage photo (of **John Rutsey**, **Geddy Lee**, Ronny Legg, **Alex Lifeson** and others) exists, marking what could very well be **John**'s final show with *Rush*.

Note: In a 1989 *Rockline* interview, **Alex Lifeson** says that **John** got out of music soon after departing *Rush* and got into amateur bodybuilding, a career he was "in and out of" over the years. **Alex** says he has infrequent contact with **John** until "about '76" when they fell out of touch for an extended period (*GuitarInternational.com* January 23, 2009).

Note: At this point, **John Rutsey** is in possession of tapes of early *Rush* recordings and around 1988/1989, he and **Alex Lifeson** listen back to them (*Rock N' Roll Reporter* February, 1996). It is unknown what became of these recordings and what the contents exactly were.

(Late July)
Neil Peart auditions for drummer of *Rush*, playing with **Geddy Lee** and **Alex Lifeson** in a warehouse in Ajax, Ontario, Canada. In a VH-1 *Hangin' With Rush* interview in 2005, **Geddy** notes is it a day of auditions and two other drummers preceded **Neil**. In *Visions*, **Alex** says **Neil** came in on the second day of auditions. Roadie Ian Grandy is also present at the audition and confirms **Neil** is the third drummer to audition, that the trio played for 40 minutes and that Grandy recorded the audition (**Alex** later says this recording is either erased to reuse the tape or is lost) (*GuitarInternational.com* January 23 & September 16, 2009).

"Anthem" – according to **Geddy** (in a 2013 *Rolling Stone* interview), he, **Alex** and **Neil** jammed to this riff during the audition. **Neil** confirms this in a 1991 *Rockline* interview. The riff was written by **Geddy** and **Alex** during the **John Rutsey** years (it's unclear exactly when), though **John** "wasn't into playing it." The *Fly By Night* lyric sheet notes the writing locations as Toronto and Beamsville. The "Toronto" portion is very likely the unfinished pre-**Neil** riff. The "Beamsville" portion then would seem to be post-**Neil**'s arrival. The song is completed by December 16nd, 1974, as it appears in a finished state during that concert performance (see the December 1974 entries).

(July 29)
According to **Neil Peart** in *Travelling Music*, he is asked to join *Rush* a few days after the audition. In the *A Farewell To Kings* tour book, he specifically states he joined on **Geddy Lee**'s 21st birthday. Various sources (including in *Rush: Beyond The Lighted Stage* and the *A Farewell To Kings* tour book) **Neil** says he has only two weeks to learn *Rush*'s repertoire. The line-up is now **Geddy Lee, Alex Lifeson** and **Neil Peart**.

Neil Peart leaves **Hush** to join *Rush*.

Note: at this point, **Neil** is sharing a farmhouse with Jackie Taylor's brothers, Steve and Keith, and Wayne Lawryk.

(August 10)
Mercury Records releases *Rush* in the US and re-issues it in Canada (replacing the Moon Records release). Added to the back cover are thank yous to Donna Halper and Cliff Burnstein.

(August 14)
Rush flies from Toronto, Ontario, Canada to Pittsburgh, Pennsylvania, US, to start their US tour.
"Fly By Night" – though written later during the US tour, the lyrics seem to encapsulate much of the same thoughts and feelings **Neil Peart** shares in *Travelling Music* about this time in his life, his drive to push his career forward and to seize the opportunity to join *Rush*, not to mention the sheer importance of this flight in his life.

Rush performs live at the Civic Arena, Pittsburgh, Pennsylvania, US, opening for Uriah Heep and Manfred Mann. This is **Neil Peart**'s first performance with the band. The setlist includes:

"Finding My Way"
"In The Mood"
"Bad Boy" – a cover of the 1959 Larry Williams song
"Working Man" – noted in a positive newspaper review of the show in the *Pittsburgh Press* the following day.

(August 15)
Rush performs live at the Public Auditorium, Cleveland, Ohio, US, opening for Uriah Heep and Manfred Mann.

(August 16)
Rush performs live at the Cincinnati Gardens, Ohio, US, opening for Uriah Heep and Manfred Mann.

(August 17)
In Cincinnati, Ohio, US, **Geddy Lee** gives an interview for *The Cincinnati Enquirer* (August 31st, 1974), wherein he talks about the debut album and how quickly the Mercury Records deal and tour happened. The piece notes that the band's second album is planned for release in the winter and **Lee** says it will have "slightly different music. Improved lyrics. Still more variety."

Note: **Geddy** says in the interview that it's given four days into the tour, placing the date here.

(August 18)
Rush performs live at the Civic Center Arena, Charleston, West Virginia, US.

(August 19)
Rush are scheduled to perform live at Bogies, Washington, D.C., US, but the show is cancelled. According to a 2009 email interview with Ian Grandy and Skip Daly, *Rush* did a short guest appearance "on some local show."

(August 20)
Rush performs live at the Stanley Theater, Pittsburgh, Pennsylvania, US, opening for Blue Öyster Cult.

(August 21 & 23)
Rush performs live in St. Louis, Missouri, US.

(Mid-August)
Rush performs live at Straughn Auditorium, Mansfield State College, Mansfield, Pennsylvania, US.

(August 26)
Rush performs live at the Agora Ballroom, Cleveland, Ohio, US, for WMMS 100.7 FM's *Nights Out At The Agora*. Reign is also on the bill. Donna Halper meets *Rush*, leading to a lifelong friendship. The show is broadcast live that evening and later released on CD as *Rush ABC (Agora Ballroom, Cleveland, Ohio, August 6, 1974)* by Left Field Media in 2011 and again on LP in 2013. Setlist as follows:

"Finding My Way"
"Best I Can"
"Need Some Love"
"In The End"
"Fancy Dancer"
"In The Mood"
"Bad Boy" – a cover of the 1959 Larry Williams song
"Here Again"
"Working Man" - features the proto-"7/4 War Furor" segment of "By-Tor & The Snow Dog"
"Drum Solo"
"What You're Doing"
"Garden Road"

"Best I Can (Live at the Agora Ballroom, August 1974)" 3:06
Written by Geddy Lee & Alex Lifeson
Appears on: Rush ABC (Agora Ballroom, Cleveland, Ohio, August 6, 1974)
The Fly By Night album is unique in that it encapsulates the periods before, during and after the personnel change that saw John Rutsey leave the band and Neil replace him on drums. "In The End" (see below) and "Best I Can" predate Neil's arrival. The riff in "Anthem" existed in the Rutsey days, but apparently he didn't like playing it, so it took Neil's joining to see it grow into a proper song. The "7/4 War Furor" battle music that would end up in "By-Tor And The Snow Dog" started appearing in live versions of "Working Man" during the post-Rutsey 1974 US tour and the rest of the songs were written in and around the tour, as well. "Fly By Night" and "Anthem" would start appearing as new songs before the year was out. "Best I Can," heard at this concert, is pretty complete, now featuring the more dynamic drumming of Neil.

"In The End (Live at the Agora Ballroom, August 1974)" 6:13
Written by Geddy Lee & Alex Lifeson
Appears on: Rush ABC (Agora Ballroom, Cleveland, Ohio, August 6, 1974)
The Fly By Night lyrics sheet says the song was written in Toronto and given it's written without Neil Peart and finished this early into the US tour, this song would seem to date from the days before Neil replaced John Rutsey. This is the earliest known live recording of the song and it's close to the eventual album recording, though with a shorter outro.

"Fancy Dancer (Live at the Agora Ballroom, August 1974)" 3:54
Written by [Undetermined]
Appears on: Rush ABC (Agora Ballroom, Cleveland, Ohio, August 6, 1974)
There's been no official confirmation as to who in Rush wrote what in this song. Lee & Lifeson almost certainly wrote the music, possibly with input from John Rutsey. Lyrics are probably Geddy's, again possibly with some work from John. It's a great uptempo bar rock song. Alex is on record saying it was good to pull out late at night in a pub gig, as it was a crowd pleaser. In the September 1988 Backstage Club newsletter, Neil says the band never recorded this song in the studio (though he may only be referring to the time *he* was in the band. It's unknown if there is a John Rutsey-era studio recording).

"Bad Boy (Live at the Agora Ballroom, August 1974)" 5:37
Written by Larry Williams
Appears on: Rush ABC (Agora Ballroom, Cleveland, Ohio, August 6, 1974)
This is another great live performance of the song, now with Neil on drums. "Bad Boy" would be the last regular cover song in Rush's set until the R30 Tour and the addition of the Feedback covers.

"Garden Road (Live at the Agora Ballroom, August 1974)" 3:03
Written by [Undetermined]
Appears on: Rush ABC (Agora Ballroom, Cleveland, Ohio, August 6, 1974)
Like with "Fancer Dancer" (and "The Loser" and "I've Been Runnin'"), there's been no official songwriting credit yet given to this song, but I'd venture to say the same as "Fancer Dancer" (Lee & Lifeson, maybe Rutsey, on music and Lee, maybe Rutsey, on lyrics. How is that for vague?). A small snippet of this song would appear again live in 2015 on the R40 Tour closing out the concerts. It's a great, high energy rocker and well worth having in your Rush collection. And if you've been keeping track, Rush had by this point seven known non-album tracks in their repertoire, likely more: "Not Fade Away," "You Can't Fight It," "The Loser," "I've Been Runnin'," Bad Boy," "Fancy Dancer" and "Garden Road," pretty much enough for an

additional album, so if you're a collector, you could assemble your own. In the September 1988 Backstage Club newsletter, Neil says the band never recorded this song in the studio (though he may only be referring to the time *he* was in the band. It's unknown if there is a John Rutsey-era studio recording).

(August 27 & 28)
Rush performs live at the Minnesota State Fair, St. Paul, Minnesota, US.

(August 29)
Rush performs live at Casino Arena, Asbury Park, New Jersey, US.

(August 30)
Rush performs live at Joint In The Woods, Parsippany, New Jersey, US. According to *Billboard*'s Sept. 21 review of the show, the setlist includes:

"In The Mood"
"Here Again"
"Need Some Love"
"Bad Boy" – a cover of the 1959 Larry Williams song

(August 31)
Rush performs live at Kee To Bala, Bala, Ontario, Canada.

(September)
Rush releases their "Finding My Way" singles on Mercury Records in North America.

7" single (M-73623):
"Finding My Way"
"Need Some Love"

US 7" Promo single (DJ-406 [73623]):
"Finding My Way (Promo Edited Version)"
"Finding My Way (Promo Edited Version)"

> "Finding My Way (Promo Edited Version)" 2:55
> Written by Geddy Lee & Alex Lifeson
> Appears on: US 7" Promo single
> I haven't heard this rare radio promo, which features a significant edit of the track (from over five minutes to under three). In a radio interview with the band on October 17, 1974, Neil Peart notes "Finding My Way" was cut down by two and a half minutes for the single, so obviously the band was informed of the edit. The label notes (for DJs to make introductions and such) that the edit's intro lasts only :09 seconds, presumably 9 seconds of music before the first verse, so it's a safe bet the opening 25 seconds were removed.

(September 1)
Rush performs live at Minden Arena, Minden, Ontario, Canada.

(September 2)
Rush performs live at Pineway Trails Park, Munson Township, Ohio, US. Also on the bill are Rare Earth, Rainbow Canyon, East Wind and Sweetleaf.

(September 6)
Rush performs live in Detroit, Michigan, US.

(September 11)
Rush performs live in Toronto, Ontario, Canada. The show is recorded for the *King Biscuit Flower Hour*, according to 2112.net.

(September 13)
Rush performs live at Gym II, University of Maryland Baltimore County, Baltimore, Maryland, US, opening for Sha-Na-Na. In a 1990 interview with *Guitar For A Practicing Musician*, **Alex Lifeson** says the band were booed throughout this show.

(September 15)
Rush performs live at Thomas Fieldhouse, Lock Haven State College, Pennsylvania, US, opening for Blue Öyster Cult and KISS.

(September 16)
Rush performs live at the Paramount Theatre, Wilkes Barre, Pennsylvania, US, opening for Blue Öyster Cult and KISS.

(September 18, 19 & 20)

Rush performs live at the Electric Ballroom, Atlanta, Georgia, US, opening for KISS. Fat Chance is also on the bill.

(September 21)
Rush performs live in St. Petersburg, Florida, US.

(September 22)
Rush performs live in Orlando, Florida, US.

(September 23)
Rush performs live in Gainesville, Florida, US.

(September 24)
Rush performs live at the Roxy Theatre, North Hampton, Pennsylvania, US.

(September 25)
One of two possible dates *Rush* could have worked on the following in Columbus, Ohio, US:
"Rivendell" – according to the *Fly By Night* lyric sheet. Lyrics by **Neil Peart**, music by **Geddy Lee**.

Rush performs live at the Agora Ballroom, Columbus, Ohio, US.

(September 27)
Rush performs live at Memorial Auditorium, Worcester, Massachusetts, US, opening for Tyrannosaurus Rex. Albatross is also on the bill.

(September 28)
Rush performs live at the Erie Country Fairgrounds, Erie, Pennsylvania, US, opening for Tyrannosaurus Rex.

(September 29)
Rush performs live at Roberts Stadium, Evansville, Indiana, US, opening for Billy Preston. Also on the bill is KISS.

(October 1)
Rush performs live at Leone Cole Auditorium, Jacksonville, Alabama, US, opening for KISS.

(October 3)
Rush performs live at War Memorial Auditorium, Nashville, Tennessee, US.

(October 4)
Rush performs live at The Music Hall, Houston, Texas, US, opening for KISS.

(October 6)
Rush performs live at the Oak Brook Forum, Oak Brook, Illinois, US, opening for Steppenwolf and Canned Heat.

(October 16)
Rush performs live as part of *Don Kirshner's Rock Concert*, Los Angeles, California, US. Setlist as follows:

"Finding My Way"
"Best I Can"
"In The Mood"
"Working Man/Drum Solo"

Note: advance advertisements in *Billboard* magazine for Rush's tour specifically say the *Don Kirshner* recording was scheduled for October 9th, which was apparently rescheduled to this date (source 2112.net).

(October 17)
Rush performs live at the Travis St. Electric Co., Dallas, Texas, US.

Note: The book *KISS Alive Forever* lists *Rush* as an opening act for KISS at Comstock Park, Grand Rapids, Michigan, US, on this date, which is incorrect. A radio interview with the band in Dallas, a Dallas print review of their show by Larry Week and a print ad for the show all definitively prove the band was in Dallas, Texas.
In the radio interview, **Geddy Lee** notes that since **Neil Peart** has joined, the band has been writing new material.

(October 18)
Rush performs live at the Soldiers & Sailors Memorial Hall, Kansas City, Kansas, US, opening for Hawkwind.

Note: A print ad lists *Rush* as opening for KISS at The Parthenon Theatre, Hammond, Indiana, US, and subsequently that date appears in various sources (including the *KISS Alive Forever* book). A more definitive *Billboard* magazine (October 12th) listing of *Rush* tour dates provided by S.R.O. Productions instead lists the Kansas City, Kansas, concert. Why the change in dates was made is unclear.

(October 19)
Rush performs live at Pershing Memorial Auditorium, Lincoln, Nebraska, US, US, opening for Hawkwind.

(October 20)
Rush performs live in Oklahoma City, Oklahoma, US.

(October 21 & 22)
Note: The book *KISS Alive Forever* lists *Rush* as performing live at The Brewery, East Lansing, Michigan, US, opening for KISS on this dates. However, official *Rush* sources list the band in Wichita, Kansas, US, supporting Hawkwind on the 22nd (see below).

(October 22)
Rush performs live at Century II Performing Arts & Convention Center, Wichita, Kansas, US, opening for Hawkwind.

(October 23)
Rush performs live at the University of Western Ontario, London, Ontario, US, opening for Nazareth.

(October 24)
Rush performs live at Massey Hall, Toronto, Ontario, Canada, opening for Nazareth.

(October 25)
Rush performs live at the Grand Hall, Queen's University, Kingston, Ontario, Canada.

(October 26)
Rush performs live at The Rock Pile, Hamilton, Ontario, Canada.

(October 28 & 29)
Rush performs live at My Father's Place, Roslyn, Now York, US.

(October 31)
Rush cancels their appearance at the Civic Centre, Ottawa, Ontario, Canada, opening for Nazareth and Hudson-Ford.

(November 1)
Rush performs live at The Forum, Montreal, Quebec, Canada, opening for Rory Gallagher and Nazareth.

(November 2)
Rush performs live in Peterborough, Ontario, Canada.

(November 3)
Rush performs live in Parsippany, New York, US.

(November 5)
Rush performs live at the Beacon Theater, New York City, New York, US, opening for Rory Gallagher. The band If is also on the bill.

(November 7)
Rush performs live at B'Ginnings, Shaumburg, Illinois, US, opening for Rory Gallagher.

(November 8)
Rush performs live at the Lyric Theater, Kitchener, Ontario, Canada.

(November 9)
Rush performs live at the Michigan Palace, Detroit, Michigan, US.

(November 10)
Rush works on the following in St. Louis, Missouri, US:
"Making Memories" – **Neil Peart** confirms song is started in a rental car south of St. Louis (*R30* press release).

Rush performs live at the Ambassador Theater, St. Louis, Missouri, US.

(November 11)
Rush works on the following in East Lansing, Michigan, US:
"Fly By Night" –According to the *Fly By Night* lyric sheet, the song is written in part in "Lansing." The December 16th, Agora Ballroom, performance features a yet-to-be-completed version of the song, suggesting the Toronto notation is when it was finished during the album sessions. **Neil Peart** says in *The Complete Tour Books* that this was one of the first songs he wrote for the band.

Rush performs live at The Brewery, East Lansing, Michigan, US.

(November 12)
Rush performs live at the Riverside Theater, Milwaukee, Wisconsin, US, opening for Rory Gallagher. Wet Willie is also on the bill.

(November 13)
Rush performs live at the Sports Arena, Toledo, Ohio, US, opening for Rory Gallagher. Carmen is also on the bill.

(November 14)
The other of two possible dates *Rush* could have worked on the following in Columbus, Ohio, US:
"Rivendell" – according to the *Fly By Night* lyric sheet. Lyrics by **Neil Peart**, music by **Geddy Lee**.

Rush performs live at Veterans Memorial Auditorium, Columbus, Ohio, US, opening for Rory Gallagher.

(November 15)
Rush performs live at the Aragon Ballroom, Chicago, Illinois, US, opening for Rory Gallagher. Wet Willie is also on the bill.

(November 16)
Rush performs live at the Orpheum Theatre, Wichita, Kansas, US.

(November 19)
Rush works on the following in Seattle, Washingston, US:
"Beneath, Between & Behind" – Lyrics by **Neil Peart**, music by **Alex Lifeson**. According to the *Fly By Night* lyrics sheet, the song is apparently started in Seattle and finished in Toronto, presumably during the album recording sessions. In the VH-1 *Hangin' With Rush* 2005 interview, **Geddy Lee** recalls this as the first song **Neil** wrote with them, which may not be entirely accurate given when and where other songs were penned according to the *Fly By Night* lyric sheet.

Rush performs live at Paramount Northwest, Seattle, Washington, US, opening for Rory Gallagher.

(November 20)
Rush performs live at Paramount Theatre, Portland, Oregon, US, opening for Rory Gallagher.

(November 22)
Rush performs live at the Tuesday Ballroom, San Diego, California, US, opening for Rory Gallagher. Earthquake is also on the bill.

(November 23)
Rush performs live at the Shrine Auditorium, Los Angeles, California, US, opening for Rory Gallagher. Wet Willie is also on the bill.

(Late November)
Rush works on the following in Los Angeles, California, US:
"Making Memories"
"By-Tor & The Snow Dog"

Rush performs live at Ventura Theater, Ventura, US. This performance was originally scheduled for November 27th.

(November 27, 28, 29, 30, December 1)
Rush performs live at Whiskey A Go Go, Los Angeles, California, US. The Butts Band is also on the bill. The November 27th setlist includes:

"Finding My Way"
"Fancy Dancer"
"In The Mood"
"In The End"
"What You're Doing"
"Bad Boy" – a cover of the 1959 Larry Williams song

(Dates Unknown)
Neil Peart works on the following in Beamsville, Ontario, Canada:
"Anthem" – the riff of the song already existed before **Neil** joined, so his lyrics would obviously come after to help shape the piece into a proper song, which was completed by December 16th. The lyrics are inspired by Ayn Rand's book *Anthem*.
"Rivendell" – inspired by J.R.R. Tolkien's books *The Hobbit* and *The Lord Of The Rings*.

Note: The *Fly By Night* insert lyrics sheet notes where the songs were worked on, many while on the tour itself. However, the band never played Beamsville, Ontario, Canada. Beamsville is just outside St. Catharines, which suggests **Neil** worked on them either before or after the first leg of the US tour. It seems unlikely **Neil** would write two new songs in August before the tour while learning their entire repertoire. "Anthem" is performed completed at the

December 16, 1974, Agora Ballroom concert, where **Geddy** introduces it as planned for the next album, which leads one to believe that since the riff already existed before **Neil** joined the band, they worked on (and completed) this song fairly quickly during the December hiatus, hence the songs' placement here.

"Rivendell" is a bit harder to pin down, not appearing anywhere until the album recording. It's entirely possible **Neil** started the song in Beamsville before the tour and continued it in Columbus.

(December)
Rush releases their "In The Mood" single in North America. At the December 22nd, Electric Lady Studios performance, **Geddy Lee** introduces this song as having been just released as a single.

7" single (73647):
"In The Mood"
"What You're Doing"

US 7" Promo single (DJ-417 [73647]):
"In The Mood (Promo Edited Version)" (Mono)
"In The Mood (Promo Edited Version)" (Stereo)

(December 6)
Rush performs live on *In Concert*, ABC TV Studio, Los Angeles, California, US.

(December 12)
Rush performs live at Convocation Hall, University of Toronto, Toronto, Ontario, Canada. Manfred Mann is also on the bill.

(December 16 & 17)
Rush works on the following in Cleveland, Ohio, US:
"By-Tor & The Snow" – The *Fly By Night* lyrics sheet notes that the song is worked on again in this city.

Rush performs live at Agora Ballroom, Cleveland, Ohio, US, on WMMS 100.7 FM's Nights Out at the Agora, supported by Law and Don Preston. The December 16th show is broadcasted live. Setlist as follows:

"Finding My Way"
"Best I Can"
"What You're Doing"
"Fly By Night" – **Geddy Lee** notes this is the first public performance of the song
"Here Again"
"Anthem"
"Bad Boy" – a cover of the 1959 Larry Williams song
"Working Man" – features the proto-"7/4 War Furor" segment of "By-Tor & The Snow Dog"
"Drum Solo"

Note: some setlists online list "In The Mood" between "Working Man" and the "Drum Solo," but available bootlegs of the broadcast don't seem to support that, unless it was edited out, but there's no break between the two songs, so it's not clear how that would be possible.

> "Best I Can (Live At The Agora Ballroom, December 1974)" 3:15
> Written by Geddy Lee & Alex Lifeson
> Appears on: Return To Cleveland (Bootleg)
> One of three songs played at this show which would feature on the next album. It was basically complete at the April Laura Secord Secondary School show in the time of John Rutsey. It was refined with Neil Peart on drums when he joined Rush and is heard here ready to be recorded for the album.
>
> "Fly By Night (Live At The Agora Ballroom, December 1974)" 3:10
> Written by Neil Peart (words) & Geddy Lee (music)
> Appears on: Return To Cleveland (Bootleg)
> Geddy announces that this is the first live performance of the song, written only "a few weeks" before (having been started in Lansing on November 11th). The lyrics are incomplete and Geddy seems a bit unsure of the next line in some places, which is probably to be expected with a brand new song still being worked on. As with most pre-album or early stage performances, it's fascinating to hear this one only partially complete, almost like a demo. There are some slightly different arrangements in places and fewer instrumental breaks between verses. The ending features a nice, slow guitar outro by Alex not heard on the album.
>
> "Anthem (Live At The Agora Ballroom, December 1974)" 4:26
> Written by Neil Peart (words), Geddy Lee & Alex Lifeson (music)
> Appears on: Return To Cleveland (Bootleg)
> Geddy announces that this song, like "Fly By Night" is planned for the next album. Unlike "Fly By Night," this song is basically done by this date, appearing very close to the finished album version. I would speculate that

the band completed this song before they started in on "Fly By Night," as the riff pre-dated Neil's arrival. As he was in his so-called "Ayn Rand" phase by most accounts, the lyrics probably came quickly. It's a great preview of what fans could expect from the next album.

(December 20 & 21)
Rush performs live at the Michigan Palace, Detroit, Michigan, co-headlining with KISS. Fancy is also on the bill.

(December 22)
Rush performs live at Electric Lady Studios, New York City, New York, US, for WQIV radio. Setlist as follows:

"Finding My Way"
"Best I Can" - **Geddy Lee** says this song will be on their next album, planned for February 1975
"In The Mood" - **Geddy** say this song is their latest single
"Anthem" - **Geddy** notes this song will be on their next album, planned for February 1975
"Need Some Love"
"Fly By Night"
"Here Again"
"Bad Boy" - a cover of the 1959 Larry Williams song
"Working Man/Drum Solo" - features the proto-"7/4 War Furor" segment of "By-Tor & The Snow Dog"

Note: An alternate track listing exists on bootlegs, which removes "In The Mood" and switches the positions of "Need Some Love" and "Anthem," but the above listing appears to be the correct one. Also, some sources list this performance as December 5th, 1974, which does not fit the available evidence and independent accounts.

"Best I Can (Live At Electric Lady Studios 1974)" 3:07
Written by Geddy Lee & Alex Lifeson
Appears on: Rush – Live At Electric Lady Studios
Rush has this song down fully now, if they didn't already by the third Agora Ballroom show in December. Not much else to report, other than it's nice to have a clean pre-album studio recording in addition to the pre-album live versions.

"Anthem (Live At Electric Lady Studios 1974)" 4:30
Written by Neil Peart (words), Geddy Lee & Alex Lifeson (music)
Appears on: Rush – Live At Electric Lady Studios
As with "Best I Can," it's nice to have a clean studio pre-album recording to go with the Agora Ballroom performance from earlier in the month. Great stuff!

"Fly By Night (Live At Electric Lady Studios 1974)" 3:10
Written by Neil Peart (words) & Geddy Lee (music)
Appears on: Rush – Live At Electric Lady Studios
The song is not really any further along compared to the December Agora Ballroom show, except maybe that the performance is more confident. The lyrics are still unfinished, but the different ending is interesting. It would appear that the song was not completed until the proper album sessions.

(December 28)
Rush begins work on their second studio album at Toronto Sound Studios, Toronto, Ontario, Canada (*Fly By Night* sessions). According to *Circus Rave* magazine in November of 1975, the sessions begin after a five day break following the Electric Lady Studio performance. The sessions last between ten days (according to the *Visions* and *Contents Under Pressure*) and approximately two weeks (Ian Grandy in an 2012 email to Skip Daly, 2112.net). The sessions last to early January, 1975.

Note: **Neil Peart** states in the *A Farewell To Kings* tour book that the *Fly By Night* sessions began in January of 1975, but at best that would reduce the number of recording days from 14 to 10, which does not seem likely.

Rush is advertised to perform live at the Orpheum Theater, Boston, Massachusetts, US, opening for Blue Öyster Cult (American Tears is also on the bill), but it's unlikely they actually did given they would be in the studio recording.

(December 29)
Rush is scheduled to perform live at the Palace, Waterbury, Connecticut, US, opening for Blue Öyster Cult, but it's unlikely they actually did as they were recording their album (*Fly By Night* sessions). American Tears is also on the bill.

FLY BY NIGHT & CARESS OF STEEL

1975

(Early January)
According to Ian Grandy (in a September 2010 email to Skip Daly, 2112.net), **Rush** completes recording work on the second album before the January 10th Humber College performance. Mixing and mastering has yet to be completed (*Fly By Night* sessions).

Tracks worked on since December include:
"Best I Can" – one of **Rush**'s oldest songs by this point, dating back to the **John Rutsey** period, is properly recorded for the album.
"In The End" – as noted previously, this song likely dates from the **John Rutsey** period and is now recorded for the album.
"Anthem" – begun by the band during the **Rutsey** days and completed with **Neil Peart**, performed live through December and recorded at last for the album.
"Fly By Night" – Played live through December in an incomplete form, the song is finished for the album.
"By-Tor & The Snow Dog" – elements of the "7/4 War Furor" segment of the song can be heard live in the instrumental jams in "Working Man" during the 1974 North American Tour.

In *The Complete Tour Books*, **Neil Peart** says one of the possible names for the album is *Aurora Borealis*.

(January 10)
Rush performs live at Humber College, Rexdale, Toronto, Ontario, Canada. A photo taken of the roadies Ian Grandy, Liam Birt and J.D. Johnson from this date later appears on the *Fly By Night* lyric sheet.

(January 14)
The master reel tapes for Sides 1 and 2 of the album are completed. According to *Visions*, **Rush** and crew finish mixing *Fly By Night* on this date (noted on the Stereo Album Master tapes), apparently working long into the night.

Tracks worked on include:
"By-Tor And The Snow Dog" – some interesting notation appears on the tape's label for this song. The run time of the song is originally noted as 8:40, which is crossed out and corrected with a time of 8:57, which is also crossed out and corrected with yet another new time of 9:20. These numbers are important because:
8:40 is close to the later standard CD track length (8:37).
8:57 is the *Archives* LP track length.
9:20 is the 2015 remaster "Extended Ending" audible time (the track length of 9:37 is actually silence after the 9:20 mark).
Note: It's likely each correction indicates the band extending the song a little further on the master tape to ensure the chime gimmick in the run-out groove has the full intended effect.
"Rivendell" – the last song mixed, according to **Geddy Lee** in an interview with Jim Ladd (April 16, 2013).

(January 15)
Rush catches a 10:30 AM flight to Winnipeg, Manitoba, Canada. The *Fly By Night* Side 1 and Side 2 Stereo Album Master tapes are sent to Masterdisk, New York City, New York, US, for mastering.

Rush performs live at Winnipeg Convention Centre, Winnipeg, Manitoba, Canada, as part of *Celebrations '75*. The Winnipeg Symphony Orchestra also performs. Rare Earth is scheduled as the headliners, but is forced to reschedule to the 18th due to the drummer's illness. The setlist includes, as noted in the *Winnipeg Free Press* (January 18th):

"Working Man"
"In The Mood"

(January 17)
Rush performs live in Etobicoke, Ontario, Canada.

(January 19)
Rush performs live at Belgian Club, Delhi, Ontario, Canada.

(January 29)
Rush performs live in Hamilton, Ontario, Canada.

(January 31)
Rush performs live at Circus Circus, Detroit, Michigan, US.

(February 14)
Rush performs two shows live at the Theatre Auditorium, Wilfrid Laurier University, Waterloo, Ontario, Canada.

(February 15)
Rush releases their album *Fly By Night* on Mercury Records in North America. Track listing as follows:

"Anthem"
"Best I Can"
"Beneath, Between & Behind"
"By-Tor And The Snow Dog (Original LP Version)
    I: At The Tobes Of Hades
    II: Across The Styx
    III: Of The Battle
        a. Challenge And Defiance
        b. 7/4 War Furor
        c. Aftermath
        d. Hymn Of Triumph
    IV: Epilogue"
"Fly By Night"
"Making Memories"
"Rivendell"
"In The End"

    "By-Tor And The Snow Dog (Original LP Version)" 8:57+
    Written by Neil Peart (words), Geddy Lee & Alex Lifeson (music)
    Appears on: Fly By Night (Original 1975 LP)
    This is one of those things which can only be done on vinyl, given the nature of the medium. LPs have at the end of each side what's called a locked groove or run-out groove. It's a continuous circle in which record player's needle can rest if you forget to lift it off the record at the end of the side. Normally, it's silent, but occasionally artists will have fun with the groove and put sounds in there, resulting in an endless cycle of the same bit over and over until you take the needle off. The Beatles famously did it with the end of their Sgt Pepper's Lonely Hearts Club Band album and even included a snippet of the loop on later CD editions. Rush got in on the fun by putting the little chimes that end of this track right into the groove so it would repeat continuously. The later CD versions end the song with a fadeout, as it would be impossible to repeat the chimes forever, so if you want to hear this (funny, but otherwise pointless) repetition, you need the record.

    Note: There are reports of some editions of *Archives* and possibly some post-1977 Anthem re-issue editions containing this version also, whereas most do not (see the *Archives*, April 1978).

Rush performs live in Owen Sound, Ontario, Canada.

(February 16)
Rush performs live in Barrie, Ontario, Canada.

(February 17)
Rush performs live at London Arena, London, Ontario, Canada. Thundermug is also on the bill.

(February 18)
Rush performs live in Kingston, Ontario, Canada.

(February 20)
Rush performs live at the Convention Center, Indianapolis, Indiana, US, opening for The Faces.

(February 21)
Rush performs live at Finch Fieldhouse, Central Michigan University, Mount Pleasant, Michigan, US, opening for ZZ Top. Setlist includes (according to a review *Central Michigan Life*, February 24, 1975):

"Anthem"
"In The End"
"Drum Solo"
"In The Mood"

(February 27)
Rush performs live at Travis St. Electric Company, Dallas, Texas, US, supported by Baked Beans.

(February 28)
Rush performs live at Sylvan Beach Pavillion, La Porte, Texas, US, supported by the Steve Long Group.

(March 5, 6, 7 & 8)

Rush performs live at the Electric Ballroom, Atlanta, Georgia, US.

(March 10)
Rush performs live at the Roxy Theatre, North Hampton, Pennsylvania, US.

(March 11)
Rush performs live at Stone Balloon, Newark, New Jersey, US.

(March 18)
Rush performs live at Morris Civic Center, South Bend, Indiana, US, opening for Aerosmith.

(March 19)
Rush performs live at The Rafters, Battle Creek, Michigan, US.

(March 22)
Rush performs live at Schmidt Fieldhouse, Xavier University, Cincinnati, Ohio, US, opening for Aerosmith. Styx is also on the bill. Setlist includes (according to *Xavier University News*, April 10, 1975):

"Working Man"
"In The Mood"

(March 24)
Rush are awarded Most Promising Group Of The Year at the Juno Awards of 1975, Canadian National Exhibition, Toronto, Ontario, Canada. *Rush* are notified by phone as they are on tour with Aerosmith in the US.

(March 26)
Rush performs live at the Memorial Coliseum, Fort Wayne, Indiana, US, opening for Aerosmith. The James Gang is also on the bill.

(March 27)
Rush performs live at Kenosha Ice Arena, Kenosha, Wisconsin, US, opening for KISS. Thin Lizzy is also on the bill.

(March 28)
Rush performs live at Aragon Ballroom, Chicago, Illinois, US, opening for Aerosmith. Pavlov's Dog is also on the bill.

(March 31)
Rush performs live at Metro Arena, Lansing, Michigan, US, opening for Aerosmith. The Amboy Dukes are also on the bill.

(April)
Rush releases their "Fly By Night" 7" promo single in North America on Mercury Records. This original release date is noted on the later *Archives* edition re-issue of the single in 1978.

7" single & Promo 7" singles:
"Fly By Night"
"Anthem"

(April 2)
Rush performs live at Veterans Memorial Auditorium, Columbus, Ohio, US, opening for Aerosmith.

(April 4)
Rush performs live at Nordic Arena, Flint, Michigan, US, opening for KISS.

(April 5)
Rush is scheduled to play the Beeghly Center, Youngstown State University, Youngstown, Ohio, US, opening for Aerosmith, with REO Speedwagon also on the bill. The show is cancelled by Aerosmith reportedly when guitarist Joe Perry falls and injures his face. The show is rescheduled for April 13, 1975, but *Rush* cannot attend as they are performing in Missouri that evening (see that entry).

(April 6)
Rush performs live at G.W. Lisner, George Washington University, Washington D.C., opening for KISS. Heavy Metal Kids are also on the bill.

(April 7)
Rush performs live at the Agora Ballroom, Cleveland, Ohio, US, for WMMS 100.7 FM's *Nights Out At The Agora*. Reign is also on the bill. The show is broadcast live that evening and later three tracks are released on CD as *Rush ABC (Agora Ballroom, Cleveland, Ohio, August 6, 1974)* by Left Field Media in 2011 and again on LP in 2013.

"Finding My Way"

"The Best I Can"
"What You're Doing"
"Anthem" – appears on the *Rush ABC* CD & LP
"Beneath, Between & Behind" - appears on the *Rush ABC* CD & LP
"In The End"
"Fly By Night" - appears on the *Rush ABC* CD & LP
"Working Man"
"In The Mood"
"Need Some Love"
"Bad Boy" – a cover of the 1959 Larry Williams song

Note: Some sources list the three *Rush ABC* bonus tracks as coming from May 1975, but *Rush* did not perform in Cleveland that month. The tracks appear to come from this date.

(April 8)
Rush performs live at Akron Civic Theatre, Akron, Ohio, US, opening for KISS. Heavy Metal Kids are also on the bill.

(April 9)
Rush performs live at Erie County Fieldhouse, Erie, Pennsylvania, US, opening for KISS. Vitale's Madmen are also on the bill.

(April 11)
Rush performs live at Michigan Concert Palace, Detroit, Michigan, US. Status Quo is also in the bill.

(April 12)
Rush performs live at Union Auditorium, Illinois State University, Normal, Illinois, US, opening for KISS.

(April 13)
Rush performs live at Aviation Field, Forest Park, St. Louis, Missouri, US, as part of KSHE Kite Fly Festival.

(April 15)
Rush performs live at Stanley Theatre, Pittsburgh, Pennsylvania, US, opening for KISS. Heavy Metal Kids are also on the bill.

(April 17)
Rush performs live at Burlington Auditorium, Burlington, Iowa, US, opening for KISS.

(April 18)
Rush performs live at the Student Activities Building, Belleville Area College, Belleville, Illinois, US, as part of the college's 3rd Annual Fine Arts Festival. Megan McDonnough and Star are also on the bill.

(April 19)
Rush performs live at Fremd High School, Palatine, Illinois, US, opening for KISS.

(April 21)
Rush performs live at Veterans Memorial Auditorium, Louisville, Kentucky, US, opening for KISS.

(April 22)
Rush performs live at the Indianapolis Convention Center, Indianapolis, Indiana, US, opening for KISS. Status Quo is also on the bill.

(April 24)
Rush performs live at Freedom Hall Civic Center, Science Hill High School, Johnson City, Tennessee, US, opening for KISS. Heavy Metal Kids are also on the bill.

(April 25)
Rush performs live at Charlotte Park Center, Charlotte, North Carolina, opening for KISS. Heavy Metal Kids are also on the bill.

(April 26)
Rush performs live at Cumberland County Memorial Arena, Fayetteville, North Carolina, US, opening for KISS.

(April 27)
Rush performs live at Richmond Arena, Richmond, Virginia, US, opening for KISS. Brian Auger & Oblivion Express and M-S Funk are also on the bill. This is Ace Frehley's (of KISS) birthday, which both KISS and Rush commemorate with a photos together.

(Date Unknown)

Mercury Records begins issuing *Rush*'s back catalogue of albums in the UK. A May 7, 1977 piece in *Melody Maker* notes the band had released their then-five albums (*Rush* to *All The World's A Stage*) "during the last two years," indicating that it took some time to get the early albums on UK store shelves.

(May)
Rush releases their 7" singles for "Fly By Night" in the US and Europe on Mercury Records.

US & Australia 7" singles:
"Fly By Night"
"Anthem"

Netherlands 7" single:
"Fly By Night"
"Best I Can"

Mercury Records also releases the following:

A Mercury "In-Store Play" Special
Featuring tracks from important, current and new Mercury albums!
US Record Store Promo LP (MK-8)
"The Whole Thing Started With Rock & Roll, Now It's Out Of Control" Ray Manzerek
"The Gambler" Ray Manzerek
"Autobahn" Kraftwerk
"Showdown" Thin Lizzy
"It's Only Money" Thin Lizzy
"Fly By Night" Rush
"Anthem" Rush
"Lonesome Fiddle Blues" Vassar Clements
"Kryptonite" Neil Merryweather
"The Groove" Neil Merryweather

Note: The Mercury Records In-Store promo LP features a track or two from artist signed to the label and was designed to be played in record shops. The black and white picture sleeve details the work and career of each artist.

(May 3)
Rush performs live at Chanel High School, Bedford, Ohio, US, with Sweat Leaf opening.

(May 6)
Rush performs live at Riverside Theatre, Milwaukee, Wisconsin, US, opening for KISS.

(May 8)
Rush performs live at Lewis University, Lockport, Illinois, US, opening for KISS.

(May 9)
Rush is scheduled to perform live at Ohio Northern University, Ada, Ohio, US, opening for KISS and James Gang. According an ONU.edu retrospective article ("Kiss Alive at ONU: 1975") about KISS's show on this date, *Rush* was intended to play, but for reasons not stated in the article they did not and The Flock performed in their place. This is corroborated by the 1975 ONU yearbook.

Note: Several sources list *Rush* performing at this show, but that would appear to be incorrect, in light of the yearbook account that they did not.

(May 10)
Rush performs live at State Farm Show Arena, Harrisburg, Pennsylvania, US, opening for Aerosmith.

(May 16)
Rush performs live at the Capitol Theatre, Port Chester, New York, US, opening for Blue Öyster Cult.

(May 17)
Rush performs live at War Memorial Arena, Johnston, Pennsylvania, US, opening for KISS.

(May 22)
Rush performs live at Capitol Theater, Yakima, Washington, US, opening for KISS.

Note: This date does not appear in the book *KISS Alive Forever*.

(May 23)
Rush performs live at the National Guard Armory, Medford, Oregon, US, opening for KISS.

(May 24)
Rush performs live at the Paramount Northwest, Portland, Oregon, US, opening for KISS.

(May 25)
Rush performs live at the Paramount Northwest, Seattle, Washington, US, opening for KISS.

(May 26)
Rush performs live at the Paramount Northwest, Portland, Oregon, US, opening for KISS.

(May 27)
Rush performs live at Spokane Coliseum, Spokane, Washington, US, opening for KISS.

(May 29)
Rush performs two shows live at Sahara Hotel Space Centre, Las Vegas, Nevada, US, opening for KISS.

(May 30)
Rush performs live at Shrine Auditorium, Los Angeles, California, US, opening for KISS and Nazareth.
"Something For Nothing" – In *Travelling Music*, **Neil Peart** says he came upon graffiti near Shrine Auditorium which read "Freedom Isn't Free," which later helped inspire this song.

(June 1)
Rush performs live at The Winterland, San Francisco California, US, opening for KISS and The Tubes.

(June 6)
Rush performs live at Warnors Theater, Warnors Center for the Performing Arts, Fresno, California, US, opening for KISS.

(June 7)
Rush performs live at the Civic Theatre, San Diego, California, US, opening for KISS.

(June 13)
Rush performs live at Cleary Auditorium, Windsor, Ontario, Canada, supported by Mendelson Joe. A review of the show by John Laycock notes the band will return to the studio in July and are planning for their third album to be released in autumn.

(June 14)
Rush performs live at Iroquois Park, Whitby, Ontario, Canada, supported by Mendelson Joe.

(June 18)
Rush performs live at Trianon Ballroom, Regina, Saskatchewan, Canada, supported by Mendelson Joe.

(June 19)
Rush is scheduled to perform live at the Winnipeg Convention Centre, Winnipeg, Manitoba, Canada, supported by Mendelson Joe and Holy Hannah, but the show is cancelled in advance due to poor ticket sales.

(June 20)
Rush performs live at Thunder Bay Arena, Thunder Bay, Ontario, Canada.

(June 21)
Rush performs live at Memorial Gardens, Sault Ste. Marie, Ontario, Canada, supported by Mendelson Joe and Trione.

(June 22)
Rush performs live at Dundas Arena, Dundas, Ontario, Canada.

(June 23)
Rush performs live at Lakefield Arena, Lakefield, Ontario, Canada.

(June 25)
Rush performs live at Massey Hall, Toronto, Ontario, Canada, supported by Max Webster. Photos from this show are used in the gatefold for *Caress Of Steel*.

(June 26)
Rush performs live at the Theatre Auditorium, Wilfrid Laurier University, Waterloo, Ontario, Canada.

Note: The promo advertisement for this leg of the tour lists the venue as "Waterloo Lutheran University," which was the previous name of Wilfrid Laurier University. The modern "Wilfrid Laurier University" name was adopted in late 1973. *Rush* did previously perform at the same university when it was "Waterloo Lutheran" on October 12, 1973. It would seem someone mistakenly used the older name for the 1975 tour list. Some online sources likewise list the wrong name.

(June 27)
Rush performs live at Centennial Hall, London, Ontario, Canada, supported by Symphonic Slam.

(June 28)
Rush performs live at Kee To Bala, Bala, Ontario, Canada.

(June 29)
Rush performs live at Summer Gardens, Port Dover, Ontario, Canada.

(Date Unknown)
Alex Lifeson marries Charlene McNicol.

(Mid-July)
Rush records their third album at Sound Studios, Toronto, Ontario, Canada (*Caress Of Steel* sessions). According to **Geddy Lee** in *Contents Under Pressure* the sessions run for "a full three weeks."
"I Think I'm Going Bald" – according to **Lee** in 2004, the title was inspired by the KISS song (with whom they'd been touring) "Goin' Blind" and **Alex Lifeson**'s preoccupation at the time with going bald.
"Lakeside Park" – according to **Neil Peart** in various sources, this song was inspired by his time working and having fun at Lakeside Park, Port Dalhousie Ward, St. Catharines, Ontario, Canada.

Also of note:
"The Twilight Zone" – Though not written until later, **Neil**'s influence from the works of Rod Serling, creator of the TV show *The Twilight Zone*, is demonstrated by the band's dedication of the album to Serling.

(August 24)
Rush performs live at the Central Canada Exhibition Bandshell, Lansdowne Park, Ottawa, Ontario, Canada.

(Late August)
Rush performs live at Places des Nations, Montreal, Quebec, Canada, opening for Nazareth.

(September)
Rush performs live in Thunder Bay, Ontario, Canada, opening for Nazareth.

(September 17)
Rush performs live at Winnipeg Arena, Winnipeg, Manitoba, Canada, opening for Nazareth.

(September 19)
Rush performs live at Saskatoon Arena, Saskatoon, Saskatchewan, Canada, opening for Nazareth.

(September 20)
Rush performs live at Kinsmen Field, Edmonton, Alberta, Canada, opening for Nazareth.

(September 21)
Rush performs live at Clearwater Beach, Calgary, Alberta, Canada, opening for Nazareth.

(September 24)
Rush releases their album *Caress Of Steel* on Mercury Records. Apparently, due to a misprinting, the cover art is green and gold instead of the intended silver tones meant to reflect the "steel" of the title. To date, this has not been corrected (despite later correcting the *Grace Under Pressure* album cover artwork). The album is dedicated to Mr. Rod Serling. Track listing as follows:

"Bastille Day"
"I Think I'm Going Bald"
"Lakeside Park"
"The Necromancer
      I: Into Darkness
      II: Under The Shadow
      III: Return Of The King"
"The Fountain Of Lamneth
      I: In The Valley
      II: Didacts And Narpets
      III: No One At The Bridge
      IV: Panacea
      V: Bacchus Plateau
      VI: The Fountain"

Note: The LP back sleeve does not list "The Fountain Of Lamneth," but instead lists the chapters by their own titles, as if they were unconnected songs. The inner gatefold liner notes do list "The Fountain Of Lamneth" as well as its individual chapters.

1975 US cassette edition:
Side 1
"Bastille Day"
"The Fountain Of Lamneth
    II: Didacts And Narpets"
"Lakeside Park"
"The Necromancer
    I: Into Darkness
    II: Under The Shadow
    III: Return Of The King"
Side 2
"The Fountain Of Lamneth
    I: In The Valley"
"I Think I'm Going Bald"
"The Fountain Of Lamneth
    III: No One At The Bridge
    IV: Panacea
    V: Bacchus Plateau
    VI: The Fountain"

Note: This cassette edition swaps "Didacts And Narpets" and "I Think I'm Going Bald," likely for time reasons, to balance the lengths of each side. Also, "The Fountain Of Lamneth" itself is not listed, just the chapter titles as if they were unconnected songs. The result of this change sees what was intended as a side-long epic piece now fractured and nonsensical.

(September 26)
Rush performs live at Pacific Coliseum Vancouver, British Columbia, Canada, opening for Nazareth.

(October 2)
Rush performs live at the Trianon Ballroom, Regina, Saskatchewan, Canada. Queen City Kids are also on the bill.

(October 5)
Rush performs live at the Brock University Gymnasium, St. Catharines, Ontario, Canada. Max Webster and Fat Rabbit are also on the bill. In an article about this show in *The St. Catharines Standard* published 10/10/75, **Neil Peart** notes that the "Return Of The King" movement of "The Necromancer" is receiving FM radio play, so he expects it to be released as a single.

(October 6)
Rush performs live at Peter Clark Hall, University of Guelph, Guelph, Ontario, Canada. Max Webster is also on the bill.

(October 11)
Rush performs live at Franklin College, Franklin, Indiana, US.

(October 13)
Rush performs live at Freedom Hall, Johnson City, Tennessee, US, opening for Aerosmith and Ted Nugent.

(October 15)
Rush performs live at Arkansas State University, Jonesboro, Arkansas, US.

(October 16)
Rush performs live at Memorial Auditorium, Joplin, Missouri, US.

(October 17)
Rush performs live at Pershing Auditorium, Lincoln, Nebraska, US.

(October 18)
Rush performs live at Municipal Auditorium, Kansas City, Missouri, US.

(October 21)
Rush performs live at Century II Performing Arts & Convention Centre, Wichita, Kansas, US.

(October 24)
Rush performs live at the Tulsa Assembly Center, Tulsa, Oklahoma, US, opening for Ted Nugent.

(October 25)

Rush performs live at the Civic Center, Amarillo, Texas, US, opening for Ted Nugent.

(October 28)
Rush performs live at Randy's Rodeo, San Antonio, Texas, US.

(October 29 & 30)
Rush performs live at Armadillo World Headquarters, Austin, Texas, US.

(October 31)
Rush performs live at Ritz Music Hall, Corpus Christi, Texas, US.

(Late 1975)
Rush releases its 7" singles for "Return Of The Prince" in Canada on Mercury Records.

Promo 7" single (M-73728-DJ):
"The Necromancer – III: Return Of The Prince (Single Edit)"
"The Necromancer – III: Return Of The Prince (Promo Edit)"

7" single (M-73728):
"The Necromancer – III: Return Of The Prince (Single Edit)"
"I Think I'm Going Bald"

> "The Necromancer – III: Return Of The Prince (Single Edit)" 3:01
> Written by Neil Peart (word), Geddy Lee & Alex Lifeson (music)
> Appears on: 7" single
> This edit removes the monologue which starts this chapter on the album, making for a more radio-friendly start to the piece. It also appears to fade out a bit earlier. Neil mentioned that this excerpt from "The Necromancer" was getting radio play following the album's release, so that likely influenced this single being issued. The single's label lists Side A as "Return Of The Prince," but notes in the credits that it is from "The Necromancer."

> "The Necromancer – III: Return Of The Prince (Promo Edit)" 2:54
> Written by Neil Peart (word), Geddy Lee & Alex Lifeson (music)
> Appears on: Promo 7" single
> I haven't heard this, but the track length suggests it's similar to the standard single edit (no intro monologue), only with a bit more instrumental removed.

(Date Unknown)
Rush begins working on the following during this tour:
"2112" – in a 1996 interview with *Guitar* magazine, **Alex Lifeson** says the band wrote the piece "while on the road."

Note: It was during this period that *Rush* felt pressure from Mercury Records to produce more commercial, mainstream material akin to their first album. The resentment and frustration was added to the Ayn Rand themes of individualism and framed in a story influenced by Samuel R. Delany's epic science fiction narratives and Rand's book *Anthem*, all done with the intent of not giving in to that pressure. As described in both the *Rush: Beyond The Lighted Stage* documentary and the *Classic Albums: 2112 & Moving Pictures* episode, *Rush* felt that by doing this epic, side-long piece against the wishes of Mercury Records, it could be their last album, but that would go out their way, uncompromising.

(November)
Rush releases its 7" singles for "Lakeside Park" in the US on Mercury Records.

7" US Promo (73737-DJ [a]) & 7" single (73737):
"Lakeside Park (Single Edit)"
"Bastille Day"

7" US Promo single (73737-DJ [b]) :
"Lakeside Park (Single Edit)" (Mono)
"Lakeside Park (Single Edit)" (Stereo)

> "Lakeside Park (Single Edit)" 3:16
> Written by Neil Peart (words), Geddy Lee & Alex Lifeson (music)
> Appears on: US & Canada 7" single
> This version cuts the song down by almost a full minute, removing a large chunk of the instrumental.

(November 1)
Rush performs live at the Electric Ballroom, Dallas, Texas, US, opening for Iron Butterfly.

(Early November)
Rush performs live at in Montreal, Quebec, Canada, as part of the Winterfest Concert Weekend).

(November 4)
Rush performs live at the Silver Dollar Saloon, Lansing, Michigan, US.

(November 5)
Rush performs live at The Rafters, Battle Creek, Michigan, US.

(November 7)
Rush performs live at Akron Civic Theatre, Akron, Ohio, US, opening for Ted Nugent. Artful Dodger is also on the bill.

(November 8)
Rush performs live at the Allen Theatre, Cleveland, Ohio, US. Ted Nugent and Artful Dodger are also on the bill. A review of the show in *Scene* by Raj Bahadur says *Rush* were the headliners.

(November 9)
Rush performs live at Kiel Auditorium, St. Louis, Missouri, US.

(November 11)
Rush performs live at Hersey High School, Arlington Heights, Illinois, US.

(November 12)
Rush performs live at Western Hall, Western Illinois University, Macomb, Illinois, US, opening for Ted Nugent.

(November 14)
Rush performs live at Memorial Coliseum, Fort Wayne, Indiana, US, opening for Frank Zappa and The Mothers.

(November 15)
Rush performs live at The Armoury, Rockford, Illinois, US, opening for KISS.

(November 16 & 17)
Rush performs live at IMA Auditorium, Flint, Michigan, US, opening for KISS.

(November 18)
Rush performs live at McMorran Arena, Port Huron, Michigan, US, opening for KISS.

(November 19)
Rush performs live at Glacier Dome, Traverse City, Michigan, US, opening for KISS.

(November 21)
Rush performs live at Hulman Centre, Indiana State University, Terre Haute, Indiana, US, opening for KISS.

(November 23)
Rush performs live at Roberts Stadium, Evansville, Indiana, US, opening for KISS and Mott.

(November 26)
Rush performs live at the Memorial Fieldhouse, Huntington, West Virginia, US, opening for KISS and Mott.

(November 27)
Rush performs live at Cumberland County Memorial Arena, Fayetteville, North Carolina, US, opening for KISS.

(November 28)
Rush performs live at the Civic Center, Asheville, North Carolina, US, opening for KISS.

(November 29)
Rush performs live at Charlotte Park Center, Charlotte, North Carolina, US, opening for KISS.

(November 30)
Rush performs live at the Capital Center, North Carolina, US, opening for KISS.

(December 2)
Rush performs live at the Municipal Auditorium, Columbus, Georgia, US, opening for KISS.

(December 3)
Rush performs live at the Civic Center, Dothan, Alabama, US, opening for KISS.

(December 5)
Rush performs live at The Omni, Atlanta, Georgia, US, opening for KISS.

(December 6)

Rush performs live at Veterans Coliseum, Jacksonville, Florida, US, opening for KISS.

(December 7)
Rush performs live at the Morris Civic Center, South Bend, US.

(December 12)
Rush performs live at the War Memorial Arena, Syracuse, New York, US, opening for KISS.

(December 14)
Rush performs live at The Orpheum, Boston, Massachusetts, US, opening for KISS.

(December 15)
Rush performs live at the Toledo Sports Arena, Toledo, Ohio, US, opening for Leslie West and Lynyrd Skynyrd.

(December 18)
Rush performs live at the Silver Dollar Saloon, Lansing, Michigan, US.

(December 19)
Rush performs live at Broome County Arena, Binghamtom, New York, US, opening for KISS.

(December 20)
Rush performs live at the Pittsburgh Civic Arena, Pittsburgh, Pennsylvania, US, opening for KISS and Mott.

(December 21)
Rush performs live at the Tomorrow Club, Youngstown, Ohio, US. Mojo is also on the bill.

(December 22)
Rush performs live at the Agricultural Hall, Allentown, Pennsylvania, US, opening for KISS and Mott.

(December 26)
Rush performs live at the Aragon Ballroom, Chicago, Illinois, US.

(December 27)
Rush performs live at Wings Stadium, Kalamazoo, Michigan, US.

(December 28)
Rush performs live at the Indianapolis Convention Centre, Indianapolis, Indiana, US, opening for Blue Öyster Cult, Ted Nugent, Mott and the Outlaws.

(December 29)
Rush performs live at Cobo Hall Arena, Detroit, Michigan, US, opening for Ted Nugent.

(December 30)
Rush is scheduled to perform live at Veterans Memorial Auditorium, Columbus, Ohio, US, but the show is rescheduled to January 3, 1976.

2112 & ALL THE WORLD'S A STAGE

1976

(January 3)
Rush performs live at Veterans Memorial Auditorium, Columbus, Ohio, US. This replaces the cancelled show from December 30, 1975.

(January 4)
Rush performs live at the Capitol Center, Landover, Maryland, US, opening for Blue Öyster Cult, Ted Nugent, REO Speedwagon and Leslie West.

(January 10)
Rush performs live at Massey Hall, Toronto, Ontario, Canada. Mainline is the opening act.

(Date Unknown)
Geddy Lee marries Nancy Young. Reportedly, the couple have a two week honeymoon in Hawaii, US.

(Early 1976)
Rush release their 7" single for "Lakeside Park" in Canada on Mercury Records.

7" single (M-73737):
"Lakeside Park (Single Edit)"
"Bastille Day"

(February)
Rush writes and rehearses their fourth studio album at a farm (likely Lakewoods Farm, Flesherton) in Ontario, Canada (*2112* sessions).
"A Passage To Bangkok" – According to **Alex Lifeson** in a 2012 *High Times* piece, the music was composed on acoustic guitar in a farmhouse on cassette, then rehearsed by the band in the basement.

Rush records their fourth studio album (*2112* sessions) at Toronto Sound Studio, Toronto, Ontario, Canada. Produced by *Rush* and Terry Brown. **Neil Peart** says in a 2014 CBC.ca interview that the band had a whole month to write, rehearse and record the album, whereas in the *Signals* tour book, he notes the album was completed in under a month. Tracks worked on include:
"2112" – The opening "space-y" sounds are performed by Hugh Syme, who improvised numerous sequences. The band then selected the best bits and assembled the intro. The track features a snippet of Tchaikovsky's Festival Overture for "The Year of 1812."
 "Lessons" – penned by Alex Lifeson
"Tears" – penned by Geddy Lee. Hugh Syme plays Mellotron on this track.
"Something For Nothing" – **Neil Peart** develops the "Freedom Isn't Free" graffiti he saw near the Shrine Auditorium on May 30, 1975.
"The Twilight Zone" – In the *Moving Pictures* tour book, **Neil** says this song was last to be written for the album and that it was created in the studio, not written and rehearsed in advance of the recording sessions. In the *Signals* tour book, he notes it was written and recorded in a day.

(February 9)
Rush performs live at Hamilton Place Great Hall, Hamilton, Ontario, Canada. Ian Thomas is the opening act.

(February 21)
Rush performs live at the Gymnasium, Brantford Collegiate Institute, Brantford, Ontario, Canada. Max Webster is the opening act.

(March 2)
Rush performs live at the Ottawa Civic Centre, Ottawa, Ontario, Canada, opening for Electric Light Orchestra (ELO).

(March 5)
Rush performs live at Randhurst Mall Ice Arena, Mt. Prospect, Illinois, US, opening for Kansas. Starcastle is also on the bill.

(March 15, 16, 17 & 18)
Rush performs live at Starwood, West Hollywood, California, US.

(March 23)
Rush performs live at Warnors Theater, Fresno, California, US. The opening acts are Styx, Sutherland Brothers and Quiver.

(March 25)

Rush performs live at The Armory, Medford, Oregon, US. The opening acts are Styx, Sutherland Brothers and Quiver.

(March 26)
Rush performs live at the Paramount Northwest, Seattle, Washington, US.

(March 27)
Rush performs live at Kennedy Pavillion, Gonzanga University, Spokane, Washington, US. The opening act is Styx.

(March 28)
Rush performs live at Paramount Theater, Portland, Oregon, US. The opening act is Sutherland Brothers & Quiver. Styx was scheduled to open, as well, but an *Oregonian* newspaper review of the show says they truck trouble in Washington and could not make it.

(March 29)
Rush performs live at Tacoma National Guard Armory, Tacoma, Washington, US. The opening act is Styx.

(April 1)
Rush releases their album *2112* on Mercury Records. Track listing as follows:

"2112
    I: Overture
    II: The Temples Of Syrinx
    III: Discovery
    IV: Presentation
    V: Oracle: The Dream
    VI: Soliloquy
    VII: Grand Finale"
"A Passage To Bangkok"
"The Twilight Zone"
"Lessons"
"Tears"
"Something For Nothing"

(April 7)
Rush performs live at the Civic Arena, Pittsburgh, Pennsylvania, US, opening for Bad Company.

(April 9)
Rush performs live at the Coliseum, Indianapolis, Indiana, US. The opening acts are Ted Nugent and Sutherland Brothers & Quiver.

(April 10)
Rush performs live at Morris Civic Center, South Bend, Indiana, US. The opening act is Starcastle.

(April 11)
Rush performs live at Ice Arena, Waukegan, Illinois, US. The opening acts is Pentwater/Starcastle.

(April 15)
Rush performs live at the Ambassador Theatre, St. Louis, Missouri, US.

(April 17)
Rush performs live at Memorial Arena, Pekin, Illinois, US. The opening acts are Thin Lizzy and Starcastle.

(April 26)
Rush performs live at the Akron Civic Theatre, Akron, Ohio, US. The opening act is Stu Daye.

(April 27)
Rush performs live at the Allen Theatre, Cleveland, Ohio, US. The opening act is Stu Daye.

(April 28)
Rush performs live at IMA Auditorium, Flint, Michigan, US, opening for Rare Earth (who failed to show up) and Journey.

(April 29)
Rush performs live at Veterans Memorial Auditorium, Columbus, Ohio, US.

(April 30)
Rush performs live at McElroy Auditorium, Waterloo, Iowa, US, opening for Aerosmith and Angel.

(May 2)
Rush performs live at Memorial Hall, Kansas City, Kansas, US.

(May 9)
Rush performs live at Tomorrow Club, Youngstown, Ohio, US. The opening act is Paris.

(May 11)
Rush performs live at Masonic Auditorium, Detroit, Michigan, US. The opening acts are Starcastle and Artful Dodger.

(May 13)
Rush performs live at Starr Auditorium, Ferris State College, Big Rapids, Michigan, US. The opening act is Pete Texas.

(May 22)
Rush performs live at RKO Orpheum Theater, Davenport, Iowa, US, opening for Blue Öyster Cult.

(May 23)
Rush performs live at Duluth Arena, Duluth, Minnesota, Iowa, US, opening for Blue Öyster Cult.

(May 24)
Rush is scheduled to perform live at Mary E Sawyer Auditorium, La Crosse, Wisconsin, US, opening for Blue Öyster Cult, but the show is cancelled.

(May 25)
Rush performs live at the Fort Wayne Memorial Coliseum, Fort Wayne, Indiana, US. Also on the bill are Thin Lizzy, Aerosmith and Stu Daye.

(May 26)
Rush performs live at Hulman Civic Center, Indiana State University, Terre Haute, Indiana, US, opening for Aerosmith.

(May 27)
Rush performs live at Brown County Arena, Green Bay, Wisconsin, US, opening for Blue Öyster Cult. Sunblind Lion is also on the bill.

(May 28)
Rush performs live at the Riviera Theater, Chicago, Illinois, US.

(May 29)
Rush performs live at the Civic Center Arena, St. Paul, Minnesota, US, opening for Blue Öyster Cult, Steve Marriot's All Stars (Humble Pie) and REO Speedwagon.

(May 30)
Rush performs live at Nelson Center, Springfield, Illinois, US.

(June 4)
Rush performs live at the Amarillo Civic Center, Amarillo, Texas, US. The opening act is Iron Butterfly.

(June 5)
Rush performs live at the Memorial Gym, University of Texas at El Paso, Texas, US. The opening act is Styx.

(June 7)
Rush performs live at Municipal Auditorium, San Antonio, Texas, US. The opening act is Thin Lizzy.

(June 11, 12 & 13)
Rush performs live at Massey Hall, Toronto, Ontario, Canada. These shows are recorded and compiled for release on the live album *All The World's A Stage*. Several tracks have also been released individually over the years.

> "Bastille Day (ATWAS – Icon 2 Version)" 4:52
> Written by Neil Peart (words), Geddy Lee (music) & Alex Lifeson (music)
> Appears on: Icon 2
> The only difference between this version and the All The World's A Stage version is that this fades out at the end, making for a good standalone cut.
>
> "Fly By Night/In The Mood (ATWAS - Single Version)" 4:53
> Written by Neil Peart (words: "Fly By Night") & Geddy Lee ("In The Mood" / music: "Fly By Night")
> Appears on: 7" single, US Promo 7" single
> A good standalone version of the medley from All The World's A Stage. It starts with a fade-in before the introduction and ends on a fade out.
>
> "Something For Nothing (ATWAS – Single Version)" 3:57
> Written by Neil Peart (words) & Geddy Lee (music)
> Appears on: "Fly By Night/In The Mood" 7" single, US Promo 7" single

As with the other live single versions, this is a good standalone cut, starting with the music and ending with a fade-out of the crowd.

"2112 (ATWAS - Icon 2 Version)" 15:49
Written by Neil Peart (words), Geddy Lee (music, except "Discovery" & "Presentation") & Alex Lifeson (music)
Appears on: Icon 2
Rush didn't play all of the "2112" epic during this tour and wouldn't play it live in its entirety until the Test For Echo Tour. Left out is most of "Discovery" (a snippet is played leading into "Presentation") and all of "Oracle: The Dream." On All The World's A Stage, the end of "Lakeside Park" segues into the spacey opening of "2112," whereas on Icon 2, the track starts just after the segue with a very quick fade-in. It ends the same as on the album, where it fades out ending Side 2 of LP 1.

"Working Man/Finding My Way (ATWAS - Early CD Version)" 14:19
Written by Geddy Lee & Alex Lifeson
Appears on: All The World's A Stage (Early CD Editions)
When Rush's back catalogue was first released on CD, the maximum allowable length on a disc was 74 minutes, which meant either All The World's A Stage would be put on 2 CDs or (the cheaper option) 1 CD with a track removed. By taking off "What You're Doing," this medley closes out the CD and thus fades out over the crowd noise, removing about 40 seconds of cheering.

"What You're Doing (ATWAS - Chronicles Version)" 5:41
Written by Geddy Lee & Alex Lifeson
Appears on: Chronicles
When Rush's back catalogue was first released on CD, the maximum allowable length on a disc was 74 minutes, which meant either All The World's A Stage would be put on 2 CDs or (the cheaper option) 1 CD with a track removed. At the same time, the Chronicles collection was planned, so when it was decided to remove this track from the original live album, the powers that be still made it available on Chronicles. This edit fades in and out at the beginning and end and omits the post-show chatter.

(June 15)
Rush performs live at the Memorial Arena, Chatham, Ontario, Canada.

(June 16)
Rush performs live at Roberts Stadium, Evansville, Indiana, US, opening for Aerosmith.

Note: This appearance would seem to have been a last minute addition as it's not listed on the original period print ads for the tour. Evansville is a more than 8 hour drive from Chatham to Evansville and another 11 hour drive from Evansville to Welland. Must have been an offer *Rush* couldn't refuse.

(June 17)
Rush performs live at Welland Arena, Welland, Ontario, Canada. Max Webster is the opening act.

(June 18)
Rush performs live at Oshawa Civic Auditorium, Oshawa, Ontario, Canada.

(Date Unknown)
Rush assembles their live album, *All The World's A Stage*, at Toronto Sound Studios, Toronto, Ontario, Canada (*The Guardian* March 24, 2011).
"Xanadu" - **Neil Peart** begins writing this song, inspired by the film *Citizen Kane*, while **Geddy Lee** and **Alex Lifeson** work on mixing the live album. The song is later overtaken by the Samuel Taylor Coleridge poem *Kubla Kahn*.

Note: in the *A Farewell To Kings* tour book, **Neil Peart** says this new song was featured in the last part of the North American tour and the UK tour prior to the recording of the album. It can be heard on the bootleg recording of the June 2, 1977, Manchester concert.

(July 6)
Rush performs live at Assembly Center, Tulsa, Oklahoma, Canada. Also on the bill are Mott and UFO.

(July 8)
Rush performs live at Hirsch Memorial Coliseum, Shreveport, Louisiana, US, opening for Blue Öyster Cult. Also on the bill are Mott and Starz.

(July 10)
Rush performs live at Moody Coliseum, Southern Methodist University, Dallas, Texas, US, opening for Blue Öyster Cult. Also on the bill are Mott and UFO.

(July 11)

Rush performs live at Sam Houston Coliseum, Houston, Texas, US, opening for Blue Öyster Cult. Also on the bill are Mott and UFO.

(July 16)
Rush performs live at West Palm Beach Auditorium, West Palm Beach, Florida, US, opening for Blue Öyster Cult. Also on the bill are Mott and Starz.

(July 18)
Rush performs live at Dothan Civic Center, Dothan, Alabama, US, opening for Blue Öyster Cult.

(July 20)
Rush performs live at Soldiers And Sailors Auditorium, Chattanooga, Tennessee, US,

(July 23)
Rush performs live at Triad Arena, Greensboro, North Carolina, US, opening for Blue Öyster Cult. Also on the bill are Mott and Starz.

(July 24)
Rush performs live at Cumberland County Arena, Fayetteville, North Carolina, US, opening for Blue Öyster Cult. Also on the bill are Mott and Starz.

(July 25)
Rush performs live at Capitol Music Hall, Wheeling, West Virginia, US, opening for Blue Öyster Cult.

(July 27)
Rush performs live at University Hall, Jackson, Mississippi, US.

(July 29)
Rush performs live at Garret Coliseum, Montgomery, Alabama, US, opening for Blue Öyster Cult at Rock Fest '76. Also on the bill is Mott.

(July 30)
Rush performs live at Municipal Auditorium, Columbus, Georgia, US.

(August)
Rush releases their 7" singles "The Twilight Zone" in North America on Mercury Records.

Canada 7" single (M-73803):
"The Twilight Zone (Single Edit)"
"Lessons (Single Edit)"

US 7" single (73803):
"The Twilight Zone (Single Edit)"
"Lessons (Single Edit)"

US promo singles (73803-DJ):
"The Twilight Zone (Single Edit)"
"Lessons (Single Edit)"

> "The Twilight Zone (Single Edit)" 2:41
> Written by Neil Peart (words) and Geddy Lee & Alex Lifeson (music)
> Appears on: Canadian 7" single, US 7" promo single
> This edit features an early fade out, cutting about 40 seconds of audible time from the track.

> "Lessons (Single Edit)" 2:58
> Written by Alex Lifeson (words and music) & Geddy Lee (music)
> Appears on: The Twilight Zone Canadian 7" single, The Twilight Zone US 7" promo single
> This edit fades out early, cutting about 50 audible seconds from the track.

(August 1)
Rush performs live in Huntsville, Alabama, US.

(August 8)
Rush performs live at Erie Stadium, Erie, Pennsylvania, US, opening for the Doobie Brothers. Heart is also on the bill.

(August 13)
Rush performs live at Municipal Auditorium, Sioux City, Iowa, US, opening for Blue Öyster Cult.

(August 14)

Rush performs live at Fargo Civic Auditorium, Fargo, North Dakota, US, opening for Blue Öyster Cult. Point Blank are also on the bill.

(August 15)
Rush performs live at All Seasons Arena, Minot, North Dakota, US, opening for Blue Öyster Cult. Point Blank are also on the bill.

(August 17)
Rush performs live at Topeka Municipal Auditorium, Topeka, Kansas, US, opening for Blue Öyster Cult. Point Blank are also on the bill.

(August 20)
Rush performs live at McElroy Auditorium, Waterloo, Iowa, US, opening for Blue Öyster Cult. Point Blank are also on the bill.

(August 26)
Rush performs live at B-Ginnings, Schaumburg, Illinois, US.

(August 27)
Rush performs live at Union Auditorium, Illinois State University, Normal, Illinois, US. The opening act is Head East.

(August 28)
Rush performs live at Glacier Dome, Traverse City, Michigan, US.

(August 29)
Rush performs live at Greater Muskegon Ice Arena, Muskegon, Michigan, US. The opening act is Styx.

(September 3)
Rush performs live at Hara Arena, Dayton, Ohio, US, opening for Blue Öyster Cult. The opening act is Styx.

(September 10)
Rush performs live at Wendler Arena, Saginaw, Michigan, US, opening for Blue Öyster Cult.

(September 13)
Rush performs live at JFK Coliseum, Manchester, New Hampshire, US, opening for Blue Öyster Cult.

(September 17)
Rush performs live at Broome County Arena, Birmingham, New York, US, opening for Blue Öyster Cult. Angel is also on the bill.

(September 18)
Rush performs live at Memorial Auditorium, Syracuse, New York, US, opening for Blue Öyster Cult. Angel is also on the bill.

(September 19)
Rush performs live at Zembo Mosque, Harrisburg, Pennsylvania, US. The opening act is Angel.

(September 20)
Rush performs live at Agricultural Hall, Allentown Pennsylvania, US. The opening act is Angel.

(September 22)
Rush performs live at The Dome Arena, Rochester, New York, US, opening for Blue Öyster Cult. Angel is also on the bill.

(September 28)
Rush performs live at Joe Louis Levesque Arena, Moncton, New Brunswick, Canada. The opening band is Wireless.

(September 29)
Rush release their live album *All The World's A Stage* on Mercury Records. The tracks are from the June 11, 12 and 13, 1976, Massey Hall shows. In a 1999 *Rockline* interview, **Geddy Lee** says there is no "doctoring" on this release (overdubs, etc.).

Rush performs live at Simmons Sports Center, Charlottetown, Prince Edward Island, Canada. The opening band is Wireless.

(October 1)
Rush performs live at Sydney Forum, Sydney, Nova Scotia, Canada. The opening band is Wireless.

(October 3)

Rush performs live at Lord Beaverbrook Rink, Saint John, New Brunswick, Canada. The opening band is Wireless.

(October 4)
Rush performs live at The Halifax Forum, Halifax, Nova Scotia, Canada. The opening band is Wireless.

(October 8)
Rush performs live at North Bay Memorial Gardens, North Bay, Ontario, Canada. The opening band is Ian Thomas.

(October 9)
Rush performs live at Sudbury Arena, Sudbury, Ontario, Canada. The opening band is Ian Thomas.

(October 10)
Rush performs live at the Civic Centre, Ottawa, Ontario, Canada. The opening acts are Max Webster and Ian Thomas.

(October 11)
Rush performs live at Kingston Memorial Centre, Kingston, Ontario, Canada. The opening act is Ian Thomas.

(October 13)
Rush performs live at Memorial Gardens, Sault Ste. Marie, Ontario, Canada.

(October 15)
Rush performs live at Fort William Gardens, Thunder Bay, Ontario, Canada. The opening act is Max Webster.

(October 17)
Rush performs live at Winnipeg Arena, Winnipeg, Manitoba, Canada. The opening act is Max Webster.

(October 19)
Rush performs live at Keystone Centre, Bandon, Manitoba, Canada. The opening act is Max Webster.

(October 20)
Rush performs live at the Agridome, Regina, Saskatchewan, Canada. The opening act may have been Queen City Kids.

(October 21)
Rush performs live at Saskatoon Arena, Saskatoon, Saskatchewan, Canada.

(October 23)
Rush performs live at the Kinsman Fieldhouse, Edmonton, Alberta, Canada.

(October 24)
Rush performs live at the Lethbridge Sportsplex, Lethbridge, Alberta, Canada. The opening act is Max Webster.

(October 26)
Rush performs live at the Pacific National, Exhibition Garden Auditorium, Vancouver, British Columbia, Canada. The opening act is Max Webster.

(October 27)
Rush performs live at Memorial Arena, Victoria, British Columbia, Canada. The opening act is Max Webster.

(October 28)
Rush performs live at Paramount Northwest, Seattle, Washington, US. The opening act is Tommy Bolin.

(October 29)
Rush performs live at Tacoma National Guard Armory, Tacoma, Washington, US. The opening act is Tommy Bolin.

(October 30 & 31)
Rush performs live at Paramount Theater, Portland, Oregon, US. The opening act is Tommy Bolin.

(November 3)
Rush performs live at Douglas Hall Fairgrounds, Roseburg, Oregon, US. The opening act is Tommy Bolin.

(November 4)
Rush performs live at the Armory, Medford, Oregon, US. The opening act is Tommy Bolin.

(November 13)
Rush performs live at the Armory, Rockford, Illinois, US. The opening acts are Cheap Trick and Paris.

(November 14)
Rush performs live at RKO Orpheum Theatre, Davenport, Iowa, US, opening for Montrose.

(November 15)
Rush performs live at Veterans Memorial Auditorium, Des Moines, Iowa, US, opening for Montrose and Kansas.

(November 19)
Rush performs live at The Tomorrow Club, Youngstown, Ohio, US.

(November 20)
Rush performs live at The Spectrum, Philadelphia, Pennsylvania, US, opening for Kansas. Robin Trower is also on the bill.

(November 24)
Rush performs live at Sacramento Memorial Auditorium, Sacramento, California, US, opening for Ted Nugent. Be-Bop Deluxe is also on the bill.

(November 26 & 27)
Rush performs live at The Winterland, San Francisco, California, US, opening for Ted Nugent. Be-Bop Deluxe is also on the bill.

(November 28)
Rush performs live at Selland Arena, Fresno, California, US, opening for Ted Nugent. Be-Bop Deluxe is also on the bill.

(November 29)
Rush release their live "Fly By Night/In The Mood" singles in the US on Mercury Records.

US 7" single (73873):
"Fly By Night/In The Mood (Live - Single Version)"
"Something For Nothing (Live – Single Version)"

US 7" promo single (73873-DJ):
"Fly By Night/In The Mood (Live - Single Version)"
"Something For Nothing (Live – Single Version)"

(November 30)
Rush performs live at Golden Hall, San Diego, California, US, opening for Ted Nugent. Rex is also on the bill.

(December 1)
Rush performs live at Great Western Forum, San Diego, California, US, opening for Ted Nugent. Rex is also on the bill.

(December 3)
Rush performs live at Auditorium Arena, Denver, Colorado, US, opening for Ted Nugent.

(December 8)
Rush performs live at the Palace Theater, Waterbury, Connecticut, US. The opening acts are Black Oak Arkansas and James Gang.

(December 9)
Rush performs live at the Springfield Civic Center, Springfield, Massachusetts, US, opening for Foghat. James Gang is also on the bill.

(December 10)
Rush performs live at the Capitol Theater, Passaic, New Jersey, US, opening for Foghat. James Gang is also on the bill. The show is audio and video recorded and later released on the *R40* boxed set in 2014. The following is released individually:

> "Anthem (Live in Passaic, 1976)" 5:00
> Written by Neil Peart (words) and Geddy Lee & Alex Lifeson (music)
> Appears on: Time Machine 2011: Live In Cleveland DVD and Blu-ray
> This cut starts with Geddy's banter and intro and ends on a fade out.

Note: The recording which appears on *R40* features what seems to be a bit of audio interference, magnetic bleed or ghosting of some sort. In the quiet parts, you can hear this audio signal faintly in the background.

(December 11)
Rush performs live at The Palladium, New York City, New York, US, opening for Foghat. Mother's Finest is also on the bill.

(December 12)
Rush performs live at the Palace Theatre, Reading, Pennsylvania, US, opening for Montrose. Black Oak Arkansas is also on the bill.

(December 15)
Rush performs live at The Forum, Montreal, Quebec, Canada, opening for Aerosmith.

(December 16)
Rush performs live at Auditorium Theatre, Chicago, Illinois, US. The opening act is Cheap Trick.

(December 18)
Rush performs live at Astor Theatre, Reading, Pennsylvania, US. The opening act is Crack The Sky.

(December 19)
Rush performs live at Century Theatre, Buffalo, New York, US.

(December 20)
Rush performs live at Winfield Dunn Center, Austin Peay State University, Clarksville, Tennessee, US, opening for Lynyrd Skynyrd.

(December 22)
Rush (for *Rush* and *All The World's A Stage*), S.R.O. Productions and CHUM FM (for supporting the band) are presented gold records by Sam "The Record Man" Sniderman and Polydor president Tim Harrold, at the Hyatt Regency Hotel, Toronto, Ontario, Canada.

Rush performs live at Agricultural Hall, Allentown, Pennsylvania, US. The opening acts are Styx and Mott.

(December 27)
Rush performs live at Market Square Arena, Indianapolis, Indiana, US. The opening acts are Bob Seger, Atlanta Rhythm Section and Roadmaster.

(December 29)
Rush performs live at Erie County Fieldhouse, Erie, Pennsylvania, US. The opening act is Diamond Reo.

(December 30)
Rush performs live at McMaster University Gym, Hamilton, Ontario, Canada. The opening acts are Max Webster and Wireless.

(December 31)
Rush performs live at Maple Leaf Gardens, Toronto, Ontario, Canada. The opening acts are Chilliwack and Wireless.

A FAREWELL TO KINGS

1977

(January)
Mercury Records releases the radio promo LP *Everything Your Listeners Ever Wanted To Hear By Rush...But You Were Afraid To Play* in the US. Track listing as follows:

"Fly By Night"
"Making Memories"
"Bastille Day"
"Something For Nothing"
"Lakeside Park"
"Anthem"
"2112: I: Overture/II: The Temples Of Syrinx"
"The Twilight Zone"
"Best I Can"
"The Fountain Of Lamneth: V: Bacchus Plateau"
"In The End"

>"2112: I: Overture/II: The Temples Of Syrinx" 6:45
>Written by Neil Peart (words), Geddy Lee & Alex Lifeson (music); Tchaikovsky ("The Year of 1812: Festival Overture" in E-flat Major [Op. 49])
>Appears on: Everything Your Listeners Ever Wanted To Hear By Rush...But You Were Afraid To Play, Rush Through Time, Rush Anthology, Chronicles, The Spirit Of Radio: Greatest Hits 1974-1987
>As you'd expect, this is the first two movements of "2112". The two parts make for a good standalone pairing.
>
>"The Fountain Of Lamneth: V: Bacchus Plateau" 3:12
>Written by Neil Peart (words) & Geddy Lee (music)
>Appears on: Everything Your Listeners Ever Wanted To Hear By Rush...But You Were Afraid To Play
>I guess this would be the most radio-friendly movement of "The Fountain Of Lamneth," but it's a little surprising that "Return Of The King" from "The Necromancer" wasn't used, having been a single itself and, according to Geddy, fairly popular on radio.

(January 3)
Rush performs live at Maple Leaf Gardens, Toronto, Ontario, Canada. The opening acts are Chilliwack and Wireless.

(January 6)
Rush performs live at The Music Hall, Houston, Texas, US.

(January 7)
Rush performs live in Corpus Christi, Texas, US.

(January 8 & 9)
Rush performs live at Municipal Auditorium, San Antonio, Texas, US, opening for Ted Nugent.

(January 10)
Rush performs live in Dallas, Texas, US,

(January 11)
Rush performs live at the Paramount Theatre, Austin, Texas, US.

(January 13)
Rush performs live in Wichita, Kansas, US.

(January 14)
Rush performs live at Fairgrounds Arena, Oklahoma City, Oklahoma, US, opening for Ted Nugent. Artful Dodger is also on the bill.

(January 15)
Rush performs live at Municipal Auditorium, Kansas City, Missouri, US, opening for Ted Nugent.

(January 16)
Rush performs live at Expo Square Pavillion, Tulsa, Oklahoma, US, opening for Ted Nugent. Artful Dodger is also on the bill.

(January 18)

Rush performs live at El Paso Coliseum, El Paso, Texas, US, opening for Ted Nugent. Artful Dodger is also on the bill.

(January 19)
Rush performs live at Lubbock Coliseum, Lubbock, Texas, US, opening for Ted Nugent. Artful Dodger is also on the bill.

(January 20)
Rush performs live at Ector County Coliseum, Odessa, Texas, US. The opening acts are Head East and Artful Dodger.

(January 21)
Rush performs live at Taylor County Coliseum, Abilene, Texas, US. The opening acts are Head East and Artful Dodger.

(January 22)
Rush performs live at Amarillo Civic Auditorium, Amarillo, Texas, US. The opening acts are Head East and Artful Dodger.

(January 24)
Rush performs live at Fair Park Coliseum, Beaumont, Texas, US. The opening acts are Head East and Artful Dodger.

(January 26 & 27)
Rush performs live at Veterans Memorial Auditorium, Columbus, Ohio, US. The opening acts are Starcastle and Max Webster.

(January 28)
Rush performs live at Louisville Gardens, Louisville, Kentucky, US, opening for Outlaws. Also on the bill is Hydra.

(January 29)
Rush performs live at Memorial Coliseum, Evansville, Indiana, US. The opening acts are Starcastle and Max Webster.

(January 30)
Rush performs live at Morris Civic Center, South Bend, Indiana, US. The opening acts are Starcastle and Max Webster.

(February 9)
Rush performs live at Wendlar Arena, Saginaw, Michigan, US. The opening act is The Runaways.

(February 10)
Rush performs live at Cobo Hall Arena, Detroit, Michigan, US. The opening acts are Max Webster and The Runaways,

(February 11)
Rush performs live at Hammond Civic Center, Hammond, Indiana, US. The opening act is Max Webster.

(February 12)
Rush performs live at the RKO Orpheum Theatre, Davenport, Iowa, US.

(February 13)
Rush performs live at Kiel Auditorium, St. Louis, Missouri, US. The opening acts are Rex and Max Webster.

(February 15)
Rush performs live at Memorial Auditorium, Chattanooga, Tennessee, US, opening for Kansas.

(February 16)
Rush performs live at Boutwell Auditorium, Birmingham, Alabama, US, opening for Blue Öyster Cult. Piper is also on the bill.

(February 17)
Rush performs live at Municipal Auditorium, Mobile, Alabama, US, opening for Blue Öyster Cult.

(February 19 & 20)
Rush performs live at The Warehouse, New Orleans, Louisiana, US, opening for Blue Öyster Cult.

(February 22)
Rush performs live at Municipal Auditorium, Columbus, Georgia, US, opening for Blue Öyster Cult.

(February 26)
Rush performs live at Cumberland County Memorial Arena, Fayetteville, North Carolina, US, opening for Blue Öyster Cult.

(February 27)
Rush performs live at The Omni, Atlanta, Georgia, US, opening for Blue Öyster Cult.

(March 2)
Rush performs live at the Auditorium, Michigan State University, East Lansing, Michigan, US. The opening acts are Nils Lofgren and Max Webster.

(March 3)
Rush performs live at Tomorrow Club, Youngstown, Ohio, US.

(March 4)
Rush performs live at Riverfront Coliseum, Cincinnati, Ohio, US. The opening acts are Boston and Starcastle.

(March 5)
Rush performs live at Straughn Auditorium, Mansfield State College, Mansfield, Pennsylvania, US. The opening act is Max Webster.

Note: The date is confirmed in the Spring 1977 issue of the MSC student newspaper *The Flashlight*.

(March 6)
Rush is scheduled to appear live at The Palladium, New York City, New York, US, but the show is postponed because headlining act Bob Seger And The Silver Bullet Band drummer Charlie Allen Martin is injured (his legs are broken) in a car accident and needs to be replaced during his recovery. The rescheduled show takes place on March 17.

(March 8)
Rush performs live at Scope Arena, Norfolk, Virginia, US, opening for Kansas. Rick Derringer is also on the bill.

(March 11)
Rush performs live at Tower Theatre, Upper Darby, Pennsylvania, US. The opening acts are Max Webster and Cheap Trick.

(March 12)
Rush performs live at the Capitol Theater, Passaic, New Jersey, US, opening for Kansas.

(March 13)
Adrian Živojinović is born to Charlene and **Alex Lifeson**.

Rush performs live in Indiana, Pennsylvania, US. The opening act is Cheap Trick.

Note: Adrian's birth is noted in a local newspaper review of the show by Pete Bishop as having occurred the Sunday before the show (on Monday), as well as that he is **Lifeson**'s second son.

(March 14)
Rush performs live at the Stanley Theater, Pittsburgh, Pennsylvania, US. The opening acts are Max Webster and Cheap Trick.

(March 17)
Rush performs live at The Palladium, New York City, New York, US, opening for Bob Seger & The Silver Bullet Band. Starz is also on the bill.

(March 18)
Rush performs live at Oshawa Civic Auditorium, Oshawa, Ontario, Canada. The opening act is Max Webster.

(March 19)
Rush performs live at University of Guelph, Guelph, Ontario, Canada.

(Mid-March)
Rush performs live at London Gardens, London, Ontario, Canada. The opening act is Max Webster.

Note: some sources note this as March 20th, such as Cygnus-X1.net.

(March 23)
Rush performs live at London Gardens, London, Ontario, Canada. The opening act is Max Webster.

(April 8)
Rush performs live at the Toledo Sports Arena, Toledo, Ohio, US. The opening acts are Angel and Max Webster.

(April 9)
Rush performs live at Hara Arena, Dayton, Ohio, US. The opening acts Rick Derringer and Max Webster.

(April 13)
Rush performs live at Wings Stadium, Kalamazoo, Michigan, US.

(April 14)
Rush performs live at Memorial Coliseum, Fort Wayne, Indiana, US. The opening acts are Starcastle and Roy Buchanan.

(April 15)
Rush performs live at the Public Hall, Cleveland, Ohio, US. The opening acts are Angel and Max Webster.

(April 16)
Rush performs live at Grove City College Arena, Grove City, Pennsylvania, US. The opening act is Max Webster.

(April 17)
Rush performs live at GW Lisner Auditorium, Washington, DC, US. The opening act is Max Webster.

(April 20)
Rush performs live at Agricultural Hall, Allentown, Pennsylvania, US. The opening acts are Angel and Max Webster.

(April 21)
Rush performs live at Mid-Hudson, Civic Center, Poughkeepsie, New York, US. The opening acts are Angel and Max Webster

(April 22)
Rush performs live at Broome County Arena, Binghamton, New York, US. The opening act is Max Webster.

(April 23)
Rush performs live at War Memorial Arena, Syracuse, New York, US. The opening act is Styx.

(April 24)
Rush performs live at Palace Arena, Albany, New York, US. The opening acts are Styx, Starcastle and Max Webster.

(May)
Ray Danniels and Vic Wilson, *Rush*'s managers and founders of S.R.O. Productions, launch Anthem Records in Canada, named after the song. The new record label also reissues *Rush*'s albums in Canada. Anthem's debut single is "Making Memories."

Canada 7" single (ANS-001):
"Making Memories"
"2112: II: The Temples Of Syrinx"

Mercury Records releases "The Temples Of Syrinx" singles in the US.

US 7" single (73912)
"2112: II: The Temples Of Syrinx"
"Making Memories"

US promo 7" single (73912-DJ):
"2112: II: The Temples Of Syrinx"
"Making Memories"

> "2112: II: The Temples Of Syrinx" 2:19
> Written by Neil Peart (words), Geddy Lee & Alex Lifeson (Music)
> Appears on: Canada 7" "Making Memories" single, US 7" single (1977), US Promo 7" single (1977), UK 7" & 12" singles (1978), Retrospective I 1974-1980, Gold
> Basically, this is "The Temples Of Syrinx" chapter of "2112," handy as a stand-alone version. Without the "Overture" preceding it, the start is a bit sudden.

(May 4)
Rush performs live at the Omaha Music Hall, Omaha, Nebraska, US. The opening acts are Angel and Max Webster.

(May 5)
Rush performs live at Fargo Civic Auditorium, Fargo, North Dakota, US. The opening act is Max Webster.

(May 6)
Rush performs live at the St. Paul Civic Center, St. Paul, Minnesota, US. The opening acts are Styx, Starcastle and Max Webster.

(May 8)
Rush performs live at Duluth Arena, Duluth, Minnesota, US. The opening act is Styx.

(May 9)

Rush performs live at Newman High School, Wausau, Wisconsin, US. The opening act is Max Webster.

(May 10)
Rush performs live at Riverside Theatre, Milwaukee, Wisconsin, US.

(May 12)
Rush performs live at Bay Theatre, Green Bay, Wisconsin, US. The opening act is Max Webster.

(May 13)
Rush performs live at McElroy Auditorium, Waterloo, Iowa, US, opening for Ted Nugent.

(May 15)
Rush performs live at Nelson Center, Springfield, Illinois, US. The opening acts are Max Webster and Cheap Trick.

(May 17)
Rush performs live at Mary E. Sawyer Auditorium, La Crosse, Wisconsin, US. The opening act is Max Webster.

(May 18)
Rush performs live at Lakeview Arena, Marquette, Michigan, US. The opening act is Max Webster.

(May 20 & 21)
Rush performs live at Aragon Ballroom, Chicago, Illinois, US. The opening act is Max Webster.

(May 22)
Rush performs live at McMorran Arena, Port Huron, Michigan, US. The opening act is Max Webster.

(June 1)
Rush performs live at City Hall, Sheffield, England. The opening act is Stray. The setlist includes the following:
"Xanadu"

(June 2)
Rush performs live at Free Trade Hall, Manchester, England. The opening act is Stray.

> "Xanadu (Live in Manchester, 1977)" 10:28
> Written by Neil Peart (words), Geddy Lee & Alex Lifeson (Music)
> Appears on: Sign Of Eth (bootleg)
> This recording shows the song was essentially finished by this point, though the closing instrumental section features a different guitar arrangement from Alex before the finale. Geddy sings the lyrics more aggressively than on the album and later live versions. Play this one loud!

(June 3)
Rush performs live at the Birmingham Odeon, Birmingham, England. The opening act is Stray.

(June 4)
Rush performs live at the Hammersmith Odeon, London, England. The opening act is Stray.

(June 6)
Rush is scheduled to perform in Frankfurt, West Germany, but the show is cancelled.

(June 8)
Rush performs live at Göta Lejon, Stockholm, Sweden.

(June 11)
Rush performs live at Newcastle City Hall, Newcastle, England. The opening act is Stray.

(June 12)
Rush performs live at The Apollo, Glasgow, Scotland.

(June 13)
Rush performs live at Liverpool Empire, Liverpool, England.

(Mid-June)
Rush records their fifth studio album at Rockfield Studios, Monmouth, Wales, UK (*A Farewell To Kings* sessions). Tracks arranged and produced by *Rush* and Terry Brown. Tracks worked on include:
"Xanadu" – according to **Alex Lifeson**, the track is played through and recorded in one take, start to finish.
"Cinderella Man" – written by **Geddy Lee** (words and music) and **Lifeson** (music). It is inspired by **Lee**'s viewing of the film *Mr. Deeds Goes To Town*.
"A Farewell To Kings" – written by **Neil Peart** (words and music) and **Lee** and **Lifeson** (music).

"Cygnus X-1" – written by **Neil Peart** (words and music) and **Lee** and **Lifeson** (music). Producer Terry Brown records the intro monologue.
"Closer To The Heart" – **Peart** shares co-writing credit of the lyrics with Peter Talbot, a friend of the band, hailing from Seattle, Washington. **Neil** bases his work on the song on a verse by Talbot.

(Summer)
Terry Brown mixes *Rush*'s album *A Farewell To Kings* at Adivision Studios, London, England, assisted by Declan O'Doherty and Ken Thomas. It is later mastered by George Graves.

Rush shoots promotional films for "Closer To The Heart," "A Farewell To Kings" and "Xanadu" at Seneca College, Toronto, Ontario, Canada.

(September 1)
Rush releases their album *A Farewell To Kings* on Anthem (Canada) and Mercury (US) Records. Track listing as follows:

"A Farewell To Kings"
"Xanadu"
"Closer To The Heart"
"Cinderella Man"
"Madrigal"
"Cygnus X-1"

Note: the liner notes list the different movements of the track by name:

"Cygnus X-1
    Book I: The Voyage
        I. Prologue
        II. 1
        III. 2
        IV. 3"

Note: The album may not have been released on this date in the US, as a *Nevada State Journal* article dated Sept. 22, 1977, says it "is due out imminently."

(September 6)
Rush performs live at Fort William Gardens, Thunder Bay, Ontario, Canada. The opening act is Max Webster.

(September 7)
Rush performs live at Winnipeg Arena, Winnipeg, Manitoba, Canada. The opening act is Max Webster.

(September 8)
Rush performs live at the Agridome, Regina, Saskatchewan, Canada. The opening act is Max Webster.

(September 9)
Rush performs live at the Kinsmen Fieldhouse, Edmonton, Alberta, Canada. The opening act is Max Webster.

(September 10)
Rush performs live at The Arena, Saskatoon, Saskatchewan, Canada. The opening act is Max Webster.

(September 11)
Rush performs live at the Stampede Corral, Calgary, Alberta, Canada. The opening act is Max Webster.

(September 13)
Rush performs live at Pacific National Exhibition Coliseum, Vancouver, British Columbia, Canada. The opening act is Max Webster.

(September 14)
Rush performs live at Victoria Arena, Victoria, British Columbia, Canada. The opening act is Max Webster.

(September 16)
Rush performs live at Spokane Coliseum, Spokane, Washington, US. The opening acts are UFO and Max Webster.

(September 17)
Rush performs live at Center Arena, Seattle Washington, US. The opening acts are UFO and Max Webster.

(September 18)
Rush performs live at Beasley Performing Arts Coliseum, Pullman, Washington, US. The opening acts are UFO and Max Webster.

(September 19, 20 & 21)
Rush performs live at the Paramount Theater, Portland, Oregon, US. The opening acts are UFO and Max Webster.

(September 22)
Rush performs live at Douglas County Fairgrounds, Rosenburg, Oregon, US. The opening acts are UFO and Max Webster.

(September 23)
Rush performs live at Jackson County Expo Pavillion, Medford, Oregon, US. The opening acts are UFO and Max Webster.

(September 24)
Rush performs live at The Winterland, San Francisco, California, US. The opening acts are UFO, Hush and Max Webster.

Note: The band Hush is not the same as **Neil Peart**'s pre-*Rush* group. This Hush is the Australian glam-rock band.

(September 25)
Rush performs live at Swing Auditorium, San Bernardino, California, US. The opening act is UFO.

(September 26)
Rush performs live at Civic Auditorium, Bakersfield, California, US. The opening acts are UFO and Dwight Tilley Band.

(September 27)
Rush is scheduled to perform live at the Washoe Fairgrounds, Reno, Nevada, US, but unsafe staging forces them to cancel the entire concert. UFO and Max Webster were also on the bill.

(September 28)
Rush performs live at Memorial Civic Auditorium, Stockton, California, US. The opening acts are UFO and Max Webster.

(September 29)
Rush performs live at Warnors Theater, Fresno, California, US. The opening acts are UFO and Dwight Tilley Band.

(September 30)
Rush performs live at San Diego Sports Arena, San Diego, California, US. The opening act is UFO.

(October)
Rush releases their "Closer To The Heart" singles in North America.

Canada 7" single (ANS-004):
"Closer To The Heart"
"Madrigal"

US 7" single (M-73958):
"Closer To The Heart"
"Madrigal"

US 7" promo single (73958-DJ):
"Closer To The Heart"
"Madrigal"

(October 1 & 2)
Rush performs live at Santa Monica Civic Auditorium, Santa Monica, California, US. The opening act is UFO.

(October 3)
Rush performs live at Starwood Amphitheatre, Hollywood, California, US.

(October 4)
Rush performs live at Mesa Amphitheatre, Mesa, Arizona, US.

(October 5)
Rush performs live at Veterans Memorial Coliseum, Phoenix, Arizona, US.

(October 7)
Rush is scheduled to perform at the Terrace Ballroom, Salt Lake City, Utah, US, but the show is cancelled because of problems with Geddy's voice.

(October 8)
Rush performs live at Auditorium Arena, Denver, Colorado, US. The opening act is Max Webster.

(October 10)
Rush performs live at the Civic Center Coliseum, Amarillo, Texas, US. The opening acts are UFO and Max Webster.

(October 11)
Rush performs live at El Paso County Coliseum, El Paso, Texas, US. The opening acts are UFO and Max Webster.

(October 12)
Rush performs live at Ector County Coliseum, Odessa, Texas, US. The opening acts are UFO and Max Webster.

(October 13)
Rush performs live at Lubbock Memorial Auditorium, Lubbock, Texas, US. The opening act is Max Webster.

(October 14)
Rush performs live at the Assembly Center, Tulsa, Oklahoma, US. The opening act is Max Webster.

(October 15)
Rush performs live at the Civic Center Music Hall, Oklahoma City, Oklahoma, US. The opening act is Max Webster.

(October 16)
Rush performs live at Taylor County Coliseum, Abilene, Texas, US. The opening acts are UFO and Max Webster.

(October 17)
Rush performs live at Municipal Center, Austin, Texas, US. The opening act is Max Webster.

(October 20)
Rush performs live at The Music Hall, Houston, Texas, US. The opening act is Max Webster.

(October 21)
Rush performs live at Will Rogers Coliseum, Fort Worth, Texas, US. The opening act is Max Webster.

(October 22 & 23)
Rush performs live at Municipal Auditorium, San Antonio, Texas, US. The opening acts are UFO and Max Webster.

(October 24)
Rush performs live at Corpus Christi Coliseum, Corpus Christi, Texas, US. The opening acts are UFO and Max Webster.

(October 25)
Rush performs live at Beaumont Civic Center, Beaumont, Texas, US. The opening act is Max Webster.

(October 27)
Rush performs live at Robinson Auditorium, Barton Coliseum, Little Rock, Arkansas, US. The opening act is Max Webster.

(October 28)
Rush performs live at Shreveport Municipal Auditorium, Shreveport, Louisiana, US. The opening acts are UFO and Max Webster.

(October 29)
Rush performs live at The Warehouse, New Orleans, Louisiana, US. The opening acts are UFO and Max Webster.

(October 30)
Rush performs live at Dixon-Myers Hall, Memphis, Tennessee, US. The opening acts are UFO and Max Webster.

(October 31)
Rush performs live at Alex Cooley's Electrical Ballroom, Atlanta, Georgia, US.

(November 1)
Rush performs live at Dothan Civic Center, Dothan, Alabama, US.

(November 10 & 11)
Rush performs live at New Century Theater, Buffalo, New York, US. The opening acts are UFO and Max Webster.

(November 12)
Rush performs live at The Palladium, New York City, New York, US. The opening acts are UFO and Cheap Trick. Following the show, *Rush*, Ray Danniels, Cliff Burnstein and Polygram/Mercury personnel Jules Abramson, Charles Fach, Steve Katz and Irwin Steinberg are presented with gold records for "A Farewell To Kings," "All The World's A Stage" and "2112." Steinberg announces that the band have re-signed with Mercury as their US, UK and European record company.

(November 13)
Rush performs live at Baltimore Civic Center, Baltimore, Maryland, US. The opening acts are UFO and Cheap Trick.

(November 16)
Rush performs live at Mid-Hudson Civic Center, Poughkeepsie, New York, US. The opening act is AC/DC.

(November 17)
Rush performs live at the Palace Theater, Albany, New York, US. The opening act is AC/DC.

(November 18)
Rush performs live at Onondaga Memorial Auditorium, Syracuse, New York, US. The opening act is AC/DC and Crawler.

(November 19)
Rush performs live at Rochester Community War Memorial, Rochester, New York, US. The opening act is Crawler. AC/DC is scheduled to perform, but cancels this (and their next show in Allentown, Pennsylvania, US, though not supporting *Rush*).

(November 22 & 23)
Rush performs live at Stanley Theater, Pittsburgh, Pennsylvania, US. The opening act is Crawler.

(November 24)
Rush performs live at War Memorial Arena, Johnstown, Pennsylvania, US. The opening acts are Cheap Trick and Mark Farner.

(November 25)
Rush performs live at the Capitol Theatre, Passaic, New Jersey, US. The opening act is Cheap Trick.

(November 26)
Rush performs live at Tower Theatre, Upper Darby, Pennsylvania, US. The opening act is Tom Petty & The Heartbreakers.

(November 27)
Rush performs live at Erie County Fieldhouse, Erie, Pennsylvania, US. The opening act is UFO. This show is originally scheduled for the following day.

(December 2)
Rush performs live at Fitchburg Theater, Fitchburg, Massachusetts, US.

(December 3)
Rush performs live at Warner Theater, Washington, D.C., US. The opening act is City Boy.

(December 5)
Rush performs live at Tomorrow Club, Youngstown, Ohio, US.

(December 8)
Rush performs live at Municipal Auditorium, Columbus, Georgia, US.

(December 9)
Rush performs live at Civic Center, Lakeland, Florida, US, opening for Bob Seger & The Silver Bullet Band.

(December 10)
Rush performs live at Hollywood Sportatorium, Hollywood, Florida, US.

(December 11)
Rush performs live at Veterans Memorial Coliseum, Jacksonville, Florida, US.

(December 12)
Rush performs live at Fox Theater, Atlanta, Georgia, US.

(December 13)
Rush performs live at Knoxville Civic Auditorium, Knoxville, Tennessee, US.

(December 14)
Rush performs live at the Civic Center, Wheeling, West Virginia, US.

(December 15)
Rush performs live at Cobo Hall, Detroit, Michigan, US.

(December 16)
Rush performs live at Toledo Sports Arena, Toledo, Ohio, US. The opening act is UFO.

(December 17)
Rush performs live at Cleveland Public Auditorium, Cleveland, Ohio, US. The opening acts are The Motors and Edgar Winter's White Trash.

(December 18)
Rush performs live at the University of Dayton Arena, Dayton, Ohio, US. The opening act is Grinderswitch.

(December 19)
Rush performs live at Wings Stadium, Kalamazoo, Michigan, US. The opening act is Legs Diamond.

(December 27)
Rush performs live at London Gardens, London, Ontario, Canada. The opening act is Max Webster.

(December 28)
Rush performs live at Kitchener Memorial Auditorium, Kitchener, Ontario, Canada.

(December 29 & 30)
Rush performs live at Maple Leaf Gardens, Toronto, Ontario, Canada. The opening act is April Wine.

HEMISPHERES

1978

(January 2)
Rush performs live at Morris Civic Center, South Bend, Indiana, US. The opening act is April Wine.

(January 3 & 4)
Rush performs live at Veterans Memorial Auditorium, Columbus, Ohio, US.

(January 5)
Rush performs live at Market Square Arena, Indianapolis, Indiana, US.

(January 6, 7 & 8)
Rush performs live at the Aragon Ballroom, Chicago, Illinois, US. The opening act is April Wine.

(January 12)
Rush performs live at the Civic Center, Providence, Rhode Island, US, opening for Blue Öyster Cult.

(January 13)
Rush performs live at Nassau Coliseum, Uniondale, Long Island, New York, US, opening for Blue Öyster Cult.

(January 14)
Rush performs live at Veterans Coliseum, New Haven, Connecticut, US, opening for Blue Öyster Cult.

(January 17)
Rush performs live at Municipal Auditorium, Kansas City, Missouri, US. The opening act is April Wine.

(January 18)
Rush performs live at Checkerdome, St. Louis, Missouri, US. The opening act is April Wine.

(January 19)
Rush performs live at Louisville Gardens, Louisville, Kentucky, US. The opening act is April Wine.

(January 21)
Rush performs live at Wendler Arena, Saginaw, Michigan, US. The opening act is Pat Travers.

(January 23)
Rush performs live at the Civic Center, Lansing, Michigan, US.

(January 24)
Rush performs live at IMA Auditorium, Flint, Michigan, US.

(January 26)
Rush performs live at Milwaukee Auditorium, Milwaukee, Wisconsin, US. The opening act is Pat Travers.

(January 27)
Rush performs live at Met Center, Bloomington, Minnesota, US. The opening acts are Starcastle and Pat Travers.

(January 28)
Rush performs live at Splash Fieldhouse, University of Wisconsin, Stevens Point, Wisconsin, US. The opening act is Pat Travers.

(January 29)
Rush performs live at Dane County Memorial Coliseum, Madison, Wisconsin, US. The opening act is Pat Travers.

(January 30)
Rush performs live at RKO Orpheum Theatre, Davenport, Iowa, US. The opening act is Pat Travers.

(January 31)
Rush performs live at Hammond Civic Center, Hammond, Indiana, US. The opening act is Pat Travers.

(Early 1978)
Rush releases their "Closer To The Heart" singles in the UK on Mercury Records.

UK 7" single [Tan] (Rush 7):
"Closer To The Heart"
"Bastille Day"

"2112: II: The Temples Of Syrinx"

UK 7" single [Silver] (Rush 7):
"Closer To The Heart"
"Bastille Day"
"2112: II: The Temples Of Syrinx"

UK 7" single [Blue] (Rush 7):
"Closer To The Heart"
"Bastille Day"
"2112: II: The Temples Of Syrinx"

UK 12" single (Rush 12):
"Closer To The Heart"
"Anthem"
"Bastille Day"
"2112: II: The Temples Of Syrinx"

Note: a piece by Bill Green about the February 12th show says "Closer To The Heart" is the recent UK single.

(February 12)
Rush performs live at the Odeon Theatre, Birmingham, England. The opening act is Tyla Gang.

(February 13)
Rush performs live at DeMontfort Hall, Leicester, England. The opening act is Tyla Gang.

(February 14 & 15)
Rush performs live at City Hall, Newcastle, England. The opening act is Tyla Gang.

(February 16 & 17)
Rush performs live at The Apollo, Glasgow, Scotland. The opening act is Tyla Gang. The 16th dated show was scheduled for Edinburgh, Scotland, but reportedly no suitable venue was available, so having already been scheduled in Glasgow on the 17th, they added an extra show to The Apollo on the 16th to make it a two-day stay.

(February 19 & 20)
Rush performs live at the Hammersmith Odeon, London, England. The opening act is Tyla Gang. The February 20th show is audio recorded and released in 1998 as part of *Different Stages*. In a November, 1998, *Vancouver Sun* magazine interview, **Alex Lifeson** says this recording was planned for a U.K. radio program, but **Geddy Lee** reportedly had problems with his voice (a cold) during the show, so the band decides not to release it.

(February 22)
Rush performs live at City Hall, Sheffield, England. The opening act is Tyla Gang.

(February 23 & 24)
Rush performs live at The Apollo, Manchester, England. The opening act is Tyla Gang.

(February 25)
Rush performs live at Liverpool Empire, Liverpool, England. The opening act is Tyla Gang.

(February 26)
Rush performs live at Colston Hall, Bristol, England. The opening act is Tyla Gang.

(February 27)
Rush performs live at Gaumont, Southhampton, England. The opening act is Tyla Gang.

(Date Unknown)
During sound checks and days off on this tour, **Rush** writes the following:
"La Villa Strangiato" – **Alex Lifeson**, in an interview with *Guitar World* in 1996, says this song was written "on the road" in advance of the recording sessions. **Neil Peart**, in a 2014 CBC.ca interview, says each part comes from a dream **Alex** would tell the band about afterwards.

(Date Unknown)
Following the tour, the tapes with the recording of the February 20, Hammersmith Odeon, **Geddy Lee** puts them in his road case and then later to his basement, where there are forgotten (*MTV News* and *Jam!Showbiz* November 9, 1998).

(March)
Mercury Records re-issues "Fly By Night" singles in the US to promote the forthcoming *Archives* 3xLP set.

US 7" re-issue single (73990):

"Fly By Night"
"Anthem"

US 7" promo single (DJ-553):
"Fly By Night"
"Fly By Night"

(March 10)
Rush performs live at the Orpheum Theatre, Boston, Massachusetts, US. The opening act is The Babys.

(March 15)
Rush performs live at the Coliseum, Knoxville, Tennessee, US. The opening acts are The Babys and Pat Travers.

(March 16)
Rush performs live at the Civic Center, Huntington, West Virginia, US.

(March 17)
Rush performs live at Freedom Hall, Johnson City, Tennessee, US. The opening acts are The Babys and Pat Travers.

(March 18)
Rush performs live at Greensboro Coliseum, Greensboro, North Carolina, US. The opening acts are The Babys and Pat Travers.

(March 19)
Rush performs live at Norfolk Civic Auditorium, Norfolk, Virginia, US. The opening act is The Babys.

(March 21)
Rush performs live at Memorial Auditorium, Chattanooga, Tennessee, US. The opening act is The Babys.

(March 22)
Rush performs live at Boutwell Auditorium, Birmingham, Alabama, US. The opening acts are The Babys and Pat Travers.

(March 24)
Rush performs live at Curtis Hixon Hall, Tampa, Florida, US. The opening acts are Pat Travers and Head East.

(March 25)
Rush performs live at Hollywood Sportatorium, Hollywood, Florida, US. The opening acts are Pat Travers and Head East.

(March 27)
A review of the March 24th concert in the *St. Petersburgh Times* notes the forthcoming *Archives* set and that it will be a "collection of old discs."

(March 30)
Rush performs live at Memorial Gardens, Guelph, Ontario, Canada. The opening act is Max Webster.

(March 31)
Rush performs live at The Forum, Montreal, Quebec, Canada. The opening act is Max Webster.

(April)
Rush releases the 3xLP set *Archives* on Anthem (Canada) and Mercury (US & Europe). The set includes the band's first three albums.

LP 1: *Rush*
LP 2: *Fly By Night*
LP 3: *Caress Of Steel*

> "By-Tor And The Snow Dog (Archives Version)" 8:57
> Written by Neil Peart (words), Geddy Lee & Alex Lifeson (Music)
> Appears on: Archives
> On the original LP, the chimes heard at the end of the track continued into the run-out groove, thereby looping until the record player's needle was lifted from the vinyl. This gimmick was not reproduced on standard editions of Archives (though some fans have reported that their copies do indeed continue into the run out groove, so perhaps the incorrect Fly By Night album master templates were used, the original format instead of the updated Archives edition). Unlike the later CD formats, the Archive cut of the track continues the chimes for about 20 extra seconds, so you still get a bit more here.

Note: the original sleeve is a faded, grey field with the Star Man logo. Later re-issues change this to a black field.

(April 1)
Rush performs live at Ottawa Civic Centre, Ottawa, Ontario, Canada. The opening act is Max Webster.

(April 2)
Rush performs live at Cornwall Civic Centre, Cornwall, Ontario, Canada. The opening act is Max Webster.

(April 3)
Rush performs live at Jock Harty Arena, Kingston, Ontario, Canada. The opening act is Max Webster.

(April 4)
Rush performs live at Peterborough Memorial Centre, Peterborough, Ontario, Canada. The opening act is Max Webster.

(April 6)
Rush performs live at Aitken Centre, University of New Brunswick, Fredericton, New Brunswick, Canada. The opening act is Max Webster.

(April 7)
Rush performs live at Joe Louis Lévesque Arena, Moncton, New Brunswick, Canada. The opening act is Max Webster.

(April 8)
Rush performs live at the Metro Centre, Halifax, Nova Scotia, Canada. The opening act is Max Webster.

(April 22)
Selena Peart Taylor is born to **Nell Peart** and Jackie Taylor.

(Spring)
Rush releases their "Cinderella Man" single in Canada on Anthem Records.

Canada 7" single (ANS-007):
"Cinderella Man"
"A Farewell To Kings"

(May 10)
Rush performs live at the Convention Center, Niagara Falls, New York, US. The opening act is Uriah Heep.

(May 11)
Rush performs live at Memorial Coliseum, Fort Wayne, Indiana, US. The opening act is Uriah Heep.

(May 12)
An article about *Rush* (including an interview with **Geddy Lee**) in the Milwaukee *Sentinel* published on this date discusses the following track:
"Cygnus X-1 Book II: Hemispheres" – the article notes that the second part of "Cygnus X-1" will appear on the next album.

Rush performs live at Riverfront Coliseum, Cincinnati, US. The opening act is Uriah Heep.

(May 13)
Rush performs live at Municipal Auditorium, Nashville, Tennessee, US. The opening act is Uriah Heep.

(May 16)
Rush performs live at Auditorium Arena, Denver, Colorado, US. The opening act is Uriah Heep.

(May 17)
Rush performs live at Salt Palace Center, Salt Lake City, Utah, US. The opening act is Uriah Heep.

(May 18)
Rush performs live at The Merchants Building, Idaho State Fairgrounds, Boise, Idaho, US. The opening act is Uriah Heep.

(May 19)
Rush performs live at Mini Dome, Idaho State University, Pocatello, Idaho, US. The opening act is Uriah Heep.

(May 20)
Rush performs live at Yellowstone Metro Arena, Billings, Montana, US. The opening act is Uriah Heep.

(May 25)

Rush performs live at the Civic Center, East Grand Forks, Minnesota, US. The opening act is Uriah Heep. Wrestler Jesse "The Body" Ventura is on the security staff for this show during a hiatus from the ring while he recovers from surgery. Ventura discusses the job on Chris Jericho's podcast *Talk Is Jericho* in 2015.

(May 26)
Rush performs live at Municipal Stadium, Sioux City, Iowa, US. The opening act is Uriah Heep.

(May 27)
Rush performs live at McElroy Auditorium. Waterloo, Iowa, US.

(May 28)
Rush performs live at Alpine Valley Music Theatre, East Troy, Wisconsin, US. The opening acts are Uriah Heep and Sweet.

(Early June)
Rush writes material for their next album (*Hemispheres* sessions). These writing sessions take place over two weeks before the band records the album, according to **Alex Lifeson** in the February 1980 issue of *Music Express* magazine.
"Cygnus X-1 Book II: Hemispheres" – the sequel to "Cygnus X-1 Book I: The Voyage." According to **Neil Peart** in *Visions*, the themes of heart and mind are inspired by the book *Powers Of Mind* by Adam Smith.
"La Villa Strangiato" – the movement sub-titled "Monsters!" (and "Monsters! [Reprise]") is based on the classical piece "Powerhouse" by Raymond Scott. Apparently, the band is unaware that the melody is not public domain. **Neil** says in a 2014 CBC.ca interview that they used "cartoon music" and got in trouble later. At some point before Scott's death in 1994, S.R.O. Productions is notified by his music publisher of the copyright infringement. According to RaymondScott.com's FAQ, the statute of limitations for the infringement had passed when the notification was made, however S.R.O. Productions did voluntarily pay a one-time fee (because it was the right thing to do) and settled with Scott. The mutual agreement also does not require *Rush* to credit Scott on the composition.
The recording of the piece is done in three parts, despite the band's efforts to record it all in one take, according to *Rush: Beyond The Lighted Stage*. **Alex Lifeson** says in a 1996 *Guitar World* feature, says the backing track was recorded in one take and his guitar solo was overdubbed. In 1980, he tells *Guitar Player* it was two parts, each recorded in one take, and that they spent a week rehearsing it before attempting to record it.
"The Trees"
"Circumstances" – appears to revisit **Neil** thoughts and feelings of the challenge of pursuing his dream back when he lived in North London, England.

(Late June to July)
Rush records their backing tracks at Rockfield Studios, Monmouth, South Wales, UK (*Hemispheres* sessions). Produced and arrangements by *Rush* and Terry Brown.

Geddy Lee records his vocals at Advision Studios, London, England (*Hemispheres* sessions).

> "The Trees (Vault Edition)" 4:54
> Written by Neil Peart (words), Geddy Lee & Alex Lifeson (music)
> Appears on: Rock Band 2 (video game)
> This is a completely different recording of the song. The differences may not immediately leap out at you, but they when played back to back with the standard version, you'll hear them right from the start. Alex's acoustic guitar intro is played a bit faster and includes little flourishes of notes not heard on the album. Geddy's vocal take is different, with his pacing and emphasis varying throughout. The entire track has a somewhat grittier feel (not unpolished, just harder and with more bite). The end of the song features a soft electric guitar extended outro. Get your hands on this one!

(August)
Hemispheres is mixed by Terry Brown and mastered by Ray Staff at Trident Studios, London, England.

(Date Unknown)
Anthem Records releases a promo LP titled *Rush: Hemispheres - Radio Special with John Donabie* (SPE-001), featuring *Rush* discussing the *Hemispheres* album with radio DJ John Donabie.

(October 14)
Rush performs live at Kingston Memorial Centre, Kingston, Ontario, Canada. This starts the band's *Tour Of The Hemispheres*.

(October 15)
Rush performs live at War Memorial Hall, University of Guelph, Guelph, Ontario, Canada.

(October 17)
Rush performs live at North Bay Memorial Gardens, North Bay, Ontario, Canada.

(October 18)
Rush performs live at Sudbury Arena, Sudbury, Ontario, Canada.

(October 20)
Rush performs live at Fort William Gardens, Thunder Bay, Ontario, Canada.

(October 21)
Rush performs live at Winnipeg Arena, Winnipeg, Manitoba, Canada. The opening act is Sweetheart.

(October 22)
Rush performs live at Keystone Centre, Brandon, Manitoba, Canada.

(October 24)
Rush performs live at the Agridome, Regina, Saskatchewan, Canada. The opening act is Sweetheart.

(October 25)
Rush performs live at Saskatoon Arena, Saskatoon, Saskatchewan, Canada. The opening act is Sweetheart.

(October 27)
Rush performs live at Northlands Coliseum, Edmonton, Alberta, Canada. The opening act is Sweetheart.

(October 28)
Rush performs live at Calgary Corral, Calgary, Alberta, Canada. The opening act is Sweetheart.

(October 29)
Rush releases their sixth studio album, *Hemispheres*, on Anthem (Canada) and Mercury Records (US, UK & Europe). Both a limited edition Picture Disc and a limited edition red vinyl (with a poster) version are released, in addition to the standard vinyl format. Track listing as follows:

"Cygnus X-1
      Book II: Hemispheres
            I. Prelude
            II. Apollo *Bringer Of Wisdom*
            III. Dionysus *Bringer Of Love*
            IV. Armageddon *The Battle Of Heart And Mind*
            V. Cygnus *Bringer Of Balance*
            VI. The Sphere *A Kind Of Dream*"
"Circumstances"
"The Trees"
"La Villa Strangiato"

Note: The liner notes list the different movements of "La Villa Strangiato" by name, as follows:

"La Villa Strangiato (An Exercise In Self-Indulgence)
I. Buenos Nochas, Mein Froinds!
II. To Sleep, perchance to dream...
III. Strangiato theme
IV. A Lerxst in Wonderland
V. Monsters! – based on "Powerhouse" by Raymond Scott
VI. The Ghost Of Aragon
VII. Danforth and Pape
VIII. The Waltz of the Shreves
IX. Never turn your back on a Monster!
X. Monsters! (Reprise) – based on "Powerhouse" by Raymond Scott
XI. Strangiato theme (Reprise)
XII. A Farewell To Things"

Anthem Records also releases a promo edition of the album as *Rush: Hemispheres (Special 12" Disc Taken From Rush 'Hemispheres' Album)* (SPE-002). Track listing same as above.

Rush performs live at Lethbridge Sportsplex, Lethbridge, Alberta, Canada.

(October 31)
Rush performs live at K.X.A. Auditorium, Kamloops, British Columbia, Canada.

(November 2)
Rush performs live at Victoria Memorial Arena, Victoria, British Columbia, Canada.

(November 3)
Rush performs live at Beban Park Arena, Nanaimo, British Columbia, Canada.

(November 4)
Rush performs live at Pacific Coliseum, Vancouver, British Columbia, Canada. The opening act is Sweetheart.

(November 6)
Rush performs live at Memorial Coliseum, Portland, Oregon, US. The opening act is Pat Travers.

(November 7)
Rush performs live at Seattle Center Coliseum, Seattle, Washington, US. The opening act is Pat Travers.

(November 8)
Rush performs live at The Coliseum, Spokane, Washington, US. The opening act is Pat Travers.

(November 10)
Rush performs live at Memorial Auditorium, Sacramento, California, US. The opening act is Pat Travers.

(November 11)
Rush performs live at Centennial Coliseum, Reno, Nevada, US. The opening act is Pat Travers.

(November 13)
Rush performs live at the Sports Arena, San Diego, California, US. The opening act is Pat Travers.

(November 14)
Rush performs live at Long Beach Arena, Long Beach, California, US. The opening act is Pat Travers.

(November 15)
Rush performs live at Warnors Theater, Fresno, California, US

(November 16)
Rush performs live at Cow Palace, San Francisco, California, US. The opening act is Pat Travers.

(November 18)
Rush performs live at Swing Auditorium, San Bernardino, California, US. The opening act is Pat Travers.

(November 19)
Rush performs live at Veterans Memorial Coliseum, Phoenix, Arizona, US. The opening act is Ambrosia.

(November 20)
Rush performs live at the Community Center, Tucson, Arizona, US.

(November 30)
Rush performs live at Market Square Arena, Indianapolis, Indiana, US. The opening act is UFO

(December 1)
Rush performs live at Hara Arena, Dayton, Ohio, US.

(December 2)
Rush performs live at Cobo Hall, Detroit, Michigan, US. The opening act is Golden Earring.

(December 3)
Rush performs live at Toledo Spot Arena, Toledo, Ohio, US. The opening act is Golden Earring.

(December 5)
Rush performs live at Palmer College, Davenport, Iowa, US.

(December 7)
Rush performs live at Milwaukee Arena, Milwaukee, Wisconsin, US. The opening act is Golden Earring.

(December 8)
Rush performs live at Brown County Arena, Green Bay, Wisconsin, US. The opening act is Golden Earring.

(December 9)
Rush performs live at the Civic Center, St. Paul, Minnesota, US.

(December 10)
Rush performs live at Veterans Memorial Auditorium, Des Moines, Iowa, US. The opening act is Golden Earring.

(December 11)
Rush performs live at Municipal Auditorium, Kansas City, Missouri, US. The opening act is Golden Earring.

(December 13)
Rush performs live at Checkerdome, St. Louis, Missouri, US. The opening act is Starz.

(December 14, 15 & 16)
Rush performs live at International Amphitheater, Chicago, Illinois, US. The opening act is Starz.

(December 17)
Rush performs live at Dane County Memorial Coliseum, Madison, Wisconsin, US.

(December 19)
Rush performs live at London Gardens, London, Ontario, Canada. The opening act is Wireless.

(December 20)
Rush performs live at Memorial Auditorium, Kitchener, Ontario, Canada. The opening act is Wireless.

(December 21)
Rush performs live at the Civic Centre, Ottawa, Ontario, Canada. The opening act is Wireless.

(December 27)
Rush performs live at The Forum, Montreal, Quebec, Canada.

(December 28 & 29)
Rush performs live at Maple Leaf Gardens, Toronto, Ontario, Canada. The opening act is Wireless.

(December 30)
Rush is scheduled to perform in Peterborough, Ontario, Canada, but the show is cancelled.

(December 31)
Rush performs live at Maple Leaf Gardens, Toronto, Ontario, Canada. The opening act is Max Webster.

'LIVE IN ENGLAND'

1979

(January)
Rush releases its "Circumstances" single in Canada on Anthem Records.

Canada 7" single (ANS-009):
"Circumstances (1979 Canadian Single Edit)"
"The Trees"

> "Circumstances (1979 Canadian Single Edit)" 2:38
> Written by Neil Peart (words), Geddy Lee & Alex Lifeson (music)
> Appears on: Canada 7" single
> This is a severe edit which cuts out an audible minute of the original track throughout. Stick with the album version.

(January 11)
Rush performs live at the Music Hall, Boston, Massachusetts, US. The opening act is Starz.

(January 12)
Rush performs live at Civic Center, Springfield, Massachusetts, US.

(January 13 & 14)
Rush performs live at The Palladium, New York City, New York, US. The opening act is Starz.

(January 16)
Rush performs live at the Palace Theatre, Albany, New York, US.

(January 17)
Rush performs live at the Capitol Theatre, Passaic, New Jersey, US. The opening act is Starz.

(January 19)
Rush performs live at the Pacific Arena, Pittsburgh, Pennsylvania, US. The opening act is Starz.

(January 20)
Rush performs live at the Baltimore Civic Center, Baltimore, Maryland, US. The opening act is Stillwater.

(January 21)
Rush performs live at The Spectrum, Philadelphia, Pennsylvania, US. The opening act is Blondie, who are reportedly booed off stage.

(January 23)
Rush performs live at the Palace Theatre, Albany, New York, US.

(January 24)
Rush performs live at Memorial Auditorium, Buffalo, US. The opening act is Starz.

(January 26)
Rush performs live at Riverfront Coliseum, Cincinnati, Ohio, US. The opening act is Starz.

(January 27)
Rush performs live at Von Braun Civic Center, Huntsville, Alabama, US. The opening act is Starz.

(January 28)
Rush performs live at Mid-South Coliseum, Memphis, Tennessee, US. The opening act is Starz.

(January 30)
Rush performs live at Louisville Gardens, Louisville, Kentucky, US. The opening act is Toto.

(January 31)
Rush performs live at I.U.A. Auditorium, Bloomington, Indiana, US. The opening act is Boyzz.

(February 1)
Rush performs live at St. John Arena, Ohio State University, Columbus, Ohio, US. The opening act is April Wine.

(February 2)
Rush performs live at Wendler Arena, Saginaw, Michigan, US. The opening act is April Wine.

(February 3)
Rush performs live at Richfield Coliseum, Richfield, Ohio, US. The opening act is April Wine.

(February 15)
Rush performs live at Township Auditorium, Columbia, South Carolina, US. The opening act is Head East.

(February 16)
Rush releases their "The Trees" singles in the US.

US 7" single (M-74051):
"The Trees"
"Circumstances"

US 7" promo single (DJ-74051):
"The Trees"
"The Trees"

US 12" promo single (MK-75):
"The Trees"
"Cygnus X-1 Book II: Hemispheres II. Prelude"
"Circumstances"

Note: a copy of the promo single is date stamped with "Feb 16 1976".

(February 17)
Rush performs live at Cumberland County Memorial Arena, Fayetteville, North Carolina, US. The opening act is Head East.

(Mid-February)
Rush performs live at Civic Center, Asheville, North Carolina, US. The opening act is Head East.

(February 20)
Rush performs live at the Civic Coliseum, Knoxville, Tennessee, US. The opening act is Head East.

(February 22)
Rush performs live at Barton Coliseum, Little Rock, Arkansas, US. The opening act is April Wine

(February 23)
Rush performs live at Hirsch Memorial Coliseum, Shreveport, Louisiana, US.

(February 24)
Rush performs live at Fairgrounds Pavillion, Oklahoma City, Oklahoma, US.

(February 25)
Rush performs live at Municipal Auditorium, Austin, Texas, US. The opening act is April Wine.

(February 27)
Rush performs live at the Coliseum, Corpus Christi, Texas, US.

(March 1)
Rush performs live at Sam Houston Coliseum, Houston, Texas, US. The opening act is April Wine.

(March 2)
Rush performs live at the Dallas Convention Center, Dallas, Texas, US. The opening act is April Wine.

(March 3)
Rush performs live at the Convention Center Arena, San Antonio, Texas, US. The opening act is April Wine.

(March 4)
Rush performs live at Fair Park Coliseum, Beaumont, Texas, US.

(March 6)
Rush performs live at Municipal Auditorium, New Orleans, Louisiana, US.

(March 8)
Rush performs live at Expo Hall, Mobile, Alabama, US. The opening act is April Wine.

(March 9)

Rush performs live at Jacksonville Civic Auditorium, Jacksonville, Florida, US. The opening act is UFO.

(March 10)
Rush performs live at the Hollywood Sportatorium, Hollywood, Florida, US. The opening act is UFO.

(March 11)
Rush performs live at Curtis Hixon Hall, Tampa, Florida, US. The opening act is UFO.

(March 13)
Rush performs live at Boutwell Auditorium, Birmingham, Alabama, US. The opening act is UFO.

(March 15)
Rush performs live at Memorial Auditorium, Chattanooga, Tennessee, US. The opening act is Molly Hatchet.

(March 16)
Rush performs live at Municipal Auditorium, Nashville, Tennessee, US. The opening act is Molly Hatchet.

(March 17)
Rush performs live at Freedom Hall Civic Center, Johnson City, Tennessee, US. The opening act is Angel.

(March 18)
Rush performs live at Wheeling Civic Center, Wheeling, West Virginia, US. The opening act is Sad Cafe.

(March 27)
Rush performs live at Salt Palace Center, Salt Lake City, Utah, US. The opening act is April Wine.

(March 28)
Rush performs live at Auditorium Arena, Denver, Colorado, US. The opening act is Wireless.

(March 29)
Rush performs live at Pershing Memorial Auditorium, Lincoln, Nebraska, US. The opening act is Angel.

(March 30)
Rush performs live at Municipal Auditorium, Topeka, Kansas, US. The opening act is Granmax. Prior to the show, the venue suffers from $3,000 damage to its doors by fans trying to get in before the doors were scheduled to open.

(April 3)
Rush performs live at Poughkeepsie Civic Center, Poughkeepsie, New York, US. The opening act is Falcon Eddie.

(April 4)
Rush performs live at Rochester War Memorial, Rochester, New York, US. The opening act is The Good Rats.

(April 6)
Rush performs live at Nassau Coliseum, Uniondale, New York, US. The opening act is The Good Rats.

(April 7)
Rush performs live at Veterans Coliseum, New Haven, US. The opening act is The Good Rats.

(April 8)
Rush performs live at Providence Civic Center, Providence, Rhode Island, US. The opening act is The Good Rats.

(April 10)
Rush performs live at Salem Civic Center, Virginia, US.

(April 11)
Rush performs live at Hampton Coliseum, Hampton, Virginia, US. The opening act is Blackfoot.

(April 13)
Rush performs live at Fox Theatre, Atlanta, Georgia, US.

(April 14)
Rush performs live at Greensboro, Coliseum, Greensboro, North Carolina, US. The opening act is Molly Hatchet.

(April 15)
Rush performs live at Providence Civic Center, Providence, Rhode Island, US. The opening act is The Good Rats.

(April 23 & 24)
Rush performs live at City Hall, Newcastle, England. The opening act is Max Webster.

(April 25 & 26)
Rush performs live at The Apollo, Glasgow, Scotland. The opening act is Max Webster.

(April 28)
Rush performs live at The Odeon, Edinburgh, Scotland. The opening act is Max Webster.

(April 29 & 30)
Rush performs live at The Apollo, Manchester, England. The opening act is Max Webster.

(May)
Advertisements first appear in Europe for the Phonogram Records *Rush* compilation *Rush Through Time*. Track listing as following:

Rush Through Time Picture Disc LP:
"Fly By Night"
"Making Memories"
"Bastille Day"
"Something For Nothing"
"Cinderella Man"
"Anthem"
"2112: I: Overture/ II: The Temples Of Syrinx"
"The Twilight Zone"
"Best I Can"
"Closer To The Heart"
"In The End"

Note: The collection is disowned by the band, who have no input into its creation or release, as it is purely an official record company product to promote the European leg of *Tour Of The Hemispheres*. Later editions in different territories are standard black vinyl.

(May 1 & 2)
Rush performs live at Liverpool Empire, Liverpool, England. The opening act is Max Webster.

(May 4, 5, 6 & 7)
Rush performs live at the Hammersmith Odeon, London, England. The opening act is Max Webster. According to the later February 1980 issue of *Music Express*, these shows are filmed for a planned *"Live In England"*-type live album (that likely would not have been the actual title). The article also notes that the band plans to assemble the live album "between touring itineraries" in 1980. It's not specified whether any post-production work was done on the project, apart from the material released as noted below. **Alex Lifeson** in the *Music Express* article sounds reluctant to release such a film, suggesting that the potential for such a film to be awful is high, citing such concert films by The Rolling Stones, Bob Dylan and Gino Vanelli. However, three tracks filmed during rehearsals are used as promotional films:

"The Trees (Live at the Hammersmith Odeon, 1979)" 4:57
Written by Neil Peart (words), Geddy Lee & Alex Lifeson (music)
Appears on: Chronicles VHS & DVD
The band is in fine form during this performance and the song has that great live energy that comes well into a tour. Both this performance and "La Villa Strangiato" are filmed either during rehearsals or the soundcheck, as there is no audience present.

"Circumstances (Live at the Hammersmith Odeon, 1979)" 3:44
Written by Neil Peart (words), Geddy Lee & Alex Lifeson (music)
Appears on: R30: 30th Anniversary World Tour Deluxe (DVD+CD Edition), R40 boxed set (Backstage Club & Best Buy Editions)
An excellent live version of the song!

"La Villa Strangiato (Live at the Hammersmith Odeon, 1979)" 10:12
Written by Geddy Lee, Alex Lifeson & Neil Peart ("Powerhouse" by Raymond Scott, arr. by Lee/Lifeson/Peart)
Appears on: R30: 30th Anniversary World Tour Deluxe DVD+CD Edition, R40 Backstage Club & Best Buy Editions
Like with "The Trees" and "Circumstances," the band rocks this track, giving it their all, as usual.

Note: There's no official source noting these promo films come from the Hammersmith Odeon dates, however the RushVEVO YouTube posting of "The Trees" has a copyright date of 1979 and the venue certainly looks like the distinctive Hammersmith Odeon (it is a theatre, rather than an arena, so the stage is narrower and there is a proscenium arch and wings stages right and left). Given the arrangements needed to set up a live venue recording, it's most probable that the shoot occurred here, rather than a separate date elsewhere.

(May 9)
Rush performs live at Coventry Theatre, Coventry, England. The opening act is Max Webster.

(May 10 & 11)
Rush performs live at The Odeon, Birmingham, England. The opening act is Max Webster.

(May 13)
Rush performs live at Southampton, Gaumont, Southampton, England. The opening act is Max Webster.

(May 14 & 15)
Rush performs live at Colston Hall, Bristol, England. The opening act is Max Webster.

(May 17)
Rush is scheduled to start the European leg of the tour in Paris, France, but a fire at the venue forces its cancellation.

(May 18)
Rush performs live at Maekeblijde, Poperinge, Belgium. The opening act is Max Webster.

(May 23)
Rush performs live at Concert House, Gothenburg, Sweden. The opening act is Max Webster.

(May 24)
Rush performs live at Chateau Neuf, Oslo, Norway. The opening act is Max Webster.

(May 25)
Rush performs live at Gröna Lund, Stockholm, Sweden. The opening act is Max Webster.

(May 27)
Rush performs live at Stadhalle, Erlangen, Germany. The opening act is Max Webster.

(May 28)
Rush performs live at Stadhalle, Offenbach, Germany. The opening act is Max Webster.
"Working Man" – a bootleg of this show (titled *Black Forest*) has the reggae intro to the song done on this tour, demonstrating the band's current interest in the genre. In a February 1980 interview with *Music Express*, **Alex Lifeson** cites the reggae intro as an influence on the reggae parts they later included in "The Spirit Of Radio."

(May 29)
Rush performs live at Musikhalle, Hamburg, Germany. The opening act is Max Webster.

(May 31)
Rush is scheduled to perform at Rosengarten, Mannheim, Germany, but the show, and the following two concerts, is cancelled because of Alex's broken finger.

(June 1)
Rush is scheduled to perform at Volkshaus, Zurich, Switzerland, but the show is cancelled because of Alex's broken finger.

(June 2)
Rush is scheduled to perform at Circus Krone, Munich, Germany, but the show is cancelled because of Alex's broken finger.

(June 4)
Rush performs live at the Pink Pop Festival, Geleen, Holland. Also on the bill are Peter Tosh, Elvis Costello And The Attractions, Dire Straits, The Police, Average White Band and Massada. Footage from backstage of this show, where **Alex Lifeson** and **Geddy Lee** say Alex's broken finger cancelled the earlier three shows, appears in the documentaries *Pink Pop - Vol. 2* and *Rush: Beyond The Lighted Stage*, along with part of their live performance of "La Villa Strangiato," during which you can see the broken finger as **Alex** plays. **Geddy**'s keyboard technician, Jack Secret, breaks both his feet at this concert jumping over a wall and into a staircase he didn't know was on the other side.

(Mid-June)
Rush takes a break following the *Tour Of The Hemispheres*.

(Mid-July)
Rush begins writing their seventh album (*Permanent Waves* sessions. The date comes from the *Permanent Waves* tour book). The work takes place at Lakewoods Farm, Flesherton, Ontario, Canada. **Geddy Lee** and **Alex Lifeson** write the music and **Neil Peart** writes lyrics separately and they then assemble the tracks.
"Entre Nous" - In the *Permanent Waves* tour book, **Neil** says the lyrics to this song were the only ones he brought to the sessions already written. Curiously, the later *Permanent Waves* liner notes, in their credit to Hugh Syme (who played piano on the album recording), refer to the song as "Between Us," indicating that may have been the original or working title.

"Uncle Tounouse" – In the *Permanent Waves* tour book, **Neil** describes this as "a giant hodge-podge of instrumental mish-mash," recorded the first day and from which the band would take some musical ideas and work them into other songs.

"The Spirit Of Radio" – the title comes from the Toronto radio station CFNY FM 102.1's slogan at the time "The Spirit of Radio." **Neil** says in a 2014 interview with CBC.ca that while driving from the Lakewoods Farm house back home to the Niagara Region on weekends, he would listen to the station and enjoyed the variety it played. In the *Permanent Waves* tour book, **Neil** says this was one of three songs completed "within the first few days." The mix of styles (punk, new wave, rock and reggae) represents the idea of changing channels between different stations. The reggae intro used in "Working Man" laid the foundation for the reggae parts written for this song, according to **Alex Lifeson**.

"Freewill" - In the *Permanent Waves* tour book, **Neil** says this was one of three songs completed "within the first few days."

"Jacob's Ladder" - In the *Permanent Waves* tour book, **Neil** says this was one of three songs completed "within the first few days."

"Sir Gawain And The Green Knight" – a song based on this story is developed and planned for the album, but dropped when it was decided the song was too different from the rest of the album and wouldn't fit.

"Different Strings" – penned by **Geddy**, the song deliberately left unrehearsed by the band so they can develop it during the actual recording session (as described in the *Permanent Waves* tour book).

Note: the February 1980 *Music Express* article is the earliest detailed description of how the band composes music, not "accumulating songs," but writing during an advance period specifically for the album.

Rough demos are then recorded at the Sound Kitchen studios, Toronto, Ontario, Canada.

Anthem Records releases a promo statement noting that **Rush** will be headlining an upcoming North American summer tour. It also says the setlists will feature material from their upcoming album, to be recorded at La Studio (Morin Heights, Quebec, Canada), mixed at Trident Studios (London, England) and is that the band is hoping to release the album in January.

Songs refined live and at sound checks following these writing and demo sessions:
"Jacob's Ladder" – this was only worked on during soundchecks, as confirmed by **Neil Peart** in the *Permanent Waves* tour book.
"Entre Nous" – a recording exists of the band working on the song at a soundcheck (said to be Dayton, Ohio).
"The Spirit Of Radio"
"Freewill"

(August 17)
Rush performs live at RKO Orpheum Theatre, Davenport, Iowa, US.

(August 18)
Rush performs live at Five Flags Arena, Dubuque, Iowa, US.

(August 19)
Rush performs live at Comiskey Park, Chicago, Illinois, US, as part of Chicago Jam II. Also on the bill are Foghat, Tubes, Southside Johnny and Roadmaster.

(August 21)
Rush performs live at Civic Center Coliseum, Charleston, West Virginia, US.

(August 22)
Rush performs live at Capital Center, Largo, Maryland, US. The opening act is Nantucket Band.

(August 24)
Rush performs live at Ivor Wynne Stadium, Hamilton, Ontario, Canada. The opening act is Sweetheart.

(August 26)
Rush performs live at the Cotton Bowl, Dallas, Texas, US, as part of A Farewell To Texas Summer. Also on the bill is Foghat, Pat Travers, Billy Thorpe, Point Blank and Little River Band.

(August 28)
Rush is scheduled to perform live at Pine Knob Music Theatre, Detroit, Michigan, US, but the show is moved to September 10th.

(August 29)
Rush performs live at Lansing Civic Center, Lansing, Michigan, US. The opening act is New England.

(August 30)
Rush performs live at Wendlar Arena, Saginaw, Michigan, US.

(August 31)

Rush performs live at Hara Arena, Dayton, Ohio, US. The opening act is Pat Travers.

> "Entre Nous (Soundcheck Version, Dayton, 1979)" 4:40
> Written by Neil Peart (words), Geddy Lee & Alex Lifeson (music)
> Appears on: Unreleased
> This bootleg recording has been floating around the internet for a while and it certainly sounds authentic. The band tears through the music and but Geddy doesn't sing much of the lyrics, resulting in a mostly instrumental live version. This is a good example of how the band worked on new songs at soundchecks in advance of the album recordings. The recording itself is pretty rough, but what can you expect? It's definitely something to have in the collection even if you don't play it too often due to audio quality.

(September 2)
Rush performs live at Varsity Stadium, University of Toronto, Toronto, Ontario, Canada. The opening act is FM.

> "The Spirit Of Radio (Live at Varsity Stadium, 1979)" 5:19
> Written by Neil Peart (words), Geddy Lee & Alex Lifeson (music)
> Appears on: Prelude To The Future (Bootleg)
> To test out the new songs before recording them for Permanent Waves, Rush performed this and "Freewill" live, introducing them as songs planned for the new album. This pre-album version of the song isn't quite as refined as it would appear on the studio recording and the guitar solo has yet to be developed, but the tempo and style changes are all there. It's very interesting to hear the song as a work in progress.

> "Freewill (Live at Varsity Stadium, 1979)" 5:35
> Written by Neil Peart (words), Geddy Lee & Alex Lifeson (music)
> Appears on: Prelude To The Future (Bootleg)
> Like with "The Spirit Of Radio," this early performance of the song is not as polished as the album version, but is more or less complete. Alex shreds through the guitar solo, as the familiar melody had not yet been written for it. It's worth tracking down this bootleg to hear the song as it was in development.

(September 5)
Rush performs live at Rupp Arena, Lexington, Kentucky, US. The opening act is Pat Travers.

(September 7)
Rush performs live at Five Seasons Theater, Cedar Rapids, Iowa, US. The opening act is Pat Travers.

(September 8)
Rush performs live at Alpine Valley Amphitheater, East Troy, Wisconsin, US. The opening act is Pat Travers.

(September 9)
Rush performs live at Rose Arena, Central Michigan University, Mount Pleasant, Michigan, US. The opening act is Pat Travers.

(September 10)
Rush performs live at Pine Knob Music Theatre, Detroit, Michigan, US. The opening act is Pat Travers.

(September 12)
Rush performs live at Allentown Fairgrounds, Allentown, Pennsylvania, US. The opening act is Pat Travers.

(Mid-September)
Various articles (publications unknown) announcing a second New Bingley Hall date for September 22, 1979, also notes that *Rush* is likely to record their next album in England (*Permanent Waves* sessions).

(September 17 to 20)
An article in *Sounds* published on September 22nd notes that band are scheduled to start recording their next album in London, England, "this week" and will end the week with the New Bingley Hall concerts. In the February 1980 *Music Express* article, **Alex Lifeson** says the band looked at working in Trident Studios, London, England, but found it was too expensive.

(September 21 & 22)
Rush performs live at New Bingley Hall, Stafford, England. The opening act is Wild Horses. A review in *New Music Express* of one of these shows notes that the following new songs are performed:

"The Spirit Of Radio"
"Freewill"

(Late September - October)
Rush begins recording their seventh studio album at Le Studio, Morin Heights, Quebec, Canada (*Permanent Waves* sessions). Produced and arrangements by *Rush* and Terry Brown. Engineered by Paul Northfield, with assistance from Adam Moseley, Craig Milliner, **Geddy Lee** and Steve S. Hort. Tracks worked on include:

"Jacob's Ladder" – worked on previously during sound checks during the summer tour and completed quickly during these sessions.
"The Spirit Of Radio" – previewed during the summer tour and completed quickly during these sessions.
"Freewill" – previewed during the summer tour and completed quickly during these sessions.
"Entre Nous" - completed quickly during these sessions.
"Different Strings" – completed (purposely) without the benefit of earlier rehearsal work. Hugh Syme plays piano on this track.
"Natural Science" – The band is forced to write a brand new song to fill the gap left by the previous removal of the "Sir Gawain" song. In the *Permanent Waves* tour book, **Neil** says he could not think of anything to write for two days while the others worked on overdubs. On the third day ideas coalesced and grew into this song, after which they started putting it to music, using parts of the "Sir Gawain" music, other unused parts (from "Uncle Tounouse"?) and new pieces.
Recording work on the album is completed three days ahead of schedule and rough mixes of the songs are made in advance of the proper mixing sessions.

During these sessions, the title of the album is decided on: *Permanent Waves*. Hugh Syme is also in contact with the band designing the album art while they work on in the studio.

(November)
A week after the recording sessions end, **Rush** and Terry Brown begin mixing *Permanent Waves* at Trident Studios, London, England. The mixing sessions take two weeks.

(December)
Geddy Lee produces Wireless's album *No Static* at Le Studio, Morin Heights, Quebec, Canada. Engineered by Paul Northfield. Terry Brown mixes the album. **Lee** also provides an "additional voice" credited as "Dirk" (his long-time nickname). The album is mixed at Soundstage, Toronto, Ontario, Canada.

Note: the recording location and date of "December 1979" is listed in the 2012 CD re-issue of the album.

The planned artwork for *Permanent Waves* features the infamous *Chicago Daily Tribune* (now *Chicago Tribune*) newspaper from November 3, 1948, with the "Dewey Defeats Truman" headline, but the *Tribune* objects to its use. Art director Hugh Syme alters the headline to read "Dewei Defeats Truman," then blurs out the words "*Chicago*" and "*Tribune*" with Arabic characters, leaving only "*Daily*" legible. The cover uses a photo of Hurricane Carla's 1961 destruction of Galveston, Texas, US, and a Coca-Cola sign visible on the distance is changed to stylized text of "Lee," "Lifeson" and "Peart" (because Coca-Cola Ltd. objects to the proximity of the sign to the cover model's nether regions).

Note: In a 1983 *Creem* magazine interview, Hugh Syme describes the problems that arose in getting the clearances from both the *Chicago Tribune* and Coca-Cola Ltd., and the subsequent necessary alterations. In a 1983 interview excerpt (available at angelfire.com/ok3/rush/albuminfo2.html) **Neil Peart** says he was the only band member available to address the legal problems being encountered as they arose with the cover art, specifically saying **Geddy Lee** was off producing (Wireless and their *No Static* album) and **Alex Lifeson** was also unavailable. He also similarly details the cover art problems in the *Permanent Waves* tour book.

PERMANENT WAVES

1980

(January 1)
Rush releases their album *Permanent Waves* on Anthem Records (Canada) and Mercury Records (UK). The Canadian and UK release features the "Dewei Defeats Truman" newspaper and the altered Coca-Cola sign (now "Lee-Peart-Lifeson" signs). Track listing as follows:

"The Spirit Of Radio"
"Freewill"
"Jacob's Ladder"
"Entre Nous"
"Different Strings"
"Natural Science"

Note: though not listed on the sleeve, the liner notes list the three movements of "Natural Science":

"Natural Science:
       I. Tide Pools
       II. Hyperspace
       III. Permanent Waves"

Note: Numerous sources claim that the original pressing of the LP in Canada and the UK featured the unaltered cover containing both the headline "Dewey Defeats Truman" and the Coca-Cola sign, however that does not appear to be the case. All known copies feature either "Dewei Defeats Truman" + Lee-Peart-Lifeson signs or the blanked-out headline + re-written Lee-Peart-Lifeson signs. France is the exception, featuring an illegible rewritten headline + the re-written Lee-Peart-Lifeson signs. Later re-issues of the album eliminates the "Dewei Defeats Truman" from the newspaper entirely in all territories. Additionally, both Hugh Syme and **Neil Peart**'s descriptions of the legal problems they had with the cover art (see December 1979) clearly demonstrate that the unaltered "Dewey Defeats Truman" and the Coca-Cola graphics never made it passed the approval stage as the *Chicago Tribune* and Coca-Cola Ltd.'s objections allowed the idea to go no further.
In Hugh Syme's 2015 book *The Art Of Rush*, the original, unaltered image used for the cover art appears, including the "Dewey" and "Coca-Cola," with no album title or band name graphics.

(January 7)
Rush releases their album *Permanent Waves* on Mercury Records in the US. The US release features the fully edited newspaper, with a white bar over the "Dewei Defeats Truman" headline. Curiously, the Lee-Peart-Lifeson signs have been altered further, featuring a different font on the names. Track listing same as above.

(January 12)
2,000 ***Rush*** fans waiting in line cause damage at Cobo Hall Arena box office, Detroit, Michigan, US, after a rumor starts that there won't be enough tickets for the upcoming concert at Joe Louis Arena, Detroit, on February 17th.

(January 17)
Rush performs live at Aitken Centre, University of New Brunswick, Fredericton, New Brunswick, Canada.

(January 18)
Rush performs live at Moncton Coliseum, Moncton, New Brunswick, Canada. The opening act is Max Webster.

(January 19)
Rush performs live at Halifax Metro Centre, Halifax, Nova Scotia, Canada. The opening act is Max Webster.

(January 20 & 21)
Rush performs live at The Forum, Montreal, Quebec, Canada. The opening act is Max Webster.

(January 22 & 23)
Rush performs live at the Palace Theatre, Albany, New York, US. The opening act is Garfield.

(January 24)
Rush performs live at the War Memorial, Rochester, New York, US. The opening act is Max Webster.

(January 26)
Rush performs live at Mid-Hudson Civic Center, Poughkeepsie, New York, US. The opening act is Max Webster. This date does not appear on the tour shirts, as it is a late addition to the schedule.

(January 27)

Rush performs live at Broome County Arena, Binghamton, New York, US. The opening act is Max Webster.

(January 29)
Rush performs live at Boutwell Auditorium, Birmingham, Alabama, US. The opening act is Max Webster.

(January 30)
Rush performs live at The Omni, Atlanta, Georgia, US. The opening act is Max Webster.

(February)
Rush releases their singles of "The Spirit Of Radio" in North America.

Canada 7" single (ANS-017):
"The Spirit Of Radio (Canadian Single Edit)"
"Circumstances (1980 Canadian Single Edit)"

Canada 7" promo single (ANS-017 PRO):
"The Spirit Of Radio (Canadian Single Edit)"
"The Spirit Of Radio (US Single Edit)"

US 7" single (M 76044):
"The Spirit Of Radio (US Single Edit)"
"Circumstances"

US 7" promo single (76044-P):
"The Spirit Of Radio (US Single Edit)"
"The Spirit Of Radio" – listed as "Long Version," this is the standard album version

US 12" promo single (MK-125):
"The Spirit Of Radio"
"The Trees"
"Working Man"

> "The Spirit Of Radio (Canadian Single Edit)" 3:40
> Written by Neil Peart (words), Geddy Lee & Alex Lifeson (music)
> Appears on: Canada 7" single;
> This edit cuts out a lot from the track throughout, mostly instrumental, but also the second "Invisible airwaves..." refrain (chorus?), so the song comes across as very truncated from start to finish.
>
> "The Spirit Of Radio (US Single Edit)" 3:00
> Written by Neil Peart (words), Geddy Lee & Alex Lifeson (music)
> Appears on: Canada 7" promo single; US 7" single; US 7" promo single; European 7" singles; UK 1988 Old Gold 7" re-issue single;
> Unlike the Canadian Single Edit, this cut takes the approach of shortening the opening, retaining the second "Invisible airwaves..." refrain, but fading out after, thereby losing the "For the words of the profits..." verse. It just goes to show that you can't edit much from a shorter Rush song and not have it fall apart or sound utterly incomplete.
>
> "Circumstances (1980 Canadian Single Edit)" 2:58
> Written by Neil Peart (words), Geddy Lee & Alex Lifeson (music)
> Appears on: Canada "The Spirit Of Radio" 7" single
> A different edit from the earlier 1979 cut, this one removes less music throughout, but is still pretty harsh.

(February 1)
Rush performs live at Myriad Convention Center, Oklahoma City, Oklahoma, US. The opening act is Max Webster.

(February 2)
Rush performs live at Tarrant County Convention Center, Fort Worth, Texas, US. The opening act is Max Webster.

(February 3)
Rush performs live at Convention Center Arena, San Antonio, Texas, US. The opening act is Max Webster.

(February 5)
Rush performs live at Sam Houston Coliseum, Houston, Texas, US. The opening act is Max Webster.

(February 6)
Rush performs live at The Coliseum, Corpus Christi, Texas, US. The opening act is Max Webster.

(February 7)
Rush performs live at Municipal Auditorium, Austin, Texas, US. The opening act is Max Webster.

(February 8)
Rush performs live at Dallas Convention Center, Dallas, Texas, US. The opening act is Max Webster.

(February 9)
Rush performs live at Assembly Center, Tulsa, Oklahoma, US. The opening act is Max Webster.

(February 10)
Rush performs live at Kansas Coliseum, Wichita, Kansas, US. The opening act is Max Webster.

(February 11, 12 & 13)
Rush performs live at Keil Auditorium, St, Louis, Missouri, US. The opening act is Max Webster. All three shows are recorded by EDR-Media for *The Source* NBC Radio's Young Adult Network and a promo 2xLP concert album is released later by Anthem Records in 1980 titled *Rush: Live In Concert From St. Louis, MOI* (SPE-003).

(February 15)
Rush performs live at Roberts Stadium, Evansville, Indiana, US. The opening act is Max Webster.

(February 16)
Rush performs live at the University of Dayton Arena, Dayton, Ohio, US. The opening act is Max Webster.

(February 17)
Rush performs live at Joe Louis Arena, Detroit, Michigan, US. The opening act is Max Webster.

(February 18)
Rush performs live at Richfield Coliseum, Richfield Coliseum, Richfield, Ohio, US. The opening act is Max Webster.

(February 19)
Rush performs live at Joe Louis Arena, Detroit, Michigan, US. The opening act is Max Webster.

(February 27)
Rush performs live at Kemper Arena, Kansas City, Missouri, US. The opening act is Roadmaster.

(Late Winter)
Anthem Records issues the promo concert album 2xLP *Rush: Live In Concert From St. Louis, MOI* (SPE-003), to NBC Radio *The Source* affiliates. The concert album was recorded live on February 11 – 13, 1980, in St. Louis.

Note: Lifted and edited directly from either the official Anthem Records promo 2xLP release or taken from the original master tapes (it's unclear which), this concert recording has been subject to numerous unofficial releases, including as *Rush: Spirit Of The Airwaves*.

(Date Unknown)
Anthem Records releases a promo LP titled *Rush: Permanent Waves - Radio Special with John Donabie* (SPE-004), featuring *Rush* discussing the *Permanent Waves* album with radio DJ John Donabie.

(March 1)
Rush performs live at McNichols Arena, Denver, Colorado, US. The opening act is Roadmaster.

(March 2)
Rush performs live at Tingley Coliseum, Albuquerque, New Mexico, US.

(March 3)
Rush performs live at Tucson Community Centre, Tucson, Arizona, US.

(March 4)
Rush performs live at Veterans Memorial Coliseum, Phoenix, Arizona, US. .38 Special is scheduled to open, but reportedly their bus broke down.

(March 6)
Rush performs live at Sports Arena, San Diego, California, US. The opening act is .38 Special.

(March 7)
Rush performs live at Swing Auditorium, San Bernardino, US. The opening act is .38 Special.

(March 9)
Rush performs live at Long Beach Arena, Long Beach, California, US. The opening act is .38 Special.

(March 10)
Rush performs live at Great Western Forum, Los Angeles, California, US. The opening act is .38 Special.

(March 11)
Rush performs live at Selland Arena, Fresno, California, US. The opening act is .38 Special.

(March 13)
Rush is scheduled to perform in Sacramento, California, US, but the show is cancelled.

(March 14)
Rush performs live at Cow Palace, San Francisco, California, US. The opening act is .38 Special.

(March 15)
Rush releases their "The Spirit of Radio" singles in the UK and Europe on Mercury.

UK 7" single (RADIO 7):
"The Spirit of Radio (US Single Edit)"
"The Trees"

UK 12" single (RADIO 12):
"The Spirit Of Radio"
"The Trees"
"Working Man"

European 7" singles:
"The Spirit of Radio (US Single Edit)"
"Circumstances"

Note: This may not be the exact date of the European single release, as release information is scarce, but it seems it was released at the same time as the UK territory.

Rush performs live at Cow Palace, San Francisco, California, US. The opening act is .38 Special.

(March 16)
Rush performs live at McArthur Court, Eugene, US.

(March 18 & 19)
Rush performs live at Seattle Center Coliseum, Seattle, Washington, US. The opening act is .38 Special.

(March 20)
Rush performs live at Memorial Coliseum, Portland, US.

(March 21)
Rush performs live at Spokane Coliseum, Spokane, Washington, US. The opening act is .38 Special.

(March 23)
Rush performs live at Northlands Coliseum, Edmonton, Alberta, Canada. The opening act is .38 Special.

(March 24 & 25)
Rush performs live at Max Bell Arena, Calgary, Alberta, Canada. The opening band is Saga.

(March 27)
Rush performs live at Memorial Arena, Victoria, British Columbia, Canada.

(March 28)
NBC Radio *The Source* station affiliates air *Rush*'s February 11-13, 1980, St. Louis, promo 2xLP concert album *Rush: Live In Concert From St. Louis, MO1*.

Rush performs live at Beban Park Arena, Nanaimo, British Columbia, Canada.

(March 29)
Rush performs live at Pacific Coliseum, Vancouver, British Columbia, Canada. The opening band is Saga.

(March 31)
Rush performs live at the Agridome, Regina, Saskatchewan, Canada.

(Date Unknown)
Vic Wilson leaves SRO Productions (*Billboard* October 26, 1996).

(Date Unknown)
Julian Weinrib is born to **Geddy Lee** and Nancy Young.

(April)
Rush releases their "Entre Nous" singles in North America.

Canada 7" single (ANS-021):
"Entre Nous (Single Edit)"
"Different Strings"

US 7" single (M-76060):
"Entre Nous (Single Edit)"
"Different Strings"

US 7" promo single (76060-DJ):
"Entre Nous (Single Edit)"
"Entre Nous (Single Edit)"

US 12" promo single (MK-137):
"Entre Nous"
"Entre Nous (Single Edit)"

> "Entre Nous (Single Edit)" 3:45
> Written by Neil Peart (words), Geddy Lee & Alex Lifeson (music)
> Appears on: Canada 7" single; US 7" single; US 7" promo single; US 12" promo single
> I have not heard this edit, but if I had to guess, I'd say it's probably similar to "The Spirit Of Radio" edits, removing portions and/or fading out early.

(April 1)
Rush performs live at Winnipeg Arena, Winnipeg, Manitoba, Canada. The opening act is Saga.

(April 3, 4, 5 & 6)
Rush performs live at the International Amphitheatre, Chicago, Illinois, US.

(April 17, 18 & 19)
Rush performs live at Milwaukee Auditorium, Milwaukee, Wisconsin, US.

(April 20)
Rush performs live at Dane County Coliseum, Madison, Wisconsin, US. The opening act is .38 Special.

(April 22)
Rush performs live at Brown County Arena, Green Bay, Wisconsin, US. The opening act is .38 Special.

(April 23)
Rush performs live at Wings Stadium, Kalamazoo, Michigan, US. The opening act is .38 Special.

(April 24)
Rush performs live at the Toledo Sports Arena, Toledo, Ohio, US. The opening act is .38 Special.

(April 26)
Rush performs live at Louisville Gardens, Louisville, Kentucky, US. The opening act is .38 Special.

(April 27)
Rush performs live at Market Square Arena, Indianapolis, Indiana, US. The opening act is .38 Special.

(April 28)
Rush performs live at Fort Wayne Coliseum, Fort Wayne, Indiana, US. The opening act is .38 Special.

(April 29)
Rush performs live at St. John Arena, Ohio State University, Columbus, Ohio, US. The opening act is .38 Special.

(May 8)
Rush performs live at The Palladium, New York City, New York, US.

(May 9)
Rush performs live at The Palladium, New York City, New York, US. According to the *Moving Pictures* tour book, the band decides prior to this show to forego working on the planned live album of the Hammersmith Odeon concerts.

(May 10 & 11)
Rush performs live at The Palladium, New York City, New York, US.

(May 13)
Rush performs live at Hersheypark Arena, Hershey, Pennsylvania, US. The opening act is Laurie And The Sighs.

(May 14)
Rush performs live at Civic Arena, Pittsburgh, Pennsylvania, US. The opening act is Sue Saad And The Next.

(May 16)
Rush performs live at Providence Civic Center, Providence, Rhode Island, US. The opening act is The Fools.

(May 17)
Rush is scheduled to play in Yarmouth, Massachusetts, US, but is cancelled because of illness.

(May 18)
Rush is scheduled to play in Portland, Maine, US, but is cancelled because of illness.

(May 20)
Rush performs live at Veterans Coliseum, New Haven, Connecticut, US.

(May 21)
Rush performs live at Memorial Auditorium, Buffalo, New York, US. The opening act is Max Webster.

(May 22)
Rush performs live at Memorial Auditorium, Utica, New York, US. The opening act is The Fool.

(May 23)
Rush performs live at Nassau Coliseum, Uniondale, New York, US. The opening act is The Fool.

(June 1 & 2)
Rush performs live at Southampton Gaumont, Southhampton, England.

(June 4, 5, 6, 7 & 8)
Rush performs live at the Hammersmith Odeon, London, England. The *Moving Pictures* tour book says these five shows were recorded, despite the band already having decided to delay putting a live album together. A February 27, 1981, interview with **Geddy Lee** in the *Milwaukee Sentinel* also notes that these shows are recorded for a planned live album.

(June 10 & 11)
Rush performs live at The Apollo, Glasgow, Scotland. The June 11th show is recorded and the following tracks appear on *Exit...Stage Left* in 1981. The recording is originally made as part of the aborted live album of the *Permanent Waves* tour.

"A Passage To Bangkok"
"Closer To The Heart"
"Beneath, Between And Behind"
"Jacob's Ladder"

>"A Passage To Bangkok (Exit...Stage Left – Rush 'N' Roulette Edit)" 2:00
>Written by Neil Peart (words), Geddy Lee & Alex Lifeson (music)
>Appears on: Rush 'N' Roulette promo LP
>This is a two minute excerpt of the track.

>"Closer To The Heart (Exit...Stage Left – Single Version)" 3:07
>Written by Neil Peart & Peter Talbot (words), Geddy Lee & Alex Lifeson (music)
>Appears on: Canada 7" single; US 7" single; US 7" promo single; UK 7" single; Ireland 7" single
>This version fades out quickly at the end before the "Beneath, Between And Behind" starts, allowing for a good standalone cut.

>"Closer To The Heart (Exit...Stage Left – Rush 'N' Roulette Edit)" 2:00
>Written by Neil Peart & Peter Talbot (words), Geddy Lee & Alex Lifeson (music)
>Appears on: Rush 'N' Roulette promo LP
>This is a two minute excerpt of the track.

(June 12 & 13)
Rush performs live at City Hall, Newcastle, England. The *Moving Pictures* tour book says these shows were recorded as part of the original plan to release a live album next, despite that plan already having been changed.

(June 15)
Rush performs live at Queens Hall, Leeds, England.

(June 16)
Rush performs live at Deeside Leisure Centre, Deeside, Wales. The opening act is Quartz.

(June 17 & 18)
Rush performs live at The Apollo, Manchester, England. The June 17th concert is recorded (as part of the aborted plan to release a live album from this tour) and the following is released individually:

> "A Passage To Bangkok (Live in Manchester, 1980)" 3:57
> Written by Neil Peart (words), Geddy Lee & Alex Lifeson (music)
> Appears on: 2112 2012 Deluxe Edition CD
> This recording comes only a week after the Glasgow show that appears on Exit...Stage Left and a great as this version is, it's not much different from that performance.

(June 20)
Rush performs live at The Odeon, Birmingham, England.

(June 21)
Rush performs live at De Montfort Hall, Leicester, England.

(June 22)
Rush performs live at Brighton Centre, Brighton, England.

(July)
A few weeks before the "Battle Scar" session, Max Webster's drummer Gary McCracken visits **Neil Peart** at **Peart**'s home in Beamsville, Ontario, Canada, to work out their drum parts for the song in advance of the recording (*Drum* November, 2007).

(July 28)
Geddy Lee, **Alex Lifeson** and **Neil Peart** work on the following with Max Webster at Phase One Studios, Toronto, Ontario, Canada:
"Battle Scar"
"Tom Sawyer" – Pye Dubois, Max Webster's lyricist, presents the band with lyrics he thinks could work well with *Rush*, later developing into this song. The working title is said to have been variously "Louis The Warrior" and "Louis The Lawyer" (according to *Merely Players*).

Note: **Neil** lists this as the recording date in the *Moving Pictures* tour book.

(August)
Rush begins songwriting for their next album at Stony Lake, Ontario, Canada. The songs written and rehearsed are:
"The Camera Eye" – in the *Moving Pictures* tour book, **Neil Peart** says this was the first song written for the album during these sessions.
"Tom Sawyer" – this song is developed from the lyrics given by Pye Dubois in July. As described in the *Classic Albums: 2112 & Moving Pictures* episode, the song was originally written at a faster tempo.
"Red Barchetta" – **Neil** is inspired by the short story *A Nice Morning Drive*.
"YYZ" – begun here by **Geddy Lee** and **Neil Peart** during the rehearsals where they jammed **Alex Lifeson** was not present according to **Lee** in *Classic Albums: 2112 & Moving Pictures* and the two of them jammed.
"Fear Trilogy" – **Neil** is quoted in the January 1994 issue of the *Rush Backstage Club* as saying he sketched out the trilogy of songs based on themes of fear and that the third part (which became "Witch Hunt") was the easiest to write, hence it was included first.

(August 31 to Early September)
Rush works at Phase One Studios, Toronto, Ontario, Canada, with Terry Brown, to record demos of the following:
"The Camera Eye"
"Tom Sawyer" – **Neil Peart** is quoted in *Merely Players* saying that "the instrumental section" developed from **Geddy Lee**'s synth melody player during soundchecks.
"Red Barchetta"
"YYZ"
"Limelight"
"Witch Hunt" - In the *Moving Pictures* tour book, **Neil Peart** says this song goes through a lot of changes until the band figures it out. It is planned as the album's studio creation, meaning it isn't designed to be played live. Note: technology advances in only a few years to allow the band to perform the song on later tours.

> "Tom Sawyer (Demo Version)"
> Written by Neil Peart & Pye Dubois (words), Geddy Lee & Alex Lifeson (music)
> Appears on: *Classic Albums: 2112 & Moving Pictures* DVD & Blu-ray
> In the *Classic Albums: 2112 & Moving Pictures* episode, Terry Brown plays the original demo recording and discusses the problems with it, namely that the song was written to be played much faster. The band decided it didn't work well that way and slowed the whole thing down. Since the summer tour performances feature

the familiar tempo (as heard during the Allentown show), this demo and the change to the speed would have occurred during these demo sessions.

Rush plans to rehearse the following outside the concerts (during soundchecks, etc.) during the upcoming tour:
"The Camera Eye"
"Tom Sawyer" - also performed in the live set of the concerts themselves
"Red Barchetta"
"YYZ"
"Limelight" - also performed in the live set of the concerts themselves

(September 11)
Rush performs live at Hampton Coliseum, Hampton, Virginia, US. The opening act is Saxon.

(September 12)
Rush performs live at Charlotte Coliseum, Charlotte, North Caroline, US. The opening act is Saxon.

(September 13)
Rush performs live at Charleston Civic Center Coliseum, Charleston, West Virginia, US. The opening act is Saxon.

(September 14)
Rush performs live at Municipal Auditorium, Nashville, Tennessee, US. The opening act is Saxon.

(September 16)
Rush performs live at Riverside Centroplex, Baton Rouge, Louisiana, US. The opening act is Saxon.

(September 18)
Rush performs live at Lee County Arena, Fort Myers, Florida, US. The opening act is Saxon.

(September 19)
Rush performs live at Hollywood Sportatorium, Hollywood, Florida, US. The opening act is Saxon.

(September 20)
Rush performs live at Civic Center Arena, Lakeland, Florida, US. The opening act is Saxon.

(September 21)
Rush performs live at Veterans Memorial Coliseum, Jacksonville, Florida, US. The opening act is Saxon.

(September 23)
Rush performs live at Riverfront Coliseum, Cincinnati, Ohio, US. The opening act is Saxon.

(September 25)
Rush performs live at The Spectrum, Philadelphia, Pennsylvania, US. The opening act is Saxon.

(September 26)
Rush performs live at Capital Centre, Largo, Maryland, US. The opening act is Saxon.

(September 27)
Rush performs live at Cape Cod Coliseum, Cape Cod, Massachusetts, US. The opening act is Saxon.

(September 28)
Rush performs live at the Civic Center, Springfield, Massachusetts, US. The opening act is Saxon.

(September 30)
Rush performs live at Allentown Fairgrounds, Allentown, Pennsylvania, US. The opening act is Saxon.

"Limelight (Live in Allentown, 1980)" 4:38
Written by Neil Peart (words), Geddy Lee & Alex Lifeson (music)
Appears on: Something Old, Something New (bootleg)
Employing the same approach as they did with the 1980 summer tour, the band again introduces two new work-in-progress songs into set, this song and "Tom Sawyer." You can hear that the song is mostly finished, but lacks the distinctive guitar solo and the synths are much higher in the mix (though this later detail is true of the entire concert, so it may be just how the sound tech mixed it that day). The performance isn't as tight as it would become, but that's to be expected, and it doesn't take away from the value of hearing what was then a yet-to-be-recorded number.

"Tom Sawyer (Live in Allentown, 1980)" 4:46
Written by Neil Peart & Pye Dubois (words), Geddy Lee & Alex Lifeson (music)
Appears on: Something Old, Something New (bootleg)

As with "Limelight," Geddy introduces this song as one planned for the upcoming album. Since this song has become one of Rush's most recognizable (if not *the* most recognizable), it's quaint to hear him tentative as he announces the title as "Tom...Sawyer." Unlike "Limelight," which is lyrically complete by this time, "Tom Sawyer" would go through further changes after this show, so what we get to hear are alternate ideas and verses. Right off the bat, "pride" and "stride" are in the opposite places, there is no shout out of "The river!" and overall, Geddy sings the song with a much more jaunty tone, which sounds a bit strange compared to the even, direct performances we're familiar with. The guitar solo is also unfinished. The real treat, however, is that the "No, his mind is not for rent..." verse is completely different after that first line, so if you're not expecting it, it'll take you by surprise. The end of the song just sort of stops without the long outro played on the standard version.

(October 1)
Rush performs live at Cumberland County Civic Center, Portland, Maine, US. The opening act is Saxon.

(October)
Rush begins recording their eighth studio album at La Studio, Morin Heights, Quebec, Canada (*Moving Pictures* sessions). Produced and arranged by *Rush* and Terry Brown. Engineered by Paul Northfield. Tracks worked on include:
"Tom Sawyer" – the song is further refined and the lyrics are changed to reflect the more familiar version. The track takes a day and a half to record, owing to the difficulty in playing it.
"Limelight"
"YYZ" – During a break in recording, *Rush* flies back to Toronto, Ontario, Canada, on a charter flight flown by **Alex Lifeson** and his flight instructor, with **Neil Peart** and **Alex Lifeson** as passengers. The Toronto International Airport identifier Morse code YYZ is audible to **Peart** and **Lee** and inspires them to include the melody and develop the 'airport' theme of the piece.
"Red Barchetta" – *Merely Players* reports that the song is recorded in one take.
"The Camera Eye"
"Witch Hunt" – Hugh Syme plays synths on this track.
"Vital Signs" – The band deliberately left themselves short a song, intending to create one brand new once in the studio recording the album proper. The song is written quickly in the studio (*Plain Dealer* April 15, 2011).

The recording sessions run a few days over schedule.

(Date Unknown)
Max Webster releases their album *Universal Juveniles*, featuring the track "Battle Scar" with *Rush*. The song is also released as a single and is credited variously as **Rush and Max Webster** and **Max Webster with Geddy Lee, Alex Lifeson and Neil Peart of Rush**.

> "Battle Scar" 5:51
> Written by Pye Dubois & Kim Mitchell
> Appears on: Universal Juveniles, The Best Of Max Webster
> A genuine collaboration between the two bands, who had been friends for a while before recording together, this recording was done live in the studio, with all the various band members performing together. Geddy and Kim share lead vocals and you can hear Neil's drums, Alex's guitar work and Geddy's bass throughout. Overall, a great, mid-tempo '80s rocker and a must for your Rush collection!

(November)
Rush is scheduled to complete mixing work on *Moving Pictures*, but technical problems cause them to run two weeks longer (Le Studio, Morin Heights, Quebec, Canada).

Note: the album liner notes say the recording sessions were from October to November, 1980, but **Neil Peart**'s account of the delays caused by equipment malfunctions notes that they finished in December. This discrepancy likely stems from the album sleeve went into production noting the original time frame, before the delays extended the band's stay at Le Studio.

(December)
Rush continues work on *Moving Pictures* at Le Studio, Morin Heights, Quebec, Canada.
"Witch Hunt" – **Alex Lifeson** notes in the January 2, 1989, episode of *In The Studio with Redbeard* that the riot vocals are recorded this month.

(December 8)
John Lennon is shot and killed outside his home, The Dakota, New York City, New York, US.
"Witch Hunt" – **Geddy Lee** later says the band works on the song on this date (*Guitar Shop* March, 1999).

(Mid-December)
Rush completes mixing *Moving Pictures* at Le Studio, Morin Heights, Quebec, Canada.

(December 31)
Geddy Lee sings and plays bass on the song "Battle Scar" with Max Webster at their concert at Maple Leaf Gardens, Toronto, Ontario, Canada.

MOVING PICTURES & EXIT...STAGE LEFT

1981

(February)
Rush releases its "Limelight" singles in North America.

Canada 7" single (ANS-031):
"Limelight (Single Edit)"
"YYZ"

US 7" single (M-76095):
"Limelight (Single Edit)"
"YYZ"

US 7" promo single (76095 DJ):
"Limelight (Single Edit)"
"Limelight (Single Edit)"

> "Limelight (Single Edit)" 3:58
> Written by Neil Peart (words), Geddy Lee & Alex Lifeson (music)
> Appears on: Canada 7" single; US 7" single; US 7" promo single
> This version fades out early.

(February 12)
Rush releases their eighth album studio, *Moving Pictures*, on Anthem Records (Canada) and Mercury Records (worldwide). Track listing as follows:

"Tom Sawyer"
"Red Barchetta"
"YYZ"
"Limelight"
"The Camera Eye"
"Witch Hunt" – part III of 'Fear'
"Vital Signs"

Note: the liner notes for "The Camera Eye" indicates two unnamed parts, commonly referred to as "New York" and "London."

Note: around this time, Anthem Records issues a 2xLP *Moving Pictures* radio promo (SPE-007) similar to the similar to the previous such album promos, featuring an interview with **Neil Peart** discussing the album intercut with all the tracks from the album itself.

(Dates Unknown)
During the *Moving Pictures* tour, concert sound man Jon Erickson begins the process of recording the band's soundcheck jams for the purpose of capturing spontaneous ideas for later use.

(February 17, 18 & 19)
Rush rehearses for the *Moving Pictures* Tour at Wings Stadium, Kalamazoo, Michigan, US.

(February 20)
Rush performs live at Wings Stadium, Kalamazoo, Michigan, US. The opening act is Max Webster.

(February 21)
Rush performs live at Five Flag Arena, Dubuque, Iowa, US. The opening act is Max Webster.

(February 24)
Rush performs live at The Center, La Crosse, Wisconsin, US. The opening act is Max Webster.

(February 26, 27, 28 & March 1)
Rush performs live at the International Amphitheater, Chicago, Illinois, US. The opening act is Max Webster.

(March 2)
Rush performs live at Mecca Arena, Milwaukee, Wisconsin, US. The opening act is Max Webster.

(March 4 & 5)
Rush performs live at The Checkerdome, St. Louis, Missouri, US. The opening act is Max Webster.

(March 7)
Rush performs live at Louisville Gardens, Louisville, Kentucky, US. The opening act is Max Webster.

(March 8)
Rush performs live at Hara Arena, Dayton, Ohio, US. The opening act is Max Webster.

(March 10)
Rush performs live at Roberts Stadium, Evansville, Indiana, US. The opening act is Max Webster.

(March 11)
Rush performs live at Market Square Arena, Indianapolis, Indiana, US. The opening act is Max Webster.

(March 13, 14 & 15)
Rush performs live at Cobo Hall Arena, Detroit, Michigan, US. The opening act is Max Webster.

(March 21)
Rush performs live at London Gardens, London, Ontario, Canada. The opening act is FM.

(March 23, 24 & 25)
Rush performs live at Maple Leaf Gardens, London, Ontario, Canada. The opening act is FM. A *Billboard* magazine piece published April 4, 1981, notes that these dates were both audio and video recorded.

Note: there is some confusion as to whether these shows were actually recorded. No material has surfaced, but looking at the approach the band had to release a *Permanent Waves* concert album and film, it makes perfect sense that *Rush* would record several shows. We also know Edmonton was at least audio recorded three months later (June 25, 1981).

(March 27)
Rush performs live at The Forum, Montreal, Quebec, Canada. The opening act is Max Webster. **Geddy Lee** comes down with a chest infection which gets worse the following date (see below). The show is audio recorded and filmed and later released on the *Exit...Stage Left* live album and concert film. The following tracks are released individually:

> "Limelight (Replay GUP Tour - Best Buy CD Version)" 4:27
> Written by Neil Peart (words), Geddy Lee & Alex Lifeson (music)
> Appears on: King Biscuit – Best Of The Best – 25 Years of Rock; Rush – Replay (DVD+CD Best Buy Edition)
> I'm going on record saying I utterly despise the concept of retailer exclusive material. It's selfish and ignorant. Taken to extremes, which some artists do, it's downright cruel to make fans hunt this material down and sometimes force them to buy different editions of the same release to get all the extras and exclusives. Rush fans fall victim to this on occasion, too, and for a band that otherwise has a long history of respecting its fans, it's even more reprehensible to see them take advantage of the loyalty of those who are the biggest factor for every artists' success.
> (Sigh.) Okay, moving on...
> The Best Buy edition of the Replay DVD+CD boxed set featured 4 unadvertised, unlisted bonus tracks added to the Grace Under Pressure Tour CD. These tracks come from the other two concert videos, Exit...Stage Left and A Show Of Hands. "Limelight" and "Closer To The Heart" (see below) come from the ESL concert video and are unique in that they didn't appear previously on the ESL album, so if you can hunt these down, you can add them to your ESL playlist to have a more complete version of the Montreal Forum concert. This cut of "Limelight" did previously appear in the King Biscuit Best Of The Best CD, so it's not entirely exclusive to the Best Buy release, but it is still pretty rare.

> "The Spirit Of Radio (Exit...Stage Left – Icon 2 Version)" 5:12
> Written by Neil Peart (words), Geddy Lee & Alex Lifeson (music)
> Appears on: Icon 2
> This cut is the same as Exit...Stage Left, but fades out nicely at the end, making for a clean standalone version.

> "The Spirit Of Radio (Exit...Stage Left – Rush 'N' Roulette Edit)" 2:00
> Written by Neil Peart (words), Geddy Lee & Alex Lifeson (music)
> Appears on: Rush 'N' Roulette promo LP
> This is a two minute excerpt of the track.

> "Red Barchetta (Exit...Stage Left – Video Version)" 6:42
> Written by Neil Peart (words), Geddy Lee & Alex Lifeson (music)
> Appears on: Chronicles VHS & DVD
> Overdubbed throughout the ESL concert video are clips of Neil discussing various tracks, including on this song. The Chronicles video version does not feature the voiceover, so you are able to enjoy the footage commentary-free!

> "Red Barchetta (Exit...Stage Left – Rush 'N' Roulette Edit)" 2:00

Written by Neil Peart (words), Geddy Lee & Alex Lifeson (music)
Appears on: Rush 'N' Roulette promo LP
This is a two minute excerpt of the track.

"Closer To The Heart (Replay GUP Tour - Best Buy CD Version)" 3:24
Written by Neil Peart & Peter Talbot (words), Geddy Lee & Alex Lifeson (music)
Appears on: Rush – Replay (DVD+CD Best Buy Edition)
The Best Buy edition of the Replay DVD+CD boxed set featured 4 unadvertised bonus tracks added to the Grace Under Pressure Tour CD. These tracks come from the other two concert videos, Exit...Stage Left and A Show Of Hands. "Limelight" (see above) and "Closer To The Heart" come from the ESL concert video and are unique in that they didn't appear previously on the ESL album, so if you can hunt these down, you can add them to your ESL playlist to have a more complete version of the Montreal Forum concert. This version does not include Geddy introducing the song.

"Vital Signs (Live at The Forum, 1981)" 5:12
Written by Neil Peart (words), Geddy Lee & Alex Lifeson (music)
Appears on: "New World Man" 7" & 12" singles (worldwide)
Recorded at The Forum concert which makes up most of the Exit...Stage Left album and all of the concert film, this track was left off both, so it's among the must-have non-album single B-sides for fans. It's a great version of the song with excellent energy in the performance. It really deserves a proper digital re-issue. Get your hands on this and add it to your Exit...Stage Left playlist!

"The Trees (Exit...Stage Left – Single Version)" 4:30
Written by Neil Peart (words), Geddy Lee & Alex Lifeson (music)
Appears on: UK 7" single; Ireland 7" single
This cut is the same as Exit...Stage Left, but fades out early nicely at the end, eliminating the extended outro that leads in to "Xanadu," making for a clean standalone version.

"The Trees (Exit...Stage Left – Rush 'N' Roulette Edit)" 2:00
Written by Neil Peart (words), Geddy Lee & Alex Lifeson (music)
Appears on: Rush 'N' Roulette promo LP
This is a two minute excerpt of the track.

"Tom Sawyer (Exit...Stage Left – Video Version)" 4:38
Written by Neil Peart & Pye Dubois (words), Geddy Lee & Alex Lifeson (music)
Appears on: Chronicles VHS
Well, if you were at all annoyed that Neil talks over the start of this song on the ESL concert VHS, at least you can turn to this version! It is the same footage, but without Neil talking.

"Tom Sawyer (Exit...Stage Left – Rush 'N' Roulette Edit)" 2:00
Written by Neil Peart & Pye Dubois (words), Geddy Lee & Alex Lifeson (music)
Appears on: Rush 'N' Roulette promo LP
This is a two minute excerpt of the track.

(March 28)
Rush releases their "Vital Signs" singles in the UK and Spain.

UK 7" single (VITAL 7):
"Vital Signs"
"In The Mood"

UK 12" single (VITAL 12):
"Vital Sign"
"A Passage To Bangkok"
"Circumstances"
"In The Mood"

UK one-sided 7" promo single (VITAL 7 DJ):
"Vital Signs (UK Promo Edit)"

Spain 7" single (61 70 089):
"Vital Signs"
"Limelight"

"Vital Signs (UK Promo Edit)" 4:00
Written by Neil Peart (words), Geddy Lee & Alex Lifeson (music)
Appears on: UK one-sided 7" promo single
I haven't heard this edit, but if I had to guess, I'd say it probably fades out early.

Rush performs live at the Ottawa Civic Centre, Ottawa, Ontario, Canada. The opening act is FM. This show is nearly cancelled because **Geddy Lee** develops laryngitis from the illness of the previous day in Montreal (noted in a post-show interview with the *Ottawa Citizen* newspaper). The show is reportedly shortened by 15 minutes because **Geddy** is unable to sing further.

(Date Unknown)
During one of the soundchecks mid-tour, *Rush* jams musical parts that later form the foundation of the following:
"Chemistry" – **Neil Peart**'s description of when and where ("Somewhere USA") this soundcheck occurred implies this was well into the tour (*Signals* tour book).

(April 3)
Rush performs live at Community Center, Tucson, Arizona, US. The opening act is Max Webster.

(April 4)
Rush performs live at Veterans Memorial Coliseum, Phoenix, Arizona, US. The opening act is Max Webster.

(April 5)
Rush performs live at Tingley Coliseum, Albuquerque, New Mexico, US. The opening act is Max Webster.

(April 7 & 8)
Rush performs live at Sam Houston Coliseum, Houston, Texas, US. The opening act is Max Webster.

(April 9)
Neil Peart, **Geddy Lee** and **Alex Lifeson** fly to Orlando, Florida, US, accepting an invitation from NASA (made long before) to attend the first launch and maiden voyage of the space shuttle *Columbia*.

(April 10)
Neil Peart, **Geddy Lee** and **Alex Lifeson** attend the aborted launch of the space shuttle *Columbia* at Cape Kennedy, Florida, US. Following the mission abort, the band hurries to the airport to fly to Dallas for their concert that evening.
"Red Sector A" – this is the name of the section from which the band is allowed to witness the launch. It would later inspire the title of the song by the same name.

Rush performs live at Reunion Arena, Dallas, Texas, US. The opening act is Max Webster.

(April 11)
Rush performs live at Convention Center Arena, San Antonio, Texas, US. The opening act is Max Webster. Immediately following the concert, the band takes a chartered flight from Dallas back to Cape Kennedy, Florida, US, to witness the launch of space shuttle *Columbia*.

(April 12)
Space shuttle *Columbia (OV-102)* launches on its maiden voyage into orbit from Cape Kennedy, Florida, US, at 7 AM EST, the first space shuttle to do so. Following the launch, *Rush* flies from Cape Kennedy to Fort Worth, Texas, US, for their concert that evening.
"Countdown" – **Neil Peart** is directly inspired by the shuttle launch to write this song.

Note: numerous sources list the date *Rush* witnessed the launch as April, 1982, which is incorrect. NASA and historical records show this date as the first orbital launch. There was no April, 1982, shuttle launch and **Neil**'s description of having to fly to and from Texas to Florida and back twice to attend the launch coincides with these touring dates and not those of April, 1982, where they were in Florida performing.

Rush performs live at Tarrant County Convention Center, Fort Worth, Texas, US. The opening act is Max Webster.

(April 14)
Rush performs live at Barton Coliseum, Little Rock, Arkansas, US. The opening act is Max Webster.

(April 15)
Rush performs live at Mississippi Coliseum, Jackson, Mississippi, US. The opening act is Max Webster.

(April 16)
Rush performs live at Mid-South Coliseum, Memphis, Tennessee, US. The opening act is Max Webster.

Note: 2112.net notes that Max Webster dissolved after this show. MaxWebster.ca lists the next few shows, up to and including the 21st, as including Max Webster.

(April 18)
Rush performs live at Municipal Auditorium, Mobile, Alabama, US.

(April 19)
Rush performs live at Municipal Auditorium, New Orleans, Louisiana, US.

(April 21)
Rush performs live at Hirsch Memorial Coliseum, Shreveport, Louisiana,

(April 23 & 24)
Rush performs live at Kemper Arena, Kansas City, Missouri, US.

(April 25)
Rush performs live at The Myriad, Oklahoma City, Oklahoma, US.

(April 26)
Rush performs live at the Assembly Center, Tulsa, Oklahoma, US.

(May 6)
Rush performs live at Civic Arena, Pittsburgh, Pennsylvania, US.

(May 7 & 8)
Rush performs live at Richfield Coliseum, Richfield, Ohio, US. The opening act is FM.

(May 9)
Rush performs live at Memorial Auditorium, Buffalo, New York, US. The opening act is FM.

(May 11)
Rush performs live at Broome County Arena, Binghamton, New York, US. The opening act is FM.

(May 12)
Rush performs live at War Memorial, Rochester, New York, US. The opening act is Saga.

(May 13)
Rush performs live at War Memorial, Syracuse, New York, US. The opening act is FM.

(May 15)
Rush performs live at Civic Center, Glens Falls, New York, US. The opening act is FM.

(May 16 & 17)
Rush performs live at the Capital Centre, Largo, Maryland, US. The opening act is FM.

(May 18)
Rush performs live at Madison Square Garden, New York City, New York, US.

(May 20)
Rush performs live at Nassau Coliseum, Uniondale, New York, US.

(May 22)
Rush performs live at The Spectrum, Philadelphia, Pennsylvania, US. The opening act is FM.

(May 23)
Rush performs live at Boston Garden, Boston, Massachusetts, US.

(May 24)
Rush performs live at the Civic Center, Providence, Rhode Island, US.

(June 1)
Rush performs live at McNichols Arena, Denver, Colorado, US. The opening act is FM.

(June 3)
Rush performs live at Salt Palace Center, Salt Lake City, Utah, US.

(June 5)
Rush performs live at The Coliseum, Oakland, California, US.

(June 6)
Rush releases their "Tom Sawyer" singles in North America.

Canada 7" single (ANS-034):
"Tom Sawyer (Single Edit)"
"Witch Hunt"

US 7" single (M-76109):

"Tom Sawyer (Single Edit)"
"Witch Hunt"

US 7" promo single (76109-DJ):
"Tom Sawyer (Single Edit)"
"Tom Sawyer (Single Edit)"

> "Tom Sawyer (Single Edit)" 4:07
> Written by Neil Peart & Pye Dubois (words), Geddy Lee & Alex Lifeson (music)
> Appears on: Canada 7" single; US 7" single; US 7" promo single
> This version removes small bits of instrumental throughout, thereby shortening the song. It's not terrible, but you're still better off with the album version.

Rush performs live at The Coliseum, Oakland, California, US. The opening act is FM.

(June 7)
Rush performs live at Selland Arena, Fresno, California, US.

(June 9)
Rush performs live at the Sports Arena, San Diego, California, US. The opening act is FM.

(June 10 & 11)
Rush performs live at Great Western Forum, Los Angeles, California, US. The opening act is FM.

(June 12)
Rush performs live at Convention Center, Anaheim, California, US. The opening act is FM.

(June 14)
Rush performs live at Long Beach Arena, Long Beach, California, US.

(June 15)
Rush performs live at Aladdin Theatre, Las Vegas, Nevada, US.

(June 16)
Rush performs live at Centennial Coliseum, Reno, Nevada, US.

(June 18 & 19)
Rush performs live at Seattle Center Coliseum, Seattle, Washington, US.

(June 20)
Rush performs live at Memorial Coliseum, Portland, Oregon, US.

(June 21)
Rush performs live at The Coliseum, Spokane, Washington, US. The opening act is FM.

(June 23)
Rush performs live at Pacific Coliseum, Vancouver, British Columbia, Canada. The opening act is Goddo.

(June 25)
Rush performs live at Northlands Coliseum, Edmonton, Alberta, Canada. This show is recorded and the following tracks are released individually:

> "2112: I: Overture (Live in Edmonton, 1981)" 4:30
> "2112: II: The Temples Of Syrinx (Live in Edmonton, 1981)" 2:20
> Written by Neil Peart (words), Geddy Lee & Alex Lifeson (Music)
> Appears on: 2112 2012 Deluxe Edition CD
> The opening two movements of "2112" also opened the set each night during the Moving Pictures Tour. Absent from Exit...Stage Left, which is mostly made up of tracks from The Forum concert in March, it's nice to have these tracks now! The performances themselves are spot on, as always. Like with The Forum performance of "Vital Signs" from the "New World Man" single, add this to the start of your Exit...Stage Left playlist where it belongs.

(July 2 & 3)
Rush performs live at the Met Center, Bloomington, Minnesota, US. The opening act is the Joe Perry Project.

(July 4 & 5)
Rush performs live at Alpine Valley Music Theatre, East Troy, Wisconsin, US. The opening act is the Joe Perry Project.

(Date Unknown)

Geddy Lee records vocals for the Bob & Doug McKenzie album *Great White North*, at either Sounds Interchange Studios or Manta Studios, Toronto, Ontario. **Lee** went to school with actor Rick Moranis (who plays Bob McKenzie) and since the album was being produced via Anthem Records, it was simple for Moranis to get a hold him. **Geddy** is quoted in *Success Under Pressure* as saying the session took him "all of a half an hour to do."

(September)
Rush assembles and mixes their live album *Exit...Stage Left* at Le Studio, Morin Heights, Quebec, Canada. According to **Alex Lifeson** (in a November 1981 *Melody Maker* article), the bulk of the work on the album is by Terry Brown, with the band "dropping in" with ideas periodically. In a 1989 *Raw* interview, **Neil Peart** discusses the band's efforts "to make a perfect live album" by "cleaning up" and repair much of the audio (suggesting overdubs are employed, via his statement that the band joked about the album being "live-ish"). In a 1999 *Rockline* interview, **Geddy Lee** says something similar, that they "tidied it up too much."
 They also work on the following:
"Tough Break" – started by **Neil Peart** and crew members Skip Gildersleeve and Jack Crymes (AKA Jack Secret), before being joined by **Alex Lifeson** and **Geddy Lee**. The track is recorded.
"Subdivisions" – **Neil Peart** starts writing this song. Separately, **Geddy** and **Alex** write music and the two are eventually combined to create the song.
"Digital Man" – **Geddy** notes the title came from an off-the-cuff comment from someone in the room made during the assignment of rooms at Le Studio, that the absence of the digital technician hired for the previous album meant they wouldn't "need a bed for the digital man." **Neil** took the phrase and developed the song around it.

(October 29)
Rush releases their live album *Exit...Stage Left* on Anthem Records (Canada) and Mercury Records (US). The album is a mix of tracks from June 11, 1980, in Glasgow (Tracks 4 to 7 [LP Side Two]) and March 27, 1981, in Montreal (Tracks 1 to 3 and 8 to 13).

Rush also releases their concert VHS, Laserdisc and Video Disc *Exit...Stage Left*. The footage comes from The Forum, Montreal, Canada, show on March 27, 1981.

Note: around this time, **Rush** and Polygram Records release the *Rush 'N' Roulette* promo LP. The gimmick here is that rather than a single groove on each side, there are actually six grooves running parallel to each other, so when you place the needle on the LP, any of the six tracks could play, you just won't know which. Monty Python did a similar gag in 1973 with their album *Free Record Given Away With The Monty Python Matching Tie And Handkerchief*, where Side Two featured two such grooves of different material. Unlike **Rush**, Python didn't advertise the fact that there were two grooves so as to deliberately confound their audience on repeat listenings. Obviously, this gag only works on the vinyl medium.

Rush 'N' Roulette promo LP
"Tom Sawyer (Exit...Stage Left – Rush 'N' Roulette Edit)"
"Closer To The Heart (Exit...Stage Left – Rush 'N' Roulette Edit)"
"A Passage To Bangkok (Exit...Stage Left – Rush 'N' Roulette Edit)"
"The Spirit Of Radio (Exit...Stage Left – Rush 'N' Roulette Edit)"
"Red Barchetta (Exit...Stage Left – Rush 'N' Roulette Edit)"
"The Trees (Exit...Stage Left – Rush 'N' Roulette Edit)"

Rush performs live at New Bingley Hall, Stafford, England. The setlist includes the following:
"Subdivisions" – This would be the live debut of the song, as it was only written the month before.

(October 30)
Rush performs live at New Bingley Hall, Stafford, England.

(October 31)
Rush performs live at Deeside Leisure Centre, Deeside, Wales.

Rush releases their "Tom Sawyer" live singles in the UK. All tracks are from the live album *Exit...Stage Left*.

Rush Live! UK 7" single (EXIT 7):
"Tom Sawyer (Exit...Stage Left)"
"A Passage To Bangkok (Exit...Stage Left)"

Rush Live! UK 7" single (EXIT 12):
"Tom Sawyer (Exit...Stage Left)"
"A Passage To Bangkok (Exit...Stage Left)"
"Red Barchetta (Exit...Stage Left)"

Note: the picture sleeve notes that the tracks are from the forthcoming album *Exit...Stage Left*.

(Date Unknown)
Rush releases their promo singles for "A Passage To Bangkok (Exit...Stage Left)" in North America.

Special Edition – Rush - Live
Canada 12" single (SPE-008):
"A Passage To Bangkok (Exit...Stage Left)"
"Freewill (Exit...Stage Left)"

Special Edition – Rush - Live
US 12" single (MK-188):
"A Passage To Bangkok (Exit...Stage Left)"
"Freewill (Exit...Stage Left)"

(November)
Rush releases their "Closer To The Heart" live singles in North America. All tracks are from the live album *Exit...Stage Left*.

Canada 7" single (ANS 039 - withdrawn):
"Closer To The Heart (Exit...Stage Left - Single Version)"
"Tom Sawyer (Exit...Stage Left)"

Canada 7" single (ANS 039):
"Closer To The Heart (Exit...Stage Left - Single Version)"
"Freewill (Exit...Stage Left)"

US 7" single (M-76124):
"Closer To The Heart (Exit...Stage Left - Single Version)"
"Freewill (Exit...Stage Left)"

US 7" promo single: (76124-DJ):
"Closer To The Heart (Exit...Stage Left - Single Version)"
"Closer To The Heart (Exit...Stage Left - Single Version)"

Anthem Records releases the Bob & Doug McKenzie album *Great White North*, featuring "Take Off" with **Geddy Lee**.

> "Take Off" 4:46
> Written by Crawford/Goldsmith/Giacomelli/Moranis/Thomas
> Appears on: Great White North
> This comedy track comes from the SCTV characters Bob & Doug McKenzie (played by Dave Thomas and Rick Moranis), whose shtick revolved around great Canadian stereotypes (toques, beer, donuts, hockey, etc.). Created for the Canadian SCTV TV series, they are still icons of the Great White North. Rush are known to be fans of SCTV (employing Count Floyd for "The Weapon" live intro on the Signals and Grace Under Pressure Tours and Rockin' Mel Slirrup for the R40 tour video), so Geddy was a natural choice to guest star on this track. Bob & Doug would reappear on the Snakes & Arrows Tour video introducing "The Larger Bowl." The "song" itself features the McKenzie Bros. bickering and Geddy singing the choruses.

> "Take Off (Single Version)" 2:42
> Written by Crawford/Goldsmith/Giacomelli/Moranis/Thomas
> Appears on: Canada 7" single, US 7" single, US 7" promo single
> This version removes the in-studio banter that opens and closes the track on the album (though isn't really part of the song anyway).

(November 2)
Rush performs live at Brighton Conference Center, Brighton, England.

(November 4, 5 & 6)
Rush performs live at Wembley Arena, London, England.

(November 8)
Rush performs live at Royal Highland Exhibition Centre, Edinburgh, Scotland.

(November 9)
Rush performs live at New Bingley Hall, Stafford, England.

(November 11)
Rush performs live at Musikhalle, Hamburg, Germany. The opening act is Girlschool.

(November 12)
Rush performs live at Hemmerleinhalle, Neunkirchen, Germany. The opening act is Girlschool.

(November 14)

Rush performs live at Ahoy Sportpaleis, Rotterdam, Holland. The opening act is Girlschool.

(November 16)
Rush performs live at Circus Krone, Munich, Germany. The opening act is Girlschool.

(November 17)
Rush performs live at Walter Kobel Halle, Rüsselsheim, Germany. The opening act is Girlschool.

(November 18 & 19)
Rush performs live at Sporthalle, Böblingen, Germany. The opening act is Girlschool. The November 18th show is not listed on print ads and may have been a late addition to the tour.

(November 20)
Rush performs live at Schwarzwaldhalle, Karlsruhe, Germany. The opening act is Girlschool.

(November 21)
Rush performs live at Grugahalle, Essen, Germany. The opening act is Girlschool.

(November 28)
Rush performs live at Hollywood Sportatorium, Hollywood, Florida, US. The opening act is Riot.

(November 29)
Rush performs live at Veterans Memorial Coliseum, Jacksonville, Florida, US. The opening act is Riot.

(Late 1981)
Rush releases their live album *Exit...Stage Left* in the UK and Europe on Mercury Records.

(December)
Rush releases their "Closer To The Heart" live singles in the UK and Ireland. All tracks are from the live album *Exit...Stage Left*.

UK 7" single (RUSH 1):
"Closer To The Heart (Exit...Stage Left - Single Version)"
"The Trees (Exit...Stage Left – Single Version)"

Ireland 7" single (RUSH 1):
"Closer To The Heart (Exit...Stage Left - Single Version)"
"The Trees (Exit...Stage Left – Single Version)"

(December 1)
Rush performs live at Birmingham-Jefferson Civic Center, Birmingham, Alabama, US. The opening act is Riot.

(December 2)
Rush performs live at Municipal Auditorium, Nashville, Tennessee, US. The opening act is Riot.

(December 4)
Rush performs live at Charlotte Coliseum, Charlotte, North Carolina, US. The opening act is Riot.

(December 5)
Rush performs live at Cumberland County Coliseum, Fayetteville, North Carolina, US. The opening act is Riot.

(December 6)
Rush performs live at Greensboro Coliseum, Greensboro, North Carolina, US. The opening act is Riot.

(December 8)
Rush performs live at Knoxville Civic Coliseum, Knoxville, Tennessee, US. The opening act is Riot.

(December 9)
Rush performs live at The Omni, Atlanta, Georgia, US. The opening act is Riot.

(December 11)
Rush performs live at Greenville Memorial Auditorium, Greenville, South Carolina, US. The opening act is Riot.

(December 12)
Rush performs live at Freedom Hall, Civic Center, Jonson City, Tennessee, US. The opening act is Riot.

(December 13)
Rush performs live at Roanoke Civic Center, Roanoke, Virginia, US. The opening act is Riot.

(December 15)
Rush performs live at Scope Arena, Norfolk, Virginia, US.

(December 18 & 20)
Rush performs live at the Hartford Civic Center, Hartford, Connecticut, US. The opening act is Riot on December 20th.

(December 21 & 22)
Rush performs live at Brendan Byrne Arena, East Rutherford, New Jersey, US. The opening act is Riot.

(Late December)
Geddy Lee and a friend named "Oscar" work on creating an assortment of synth and electronic-based music at **Lee** home north of Toronto, Ontario, Canada.
"The Weapon" - **Geddy Lee** develops an "extended electronic intro" planned for "Vital Signs" live which would later grow to become part of this track.

SIGNALS

1982

(January)
Aboard the *Orlando* at the British Virgin Islands, *Rush* works on the following (*Signals* tour book):
"The Analog Kid" – **Neil Peart** notes in the *Signals* tour book that he developed the song as a "companion" to "Digital Man."
"The Weapon" – **Neil** writes lyrics for this song, developing the second part of his fear-themed three-part series and shares them with **Geddy Lee. Lee** plays for **Peart** some of the electronic pieces he wrote in December which would later contribute to this song.

(March)
Rush begins writing and rehearsing new songs for their ninth studio album at The Grange, Muskoka Lakes, Ontario, Canada (*Signals* sessions). Tracks worked on include:
"Chemistry" – **Geddy Lee** and **Alex Lifeson** scour the previous tour's soundcheck tapes and discover three nearly complete instrumental parts which they craft into this song. They come up with the title and theme for the song and contribute lyric ideas before handing it off to **Neil** to complete. **Peart** says in the *Signals* tour book that this was the easiest song on the album to write and is the first to be a full collaboration between all three on lyrics. A demo of the nearly completed song is recorded. Note: it's unclear from **Neil**'s description exactly when creation of the song occurred, but I would hazard a guess it was post-tour during these sessions.
"Digital Man" – work continues on this song.
"Losing It" – written and arranged during these sessions. A demo is recorded with just keyboards and drums.

(April 1)
Rush performs live at Barton Coliseum, Little Rock, Arkansas, US. The opening act is Riggs.

(April 2)
Rush performs live at Mississippi Coliseum, Jackson, Mississippi, US. The opening act is Riggs.

(April 3)
Rush performs live at Civic Center Arena, Monroe, Louisiana, US. The opening act is Riggs.

(April 5)
Rush performs live at the Civic Center, Lake Charles, Louisiana, US. The opening act is Riggs.

(April 6)
Rush performs live at Riverside Centroplex, Baton Rouge, Louisiana, US. The opening act is Riggs.

(April 7)
Rush performs live at Mississippi Coast Coliseum, Biloxi, Mississippi, US. The opening act is Riggs.

(April 8)
Rush performs live at Mirsch Memorial Coliseum, Shreveport, Louisiana, US. The opening act is Krokus.

(April 9)
Rush performs live at Leon County Civic Center, Tallahassee, Florida, US. The opening act is Krokus.

(April 10 & 11)
Rush performs live at Civic Center Arena, Lakeland, Florida, US. The opening act is Krokus.

> "Subdivisions (Live in Lakeland, 1982)" 5:36
> Written by Neil Peart (words), Geddy Lee & Alex Lifeson (music)
> Appears on: Live In Lakeland (bootleg)
> The first new song written for Signals in the summer of 1981, it debuted live in England that fall, so by this point the song is finished. The only real difference between this performance and the album recording is the guitar solo isn't quite there yet.

> "The Analog Kid (Live in Lakeland, 1982)" 5:05
> Written by Neil Peart (words), Geddy Lee & Alex Lifeson (music)
> Appears on: Live In Lakeland (bootleg)
> The newer of the two new songs played at this concert, "The Analog Kid" is also just as complete as "Subdivisions" (even the guitar solo is pretty close to the finished version!).

(April 12)
Rush performs live at Bayfront Center Arena, St. Petersburg, Florida, US. The opening act is Krokus.

(April 21)
Rush begins recording their ninth studio album at Le Studio, Morin Heights, Quebec, Canada (*Signals* sessions). Arranged and produced by ***Rush*** and Terry Brown. Engineered by Paul Northfield. Note: the date comes from *Visions*.

(Date Unknown)
Anthem Records issues a 2xLP radio promo titled *The Rush Special* (SPE-2-009).

Note: I haven't heard or seen this myself, but a description at the website archive.is/poyn says it features music and interview clips and came with 5 pages of cue sheets for DJs.

(May)
During recording sessions for their ninth studio album at Le Studio, Morin Heights, Quebec, Canada (*Signals* sessions), ***Rush*** completes the basic tracks for the following:
"Subdivisions"
"The Analog Kid"
"Chemistry"
"Digital Man"
"The Weapon"
"Losing It"
"Countdown"

The band also works on the following:
"New World Man" – the working title is "Project 3:57," because the band realizes they have a shorter amount of material than they'd like for a full album and the song they want to write to fill the gap must be no more than this length. **Neil Peart** spends several days writing lyrics. The band then spends a day writing the music and a day recording it.

(June)
During recording sessions for their ninth studio album at Le Studio, Morin Heights, Quebec, Canada (*Signals* sessions), ***Rush*** works on the following, among much else:
"Losing it" – Ben Mink of FM records his violin parts.
"Subdivisions" – **Neil Peart** provides the deep voice vocal part that says "Subdivisions" in the chorus. Note: it is a longstanding rumour that CityTV news broadcaster and local personality Mark Dailey provided this voice and this factoid still appears on several otherwise accurate and detailed online sources. The truth is that **Neil** provided the vocal. He confirms this fact via *Jam!Showbiz* on March 26, 2010. Mark Dailey also denied doing it, specifically via CityTV.com March 23, 2009.

(July 15)
Rush completes work on their ninth studio album *Signals* at Le Studio, Morin Heights, Quebec, Canada (*Signals* sessions). Tracks worked on between April and July include:
"The Weapon" – an alternate master of this song is put to tape, featuring a slightly different mix of the song. The missing vocal here is present on the standard album version master.

>"The Weapon (Alternate Album Master Version)" 6:29
>Written by Neil Peart (words), Geddy Lee & Alex Lifeson (music)
>Appears on: Signal (1994 MFSL Ultradisc II Edition)
>Apparently made before part of the chorus was added to the final album master (the line at 3:13, "...and the things that he fears are a weapon to be used against him"), this alternate master tape is later sent to Mobile Fidelity Sound Labs for the creation of their Ultradisc II Edition in 1994. This is definitely worth having to hear a different version of the song.

(August)
Rush releases their "New World Man" singles in the UK and Europe.

UK 7" single (RUSH 8):
"New World Man"
"Vital Signs (Live at The Forum, 1981)"

UK 12" single (RUSH 812):
"New World Man"
"Vital Signs (Live at The Forum, 1981)"
"Freewill (Exit...Stage Left)"

Netherlands 7" single (6170 227):
"New World Man"
"Vital Signs (Live at The Forum, 1981)"

(Date Unknown)

Anthem Records releases a 2xLP promo titled *Rush 'Signals' Radio Special* (SPE-012) to North American radio stations. It features interviews clips intercut with all the tracks from the album. The interviews are with **Rush** speaking to CFNY radio DJ Andre Tilk.

(September)
Rush releases their "New World Man" singles in North America.

Canada 7" single (ANS-046):
"New World Man"
"Vital Signs (Live at The Forum, 1981)"

Canada 12" single (SPE-011):
"New World Man"
"Vital Signs (Live at The Forum, 1981)"

US 7" single (M-76179):
"New World Man"
"Vital Signs (Live at The Forum, 1981)"

US 7" promo single (76179-DJ):
"New World Man"
"New World Man"

US 12" promo single (MK 216) (clear vinyl):
"New World Man"
"Vital Signs (Live at The Forum, 1981)"

(September 3)
Rush performs live at Brown County Arena, Green Bay, Wisconsin, US. The opening act is Rory Gallagher.

(September 4)
Rush performs live at La Crosse Center, La Crosse, Wisconsin, US. The opening act is Rory Gallagher.

(September 5)
Rush performs live at Five Flags Arena, Sioux Falls, South Dakota, US. The opening act is Rory Gallagher.

(September 7)
Rush performs live at Sioux Falls Arena, Sioux Falls, South Dakota, US. The opening act is Rory Gallagher.

(September 8)
Rush performs live at Veterans Memorial Auditorium, Des Moines, Iowa, US. The opening act is Rory Gallagher.

(September 9)
Rush releases its ninth studio album *Signals* on Anthem Records (Canada) and Mercury Records (US). Track listing as follows:

"Subdivisions"
"The Analog Kid"
"Chemistry"
"Digital Man"
"The Weapon" - part II of 'Fear'
"New World Man"
"Losing It"
"Countdown"

Rush performs live at Civic Auditorium Arena, Omaha, Nebraska, US. The opening act is Rory Gallagher.

(September 11)
Rush performs live at Rushmore Plaza Civic Center, Rapid City, South Dakota, US. The opening act is Rory Gallagher.

(September 12)
Rush performs live at Bismarck Civic Center, Bismarck, North Dakota, US. The opening act is Rory Gallagher.

(September 14)
Rush performs live at MetraPark, Billings, Montana, US. The opening act is Rory Gallagher.

(September 15)
Rush performs live at Casper Events Center, Casper, Wyoming, US. The opening act is Rory Gallagher.

(September 17)
Rush performs live at McNichols Arena, Denver, Colorado, US. The opening act is Rory Gallagher.

(September 19)
Rush performs live at ISU Minidome, Pocatello, Idaho, US. The opening act is Rory Gallagher.

(September 20)
Rush performs live at BSU Pavilion, Boise, Idaho, US. The opening act is Rory Gallagher.

(September 21)
Rush performs live at Salt Palace Center, Salt Lake City, Utah, US. The opening act is Rory Gallagher.

(September 30)
Rush performs live at Pacific Coliseum, Vancouver, British Columbia, Canada. The opening act is Wrabit.

(October 2)
Rush performs live at Calgary Corral, Calgary, Alberta, Canada. The opening act is Wrabit.

(October 3)
Rush performs live at Northlands Coliseum, Edmonton, Alberta, Canada. The opening act is Wrabit.

(October 5)
Rush performs live at Winnipeg Arena, Winnipeg, Manitoba, Canada. The opening act is Wrabit.

(October 8)
Rush performs live at Duluth Arena, Duluth Arena, Duluth, Minnesota, US. The opening act is Rory Gallagher.

(October 9)
Rush performs live at Mecca Arena, Milwaukee, Wisconsin, US. The opening act is Rory Gallagher.

(October 10)
Rush performs live at Dane County Memorial Coliseum, Madison, Wisconsin, US. The opening act is Rory Gallagher.

(October 12)
Rush performs live at The Checkerdome, St. Louis, Missouri, US. The opening act is Rory Gallagher.

(October 13)
Rush performs live at University of Illinois Assembly Hall, Champaign, Illinois, US. The opening act is Rory Gallagher.

(October 15)
Rush performs live at The Checkerdome, St. Louis, Missouri, US. The opening act is Rory Gallagher. This show is a late addition to the tour, made possible by the moving of the Kemper Arena, Kansas City, show from this date (as originally scheduled) to October 16th (see below).

(October 16)
Rush performs live at Kemper Arena, Kansas City, Missouri, US. The opening act is Rory Gallagher. This show was originally scheduled for October 15th, but was moved to the 16th to allow for a second St. Louis show to take place on the 15th.

(October 17)
Rush performs live at Kansas Coliseum, Wichita, Kansas, US. The opening act is Rory Gallagher.

(October 19)
Rush performs live at Mid-South Coliseum, Memphis, Tennessee, US. The opening act is Rory Gallagher.

(October 20)
Rush performs live at Municipal Auditorium, Nashville, Tennessee, US. The opening act is Rory Gallagher.

(October 21)
An article in *The Nashville Banner* says *Rush* will take a 10-day Caribbean vacation during this hiatus in the tour.

(October 30)
Rush releases their "Subdivisions" singles in the UK and Europe.

UK 7" single (RUSH 9):
"Subdivisions"
"Red Barchetta"

UK 10" single (picture disc) (RUSHP 9):

"Subdivisions"
"Red Barchetta"

Rush performs live at Rupp Arena, Lexington, Kentucky, US. The opening act is Rory Gallagher.

(October 31)
Rush performs live at Roberts Stadium, Evansville, Indiana, US. The opening act is Rory Gallagher.

(November)
Rush releases their "Subdivisions" singles in North America.

Canada 7" single (ANS-048):
"Subdivisions (Single Edit)"
"Countdown"

US 7" single (M-76196):
"Subdivisions"
"Countdown"

US 7" promo single (76196-DJ):
"Subdivisions (Single Edit)"
"Subdivision"

> "Subdivisions (Single Edit)" 4:42
> Written by Neil Peart (words), Geddy Lee & Alex Lifeson (music)
> Appears on: Canada 7" single; US 7" promo single
> This edit cuts out instrumental sections throughout, removing nearly a minute of the song and as usual, the track suffers for it.

(November 1)
Rush performs live at Market Square Arena, Indianapolis, Indiana, US. The opening act is Rory Gallagher.

(November 3 & 4)
Rush performs live at Richfield Coliseum, Richfield, Ohio, US. The opening act is Rory Gallagher on the 4th.

(November 5)
Rush performs live at Joyce Athletic And Convocation Center, University of Notre Dame, South Bend, Indiana, US. The opening act is Rory Gallagher.

(November 7 & 8)
Rush performs live at Joe Louis Arena, Detroit, Michigan, US. The opening act is Rory Gallagher.

(November 9)
Rush performs live at University of Dayton Arena, Dayton, Ohio, US. The opening act is Rory Gallagher.

(November 11)
Rush performs live at Wings Stadium, Kalamazoo, Michigan, US. The opening act is Rory Gallagher.

(November 12)
Rush performs live at the Sports Arena, Toledo, Ohio, US. The opening act is Rory Gallagher.

(November 15, 16 & 17)
Rush performs live at Maple Leafs Gardens, Toronto, Ontario, Canada. The opening act is The Payolas.

(November 19, 20 & 21)
Rush performs live at Rosemont Horizon, Rosemont, Illinois, US. The opening act is Rory Gallagher.

(November 29)
Rush performs live at Capital Centre, Largo, Maryland, US. The opening act is Rory Gallagher.

(November 30)
Rush performs live at Hampton Coliseum, Hampton, Virginia, US. The opening act is Rory Gallagher.

(December 2 & 3)
Rush performs live at Madison Square Garden, New York City, New York, US. The opening act is Rory Gallagher.

(December 5)
Rush performs live at Civic Center, Providence, Rhoda Island, US. The opening act is Rory Gallagher.

(December 6)
Rush performs live at Boston Garden, Boston, Massachusetts, US. The opening act is Rory Gallagher.

(December 8 & 9)
Rush performs live at Nassau Coliseum, Uniondale, New York, US. The opening act is Rory Gallagher.

(December 11)
Rush performs live at Veterans Coliseum, New Haven, Connecticut, US. The opening act is Rory Gallagher.

(December 13 & 14)
Rush performs live at The Spectrum, Philadelphia, Pennsylvania, US. The opening act is Rory Gallagher.

(December 15)
Rush performs live at The Centrum, Worcester, Massachusetts, US. The opening act is Rory Gallagher.

COUNTDOWN

1983

(Date Unknown)
Geddy Lee produces the band Boys Brigade for the self-titled, debut album, venue unknown. The band is from Toronto, Ontario, Canada, and had previously signed Howard Ungerleider on as their manager before moving to SRO Productions, bringing them in contact with **Lee**. Reportedly, the sessions take place over six months accommodating **Geddy**'s tour schedule.

(Date Unknown)
Geddy Lee records bass on the tracks "All The Horses Running" and "Over Queen Charlotte Sound" for Marie-Lynn Hammond's forthcoming album (*Vignettes* sessions). Produced and co-arranged by Ben Mink.

(February 11 & 12)
Rush performs live at Tingley Coliseum, Albuquerque, New Mexico, US. The opening act is Golden Earring.

(February 14 & 15)
Rush performs live at Long Beach Arena, Long Beach, California, US. The opening act is Golden Earring.

(February 17 &18)
Rush performs live at Great Western Forum, Los Angeles, California, US. The opening act is Golden Earring.

(February 21)
Rush performs live at Sport Arena, San Diego, California, US. The opening act is Golden Earring.

Note: in interviews both at the time (with Dennis Hunt) and later (also with Hunt in *The Sun*, 1985), the band indicates that they are feeling in something of a rut during this period and feel it's affecting their studio work and live performances. It is apparently the catalyst that moves them to want to make changes when recording their next album (such as wanting to work with a different producer than Terry Brown on their next album).

(February 23)
Rush performs live at the Tucson Community Center, Tucson, Arizona, US. The opening act is Golden Earring.

(February 24)
Rush performs live at Veterans Memorial Coliseum, Phoenix, Arizona, US. The opening act is Golden Earring.

(February 26)
Rush performs live at Pan American Center, Las Cruces, New Mexico, US. The opening act is Golden Earring.

(February 28 & March 1)
Rush performs live at Reunion Arena, Dallas, Texas, US. The opening act is Golden Earring.

(March 2)
Rush performs live at Convention Center Arena, San Antonio, Texas, US. The opening act is Golden Earring.

(March 4)
Rush performs live at The Myriad, Oklahoma City, Oklahoma, US. The opening act is Golden Earring.

(March 6 & 7)
Rush performs live at The Summit, Houston, Texas, US. The opening act is Golden Earring.

(March 16)
Rush performs live at Jacksonville Coliseum, Jacksonville, Florida, US. The opening act is The Jon Butcher Axis.

(March 17 & 18)
Rush performs live at Hollywood Sportatorium, Hollywood, Florida, US. The opening act is The Jon Butcher Axis.

Note: in the *Grace Under Pressure* tour book, **Neil Peart** says it was in Florida during this tour when *Rush* informs Terry Brown that they plan to work with a different producer on the next album in order to broaden their experience.

(March 20 & 21)
Rush performs live at the Lakeland Civic Center, Lakeland, Florida, US. The opening act is The Jon Butcher Axis.

(March 23)
Rush performs live at The Omni, Atlanta, Georgia, US. The opening act is The Jon Butcher Axis.

(March 25)
Rush performs live at Charlotte Coliseum, Charlotte, North Carolina, US.

(March 26)
Rush performs live at the University of South Carolina Coliseum, Columbia, South Carolina, US.

(March 27)
Rush performs live at Greensboro Coliseum, Greensboro, North Carolina, US. The opening act is The Jon Butcher Axis.

(March 29)
Rush performs live at Civic Center Coliseum, Charleston, West Virginia, US. The opening act is The Jon Butcher Axis.

(March 30)
Rush performs live at Riverfront Coliseum, Cincinnati, Ohio, US. The opening act is The Jon Butcher Axis.

(April)
Rush releases their "Countdown" and "New World Man" AA-side singles in the UK.

UK 7" single (RUSH 10):
A: "Countdown"
AA: "New World Man"

UK 7" single (shaped picture disc) (RUSHP 10):
A: "Countdown"
AA: "New World Man"

UK 12" single (RUSH 1012):
A: "New World Man"
B: "The Spirit Of Radio (Exit...Stage Left)"
BB: "Excerpts From An Interview"
AA: "Countdown"

> "Excerpts From An Interview" 2:55
> Written by N/A
> Appears on: UK 12" single
> These 'Excerpts' come from the 2xLP promo Rush 'Signals' Radio Special. Interesting, but not something you'd probably listen to over and over.

(April 1)
Rush performs live at the Civic Center, Hartford, Connecticut, US. The opening act is The Jon Butcher Axis.

(April 2)
Rush performs live at Carrier Dome, Syracuse, New York, US. The opening act is The Jon Butcher Axis.

(April 4)
Rush performs live at the Civic Arena, Pittsburgh, Pennsylvania, US. The opening act is The Jon Butcher Axis.

(April 5)
Rush performs live at Memorial Auditorium, Buffalo, New York, US. The opening act is The Jon Butcher Axis.

(April 7)
Rush performs live at The Coliseum, Quebec City, Quebec, Canada. The opening act is The Tenants.

(April 8 & 9)
Rush performs live at The Forum, Montreal, Quebec, Canada. The opening act is The Tenants. These are roadie Ian Grandy's last show with the band.

(Early May)
Assistant Recording Engineer and friend of *Rush*, Robbie Whelan, is killed in a car accident on his way to work at Le Studio, Morin Heights, Quebec, Canada.
"Afterimage" – In *Roadshow*, **Neil Peart** says this song was written for him.

(May 3)
Rush performs live at Ahoy Sportpaleis, Rotterdam, Holland. The opening act is Vanderburg.

(May 4)
Rush is scheduled to perform at Le Zenith, Paris, France, but the show is cancelled.

(May 6)

Rush performs live at Spothalle, Böblingen, Germany. The opening act is Nazareth.

(May 7)
Rush performs live at Festhalle, Frankfurt, Germany. The opening act is Nazareth.

(May 8)
Rush performs live at Congress Centrum, Hamburg, Germany. The opening act is Nazareth.

(May 10)
Rush performs live at Philipshalle, Dusseldorf, Germany. The opening act is Nazareth.

(May 11)
Rush performs live at Rhein-Neckar-Halle, Heidelberg, Germany. The opening act is Nazareth.

(May 12)
Rush performs live at Forest National, Brussels, Belgium.

(May 14 & 15)
Rush performs live at National Exhibition Centre, Birmingham, England. During one of these shows, **Alex Lifeson**'s guitar cuts out just before his solo in "The Analog Kid."

Note: during the England dates, the band interviews prospective producers for their next album.

(May 17, 18, 20 & 21)
Rush performs live at Wembley Arena, London, England.

(May 22)
Rush performs live at National Exhibition Centre, Birmingham, England. This show is added after a fire at Deeside Leisure Centre cancelled the May 23rd date.

(May 23)
Rush is scheduled to perform live at Deeside Leisure Centre, Deeside, Wales, but a fire at the venue forces its cancellation and it is rescheduled to May 22nd, National Exhibition Centre.

(May 24 & 25)
Rush performs live at Royal Highland Exhibition Centre, Edinburgh, Scotland.

(Date Unknown)
Marie-Lynn Hammond releases her album *Vignettes*, featuring **Geddy Lee** on the tracks "All The Horses Running" and "Over Queen Charlotte Sound."

> "All The Horses Running" 3:16
> Written by Marie-Lynn Hammond
> Appears on: Vignettes
> A good folk rock number, this song features Geddy's bass very present in the mix, but not overpowering. The song is full of atmosphere and mood and is quite good, though may not be everyone's taste. Recommended!

> "Over Queen Charlotte Sound" 2:44
> Written by Marie-Lynn Hammond
> Appears on: Vignettes
> A slower, light pop-folk song, Geddy's bass playing is more subdued (you can hear it, but it blends nicely in the backing track). On the original LP release, this song is listed separately from the next track, "Where The Grey Sky Meets The Sea," but because the two pieces segue seamlessly, the CD edition combines them into a single track. Geddy only appears on this song of the two.

(Summer)
In advance of beginning the sessions for their tenth studio album, *Rush* contacts a number of producers to work on the project. This process takes longer than anticipated and the scheduled studio time is pushed back.

In a 1989 *Rockline* interview, **Geddy Lee** says Rupert Hine is among those producers with whom the band was interested in working on the album. **Lee** doesn't specify why he did not produce the album, but he would later go on to produce *Presto* and *Roll The Bones*.

One of the producers with whom the band meets is Steve Lillywhite, who later talks about his relationship with Rush (in both *Sounds* magazine, 1984, and *Mohr Talk*, July 5, 2013). Lillywhite's description of not wanting to work with *Rush* (because he apparently didn't think highly of their work) and his pulling out of the project at the last minute seems to parallel **Neil Peart**'s description of the unnamed producer who had agreed to the job but then dropped out, citing that he didn't feel he was a good fit (*Grace Under Pressure* tour book). Reportedly, there were a lot of angry words and exchanges between the band's management and Lillywhite (also see "Kid Gloves" below).

(Date Unknown)
Rush releases is promo 12" single "The Weapon" in Canada.

Canada 12" promo single (SPE-14):
"The Weapon (12" Version)"
"Digital Man"

> "The Weapon (12" Version)" 4:18
> Written by Neil Peart (words), Geddy Lee & Alex Lifeson (music)
> Appears on: Canada 12" promo single
> This version features audio from the video intro by Count Floyd (SCTV actor Joe Flaherty) used during the Signals tour to introduce the song (this intro was also used during the Grace Under Pressure Tour). Not only that, the song is cut down to at the beginning and end, removing most of the intro synths and the outro, making for a not too bad radio edit. This is definitely one of the more interesting alternate versions in Rush's catalogue.

(Date Unknown)
Boys Brigade release their self-titled debut album, produced by **Geddy Lee**, on Anthem Records (Canada) and Capitol Records (worldwide).

Note: around this time, Anthem Records releases a promo interview LP titled *Interview With Boys Brigade And Geddy Lee* (SPE-018), where in the band and **Lee** discuss with radio DJ Andre Tilk their collaboration. Track listing as follows:

"Melody" Boys Brigade
"The Cut Up (Breaking Glass)" Boys Brigade
"Part One" Interview with Boys Brigade And Geddy Lee
"Part Two" Interview with Boys Brigade And Geddy Lee

(Mid-August to Early September)
Rush, still in search of a producer, begins writing and rehearsing new material, Horseshoe Valley, Ontario, Canada (*Grace Under Pressure* sessions). Demos are recorded and the sessions last three weeks, as noted in the *Grace Under Pressure* tour book. Tracks worked on include:
"Between The Wheels" - The "three parts" of the song come from a jam done on the first night, which form the foundation of the song. The lyrics later develop out of **Neil Peart** reading the *Globe & Mail* newspaper each morning.
"Kid Gloves" - was written within a few days (*Grace Under Pressure* tour book) and was motivated by the difficulties the band were experiencing finding a producer (**Alex Lifeson** in *Circus* magazine).
"Afterimage" - was written within a few days about the loss in May of their friend and Le Studio staff member Robbie Whelan.
"Red Sector A" - the title for this song comes from the name of the area at Cape Kennedy where the band watched the maiden voyage of space shuttle *Columbia* in April of 1981.
"The Body Electric" - the title comes from the Walt Whitman poem "I Sing The Body Electric."

(Mid September)
Rush spends a week rehearsing for their Radio City Music Hall dates.

(September 18, 19, 21, 22 & 23)
Rush performs live at Radio City Music Hall, New York City, New York, US. The opening at is Marillion.

> "Kid Gloves (Live at Radio City Music Hall, 1983)" 4:30
> Written by Neil Peart (words), Geddy Lee & Alex Lifeson (music)
> Appears on: Countdown PE (bootleg)
> One of the most remarkably different "pre-release" versions of a Rush song, this one finds Geddy singing the familiar lyrics with a much different cadence than he would on the album. Certainly an interesting insight into how the song originally sounded at the demo stage.

> "Red Sector A (Live at Radio City Music Hall, 1983)" 5:42
> Written by Neil Peart (words), Geddy Lee & Alex Lifeson (music)
> Appears on: Countdown PE (bootleg)
> This version of the song is not all that far from the finished album version, but (and you may see a recurring theme here) the guitar solo has yet to be completed.

> "The Body Electric (Live at Radio City Music Hall, 1983)" 5:11
> Written by Neil Peart (words), Geddy Lee & Alex Lifeson (music)
> Appears on: Countdown PE (bootleg)
> More or less complete, barring a few variations in lyrics and a rougher, wilder guitar solo that has Alex simply shredding through it.

(Late September to October)

Rush, still absent a producer, returns to Horseshoe Valley, Ontario, Canada and continues writing and rehearsing new material for their ninth studio album (*Grace Under Pressure* sessions). Songs worked on during these sessions include:
"Distant Early Warning" - The lyrics develop out of **Neil Peart** reading the *Globe & Mail* newspaper each morning. According to *Merely Players*, the working title is "Red Alert."
"The Enemy Within" – the original first part of **Neil Peart** planned 'Fear' trilogy.
"Red Lenses" – started at this time and the lyrics develop out of **Neil Peart** reading the *Globe & Mail* newspaper each morning. **Peart** also notes that the song was difficult to write and went through many lyric and title changes.

In the *Grace Under Pressure* tour book, **Neil Peart** notes that by the end of the writing and demoing sessions, the songs had gone through many variations and rearrangements, each with multiple demos made.

Rush meets with producer Peter Henderson and the next day they offer him the job on this album.

(November)
Rush begins recording their tenth studio album at Le Studio, Morin Heights, Quebec, Canada (*Grace Under Pressure* sessions). Produced by ***Rush*** and Peter Henderson. Engineered by Peter Henderson. In the *Grace Under Pressure* tour book, **Neil Peart** notes that the title *Grace Under Pressure* is suggested around this time. The sessions run until March, 1984.

GRACE UNDER PRESSURE

1984

(Early 19834)
Rush takes a break from recording *Grace Under Pressure* to be photographed for the album sleeve by famed photographer Yousuf Karsh in Ottawa, Ontario, Canada.

Mercury Records releases a compilation titled *Rush Anthology* in Venezuela. Track listing as follows:

"2112: I: Overture/ II: The Temples Of Syrinx"
"Closer To The Heart"
"The Trees"
"The Spirit Of Radio"
"Tom Sawyer"
"Limelight"
"Subdivisions"
"The Analog Kid"

(March 13)
Rush completes recording work on *Grace Under Pressure* at Le Studio, Morin Heights, Quebec, Canada.

Note: the date comes from the album's master tape boxes.

(April)
Rush releases their single "Distant Early Warning" in North America and Europe.

Canada 7" single (ANS-057):
"Distant Early Warning"
"Between The Wheels"

US 12" promo single (PRO 276-1):
"Distant Early Warning"
"Between The Wheels"

Spain 7" single (880-050-7):
"Distant Early Warning"
"Between The Wheels"

(April 12)
Rush releases their tenth studio album, *Grace Under Pressure*, on Anthem Records (Canada), Mercury Records (US and most other territories) and Vertigo Records (UK). Track listing as follows:

"Distant Early Warning"
"Afterimage"
"Red Sector A"
"The Enemy Within" – part I of 'Fear'
"The Body Electric"
"Kid Gloves"
"Red Lenses"
"Between The Wheels"

Note: the cover art painting by Hugh Syme appears slightly over-exposed and miscoloured on the original release and subsequent releases until the 1997 Rush Remaster series fixed the problem, featuring the correct, darker tones.

Note: around this time Anthem Records issues a promo radio *Grace Under Pressure* interview LP (SPE-021), featuring interview clips with radio DJ David Pritchard and *Rush* and music from the album.

(May 7)
Rush performs live at Tingley Coliseum, Albuquerque, New Mexico, US.

(May 9)
Rush performs live at Tucson Community Center, Tucson, Arizona, US. The opening act is Gary Moore. **Geddy Lee** is struck by a bottle thrown by an audience member mid-concert.

(May 10)
Rush performs live at Thomas & Mack Center, Las Vegas, Nevada, US. The opening act is Gary Moore.

(May 12)
Rush performs live at Lawlor Events Center, Reno, Nevada, US. The opening act is Gary Moore.

(May 14)
Rush performs live at Salt Palace Center, Salt Lake City, Utah, US. The opening act is Gary Moore.

(May 15)
Rush performs live at BSU Pavilion, Boise, Idaho, US. The opening act is Gary Moore.

(May 17)
Rush performs live at Memorial Coliseum, Portland, Oregon, US. The opening act is Gary Moore.

(May 18)
Rush performs live at Tacoma Dome, Tacoma, Washington, US. The opening act is Gary Moore.

(May 19)
Rush performs live at Pacific Coliseum, Vancouver, British Columbia, Canada. The opening act is Gary Moore.

(May 24, 25 & 26)
Rush performs live at Cow Palace, San Francisco, California, US. The opening act is Gary Moore on the 25th and 26th.

(May 28)
Rush performs live at San Diego Sports Arena, San Diego, California, US. The opening act is Gary Moore.

(May 29 & 30)
Rush performs live at Great Western Forum, Los Angeles California, US. The opening act is Gary Moore.

(June)
Gary Moore & Phil Lynott release their single "Out In The Fields," produced by Peter Collins. Collins later says it is his production work on this track that gets him the producer job for *Rush*'s next album (*Power Windows*), when Gary Moore was touring with the band.

(Date Unknown)
Jeff Berlin contacts **Geddy Lee** while *Rush* are in California, US, and **Lee** invites Berlin to visit the band backstage during one of their concerts.

(June 2)
Rush performs live at Irvine Meadows Amphitheater, Irvine, California, US. The opening act is Gary Moore.

(June 4)
Rush performs live at Veterans Memorial Coliseum, Phoenix, Arizona, US. The opening act is Gary Moore.

(June 5)
Rush performs live at Pan American Center, Las Cruces, New Mexico, US. The opening act is Gary Moore.

(June 6)
Rush performs live at Ector County Coliseum, Odessa, Texas, US.

(June 8)
Rush performs live at Astrodome, Houston, Texas, US, as part of the Texxas World Music Festival.

(June 10)
Rush performs live at Cotton Bowl, Dallas, Texas, US, as part of the Texxas World Music Festival. Also on the bill is .38 Special, Ozzy Osbourne, Bryan Adams and Gary Moore.

(June 12)
Rush performs live at Barton Coliseum, Little Rock, Arkansas, US. The opening act is Gary Moore.

(June 13)
Rush performs live at Convention Center, Tulsa, Oklahoma, US. The opening act is Gary Moore.

(June 15)
Rush performs live at Kansas Coliseum, Wichita, Kansas, US. The opening act is Gary Moore.

(June 16)
Rush performs live at Kemper Arena, Kansas City, Missouri, US. The opening act is Gary Moore.

(June 25)

Rush performs live at Mecca-Milwaukee Arena, Milwaukee, Wisconsin, US.

(June 26 & 27)
Rush performs live at Met Center, Bloomington, Minnesota, US. The opening act is Gary Moore.

(June 29 & 30)
Rush performs live at Rosemont Horizon. Rosemont, Illinois, US. The opening act is Gary Moore.

(July 2)
Rush performs live at The Arena, St. Louis, Missouri, US. The opening act is Gary Moore.

(July 3)
Rush performs live at Market Square Arena, Indianapolis, Indiana, US. The opening act is Pat Travers Band.

(July 5 & 6)
Rush performs live at Richfield Coliseum, Richfield, Ohio, US. The opening act is Gary Moore.

(July 7)
Rush is apparently scheduled to perform live at Memorial Auditorium, Buffalo, New York, US, but at some point the show is re-scheduled to July 12th.

Rush performs live at Ohio Center, Columbus, Ohio, US. The opening act is Pat Travers Band.

(July 8)
Rush performs live at Civic Arena, Pittsburgh, Pennsylvania, US. The opening act is Pat Travers Band.

(July 9)
Rush performs live at Joe Louis Arena. Detroit, Michigan, US. The opening act is Pat Travers Band.

(July 12)
Rush performs live at Memorial Auditorium, Buffalo, New York, US. The opening act is Red Rider. This show is reportedly re-scheduled from July 7th.

(July 14 & 15)
Rush performs live at The Forum, Montreal, Quebec, Canada. The opening act is Red Rider. Bills for this show advertise the release of the new *Rush* single "The Body Electric."

Canada 7" single (ANS 059):
"The Body Electric"
"Between The Wheels"

Canada 12" promo single (SPE-022):
"The Body Electric (Single Edit)"
"The Body Electric"

US 7" single (880-050-7):
"The Body Electric"
"Between The Wheels"

US 7" promo single (880-050-7 DJ):
"The Body Electric (Single Edit)"
"The Body Electric (Single Edit)"

US 12" promo single (PRO 290-1):
"The Body Electric"
"The Body Electric"

UK 7" single (RUSH 11):
"The Body Electric"
"The Analog Kid"

UK 7" promo single (RUSDJ 11):
"The Body Electric (Single Edit)"
"The Body Electric"

UK 10" single (limited edition red vinyl) (RUSH 1110):
"The Body Electric"
"The Analog Kid"
"Distant Early Warning"

UK 12" single (RUSH 1112):
"The Body Electric"
"The Analog Kid"
"Distant Early Warning"

> "The Body Electric (Single Edit)" 4:16
> Written by Neil Peart (words), Geddy Lee & Alex Lifeson (music)
> Appears on: Canada 12" promo single, US 7" single, US 7" promo single, UK 7" promo single
> This edit removes sections of instrumental from the opening and closing of the song.

(July 16)
Rush performs live at The Coliseum, Quebec City, Quebec, Canada.

(September)
Neil Peart receives a letter from drummer Paul Siegel proposing **Neil** put together a drum instructional video. This proposal is later revisited and becomes *A Work In Progress* (*AWIP*) liner notes.

(September 14)
Rush performs live at Cumberland County Civic Center, Portland, Maine, US. The opening act is Fastway.

(September 15)
Rush performs live at Civic Center, Glens Falls, New York, US. The opening act is Fastway.

(September 17)
Rush performs live at Madison Square Garden, New York, New York, US. The opening act is Fastway.

(September 18)
Rush performs live at Olympic Center, Lake Placid, New York, US. The opening act is Fastway.

(September 21 & 22)
Rush performs live at Maple Leaf Gardens, Toronto, Ontario, US. The opening act is Red Rider. The show on the 21st is audio recorded and filmed and released as Grace Under Pressure Tour VHS in 1986 (and on DVD and CD in 2007). The following tracks have been release individually over the years:

> "The Enemy Within (GUP Tour - Single Version)" 4:40
> Written by Neil Peart (words), Geddy Lee & Alex Lifeson (music)
> Appears on: UK "Time Stand Still" 12" promo single, UK (?) & Europe CD single, UK & Europe 12" single, UK 12" Picture Disc single
> A good stand-alone cut of the track from the Grace Under Pressure Tour video (and later CD), opening and closing with a fade. It fades in after the intro.

> "Witch Hunt (GUP Tour - Single Version)" 4:45
> Written by Neil Peart (words), Geddy Lee & Alex Lifeson (music)
> Appears on: UK "Time Stand Still" 12" promo single, UK (?) & Europe CD single, UK & Europe 12" single
> This version fades in as the opening chimes are heard and fades out before "New World Man" starts.

> "New World Man (GUP Tour - Single Version)" 4:02
> Written by Neil Peart (words), Geddy Lee & Alex Lifeson (music)
> Appears on: "Prime Mover" UK 12" & CD single
> A good stand-alone cut of the track from the Grace Under Pressure Tour video (and later CD), opening and closing with a fade.

> "New World Man (GUP Tour - Icon 2 Version)" 4:03
> Written by Neil Peart (words), Geddy Lee & Alex Lifeson (music)
> Appears on: Icon 2
> Nearly identical to the "Single Version" from "Prime Mover," the fade in is ever so slightly longer here.

> "Distant Early Warning (GUP Tour - Single Version)" 6:12
> Written by Neil Peart (words), Geddy Lee & Alex Lifeson (music)
> Appears on: "Prime Mover" UK 7" single (white vinyl); "Prime Mover" UK 12" & CD single
> A good stand-alone cut of the track from the Grace Under Pressure Tour video (and later CD), opening and closing with a fade.

> "Red Sector A (GUP Tour - Single Version)" 5:25
> Written by Neil Peart (words), Geddy Lee & Alex Lifeson (music)
> Appears on: "The Big Money" Canada 7" single; "The Big Money" US 7" single; "The Big Money" UK 12" single; "The Big Money" Netherlands 7" single, UK & Europe CDV

A good stand-alone cut of the track from the Grace Under Pressure Tour video (and later CD), opening and closing with a fade.

"Red Sector A (GUP Tour – Video Version)" 5:20
Written by Neil Peart (words), Geddy Lee & Alex Lifeson (music)
Appears on: Chronicles VHS & DVD
An excerpt from this concert video, this version has the same footage, but fades in and out nicely, almost identically to the "Single Version."

"Closer To The Heart (GUP Tour – Icon 2 Version)" 3:37
Written by Neil Peart & Peter Talbot (words), Geddy Lee & Alex Lifeson (music)
Appears on: Icon 2
A good stand-alone cut of the track from the Grace Under Pressure Tour video (and later CD), opening and closing with a fade.

"Vital Signs (GUP Tour – Icon 2 Version)" 4:59
Written by Neil Peart & Peter Talbot (words), Geddy Lee & Alex Lifeson (music)
Appears on: Icon 2
Unlike the stand-alone versions noted above, this one starts with a nice fade in, but because there's no real pause in the show before the band goes into the "Finding My Way/In The Mood" medley, the end of this track has a really fast fade-out right after the last note. The performance is good, but if you want a better live edit of this song, you should hunt down earlier version from the "New World Man" single.

(September 24)
Rush is scheduled to perform live at Veterans Coliseum, New Haven, Connecticut, US, but the show is postponed until the 28th because **Geddy Lee** is ill.

(September 25)
Rush is scheduled to perform live at Civic Center. Providence, Rhode Island, US, but the show is postponed until the Nov 7th, because **Geddy Lee** is ill.

(September 27)
Rush performs live at Capital Centre, Largo, Maryland, US. The opening act is Helix.

(September 28)
Rush performs live at Veterans Coliseum, New Haven, Connecticut, US. The opening act is Fastway. This show replaces the postponed show from the 24th.

(September 29)
Rush performs live at Brendan Byrne Arena, East Rutherford, New Jersey, US. The opening act is Helix.

(September 30)
Rush performs live at Nassau Coliseum, Uniondale, New York, US. The opening act is Helix.

(October 2 & 3)
Rush performs live at The Centrum, Worcester, Massachusetts, US. The opening act is Fastway.

(October 4)
Rush performs live at War Memorial, Rochester, New York, US. The opening act is Fastway.

(October 6)
Rush performs live at University of Dayton Arena, Dayton, Ohio, US. The opening act is Fastway.

(October 7)
Rush performs live at Ohio Center, Columbus, Ohio, US. The opening act is Fastway.

(October 18)
Rush performs live at Toledo Sports Arena, Toledo, Ohio, US. The opening act is Fastway.

(October 19)
Rush performs live at Wendler Arena, Saginaw, Michigan, US. The opening act is Fastway.

(October 21)
Rush performs live at Rupp Arena, Lexington, Kentucky, US. The opening act is Fastway.

(October 23)
Rush performs live at Mid-South Coliseum, Memphis, Tennessee, US. The opening act is Fastway.

(October 24)

Rush performs live at Mississippi Coliseum, Jackson, Mississippi, US. The opening act is Fastway.

(October 26)
Rush performs live at Mississippi Coast Coliseum, Biloxi, Mississippi, US. The opening act is Fastway.

(October 27)
Rush performs live at UNO Lakefront Arena, New Orleans, Louisiana, US. The opening act is Fastway.

(October 29)
Rush performs live at Municipal Auditorium, Nashville, Tennessee, US. The opening act is Fastway.

(October 30)
Rush performs live at The Omni, Atlanta, Georgia, US. The opening act is Fastway.

(Date Unknown)
Rush releases its "Red Sector A" singles in North America.

Canada 7" single (ANS-060):
"Red Sector A (Single Edit)"
"Red Lenses"

Canada 7" promo single (SPE-023):
"Red Sector A (Single Edit)"
"Red Lenses"

US 7" promo single (red vinyl) (PRO 319-7):
"Red Sector A (Single Edit)"
"Red Sector A (Single Edit)"

US 12" promo single (red vinyl) (PRO 320-1):
"Red Sector A (Single Edit)"
"The Enemy Within"

> "Red Sector A (Single Edit)" 4:10
> Written by Neil Peart (words), Geddy Lee & Alex Lifeson (music)
> Appears on: Canada 7" single, Canada 7" promo single, US 7" promo single, US 12" promo single.
> I have not heard this, but I expect it removes instrumental material throughout in order to cut the running time down by a minute.

(November 1)
Rush performs live at Civic Center Coliseum, Charleston, West Virginia, US. The opening act is Y&T.

(November 2)
Rush performs live at Freedom Hall Civic Center, Johnson City, Tennessee, US.

(November 3)
Rush performs live at Hampton Coliseum, Hampton, Virginia, US. The opening act is Y&T.

(November 5 & 6)
Rush performs live at The Spectrum. Philadelphia, Pennsylvania, US. The opening act is Y&T.

(November 7)
Rush performs live at the Civic Center. Providence, Rhode Island, US. The opening act is Y&T. This is rescheduled from the cancelled September 25th concert. Producer Peter Collins is in attendance (*Musician* magazine, December 1985).

(November 16)
Rush performs live at Seto-shi Bunka Center, Seto, Aichi, Japan.

(November 18)
Rush performs live at Fukuoka Sun-Palace Hall, Fukuoka-shi, Fukuoka, Japan.

(November 20)
Rush performs live at Osaka-shi, Osaka, Japan.

(November 21)
Rush performs live at Nippon Budokan, Tokyo, Japan.

(November 24 & 25)
Rush performs live at Honolulu NBC Arena, Honolulu, Hawaii, US. The opening act is Strict-Neine.

POWER WINDOWS

1985

(February)
Rush begins writing and rehearsing new material for their eleventh studio album at Elora Sound Studio, Elora, Ontario, Canada (*Power Windows* sessions). Songs worked on are:
"The Big Money" – **Neil Peart** had outlined this song prior to arriving. The band develops the song within the first week. A demo is recorded. The title comes from the Jon Dos Passos novel of the same name, as suggested by **Peart** in the January 1988 *Backstage Club* newsletter.
"Mystic Rhythms" – **Neil Peart** had outlined this song prior to arriving. The band develops the song within the first week. A demo is recorded.
"Marathon" – **Neil Peart** had outlined this song prior to arriving. The band develops the song within the first week. A demo is recorded.
"Middletown Dreams"
"Manhattan Project" – **Neil** begins research for this song.
"Grand Designs"

Neil Peart writes the following:
"Pieces Of Eight" – while experimenting on the midi marimba, **Neil** writes this piece (*Anatomy Of A Drum Solo*).

In a January 1989 *Music Express* interview, **Alex Lifeson** says about 60% of the musical ideas are culled from the *Grace Under Pressure* tour soundcheck recordings.

David Foster contacts SRO Productions to invite **Geddy Lee** record with Northern Lights, the Canadian recording artists who are a part of the famine relief for Ethiopia (*Rockline*). **Geddy Lee** notes ***Rush*** was writing *Power Windows* when the call came.

(February 10)
Geddy Lee records his vocal part for "Tears Are Not Enough" with **Northern Lights** as part of the famine relief benefit for Ethiopia, at Sound Studios, Toronto, Ontario, Canada. Other artists involved include Gordon Lighhtfoot, Burton Cummings, Anne Murray, Joni Mitchell, Neil Young, Bryan Adams, Corey Hart, Dalbello and Mark Holmes.

(March)
Rush travels to Lakeland, Florida, US, in advance of the warm-up tour dates. Around this time, **Neil Peart** begins working on the following:
"Territories" - In the *Power Windows* tour book, **Neil** says that by late March he had been struggling with these lyrics for a couple of weeks already.

Northern Lights release their "Tears Are Not Enough" singles. The song also later appears on the USA For Africa collection *We Are The World*.

Canada 7" single (7BEN-7073):
"Tears Are Not Enough (Single Edit)"
"Tears Are Not Enough (Instrumental)"

Canada 12" single (12BEN-7074):
"Tears Are Not Enough (12" Version)"
"Tears Are Not Enough (Single Edit)"
"Tears Are Not Enough (Instrumental)"

> "Tears Are Not Enough (12" Version)" 5:17
> Written by David Foster, Bryan Adams, Jim Vallance
> Appears on: Canada 12" single
> The mid-1980s saw the music world rally to the cause of famine relief for Ethiopia, kicked of by the 1984 charity supergroup single "Do They Know It's Christmas" and followed up by the We Are The World album and singles (including "Tears Are Not Enough"), and Live Aid. The cause was genuine and the concern heartfelt, but the supergroup charity songs were so heartfelt and direct that a generation or so later, the approach of the benefit single is in many quarters considered a bit hokey now. Parodies exist anywhere from The Simpsons to Odd Job Jack to Saturday Night Live to "Weird Al" Yankovic. The website TV Tropes even has a page for these, titled: Charity Motivation Song. In "Tears Are Not Enough," Geddy has a solitary solo line which does little to cut through the naked earnestness on display here. The 12" version is the most complete cut of the song, with all the finale choruses taking it past the five minute mark.
>
> "Tears Are Not Enough (We Are The World Version)" 4:23
> Written by David Foster, Bryan Adams, Jim Vallance
> Appears on: We Are The World

> The version that appears on the album is the same recording as the "12" Version," fades out much earlier, removing most of the finale choruses.
>
> "Tears Are Not Enough (Single Edit)" 3:56
> Written by David Foster, Bryan Adams, Jim Vallance
> Appears on: Canada 12" single, Canada 7" single
> This edit is again the same recording, only fading out even earlier than the album version.
>
> "Tears Are Not Enough (Instrumental)" 4:53
> Written by David Foster, Bryan Adams, Jim Vallance
> Appears on: Canada 12" single, Canada 7" single
> This is the instrumental backing track, fading out earlier than the "12" Version. Obviously, there are no Geddy Lee vocals.

(March 10)
Rush rehearses at the Civic Center, Lakeland, Florida, US.

(March 11)
Rush performs live at the Civic Center, Lakeland, Florida, US.

(March 12)
Rush performs live at the Civic Center, Lakeland, Florida, US. In the *Power Windows* tour book, **Neil Peart** says on this date he listens to a tape of the five demoed songs:
"The Big Money"
"Mystic Rhythms"
"Marathon"
"Middletown Dreams"
"Grand Designs"

(March 14)
Rush performs live at Lee Civic Center, Ft. Meyers, Florida, US.

(March 15)
Rush performs live at Hollywood Sportatorium, Hollywood, Florida, US.

> "Middletown Dreams (Live in Florida, 1985)" 5:50
> Written by Neil Peart (words), Geddy Lee & Alex Lifeson (music)
> Appears on: Unreleased
> This bootleg recording from the Sportatorium features a version of the song dating from before the proper recording sessions. The lyrics are all there and the basic arrangement is similar to the album recording, with a few differences, such as the beat breaks in the opening being absent and the guitar work being much rougher.
>
> "The Big Money (Live in Florida, 1985)" 5:22
> Written by Neil Peart (words), Geddy Lee & Alex Lifeson (music)
> Appears on: Unreleased
> As with "Middletown Dreams," there wouldn't be much more to develop after this, it's all pretty much here, including the little fills in the intro. The synths are less prominent, though, which could be the quality of the bootleg, it's hard to say. Also, I'm not 100% certain this track comes from this show, but in all likelihood it does (it's definitely a Florida pre-release performance and it makes sense that whomever taped "Middletown Dreams" also taped this song).

(Mid-March)
Geddy Lee attends Major League Baseball pre-season games in Florida, US.

Neil Peart records drum parts for Jeff Berlin & Vox Humana's album *Champion*, on the tracks "Marabi" (a cover of the 1968 Cannonball Adderley piece) and "Champion (Of The World)," at Music Annex, Menlo, California, US. His sessions take a day and a half.

(Late-March)
Rush continues writing and rehearsing new material for their eleventh studio album at Elora Sound Studio, Elora, Ontario, Canada (*Power Windows* sessions). Songs worked on are:
"Emotion Detector" – Developed on the first day back, a result of the band wanting to write a "ballad."
"Territories" – the music is written for the song during this period.
"Manhattan Project" – the last song completed after some struggles with it. Producer Peter Collin helps with it.

(Date Unknown)

Alex Lifeson records guitar solos on the tracks "Holy Water" and "Crying Over You" for Platinum Blonde's forth coming album, *Alien Shores*, at MetalWorks Studios, Mississauga, Ontario, Canada. Of note, Dalbello also appears on this album, who will later appear on **Alex**'s solo project **Victor**.

(Date Unknown)
PolyGram Video releases the *Rush* video collection *Through The Camera Eye* on VHS and laserdisc worldwide. It contains videos (not all) from *Moving Pictures, Signals, Grace Under Pressure* and an excerpt from the *Exit…Stage Left* concert film.

North American VHS & Japan laserdisc:
"Distant Early Warning"
"Vital Signs" – Le Studio
"The Body Electric"
"Afterimage"
"Subdivisions"
"Tom Sawyer (Exit…Stage Left – Video Version)"
"The Enemy Within"
"Countdown"

UK VHS:
"Distant Early Warning"
"Subdivisions"
"Vital Signs" – Le Studio
"Tom Sawyer (Exit…Stage Left – Video Version)"
"The Body Electric"
 "The Enemy Within"
"Afterimage"
"Countdown"

(April)
Rush begins recording their eleventh studio album at The Manor, Shipton-on-Cherwell, Oxfordshire, England (*Power Windows* sessions). Produced by Peter Collins. Engineered by James Barton. The basic tracks are recorded in a few weeks. Andy Richard then programs and records some keyboard work on the album.

(May)
Rush continues work on their eleventh studio album at AIR Studios, Montserrat, West Indies (*Power Windows* sessions). Guitar overdubs are recorded.

(June to July)
Rush continues work on their eleventh studio album at Sarm East Studios, London, England (*Power Windows* sessions). Guitar solos and vocals are recorded.

(Mid-July)
Rush continues work on their eleventh studio album at Studio 1, Abbey Road Studios, London, England (*Power Windows* sessions), to record the strings for the following:
"Marathon" – string arrangements by Anne Dudley

(August)
Rush continues work on their eleventh studio album at Angel Studios, London, England (*Power Windows* sessions), to record the choir for the following:
"Marathon" – choral arrangements and conducted by Andrew Jackman

Recording of the album is apparently completed this month.

(Summer)
Platinum Blonde releases their album *Alien Shores*, featuring **Alex Lifeson** on the tracks "Crying Over You" and "Holy Water." "Crying Over You" is also released as a single.

> "Crying Over You" 3:36
> Written by Mark Holmes
> Appears on: Alien Shores
> This was the height of new wave, where loud suits and big hair dominated male pop and rock stars. Platinum Blonde was no exception and their synth-rock-pop sound was indicative of the time. They were pretty big at this point in Canada, but apparently never made much of a dent in the US beyond this song during the one hit wonder '80s. Alex's guitar solo is the only thing that doesn't feel dated in this song, though if you have a soft spot for glittery synth power ballads, this one's right up your alley.
>
> "Holy Water" 3:14
> Written by Mark Holmes & Kenny MacLean

Appears on: Alien Shores
A synth-rock power ballad, this song features another guitar solo from Alex, which adds a bit of flavour to an otherwise middling album track that seems to musically borrow bits from Cindy Lauper's "Time After Time" and Duran Duran's "Rio" in places.

"Crying Over You (Radical Mix)" 6:07
Written by Mark Holmes
Appears on: Canada 12" single
Alex's guitar solo survives this version, but seems to be lower in the mix, that favours the drum track, percussion and synth horns and effects. There are a lot of breakdowns in this mix, which strangely help to elevate the song and make it more listenable overall than the original, odd as that may sound (and that depends on your tastes. If you don't like the original at all, this one probably won't win you over).

"Crying Over You (Dub Version)" 5:27
Written by Mark Holmes
Appears on: Canada 12" single
This is basically an extended, mostly instrumental mix, with some nice breakdowns and only a few bits of vocal here and there, including the choruses. Alex's guitar solo, sadly, doesn't appear in this version.

"Crying Over You (Instrabeat Mix)" 4:33
Written by Mark Holmes
Appears on: Canada 12" single
What we have here is a mix made up entirely of an extended instrumental breakdown. There are almost no vocals. And no Alex Lifeson.

(September)
Geddy Lee oversees the mastering of *Power Windows* at Masterdisk, New York, City, New York, US. Engineered by Bob Ludwig. In a June 1986 *Circus* magazine feature, it is reported that Ludwig rejected the mastering heard on at least two test pressings before approving the final mix.

(September 18)
Neil Peart embarks on a two-week bicycle tour of China.
"Tai Shan" – **Peart** climbs Mount Tai during his tour and the experience later inspires this song.

Neil later privately publishes a travelogue of his trip titled *Riding The Golden Lion*.

(Autumn)
Jeff Berlin & Vox Humana release their album *Champion*, featuring **Neil Peart** on the tracks "Marabi" and "Champion (Of The World)."

"Marabi" 5:34
Written by Julian "Cannonball" Adderley
Appears on: Champion
This is an excellent fusion rendition of the Cannonball Adderley number from his 1968 album Accent On Africa. Neil's drum parts come in on the "chorus" sections, beefing up the Steve Smith's drum parts and adding a lot of power. Highly recommended! Smith would also later participate in Peart's Burning For Buddy tribute.

"Champion (Of The World)" 4:37
Written by Jeff Berlin
Appears on: Champion
A great jazz-fusion track here that really let's Neil shine in a genre that he would later explore in more detail via Burning For Buddy. There are plenty of signature drum fills, but he doesn't overdue it and lets the song stay airy and light. Also highly recommended!

(October)
Rush releases its singles for "The Big Money" in Canada.

Canada 7" single (ANS-067):
"The Big Money"
"Red Sector A (Grace Under Pressure Tour – Single Version)"

Canada 12" Promo single (SPE-028):
"The Big Money"
"The Big Money"

Canada 7" Promo single (SPE-029-DJ):
"The Big Money (Promo Edit)"
"The Big Money (Promo Edit)"

"The Big Money (Promo Edit)" 4:32
Written by Neil Peart (words), Geddy Lee & Alex Lifeson (music)
Appears on: Canada 7" promo single, US 7" promo single
I haven't heard this, but at a guess, I'd say it's similar to the video edit, which, if the finale was removed, would bring the run time in line with this edit.

"The Big Money (Video Edit)" 4:47
Written by Neil Peart (words), Geddy Lee & Alex Lifeson (music)
Appears on: Chronicles VHS & DVD
This edit removes bits of instrumental throughout the song, shaving off about 45 audible seconds. Needless to say, it doesn't do the song justice, but isn't particularly bad. Curiously, the October 12, 1985, Billboard article describes the video production and concept, stating it stars actor Howard Busgang as "Mr. Big Money, a man obsessed with business success." This version of the video would appear to not have seen the light of day.

Note: a *Billboard* magazine article from October 12, 1985, discusses both "The Big Money" video and single.

(October 12)
Rush releases its singles for "The Big Money" in the UK.

UK 7" single (RUSH 12):
"The Big Money"
"Territories"

UK 2x7" single (double pack) (RUSHD 12):
"The Big Money"
"Territories"
"Closer To The Heart"
"The Spirit Of Radio"

UK 7" Gatefold single (RUSHG 12):
"The Big Money"
"Middletown Dreams"

UK 12" single (RUSH12 12):
"The Big Money"
"Territories"
"Red Sector A (Grace Under Pressure Tour – Single Version)"

(October 29)
Rush releases their album *Power Windows* on Anthem Records (Canada), Mercury Records (worldwide) and Vertigo Records (UK). Additional keyboards by Jim Burgess. Track listing as follows:

"The Big Money"
"Grand Designs"
"Manhattan Project"
"Marathon"
"Territories"
"Middletown Dreams"
"Emotion Detector"
"Mystic Rhythms"

(Late 1985)
According to a *Pittsburgh Press* article (December 12, 1985), **Geddy Lee** spends two week prior to the tour programming his synthesizers and **Neil Peart** spends the same time setting up his electronic drums and getting physically ready.

(November)
Rush releases its singles for "The Big Money" in the US.

US 7" single (884-191-7):
"The Big Money"
"Red Sector A (Grace Under Pressure Tour – Single Version)"

US 12" Promo single (PRO-382-1):
"The Big Money"
"The Big Money"

US 7" Promo single (PRO-383-7-DJ):
"The Big Money"
"The Big Money (Promo Edit)"

(December 4)
Rush performs live Cumberland County Civic Center, Portland, Maine, US.

(December 5)
Rush performs live Civic Center, Providence, Rhode Island, US. The opening act is Steve Morse.

(December 7)
Rush performs live Veterans Coliseum, New Haven, Connecticut, US. The opening act is Steve Morse.

(December 8)
Rush performs live Civic Center, Hartford, Connecticut, US. The opening act is Steve Morse.

(December 10)
Rush performs live War Memorial, Rochester, New York, US. The opening act is Steve Morse.

(December 12 & 13)
Rush performs live The Centrum, Worcester, Massachusetts, US. The opening act is Steve Morse.

(December 15)
Rush performs live Richmond Coliseum, Richmond, Virginia, US. The opening act is Steve Morse.

(December 16)
Rush performs live Capital Centre, Largo, Maryland, US. The opening act is Steve Morse.

(December 18)
Rush performs live Civic Arena, Pittsburgh, Pennsylvania, US. The opening act is Steve Morse. Prior to the concert, **Neil Peart** says in an interview that the band "jams freely" at soundchecks and these are recorded for future musical ideas.

(December 19)
Rush performs live Richfield Coliseum, Richfield, Ohio, US.

MYSTIC RHYTHMS

1986

(January)
In a *Modern Drummer* interview published his month, **Neil Peart** says he recorded on a track with artist Ken Ramm. In 2002, Ramm states in an email to *Power Windows - A Tribute To Rush* that the tracks title is "Economy In Motion" and that it remains unreleased.

(January 9)
Rush performs live at Pensacola Civic Center, Pensacola, Florida, US. The opening act is Steve Morse.

(January 10)
Rush performs live at Cajundome, Lafayette, Louisiana, US. The opening act is Steve Morse.

(January 12 & 13)
Rush performs live at Reunion Arena, Dallas, Texas, US. The opening act is Steve Morse.

(January 15 & 16)
Rush performs live at The Summit, Houston, Texas, US. The opening act is Steve Morse.

(January 18)
Rush performs live at Erwin Special Events Center, Austin, Texas, US. The opening act is Steve Morse.

(January 19)
Rush performs live at Convention Center Arena, San Antonio, Texas, US. The opening act is Steve Morse.

(January 30)
Rush performs live at Cow Palace, San Francisco, California, US. The opening act is Steve Morse.

(January 31)
Rush performs live at Oakland Coliseum. Oakland, California, US. The opening act is Steve Morse.

(Date Unknown)
Rush releases its concert film on VHS of the *Grace Under Pressure Tour* worldwide. The North American edition via RCA/Columbia Home Video includes the rare, full-length music video for "The Big Money." The Castle Communications, Channel 5 Video and PolyGram Video editions (UK and Europe) do not include this bonus video.

(February 2)
Rush performs live at Thomas & Mack Center, Las Vegas, Nevada, US. The opening act is Steve Morse.

(February 3)
Rush performs live at Sports Arena, San Diego, California, US. The opening act is Steve Morse.

(February 5 & 6)
Rush performs live at Great Western Forum, Los Angeles, California, US. The opening act is Steve Morse.

(February 8)
Rush performs live at Veterans Memorial Coliseum, Phoenix, Arizona, US. The opening act is Steve Morse.

(February 10)
Rush performs live at Community Center, Tucson, Arizona, US.

(February 12)
Rush performs live at Tingley Coliseum, Albuquerque, New Mexico, US.

(February 13)
In a 1990 *Guitar For A Practicing Musician* interview, **Alex Lifeson** says on this night *Rush* and Steve Morse's band go out to dinner at a Moroccan restaurant, Denver, Colorado, US. There he eats something that would later trigger an allergic reaction.

(February 14)
Alex Lifeson awakens this day feeling ill as a result of an allergic reaction from the Moroccan dinner eaten the night before. By soundcheck time, he has gotten worse and takes an antihistamine, which is difficult on his system, but he goes ahead with the show.

Rush performs live at McNichol's Arena, Denver, Colorado, US. The opening act is Steve Morse. **Alex Lifeson** believes he didn't play well this concert as a result of the medication.

(February 27)
Rush performs live at Memorial Auditorium, Buffalo, New York, US. The opening act is Marillion.

(February 28)
Rush performs live at Copps Coliseum, Hamilton, Ontario, Canada.

(March 1)
Rush performs live at Civic Center, Ottawa, Ontario, Canada. The opening act is FM.

(March 3)
Rush performs live at The Coliseum, Quebec City, Quebec, Canada. The opening act is Marillion.

(March 4)
Rush performs live at The Forum, Montreal, Quebec, Canada. The opening act is Marillion.

A June 1986 feature in *Circus* suggests "Mystic Rhythms" is the recent single around the time of this concert.

Canada 7" single (ANS-069):
"Mystic Rhythms"
"Emotion Detector"

Canada 7" Promo single (SPE-031-DJ):
"Mystic Rhythms"
"Mystic Rhythms"

US 7" single (884 520-7):
"Mystic Rhythms"
"Emotion Detector"

(March 6 & 7)
Rush performs live at Maple Leaf Gardens, Toronto, Ontario, Canada. The opening act is FM.

(March 20)
Rush performs live at Market Square Arena, Indianapolis, Indiana, US. The opening act is Marillion.

(March 21 & 22)
Rush performs live at Rosemont Horizon, Rosemont, Illinois, US. The opening act is Marillion.

(March 24)
Rush performs live at Mecca Arena, Milwaukee, Wisconsin, US. The opening act is Marillion.

(March 25)
Rush performs live at Civic Center, St. Paul, Minnesota, US. The opening act is Marillion.

(March 28)
Rush performs live at Joe Louis Arena, Detroit, Michigan, US. The opening act is Marillion.

(March 29)
Rush performs live at Riverfront Coliseum, Cincinnati, Ohio, US. The opening act is Marillion.

(March 31 & April 1)
Rush performs live at Brendan Byrne Arena, East Rutherford, New Jersey, US. The opening act is Marillion. Both shows are recorded. The following tracks later appear on the live album *A Show Of Hands*:

"Mystic Rhythms"
"Witch Hunt"

> "Mystic Rhythms (ASOH - Chronicles Version)" 5:42
> Written by Neil Peart (words), Geddy Lee & Alex Lifeson (music)
> Appears on: Chronicles
> Unlike the A Show Of Hands CD, this track doesn't start with the opening drums, but instead fades in on the crowd noise leading into the drums and fades out over the crowd at the end, making for a clean cut.
>
> "Mystic Rhythms (ASOH - Icon 2 Version)" 5:36
> Written by Neil Peart (words), Geddy Lee & Alex Lifeson (music)
> Appears on: Icon 2

Similar to the "Chronicles Version," this edit fades in fast at the opening, almost right at the drum intro and fades out almost as fast at the end. It's hair-splitting and maybe I'm just more used to the Chronicles edit, but I prefer the slightly longer fades, they seem less ~~rushed~~ hurried.

"Witch Hunt (ASOH – Single Version)" 3:55
Written by Neil Peart (words), Geddy Lee & Alex Lifeson (music)
Appears on: "Closer To The Heart (ASOH)" Canada 7" single
This edit fades in on the opening chimes and fades out over the crowd noise at the end.

(April)
Mercury Records re-issues the following *Rush* album on CD in the US.

Fly By Night (822 542-2) – contains "By-Tor And The Snow Dog (Standard CD Version)"

"By-Tor And The Snow Dog (Standard CD Version)" 8:37
Written by Neil Peart (words), Geddy Lee & Alex Lifeson (music)
Appears on: Fly By Night CD Editions and Remasters (most, if not all, formats), Time Stand Still: The Collection
If your first or only exposure to Rush is by way of the digital variety, congratulations on being born around 1990. That being the case this version of "By-Tor" is probably the one you know best, but it is, in fact, an edit. The original 1975 LP extended the chimes at the end into the run-out groove, allowing them to go past the 8:57 run time ad infinitum. The Archives edition pared that down to 8:57 by not extending into the groove, but the CD edition shaved off 20 more seconds for reasons unknown and this has become the standard for CD re-issues everywhere, it would seem, across the various remasters, including the 2013 digital Mastered For iTunes edition of the track.

Note: Date comes from Discogs.com

(April 3)
Rush performs live at Civic Center, Springfield, Massachusetts, US. The opening act is Marillion.

(April 4)
Rush performs live at Nassau Coliseum, Uniondale, New York, US. The opening act is Marillion.

(April 13)
Rush performs live at Broome County Arena, Binghamton, New York, US. The opening act is Blue Öyster Cult.

(April 14 & 16)
Rush performs live at The Spectrum, Philadelphia, Pennsylvania, US. The opening act is Blue Öyster Cult.

(April 17)
Rush performs live at Baltimore Civic Center, Baltimore, Maryland, US.

(April 19)
Rush performs live at Hampton Coliseum, Hampton, Virginia, US. The opening act is Blue Öyster Cult.

(April 20)
Rush performs live at Charlotte Coliseum, Charlotte, North Carolina, US. The opening act is Blue Öyster Cult.

(April 22)
Rush performs live at Greensboro Coliseum, Greensboro, North Carolina, US. The opening act is Blue Öyster Cult.

(April 23)
Rush performs live at Augusta Civic Center, Augusta, Georgia, US. The opening act is Blue Öyster Cult.

Note: there is some speculation as to whether *Rush* might have actually played in Greenville, North Carolina, US, on this date.

(April 25)
Rush performs live at The Omni, Atlanta, Georgia, US. The opening act is Blue Öyster Cult.

(April 26)
Rush performs live at Jefferson Civic Center, Birmingham, Alabama, US. The opening act is Blue Öyster Cult.

(April 28)
Rush performs live at The Arena, St. Louis, Missouri, US.

(April 29)
Rush performs live at Kemper Arena, Kansas City, Missouri, US. The opening act is Blue Öyster Cult.

(May 1)
Rush performs live at The Myriad, Oklahoma City, Oklahoma, US. The opening act is Blue Öyster Cult.

(May 2)
Rush performs live at Kansas Coliseum, Wichita, Kansas, US. The opening act is Blue Öyster Cult.

(May 11)
Rush is scheduled to perform live at in Winnipeg, Manitoba, Canada. The show is cancelled.

(May 12)
Rush performs live at Salt Palace Center, Salt Lake City, Utah, US. The opening act is The Fabulous Thunderbirds.

(May 14)
Rush is scheduled to perform live at Northlands Coliseum, Edmonton, Alberta, Canada, but the show is cancelled due to a blizzard in Calgary stranding the band's equipment trucks in Calgary. Of note, this concert appears to have originally been scheduled for May 15th, according to print ads with that date.

(May 15)
Rush performs live at The Olympic Saddledome, Calgary, Alberta, Canada. The opening act is Kick Axe.

(May 17)
Rush performs live at Pacific Coliseum, Vancouver, British Columbia, Canada. The opening act is Kick Axe.

(May 19)
Rush performs live at Memorial Coliseum, Portland, Oregon, US. The opening act is The Fabulous Thunderbirds.

(May 21)
Rush performs live at Seattle Center Coliseum, Seattle, Washington, US. The opening act is The Fabulous Thunderbirds.

(May 24)
Rush performs live at Cal Expo, Sacramento, California, US. The opening act is The Fabulous Thunderbirds.

(May 25 & 26)
Rush performs live at Pacific Amphitheater, Costa Mesa, California, US. The opening act is The Fabulous Thunderbirds.

(Date Unknown)
PolyGram re-issues the following ***Rush*** albums on CD in the US.

Fly By Night (PS 22542) – contains "By-Tor And The Snow Dog (Standard CD Version)"
Caress Of Steel (PS 22543)
2112 (PS 22545)
A Farewell To Kings (PS 22546)
Hemispheres (PS 22547)
Permanent Waves (PS 22548)
Moving Pictures (PS 00048)
Signals (PS 10002)
Grace Under Pressure (PS 18476)

Note: these PolyGram CD editions are mastered at Masterdisk, New York City, New York, US, and it would appear most subsequent CD re-issues employ this mastering until the 1997 Rush Remasters series.

Note: year comes from Discogs.com.

(Summer)
Alex Lifeson also begins working on musical ideas for the next album in advance of the band's formal songwriting sessions, as described in the *Hold Your Fire* tour book, at his home studio, Toronto, Ontario, Canada.

(Early September)
At a lakeside cottage, **Neil Peart** begins writing lyrics in advance of the band's formal songwriting sessions, as described in the *Hold Your Fire* tour book.
"Time Stand Still" – the first song started during this period.
"Second Nature"
"High Water"

Geddy Lee begins working on musical ideas for the next album in advance of the band's formal songwriting sessions, as described in the *Hold Your Fire* tour book, at his home studio, Toronto, Ontario, Canada. **Lee** also catalogues the bands sound check jam sessions from the previous tour and organizes the material for future potential use on the next album.

Note: in a November 1987 interview with *The Buffalo News*, **Neil Peart** says this advance work was two weeks before they started rehearsing together.

(Mid-September)
Neil Peart and **Geddy Lee** meet at **Lee**'s home studio, Toronto, Ontario, Canada, to work on ideas in advance of the band's formal songwriting sessions, as described in the *Hold Your Fire* tour book.
"Mission"
"Open Secrets"
"Turn The Page"

(October)
Rush begins writing and rehearsing for their next album at Elora Sound Studios, Elora, Ontario, Canada (*Hold Your Fire* sessions). **Geddy Lee** presents the band with the organized sound check jam material from the *Power Windows* tour, from which they can cull ideas during these sessions.
"High Water" – in the *Hold Your Fire* tour book, **Neil Peart** describes spending three days on rewrites, only to be dissatisfied and throwing eight pages worth of lyrics away.

(Late October)
Rush takes a break from writing and rehearsing for the next album.

(November)
Rush continues writing and rehearsing for their next album at Elora Sound Studios, Elora, Ontario, Canada (*Hold Your Fire* sessions). In the *Hold Your Fire* tour book, **Neil Peart** says the band has eight songs by this point. They also decided to extend the album length from 40 minutes to 50 minutes and aim for ten songs.

(Late 1986)
Rik Emmett gets the go-ahead to assemble the Canadian Guitar Summit recording for *Guitar Magazine*. He contacts Liona Boyd, Ed Bickerton and **Alex Lifeson** to work on the project. Emmett sends them a home demo recording of his basic idea.
"In The Mood (1986 12" Remix)" - During a 1990 *Rockline* interview, when asked about the Canadian Guitar Summit project, **Alex Lifeson** and **Geddy Lee** say the call came in when they were in the studio working on a remix apparently for a 12" "In The Mood" single.

> "In The Mood (1986 12" Remix)"
> Written by Geddy Lee
> Appears on: Unreleased
> Nothing is really known about this, or if any such completed mix exists. Alex and Geddy mention the remix for the 12" single in the 1990 Rockline interview, but not such single or mix seems to have surfaced. In the same interview, both men discuss liking playing "In The Mood" live and that it has been in every tour setlist from the start (which is true, in one form or another it has been), so *maybe* they planned to put the song back out there in remix form? But I'm just a guessing. If such a mix exists in the vaults, I'm sure fans would love to hear it.

(December)
Rush continues writing and rehearsing for their next album at Elora Sound Studios, Elora, Ontario, Canada (*Hold Your Fire* sessions). Producer Peter Collins joins these sessions.
"Mission" – lyrics are rewritten during this month.
"Open Secrets" – the chorus undergoes changes.

(December 14)
At the end of the *Hold Your Fire* pre-production sessions, *Rush* works on the following:
"Force Ten" – the last song written for the album, as the in-studio creation. In the *Hold Your Fire* tour book, **Neil Peart** says this song was put together in the last two days of session time. Pye Dubois had sent lyrics (according to *Visions*), from which **Neil** works in assembling the song by adding the verses. *Visions* quotes **Geddy Lee** as saying that it was Peter Collins suggestion to write "one more song."

HOLD YOUR FIRE

1987

(January 5)
Rush begins recording sessions for their twelfth studio album at The Manor, Shipton-on-Cherwell, Oxfordshire, England (*Hold Your Fire* sessions). Produced and arranged by *Rush* and Peter Collins. The band lays down the bed tracks (drums, bass, basic keyboards, guide guitar and guide vocals).
"Mission" – Peter Collins spearheaded the addition of an English band to the arrangement and hired The William Faerey Engineering Brass Band to record their parts for the track at Mirage Studio, Oldham, England. Brass orchestrations arranged and conducted by Andrew Jackman.

Around this time, according to Rik Emmet's description of events in the July issue of *Guitar Player* magazine, he and **Alex Lifeson** had been exchanging tape recording via mail in advance of the **Canadian Guitar Summit** project.

(February 7)
Rush continues their recording sessions at Ridge Farm Studios, Surrey, England. Andy Richards adds additional keyboard work during these sessions. **Alex Lifeson** records guitar overdubs.

Alex Lifeson records guitar parts for the **Canadian Guitar Summit** recording of the following at Metalworks Studios, Mississauga, Ontario, Canada:
"Beyond Borders" – written by Rik Emmett (titled by Liona Boyd) for a *Guitar Player* magazine exclusive, the other artists who appear on the recording are Emmett himself, Boyd and Ed Bickerton.

Note: the **Canadian Guitar Summit** recording date comes from **Alex** in the July *Guitar Player* magazine interview, meaning he must have flown back to Canada during or between *Hold Your Fire* sessions this month. **Alex** is also present for the mixing of the track, which may have occurred during these sessions.

(March 1)
Rush continues their recording sessions at AIR Studios, Montserrat, West Indies.

(Late March to April)
Rush continues their recording sessions at McClear Place Studios, Toronto, Ontario, Canada. At the latter venue, vocals are recorded and the last guitar parts are put down.
"Time Stand Still" – Aimee Mann records her vocal parts
"Prime Mover" - Aimee Mann records her vocal parts
"High Water" – Steve Margoshes' orchestral arrangements are recorded
"Mission" – Steve Margoshes' orchestral arrangements are recorded
"Second Nature" – Steve Margoshes' orchestral arrangements are recorded

(April)
Mercury Records releases the following *Rush* albums on CD in the US.

Rush (822-541-1 M-1)
Fly By Night 822-542-2 M-1) – contains "By-Tor And The Snow Dog (Standard CD Edition)"
Caress Of Steel (822-543-2 M-1)
2112 (822-545-2 M-1)
All The World's A Stage (822 552-2 M-1) – omits "What You're Doing"
A Farewell To Kings (822 546-2 M-1)
Hemispheres (822 547-2 M-1)
Permanent Waves (822 548-2 M-1)
Moving Pictures (800 048-2)
Exit...Stage Left (822 551-2 M-1) – omits "A Passage To Bangkok"
Signals (810 002-2 M-1)
Grace Under Pressure (818 476-2)

Note: year comes from Discogs.com, though the variations in catalogue numbers suggest different batches on different release dates, particularly for *Moving Pictures* and *Signals*.

(April 24)
Rush finishes their recording sessions for *Hold Your Fire* at McClear Place Studios, Toronto, Ontario, Canada.

(May)
This month's issue of *Modern Drummer* includes the "Pieces Of Eight" Flexi disc single by **Neil Peart**.

"Pieces Of Eight" 4:51
Written by Neil Peart

Appears on: Modern Drummer (May 1987) Flexi disc single, Anatomy Of A Drum Solo DVD
This drum piece will sound familiar to fans, as it features in Neil's live drum solos. It's nearly 5 minutes of drumming excellence, with standard drums and synth drum pads. You'll hear some bits and pieces (no pun intended) not heard in the live performances, too.

(May 7)
Rush begins mixing sessions at Studio Guillaume Tell, Paris, France.

(June)
Neil Peart takes a ten-day cycling & train trip across the Pyrenees, Spain. He later writes a privately published travelogue about the journey, titled: *Pedals Over The Pyrenees (or: Spain and Spokes and Trains)*.

(July)
This month's issue of *Guitar Player* magazine includes an exclusive Flexi disc single, "Beyond Borders" by the **Canadian Guitar Summit** featuring **Alex Lifeson**.

Flexi disc 7" one-side single (July 1989):
"Beyond Borders"

> "Beyond Borders" 6:03
> Written by Rik Emmett
> Appears on: Guitar Player July 1989 Flexi disc single
> Made up entirely of Lifeson, Boyd, Bickerton and Emmett's guitar playing (no drums or keyboards, etc.), this piece shifts moods and showcases each player both individually and together. It's a bit on the experimental side, but certainly adventurous and listenable. It doesn't really rock out much, except near the beginning. Alex's parts are identifiable by the thick, smoky sound complimenting Liona's classical guitar playing. Some great stuff!

(Mid-July)
Geddy Lee and engineer Bob Ludwig master *Hold Your Fire* at Masterdisk, New York City, New York, US.

(September 8)
Rush releases their album *Hold Your Fire* on Anthem Records (Canada) and Mercury Records (US & Europe). Track listing as follows:

"Force Ten"
"Time Stand Still"
"Open Secrets"
"Second Nature"
"Prime Mover"
"Lock And Key"
"Mission"
"Turn The Page"
"Tai Shan"
"High Water"

(October)
Geddy Lee records vocals for the track "Look!...Here Comes The (Fat) Uncle" on this album *From Ship To Shore* by Klezmer orchestra Finjan, in Winnipeg, Manitoba, Canada. Produced and co-written by Ben Mink (Mendelson Joe is also a co-writer of this track).

(October 29 & 30)
Rush performs live at Memorial Stadium, St. John's, Newfoundland, Canada. The opening act is Chalk Circle.

Note: A March 1989 *Keyboard* magazine article claims the band recorded 20 shows on this tour in an effort to capture high quality performances for their next live album.

(October 31)
Rush releases their "Time Stand Still" singles in North America, the UK, Europe and Australasia.

Canada 7" single (ANS-075):
"Time Stand Still"
"High Water"

Canada 12" promo single (SPE-037):
"Time Stand Still"
"Time Stand Still"

Canada 7" promo single (SPE-038):

"Time Stand Still (DJ Edit)"
"Time Stand Still (DJ Edit)"

US 7" single (888-891-7):
"Time Stand Still"
"High Water"

US 7" promo single (888-891-7 DJ):
"Time Stand Still"
"Time Stand Still (DJ Edit)"

US CD promo single (CDP 05):
"Time Stand Still"
"Time Stand Still (DJ Edit)"

UK & Europe 7" single (silver) (RUSH 13)/(888-941-1):
"Time Stand Still"
"Force Ten"

UK & Europe 7" single (tan) (RUSH 13)/(888-941-1):
"Time Stand Still"
"Force Ten"

UK 7" Die Cut sleeve single (RUSHD 13):
"Time Stand Still"
"Force Ten"

UK 7" promo single (RUSH 13 DJ):
"Time Stand Still (DJ Edit)"
"Force Ten"

UK & Europe 12" single (RUSH 13 12)/(888-941-1):
"Time Stand Still"
"Force Ten"
"The Enemy Within (Grace Under Pressure Tour - Single Version)"
"Witch Hunt (Grace Under Pressure Tour - Single Version)"

UK (?) & Europe 12" Picture Disc single (RUSHP 13 12):
"Time Stand Still"
"Force Ten"
"The Enemy Within (Grace Under Pressure Tour - Single Version)"

UK 12" single (RUSH 13 12 DJ):
"Time Stand Still"
"Force Ten"
"The Enemy Within (Grace Under Pressure Tour - Single Version)"
"Witch Hunt (Grace Under Pressure Tour - Single Version)"

UK (?) & Europe CD single (RUSCD 13):
 "Time Stand Still"
"Force Ten"
"The Enemy Within (Grace Under Pressure Tour - Single Version)"
"Witch Hunt (Grace Under Pressure Tour - Single Version)"

Australasia 7" single (888-891-7):
"Time Stand Still"
"High Water"

> "Time Stand Still (DJ Edit)" 4:40
> Written by Neil Peart (words), Geddy Lee & Alex Lifeson (music)
> Appears on: Canada 7" promo single, US 7" promo single, US CD promo single, UK 7" promo single
> This edit removes about 20 seconds of instrumental bits throughout, similar to the other single edits. This is sometimes referred to as the "Video Edit," which is curious because the song's video features the full, uncut track. The North American singles list it as the "Edited Version."

(November 1)
Rush performs live at Centre 200, Sydney, Nova Scotia, Canada. The opening act is Chalk Circle.

(November 2)

Rush performs live at Metro Centre, Halifax, Nova Scotia, Canada. The opening act is Chalk Circle.

(November 4)
Rush performs live at Moncton Coliseum, Moncton, New Brunswick, Canada. The opening act is Chalk Circle.

(November 6 & 7)
Rush performs live at Civic Center, Providence, Rhode Island, US.

(November 9)
Rush performs live at Civic Center, Springfield, Massachusetts, US.

(November 10)
Rush performs live at Memorial Auditorium, Utica, New York, US. The opening act is McAuley Schenker Group.

(November 12)
Rush performs live at RPI Fieldhouse. Troy, New York, US. The opening act is McAuley Schenker Group.

(November 13)
Rush performs live at Broome County Arena, Binghamton, New York, US. The opening act is McAuley Schenker Group.

(November 14)
Rush performs live at Memorial Auditorium, Buffalo, New York, US.

(November 16)
Rush performs live at Hartford Civic Center, Hartford, Connecticut, US. The opening act is McAuley Schenker Group. It's unclear if this concert went ahead or was cancelled.

(Date Unknown)
Alex Lifeson records guitar for the track "Hands Of Man," for the forthcoming Olympic compilation *The Big Picture - Dream On The Horizon (A Tribute To The Olympic Spirit)*. Also on the track is Joel Wade, Rik Emmett and Liona Boyd.

(November 25)
Rush performs live at The Omni, Atlanta, Georgia, US. The opening act is McAuley Schenker Group.

(November 27)
Rush performs live at Charlotte Coliseum, Charlotte, North Carolina, US. The opening act is McAuley Schenker Group.

(November 28)
Rush is scheduled to perform at Hampton Coliseum, Hampton, Virginia, US, but is postponed to January 14, 1988, due to **Geddy Lee** being ill.

(November 30)
Rush performs live at Capital Centre, Largo, Maryland, US. The opening act is McAuley Schenker Group.

(December 2 & 3)
Rush performs live at The Centrum, Worcester, Massachusetts, US. The opening act is Tommy Shaw.

(December 5)
Rush performs live at Veterans Coliseum. New Haven, Connecticut, US. The opening act is Tommy Shaw. Footage of "Lock And Key" is filmed during this show and later used in the promo video.

(December 6)
Rush is scheduled to perform at Brendan Byrne Arena, East Rutherford, New Jersey, US, but the show is moved to December 7th to accommodate a concert by Frank Sinatra this evening.

(December 7)
Rush performs live at Brendan Byrne Arena, East Rutherford, New Jersey, US. The opening act is Tommy Shaw.

(December 9)
Rush performs live at Nassau Coliseum, Uniondale, New York, US. The opening act is Tommy Shaw.

(December 11)
Rush performs live at Madison Square Garden, New York, New York, US. The opening act is Tommy Shaw.

(December 13 & 14)
Rush performs live at The Spectrum, Philadelphia, Pennsylvania, US. The opening act is Tommy Shaw.

(December 16)
Rush performs live at Civic Arena, Pittsburgh, Pennsylvania, US.

(December 17)
Rush performs live at Richfield Coliseum, Richfield, Ohio, US. The opening act is Tommy Shaw.

A SHOW OF HANDS

1988

(Early 1988)
Chartwell Records Ltd. releases *The Big Picture - Dream On The Horizon (A Tribute To The Olympic Spirit)*, featuring "Hands Of Man" with **Alex Lifeson**.

(January 14)
Rush performs live at Hampton Coliseum, Hampton, Virginia, US. The opening act is Tommy Shaw.

(January 15)
Rush performs live at Reynolds Coliseum, Raleigh, North Carolina, US. The opening act is Tommy Shaw.

(January 17)
Rush performs live at Birmingham-Jefferson Civic Center, Birmingham, Alabama, US. The opening act is Tommy Shaw.

(January 18)
Rush performs live at Mississippi Coliseum, Jackson, Mississippi, US. The opening act is Tommy Shaw.

(January 19)
Rush (maybe) performs live at Reunion Arena, Dallas, Texas, US. The opening act is Tommy Shaw. An eyewitness account says the show was at a late stage rescheduled to the following night, January 20th, and that the band only performed once in Dallas on this tour.

(January 20)
Rush (maybe) performs live at Reunion Arena, Dallas, Texas, US. The opening act is Tommy Shaw.

(January 21)
Rush performs live at Convention Center Arena, San Antonio, Texas

(January 23)
Rush performs live at The Myriad, Oklahoma City, Oklahoma

(January 24)
Rush performs live at Hirsch Memorial Coliseum, Shreveport, Louisiana

(January 25)
Rush performs live at Barton Coliseum. Little Rock, Arkansas, US.

(January 26)
Rush performs live at Barton Coliseum. Little Rock, Arkansas, US. The opening act is Tommy Shaw.

(January 27)
Rush performs live at Lakefront Arena, New Orleans, Louisiana, US. The show is recorded and the following track appears in the live album *A Show of Hands*:

"Turn The Page"

(January 29)
Rush performs live at The Summit, Houston, Texas, US. The opening act is Tommy Shaw.

(January 30)
Rush performs live at Erwin Special Events Center, Austin, Texas, US. The opening act is Tommy Shaw.

(February)
Old Gold releases "The Spirit Of Radio" 7" single in the UK.

UK 7" single:
"The Spirit Of Radio (US Single Edit)"
"Closer To The Heart"

(February 1)
Rush performs live at Veterans Memorial Coliseum, Phoenix, Arizona, US. The show is recorded and the following track appears in the live album *A Show of Hands*:

"Manhattan Project"

"Force Ten"

> "Force Ten (ASOH – LP Version)" 4:57
> Written by Neil Peart & Pye Dubois (words), Geddy Lee & Alex Lifeson (music)
> Appears on: A Show Of Hands LP & cassette
> For the vinyl and cassette releases of A Show Of Hands album, both media still had 'sides' to consider, so where the CD could run uninterrupted from start to finish, these could not. "Force Ten," which starts Side Four, fades in at the beginning over the crowd noise before continuing normally.

> "Force Ten (ASOH – Single Version)" 4:58
> Written by Neil Peart & Pye Dubois (words), Geddy Lee & Alex Lifeson (music)
> Appears on: Canada "Show Don't Tell" cassette single
> Starting similarly to the LP Version, this cut fades out over the crowd noise at the end, making for a good standalone version of the song.

(February 3)
Rush performs live at Sports Arena, San Diego, California, US. The opening act is Tommy Shaw The show is recorded and the following track appears in the live album *A Show of Hands*:

"Mission"

> "Mission (ASOH – LP Version)" 5:59
> Written by Neil Peart (words), Geddy Lee & Alex Lifeson (music)
> Appears on: A Show Of Hands LP & cassette
> For the vinyl and cassette releases of A Show Of Hands album, both media still had 'sides' to consider, so where the CD could run uninterrupted from start to finish, these could not. "Mission," which ends Side Two, actually starts with the song's intro by Geddy, according to the track time on the label. This differs from the CD (though there is no audible difference), which separates the tracks and has that intro at the end of "Manhattan Project." The track ends with a fade out over the crowd noise.

> "Mission (ASOH – Single Version)" 5:44
> Written by Neil Peart (words), Geddy Lee & Alex Lifeson (music)
> Appears on: Canada 12" Promo single
> Beginning with a fade in (no intro by Geddy), this track continues identically to A Show Of Hands and closes with a fade out over the crowd noise.

(February 4 & 5)
Rush performs live at Great Western Forum, Los Angeles, California, US. The opening act is Tommy Shaw. In a January 1989 *Music Express* article, Alex Lifeson says these shows were recorded, but the sound quality between dates was not consistent, so they were not used for *A Show Of Hands*.

(February 13)
Rush is scheduled to perform live at Hollywood Sportatorium, Hollywood, Florida, US, but is the show date is later moved to the 16th.

Alex Lifeson performs "Hands Of Man" with Liona Boyd and Rik Emmett at the XV Olympic Winter Games Opening Ceremonies, Olympic Saddledome, Calgary, Alberta, Canada.

(February 15)
Rush performs live at Civic Center, Lakeland, Florida, US. The opening act is Tommy Shaw.

(February 16)
Rush is scheduled to perform live at Bayfront Centre, St. Petersburg, Florida, US, but due to poor ticket sales, this show is cancelled.

Rush performs live at Hollywood Sportatorium, Hollywood, Florida, US. The opening act is Tommy Shaw. This concert replaces the Hollywood show originally scheduled for the 13th.

(February 18)
Rush performs live at Memorial Coliseum, Jacksonville, Florida, US.

(February 19)
Rush performs live at Civic Center, Pensacola, Florida, US. The opening act is Tommy Shaw.

(February 21)
Rush performs live at Mid-South Coliseum, Memphis, Tennessee, US. The opening act is Tommy Shaw.

(February 22)
Rush performs live at Municipal Auditorium, Nashville, Tennessee, US.

(February 23 & 24 [possibly])
Rush performs live at Riverfront Coliseum, Cincinnati, Ohio, US. The opening act is Tommy Shaw.

(February 25 & 26)
Rush performs live at Rosemont Horizon, Rosemont, Illinois, US. The opening act is Tommy Shaw.

(February 28)
Rush performs live at Civic Center, Peoria, Illinois, US. The opening act is Tommy Shaw.

(March)
In advance of the UK tour, *Rush* releases their "Prime Mover" singles in the UK and Europe.
As with the print ads for those shows (which advertise the singles), some of the singles sleeves advertise the UK tour dates, as well.

UK & Europe 7" single (RUSH 14)/(870-108-7):
"Prime Mover"
"Tai Shan"

UK & Europe 7" white vinyl single (RUSHR 14)/(870-131-7):
"Prime Mover"
"Distant Early Warning (Grace Under Pressure Tour – Single Version)"

UK 7" promo single (RUSDJ 14):
"Prime Mover"
"Tai Shan"

UK 12" single (RUSH 14 12):
"Prime Mover"
"Open Secrets"
"Tai Shan"

UK 12" single (RUSHR 14 12):
"Prime Mover"
"Tai Shan"
"Distant Early Warning (Grace Under Pressure Tour – Single Version)"
"New World Man (Grace Under Pressure Tour – Single Version)"

UK CD single (RUSCD 14):
"Prime Mover"
"Tai Shan"
"Distant Early Warning (Grace Under Pressure Tour – Single Version)"
"New World Man (Grace Under Pressure Tour – Single Version)"

(March 1)
Rush performs live at The Arena, St. Louis, Missouri, US. The opening act is Tommy Shaw.

(March 2)
Rush performs live at Market Square Arena, Indianapolis, Indiana, US. The opening act is Tommy Shaw.

(March 4 & 5)
Rush performs live at Joe Louis Arena, Detroit, Michigan, US. The opening act is Tommy Shaw.

(March 7 & 8)
Rush performs live at Maple Leaf Gardens, Toronto, Ontario, Canada. The opening act is Chalk Circle.

Note: an article in *Now* magazine about these shows notes that *Rush* plans to record their forthcoming England dates.

(March 10)
Rush performs live at The Forum, Montreal, Quebec, Canada. The opening act is Chalk Circle.

(March 11)
Rush performs live at Colisée de Québec, Quebec City, Quebec, Canada. The opening act is Chalk Circle.

(April 2)
Rush performs live at Civic Auditorium Arena, Omaha, Nebraska, US. The opening act is The Rainmakers.

(April 4)
Rush performs live at Met Center, Bloomington, Minnesota, US. The opening act is The Rainmakers.

(April 5)
Rush performs live at Mecca Arena, Milwaukee, Wisconsin, US. The opening act is The Rainmakers.

(April 7)
Rush performs live at Kemper Arena, Kansas City, Missouri, US. The opening act is The Rainmakers.

(April 9)
Rush performs live at Louisville Gardens, Louisville, Kentucky, US.

(April 10)
Rush performs live at Hara Arena, Dayton, Ohio, US.

(April 21, 23 & 24)
Rush performs live at National Exhibition Centre, Birmingham, England. The 21st is recorded as test footage, according to **Alex Lifeson** (*Music Express* Jan. 1989) The 23rd & 24th dates make up the bulk of the *A Show of Hands* live album and all of the concert film. The following tracks are released individually:

"The Big Money (ASOH - Icon 2 Version)" 6:00
Written by Neil Peart (words), Geddy Lee & Alex Lifeson (music)
Appears on: Icon 2
Same as the album version, but this cut fades out over the crowd noise at the end.

"Marathon (ASOH – LP Version)" 6:43
Written by Neil Peart (words), Geddy Lee & Alex Lifeson (music)
Appears on: A Show Of Hands LP & cassette
For the vinyl and cassette releases of A Show Of Hands album, both media still had 'sides' to consider, so where the CD could run uninterrupted from start to finish, these could not. "Marathon," which ends Side One, fades out over the crowd noise at the end, similar to the Single Version."

"Marathon (ASOH – Single Version)" 6:32
Written by Neil Peart (words), Geddy Lee & Alex Lifeson (music)
Appears on: Canada 12" single, US CD promo single
This version is the same as the album version, starting with the music, though ends with a fade out over the crowd at the end.

"Marathon (ASOH – Video Edit)" 5:52
Written by Neil Peart (words), Geddy Lee & Alex Lifeson (music)
Appears on: N/A
The video promoting the live album and "Marathon" single pares down the musical interlude and Alex's guitar solo in the middle.

"Turn The Page (ASOH – LP Version)" 4:46
Written by Neil Peart (words), Geddy Lee & Alex Lifeson (music)
Appears on: A Show Of Hands LP & cassette
For the vinyl and cassette releases of A Show Of Hands album, both media still had 'sides' to consider, so where the CD could run uninterrupted from start to finish, these could not. "Turn The Page," which starts Side Two," fades in over the crowd noise and then continues normally.

"Closer To The Heart (ASOH – Single Version)" 4:53
Written by Neil Peart & Peter Talbot (words), Geddy Lee & Alex Lifeson (music)
Appears on: Canada 7" single
Ever slightly different from the way it appears on the album, the single fades quickly on the crowd noise at the start and fades out the same as the album.

"Time Stand Still (ASOH - Icon 2 Version)" 5:14
Written by Neil Peart (words), Geddy Lee & Alex Lifeson (music)
Appears on: Icon 2
Same as the album version, but this cut fades in quickly over the crowd at the beginning before the bass drum count-in and faded out over the crowd noise at the end.

"Distant Early Warning (ASOH – LP Version)" 5:22
Written by Neil Peart (words), Geddy Lee & Alex Lifeson (music)
Appears on: A Show Of Hands LP & cassette
For the vinyl and cassette releases of A Show Of Hands album, both media still had 'sides' to consider, so where the CD could run uninterrupted from start to finish, these could not. "Distant Early Warning," which begins Side Three, fades in over the crowd noise, which actually adds about 9 audible (and listed) seconds to the track.

"Lock And Key (ASOH - US Laserdisc Exclusive)" 6:13
Written by Neil Peart (words), Geddy Lee & Alex Lifeson (music)
Appears on: A Show Of Hands (US 1st Pressing Laserdisc Edition), R40
On the Laserdisc, this song appears between "Force Ten" and "Mission." It starts with a clip from the 1932 film "The Last Mile" (some footage also appears in the song's video). The film looks at death row prisoners, which befits the themes in the song. The performance of the song itself is pretty good and is worth seeking out.

"Lock And Key (ASOH – R40 Version)" 5:24
Written by Neil Peart (words), Geddy Lee & Alex Lifeson (music)
Appears on: R40
The version which appears on the R40 boxed set does not include "The Last Mile" footage preceding the song, which *does* appear on the 1st Pressing Laserdisc Edition, so while it's nice to get the song itself, viewers don't get the full experience.

"The Rhythm Method (ASOH – LP Version)" 4:40
Written by Neil Peart (words), Geddy Lee & Alex Lifeson (music)
Appears on: A Show Of Hands LP & cassette
For the vinyl and cassette releases of A Show Of Hands album, both media still had 'sides' to consider, so where the CD could run uninterrupted from start to finish, these could not. Neil's drum solo ends Side Three, fading out over the crowd noise

"The Rhythm Method (ASOH – Video Version)" 3:41
Written by Neil Peart (words), Geddy Lee & Alex Lifeson (music)
Appears on: A Show Of Hands VHS, Laserdisc & DVD
The concert film edits Neil's drum solo, removing the portion following the bit with the horn samples, so the on the video the horns appear to end the solo, whereas the album version continues onto into a future-y sounding section to end it off.

"The Rhythm Method (ASOH – AOADS Version)" 3:32
Written by Neil Peart (words), Geddy Lee & Alex Lifeson (music)
Appears on: Anatomy Of A Drum Solo DVD
This version is slightly shorter, fading in and out at the beginning and end.

"The Spirit Of Radio (ASOH - Replay GUP Tour Best Buy CD Version)" 5:00
Written by Neil Peart (words), Geddy Lee & Alex Lifeson (music)
Appears on: Rush – Replay (DVD+CD Best Buy Edition)
The Best Buy edition of the Replay DVD+CD boxed set featured 4 unadvertised bonus tracks added to the Grace Under Pressure Tour CD. These tracks come from the other two concert videos, Exit...Stage Left and A Show Of Hands. "The Spirit Of Radio" and "Tom Sawyer" come from the ASOH film and as neither appear the album, feel free to add them to your ASOH playlist. This version starts with the music and fades out at the end.

"Tom Sawyer (ASOH - Replay GUP Tour Best Buy CD Version)" 5:00
Written by Neil Peart & Pye Dubois (words), Geddy Lee & Alex Lifeson (music)
Appears on: Rush – Replay (DVD+CD Best Buy Edition)
The Best Buy edition of the Replay DVD+CD boxed set featured 4 unadvertised bonus tracks added to the Grace Under Pressure Tour CD. These tracks come from the other two concert videos, Exit...Stage Left and A Show Of Hands. "The Spirit Of Radio" and "Tom Sawyer" come from the ASOH film and as neither appear the album, feel free to add them to your ASOH playlist. This version starts with the music and fades out at the end.

Note: Print ads for the UK tour dates include promotion for the "Prime Mover" 12" 3D effect sleeve single and 7" white vinyl single.

(April 26)
Rush performs live at Scottish Exhibition Centre, Glasgow, Scotland.

(April 28, 29 & 30)
Rush performs live at Wembley Arena, London, England.

(Date Unknown)
Vertigo Records releases *Rush*'s "The Big Money" CDV single in the UK and Europe.

CDV single (080-084-2):
"The Big Money"
"Red Sector A (Grace Under Pressure Tour – Single Version)"
"Marathon"
CD-ROM "Marathon" (Full Video) - this is the rare complete video

(May 2)
Rush performs live at Ahoy Sportpaleis, Rotterdam, Holland.

(May 4)
Rush performs live at Festhalle, Frankfurt, Germany. The opening act is Wishbone Ash.

(May 5)
Rush performs live at Hanns Martin Schleyer Halle, Stuttgart, Germany. The opening act is Wishbone Ash.

(Mid-May to June)
In a June 8 published interview with *The Stars And Strips*, **Alex Lifeson** says that after they finish the German tour dates, they are scheduled to work on assembling the next live album (what will become *A Show Of Hands*). According to a *Music Express* 1989 interview with **Alex**, Mercury Records required them to release either a 'Greatest Hits' collection or a live album. This release would also me their last original release on the Mercury label. **Neil Peart** later tells the *Backstage Club* newsletter this year that the intent is to focus on songs which hadn't previously appeared on the other two live albums and to keep the content to a single CD. Mixing sessions for the live album take place a week later at McClear Place Studios, Toronto, Ontario, Canada. In a *Music Express* article (January 1989), **Lifeson** says the session finished in June. A February 1989 *Toronto Star* article with **Geddy Lee** says the sessions took six weeks.
Presto - **Geddy** says in a December 1989 *Rockline* interview that *A Show Of Hands* was very nearly called *Presto*.

(Summer)
The mastering of *A Show Of Hands* takes place at Gateway Mastering Studios, Portland, Maine, US, by Bob Ludwig and Brian Lee.

Note: for the rest of the year, according to **Neil Peart** in the *Presto* tour book, the band takes a well-deserved break after working on the live album. **Alex Lifeson**, in *Music Express* (January 1989) says the band was "tired and disillusioned" following the completion of the live album, which led to the six month break. **Peart** says in a Jan. 1989 *Toronto Star* interview that the band left its future "open-ended" at this point, as there were no record company obligations after *A Show Of Hands*' completion.

(Date Unknown)
Finjan releases its album *From Ship To Shore* on Fat Uncle Records, featuring **Geddy Lee** on the track "Look! Here Comes The (Fat) Uncle."

> "Look! Here Comes The (Fat) Uncle" 3:50
> Written by Ben Mink, Jack Soberman & Mendelson Joe
> Appears on: From Ship To Shore
> I haven't heard this piece, but 2112.net reports that Lee's involvement has him in a talking role, rather than singing, on this track.

(August)
A weather report in one evening inspired **Neil Peart** to later write the following at his home in Wentworth-Nord, Quebec, Canada:
"Chain Lightning" - the report separately discusses the weather phenomena "sun dogs" and a forthcoming meteor shower, which **Neil** witnesses with his daughter, Selena.

Note: date comes from *Canadian Geographic* January, 2006.

(Date Unknown)
Alex Lifeson produces the band Clean Slate. He is also re-mix engineer for their self-titled mini-LP.

(Date Unknown)
Geddy Lee records his vocal parts on "Who's Missing Who," for Climb's album *Take A Chance*, at High Five Studio, Miami, Florida, US.

(September)
In the *Rush Backstage Club* newsletter this month, **Neil Peart** announces that the *A Show Of Hands* live album is complete. He also notes that **Geddy Lee** is working on the accompanying concert film.

(Dates Unknown)
Neil Peart takes cycling tours of Togo, Ghana and the Ivory Coast during the six month break from *Rush*.

(Autumn)
Geddy Lee and his family vacation in East Africa.

(Date Unknown)
Clean Slate release their self-titled debut mini-LP, produced and re-mixed by **Alex Lifeson**.

(November)
Neil Peart embarks on a month-long cycling tour of Cameroon and into Chad.
"The Larger Bowl" – during his adventure, **Neil** has a bout of dysentery and in a vivid dream hears a mourn song with this title.

Note: this cycling tour would later be documented in **Peart**'s book *The Masked Rider*.

(November 28)
Climb releases their album *Take A Chance* in Japan, featuring **Geddy Lee** on the track "Who's Miss Who."

> "Who's Missing Who" 4:09
> Written by G. Terry, W. Cromartie, K. Terry
> Appears on: Take A Chance
> Climb was Warren Cromartie's band. Cromartie (the band's drummer) formerly played baseball with the Montreal Expos and Geddy Lee being a huge baseball fan, Warren got to be friends with Rush. He is both thanked in the Signals liner notes and the high school on the blue prints is named after him. Geddy's only line in the song comes around the 34-second mark ("I break out in a cold, cold sweat!"). The song is a typical '80s pop power ballad, and while it's not especially bad, it's not particularly memorable, either.

(Date Unknown)
PolyGram Music Video re-issues **Rush**'s live concert video *Grace Under Pressure Tour* on laserdisc. This edition also features the complete video of "The Big Money."

(Date Unknown)
Rush releases its promo single for the *A Show Of Hands* version of "Marathon" in the US.

US 12" promo single (PRO 689-1)
"Marathon (ASOH – Single Version)"
"Marathon (ASOH – Single Version)"

(December)
According to a January 1989 *Toronto Star* interview, **Neil Peart** begins working on lyric ideas.

(December 7)
A devastating earthquake hits the northern region of Armenia. The plight of those affected by the earthquake prompts charity campaigner Jon Dee to later organise the super-group Rock Aid Armenia. **Neil Peart** is asked to participate in the recording of a cover of Deep Purple's "Smoke On The Water" and agrees.

PRESTO

1989

(January)
In a *Music Express* article published this month, **Alex Lifeson** says he currently works out with former *Rush* drummer **John Rutsey**. In a February *Rockline* interview, **Alex** says he works out with **John** a few times a week at Gold's Gym, Toronto, Ontario, Canada. He also says that he and **Geddy Lee** have, separately, recently been working in their respective home studios on new material, and that **Neil Peart** has similarly been writing some lyrics. **Neil** says in a February *Kerrang* interview that this work took place at his log cabin in the mountains. He also notes that producer Peter Collins has chosen to not work with the band on their next project, citing the recording timeframe and wanting to focus again on bands' singles work instead of albums. **Peart** says in a January interview with *Metal Hammer* for their April 1989 'Fan Mag' supplement, that for the next six months, the band will be writing new material.
"Show Don't Tell" – **Alex** says in a 1996 *Guitar World* interview that he had been working on the basic music prior to the band re-joining for the writing sessions.
"Available Light" – **Geddy** says in an April 1990 *Rockline* interview that **Alex** wrote the music for the music parts which would become the chorus at his home studio during this period.

Note: **Alex Lifeson** later says that during the period of hanging out with **John Rutsey**, **Rutsey** had old tapes of *Rush* recording and that they listened to them around this time (*Rock N' Roll Reporter* February, 1996)

(January 9)
Rush releases their live album *A Show Of Hands* worldwide. It is made up primarily of the April 23 & 24, 1988, Birmingham, England concerts, as well as Phoenix, AZ, New Orleans, LA, and San Diego, CA, 1988 dates and East Rutherford, NJ, from the *Power Windows* tour.

(January 20)
Rush begins writing and rehearsing songs for their thirteenth studio album at Chalet Studio, Pickering, Ontario, Canada. The band records demos of their songs during these sessions.
"Show Don't Tell" – **Geddy Lee**, in *Guitar For The Practicing Musician* magazine (June 1990), says this was the first song he and **Alex Lifeson** write for the album.
"Available Light" - **Geddy Lee** writes musical parts for what will eventually become the verses to this song "in the very early stages" of the writing sessions. **Neil Peart**'s lyrics would come later and both **Alex** and **Geddy**'s parts would be combined "virtually remain[ing] untouched" for the finished song.

In a 1990 interview with *Guitar For A Practicing Musician* magazine, **Alex Lifeson** says there were about four songs lyrically written prior to the star of the sessions.

(Late January)
In a February *Kerrang* interview, **Neil Peart** says work on the new album is in the early stage, but notes that "lyrics and music are buzzing around Toronto."

(February 6)
In a *Rockline* interview on this date, **Geddy Lee** says the band is currently writing material for the next album, which they started "about a week ago" and plan to start recording in June. He also says they are currently talking to producers about working on the next album. When asked about a new record company, **Geddy** says "No comment." Both **Lee** and **Alex Lifeson** they have discussed doing another instrumental piece for the forthcoming album.

(February 21)
Rush releases their live concert *A Show Of Hands* via Anthem/Polgram. It is made up of footage shot during the April 23 & 24, 1988, Birmingham, England, concerts. The track listing and order differ from the earlier album of the same name. There are several editions released:

VHS Edition
- This is the standard version and does NOT include "Lock And Key," nor is it listed on the sleeve.

Laserdisc 1st Pressing (lavender disc label)
- This version feature "Lock And Key."

Laserdisc 2nd Pressing and beyond (white disc label)
- This version does NOT include "Lock And Key," despite being listed on the sleeve. The manufacturer put a sticker on the shrink wrap notifying buyers of the error.

Note: efforts have been made to better track on the second-hand market which laserdisc pressings have "Lock And Key" and which don't, since all the laserdisc sleeves list it. The "lavender label" clue seems to be the only reliable method short of watching the laserdisc. Reports of a UK pressing with the catalogue number CDV 082 575-1 which contains "Lock And Key" have surfaced, but I cannot confirm nor deny their accuracy. The best method in determining the laserdisc's contents would be to play it and see if the song is actually on it.

(Early 1989)
Rush signs with Atlantic Records as their new international record company. Anthem Records remains their record company in Canada.

(Dates Unknown)
Anthem Records re-issues the following **Rush** albums on CD in Canada:

Rush (ANC-1-1001)
Fly By Night (ANC-1-1002) – contains "By-Tor And The Snow Dog (Standard CD Version)"
Caress Of Steel (ANC-1-1003)
2112 (ANC-1-1004)
All The World's A Stage (ANC-2-1005) – omits "What You're Doing"
A Farewell To Kings (ANC-1-1010)
Hemispheres (ANC-1-1014)
Permanent Waves (ANC-1-1021)
Moving Pictures (ANC-1-1030)
Exit...Stage Left (ANC-1-1035) – omits "A Passage To Bangkok"
Signals (ANC-1-1038)
Grace Under Pressure (ANC-1-1045)

Note: The catalogue numbers starting with ANC were used by Anthem Records while distributing through Capitol-EMI until October 1989, placing these re-issues this year.

(Spring)
Rush brings producer Rupert Hine on board for their next album. In the *Presto* tour book, **Neil Peart** says they had demos of songs recorded at this point. **Alex Lifeson** notes in a 1989 *Kerrang* interview that Hine had just completed work with Stevie Nicks (on her *Other Side Of The Mirror*), which places his arrival around this time.
"Scars" – in a 1989 *Modern Drummer* interview, **Peart** says this is one of the demos played for Hine.

(Date Unknown)
Rush releases its promo single for "Mission" in Canada.

Canada 12" promo single (SPE 050):
"Mission (ASOH – Single Version)"
"Mission (ASOH – Single Version)"

(May 1)
Hal Leonard Publishing Corporation publishes the book+CD set *Standing In The Shadows Of Motown: The Life And Music Of Legendary Bassist James Jamerson*, featuring **Geddy Lee** on the track "Get Ready."

> "Get Ready" 1:12
> Written by N/A ("Get Ready" by Smokey Robinson)
> Appears on: Standing In The Shadows Of Motown: The Life And Music Of Legendary Bassist James Jamerson (Book+CD)
> This book and 2xCD set looks at the bass work of Motown session player James Jamerson. Geddy details the bass line of this Temptations 1966 hit.

(June)
Rush begins recording their thirteenth studio album at Le Studio, Morin Heights, Quebec, Canada (*Presto* sessions). Co-produced and arrangements by Rush and Rupert Hine. Engineered by Stephen W. Tayler.

(July 8)
Neil Peart, having been asked to contribute drum parts to Rock Aid Armenia's "Smoke On The Water" benefit single, in unable to do so as he is working on the new **Rush** album at either Le Studio, Morin Heights, Quebec, or McClear Place Studios, Toronto, Canada (it's unclear which. *Presto* sessions). The first Rock Aid Armenia recording session, at which **Peart** was to record, is scheduled on this date at Metropolis Studios, London, England. Prior to this date, **Neil** informed organizer Jon Dee by faxed letter of his inability to attend.

(August)
Rush completes recording their thirteenth studio album. Since June, sessions took place at Le Studio, Morin Heights, Quebec, and McClear Place Studios, Toronto, Ontario, Canada (*Presto* sessions). According to a December 1989 *Modern Drummer* piece, the drum parts are completed before **Alex Lifeson** begins his guitar overdubs. Producer Rupert Hine contributes additional background vocals and keyboards. Jason Sniderman also provides additional keyboards. **Alex Lifeson** in a November *Kerrang* interview that the band finished work on the album "about three or four week early."

"Hand Over Fist" – In a December 1989 *Rockline* interview, **Geddy Lee** says the planned instrumental (noted in the February *Rockline* interview) was given lyrics when **Neil Peart** had written so much material and the lyrics fit this music.
"Presto" - **Geddy** says in a December 1989 *Rockline* interview that the title of the song coincides with the band deciding to use title for the album (after not using it for *A Show Of Hands*).

In the same *Modern Drummer* piece, **Neil Peart** says he played drums on incidental music written for a soap opera, at the request of the composer, who is a friend of his.
Generations – **Neil**'s description of the soap opera is that it is set in Chicago and the music used old blues patterns, which would certainly fit this series, making it the likely candidate.

(September)
Rush mixes *Presto* at Metropolis Studios, London, England. In an interview with *Kerrang* magazine (November 25, 1989), **Alex Lifeson** says the end of mixing sessions were in the last week of September and it was then when they first discussed touring the album. **Geddy Lee** on *Rockline*, 1992, says the tour was planned to be short due to their weariness of touring by this point.

(September 24)
During their mixing sessions for *Presto*, **Alex Lifeson** is asked by Jon Dee, organizer of Rock Aid Armenia, to contribute guitar work for the benefit single, Metropolis Studios, London, England.
"Smoke On The Water" - Jon Dee describes the sessions' recordings for the single in great detail on the official site RockAidArmenia.com, and **Alex** later discusses his involvement in a 1990 *Rockline* interview. **Alex** is approached as the band is mixing *Presto* in the studio adjacent to the one where Jon Dee and company are working on the Rock Aid Armenia single. **Alex**'s guitar work is the very last thing recorded. It is "guitar underpinnings" rather than being another guitar solo. Geoff Downing is also at the session and both he and **Lifeson** are filmed for the promotion material. Jon Dee also meets **Neil Peart**, who previously wasn't able to work on the single. As Queen's Roger Taylor had already recorded drums for the track, Dee felt there wasn't need for a second drummer.

(Autumn)
Bob Ludwig masters *Presto* at Masterdisk, New York City, New York, US.

(November)
Rush releases their singles for "Show Don't Tell" in North America.

Canada CD promo single (PRO-CD-3):
"Show Don't Tell (Promo Edit)"

Canada cassette single (ANCS-001):
"Show Don't Tell"
"Red Tide"
"Force Ten (ASOH – Single Version)"

US CD promo single (PR-3082-2):
"Show Don't Tell"

> "Show Don't Tell (Promo Edit)" 4:47
> Written by Neil Peart (words), Geddy Lee & Alex Lifeson (music)
> Appears on: Canada CD promo single
> This edit removes the quiet opening percussion, so the track starts with burst of music, which can be startling if you're not expecting it.

Additionally, *Rush* releases their promo singles for "The Pass" in North America.

Canada CD promo single (PRO7):
"Superconductor"

US CD promo single (PRCD 3331-2):
"Superconductor"

This month, **Neil Peart** takes a cycling trip through Togo.
"Heresy" – During the trip, **Peart** hears a drum pattern performed in the distance as he falls asleep and uses it later for this song.

(November 21)
Rush releases their thirteen studio album, *Presto*, in Canada (Anthem Records) and worldwide (Atlantic Records). Track listing as follows:

"Show Don't Tell"
"Chain Lightning"

"The Pass"
"Scars"
"Presto"
"Superconductor"
"Anagram (for Mongo)"
"Red Tide"
"Hand Over Fist"
"Available Light"

(November 25)
In an interview with *Kerrang* magazine published on this date, **Alex Lifeson** discusses the forthcoming Mercury/PolyGram-planned *Rush* compilation *Chronicles*, scheduled for release in the summer of 1990. He says the band has no control over the content and that they've fought with the record company over it. Atlantic Records worked out a deal whereby *Rush* has a say in the packaging and artwork. In the same article, **Alex** says they just shot their promo video for "Show Don't Tell."

(Late 1989)
In a November 1989 interview with *Kerrang* magazine, **Alex Lifeson** says he is vacationing in Papua New Guinea for about three weeks during this time.

(Dates Unknown)
Anthem Records re-issues the following *Rush* albums on CD in Canada:

Rush (WANK 1001)
Fly By Night (WANK-1002) – contains "By-Tor And The Snow Dog (Standard CD Version)"
Caress Of Steel (WANK-1003)
2112 (VANK-1004)
All The World's A Stage (WAGK-1005) – omits "What You're Doing"
A Farewell To Kings (WANK-1010)
Hemispheres (WANK-1014)
Permanent Waves (VANK-1021)
Moving Pictures (VANK-1030)
Exit...Stage Left (WAGK-1035) – omits "A Passage To Bangkok"
Signals (VANK-1038)
Grace Under Pressure (VANK-1045)
Power Windows (VANK-1049)
Hold Your Fire (VANK-1051)

Note: the W and V prefixes from ANK Anthem remastered came into use in October 1989 (until October 1995), when Anthem Records began distribution with CBS/Sony. At the time, CD total runtime lengths were at the 74 minute mark, which forced the exclusions of "What You're Doing" from ATWAS and "A Passage To Bangkok" from ESL. The increase to 80 minutes wouldn't occur until 1990 thereabouts, placing some or all of this series of re-issues around this time.

(December)
Rock Aid Armenia releases "Smoke On The Water" singles for charity in the UK (and some in France and the Netherlands):
7" single & CD single:
"Smoke On The Water (Radio Version)" Rock Aid Armenia
"Paranoid" Black Sabbath

12" single:
"Smoke On The Water (Radio Version)" Rock Aid Armenia
"Paranoid" Black Sabbath

12" single:
"Smoke On The Water (Mega Rock Remix)" Rock Aid Armenia
"Paranoid" Black Sabbath

12" single:
"Smoke On The Water (Mayhem Mix)" Rock Aid Armenia
"Smoke On The Water (Extended Version)" Rock Aid Armenia

> "Smoke On The Water (Radio Mix)" 5:08
> Written by Blackmore/Gillan/Glover/Lord/Paice
> Appears on: UK Smoke On The Water 7" vinyl (1989), UK Smoke On The Water CD single (1989), UK Smoke On The Water '90 Mayhem Mix 12" vinyl, UK Smoke On The Water '90 7" vinyl
> The original Smoke On The Water release was the Radio Mix, found on the 7" vinyl and CD single from 1989. Note that the 2010 re-release lists the 1990 Radio Mix. It is not this mix, but rather it is The Earthquake

Album version. This mix is also labelled as the "original extended version" on the UK/French Smoke On The Water '90 12" vinyl single.

"Smoke On The Water (Extended Mix)" 5:52
Written by Blackmore/Gillan/Glover/Lord/Paice
Appears on: UK Smoke On The Water 12" vinyl (1989), UK Smoke On The Water CD single (1989), UK Smoke On The Water '90 Mayhem Mix 12" vinyl, Smoke On The Water: The Metropolis Sessions
The extended mix of Smoke On the Water first appeared on the 1989 12" vinyl single and on the 1989 CD single. It was later released again in 1990 in various formats as "The Mayhem Mix". It features the chorus repeated a a few times and some additional instrumental bits. Note: this is labelled as the "Original 1989 Mix" on the 2010 re-release.

"Smoke On The Water (Mayhem Mix)" 5:52
Written by Blackmore/Gillan/Glover/Lord/Paice
Appears on: UK Smoke On The Water 12" vinyl (1989), UK Smoke On The Water CD single (1989), UK Smoke On The Water '90 Mayhem Mix 12" vinyl, Smoke On The Water: The Metropolis Sessions
As mentioned in the previous entry, this is a renaming of the original 1989 Extended Mix.

"Smoke On The Water (Mega-Rock Remix)" 6:02
Written by Blackmore/Gillan/Glover/Lord/Paice
Appears on: UK Smoke On The Water Mega-Rock Remix 12" vinyl
The Mega Rock Remix appears only it's own, blue 12" vinyl release. It is very similar to the extended version. This version extends The Earthquake Album version. The intro instrumental is quite a bit longer. There are some other minor mix differences at the beginning.

(December 4)
Geddy Lee appears on the radio call-in show *Rockline*.

CHRONICLES

1990

(January 3)
A *Canadian Press* article published on this date says **Neil Peart** recently climbed Mount Kilimanjaro, Tanzania.

(January 18)
Geddy Lee writes his equipment list profile for the *Presto* tour book.

(Date Unknown)
Rock Aid Armenia releases *The Earthquake Album* in the UK, featuring "Smoke On The Water '90." The compilation also features "The Spirit Of Radio" by **Rush**.

> "Smoke On The Water '90" (a.k.a The Earthquake Album Version, a.k.a. '90 Radio Mix) 4:06
> Written by Blackmore/Gillan/Glover/Lord/Paice
> Appears on: UK The Earthquake Album, UK Smoke On The Water '90 7" vinyl, Netherlands Smoke On The Water '90 7" vinyl, Smoke On The Water: The Metropolis Sessions
> The Earthquake Album version is a remix of the 1989 7" release. It loses the final two verses and some instrumental bits. This is called the 1990 Radio Mix on the 2010 re-release.

(Early 1990)
Rush releases their singles for "The Pass" in North America and Australia.

Canada cassette single (ANCS-002):
"The Pass"
"Presto"

US CD promo single (PR 3165-2):
"The Pass (Promo Edit)"
"The Pass"

US CD promo single (PR 3175-2):
"The Pass"

Australia 7" single (7-87986):
"The Pass"
"Presto"

> "The Pass (Promo Edit)" 4:04
> Written by Neil Peart (words), Geddy Lee & Alex Lifeson (music)
> Appears on: US CD promo single
> I haven't heard this, but it appears nearly 50 seconds have been edited.

Note: some source list this release as November 1989, but the copyright year is 1990 and the CD singles promote the upcoming tour dates, placing more likely around this time.

(February 10)
Neil Peart writes a piece and answers letters for the March *Rush Backstage Club* newsletter. He notes the band has been in rehearsals "for weeks."

(February 15)
Rush rehearses at Memorial Auditorium, Greenville, South Carolina, US.

(February 17)
Rush performs live at Memorial Auditorium, Greenville, South Carolina, US. The opening act is Mr. Big.

(February 19)
Rush performs live at Memorial Coliseum, Jacksonville, Florida, US. The opening act is Mr. Big.

(February 20)
Rush performs live at Bayfront Center, St. Petersburg, Florida, US. The opening act is Mr. Big.

(February 22)
Rush performs live at Miami Arena, Miami, Florida, US. The opening act is Mr. Big.

(February 23)

Rush performs live at Orlando Arena, Orlando, Florida, US. The opening act is Mr. Big.

(February 25)
Rush performs live at Lakefront Arena, New Orleans, Louisiana, US. The opening act is Mr. Big.

(February 26)
Rush performs live at The Summit, Houston, Texas, US. The opening act is Mr. Big.

(February 28)
Rush performs live at Convention Center Arena, San Antonio, Texas, US. The opening act is Mr. Big.

(March 1)
Rush performs live at Reunion Arena, Dallas, Texas, US. The opening act is Mr. Big.

(March 3)
Rush performs live at Kemper Arena, Kansas City, Missouri, US. The opening act is Mr. Big.

(March 5)
Rush performs live at The Arena, St. Louis, Missouri, US. The opening act is Mr. Big.

(March 6)
Rush performs live at Riverfront Coliseum, Cincinnati, Ohio, US. The opening act is Mr. Big.

(March 8 & 9)
Rush performs live at The Palace, Auburn Hills, Michigan, US. The opening act is Mr. Big.

(March 20)
Rush performs live at Northlands Coliseum, Edmonton, Alberta, US. The opening act is Mr. Big.

(March 21)
Rush performs live at Calgary Saddledome, Calgary, Alberta, US. The opening act is Mr. Big.

(March 23)
Rush performs live at Pacific Coliseum, Vancouver, British Columbia, US. The opening act is Mr. Big.

(March 24)
Rush performs live at Memorial Coliseum, Portland, Oregon, US.

(March 26)
Rush performs live at Seattle Center Coliseum, Seattle, Washington, US. The opening act is Mr. Big.

(March 28)
Rush performs live at Arco Arena, Sacramento, California, US. The opening act is Mr. Big.

(March 30)
Rush performs live at Oakland Coliseum, Oakland, California, US. The opening act is Mr. Big.

(March 31)
Oakland Coliseum. Oakland, California, US. The opening act is Mr. Big.

(April 2)
Rush performs live at Great Western Forum, Los Angeles, California, US. The opening act is Mr. Big.

(April 3)
Great Western Forum. Los Angeles, California, US. The opening act is Mr. Big.

(April 5)
Rush performs live at Sports Arena, San Diego, California, US. The opening act is Mr. Big.

(April 7)
Rush performs live at Pacific Amphitheater, Costa Mesa, California, US. The opening act is Mr. Big.

(April 8)
Rush performs live at Veterans Memorial Coliseum, Phoenix, Arizona, US. The opening act is Mr. Big.

(Mid-April)
During a hiatus in the tour, **Geddy Lee** travels back to Toronto, Ontario, Canada. There he catches a cold.

(Date Unknown)

Alex Lifeson records guitar parts for Gowan's album *Lost Brotherhood*. **Lifeson** appears on each track of the album. Sessions take place at either The Metalworks or McClear Place, Toronto, Ontario, Canada.

(April 19)
Rush is scheduled to perform live at War Memorial, Rochester, New York, US, but the show is cancelled due to **Geddy Lee's** cold. It is rescheduled to April 28th.

(April 20)
Rush performs live at Brendan Byrne Arena, East Rutherford, New Jersey, US. The opening act is Mr. Big.

(April 22)
Rush performs live at Nassau Coliseum, Uniondale, New York, US. The opening act is Mr. Big.

(April 24)
Rush performs live at The Spectrum, Philadelphia, Pennsylvania, US. The opening act is Mr. Big.

(April 25)
Rush performs live at Brendan Byrne Arena, East Rutherford, New Jersey, US.

(April 27)
Rush performs live at The Spectrum, Philadelphia, Pennsylvania, US. The opening act is Mr. Big.

(April 28)
Rush performs live at War Memorial, Rochester, New York, US. The opening act is Mr. Big. This show replaces the cancelled show from April 19th.

(April 30)
Geddy Lee and **Alex Lifeson** appear on *Rockline* promoting *Presto*.

(May 1)
Rush performs live at The Omni, Atlanta, Georgia, US. The opening act is Mr. Big.

(May 2)
Rush performs live at Charlotte Coliseum, Charlotte, North Carolina, US. The opening act is Mr. Big.

(May 4)
Rush performs live at Richmond Coliseum, Richmond, Virginia, US. The opening act is Mr. Big.

(May 5)
Rush performs live at Capital Centre, Largo, Maryland, US. The opening act is Mr. Big.

(May 7)
Rush performs live at Civic Center, Providence, Rhode Island, US. The opening act is Mr. Big.

(May 8)
Rush performs live at Hartford Civic Center, Hartford, Connecticut, US. The opening act is Mr. Big.

(May 10 & 11)
Rush performs live at The Centrum, Worcester, Massachusetts, US. The opening act is Mr. Big.

(May 13)
Rush performs live at Colisée de Quebec, Quebec City, Quebec, Canada. The opening act is Chalk Circle.

(May 14)
Rush performs live at The Forum, Montreal, Quebec, Canada. The opening act is Voivod.

(May 16 & 17)
Rush performs live at Maple Leaf Gardens, Toronto, Ontario, Canada. The opening act is Voivod.

(June 1)
Rush is scheduled to perform live at Old Orchard Beach, Maine, US, but the show is cancelled.

(June 2)
Rush performs live at Knickerbocker Arena, Albany, New York, US. The opening act is Mr. Big.

(June 4)
Rush performs live at Baltimore Arena, Baltimore, Maryland, US. The opening act is Mr. Big.

(June 5)

Rush performs live at Hampton Coliseum, Hampton, Virginia, US. The opening act is Mr. Big.

(June 7)
Rush performs live at Civic Arena, Pittsburgh, Pennsylvania, US. The opening act is Mr. Big.

(June 8)
Rush performs live at Richfield Coliseum, Richfield, Ohio, US. The opening act is Mr. Big.

(June 10)
Rush performs live at Blossom Music Center, Cuyahoga Falls, Ohio, US. The opening act is Mr. Big.

(June 11)
Rush performs live at Riverbend Music Center, Cincinnati, Ohio, US. The opening act is Mr. Big.

(June 12)
On his day off between shows **Neil Peart** cycles from Cincinnati to Columbus, Ohio, US.
"Dreamline" - once in Columbus, while watching *Nova*, the documentary inspires some lines he later uses in the song.

(June 13)
The demolition of the Anti-Fascist Protection Rampart (The Berlin Wall) begins between East & West Berlin, Germany.
"Heresy" – The fall of communism during this period and the tearing down of the wall in particular later inspires **Neil Peart** to write the lyrics for this song.

Rush performs live at Cooper Stadium, Columbus, Ohio, US. The opening act is Mr. Big.

(June 14)
Rush performs live at Deercreek Amphitheater, Noblesville, Indiana, US.

(June 16 & 17)
Rush performs live at Alpine Valley Music Theatre, East Troy, Wisconsin, US. The opening act is Mr. Big.

(June 19)
Rush performs live at Met Center, Bloomington, Minnesota, US. The opening act is Mr. Big.

(June 20)
Rush performs live at Civic Auditorium Arena, Omaha, Nebraska, US. The opening act is Mr. Big.

(June 22)
Rush performs live at Fiddler's Green Amphitheatre, Englewood, Colorado, US. The opening act is Mr. Big.

(June 24)
Rush performs live at Salt Palace Center, Salt Lake City, Utah, US. The opening act is Mr. Big.

(June 26)
Rush performs live at Cal Expo. Sacramento, California, US. The opening act is Mr. Big.

(June 27)
Rush performs live at Shoreline Amphitheater, Mountain View, California, US. The opening act is Mr. Big.

(June 29)
Rush performs live at Irvine Meadows Amphitheater, Irvine, California, US. The opening act is Mr. Big.

(Dates Unknown)
Anthem Records re-issues the following *Rush* albums on CD in Canada:

All The World's A Stage (ANK 1005) – restores "What You're Doing"
A Farewell To Kings (ANK-1010)
Hemispheres (ANK-1014)
Permanent Waves (ANK-1021)
Moving Pictures (ANK-1030)
Exit...Stage Left (ANK-1035) – omits "A Passage To Bangkok"
Grace Under Pressure (ANK-1045)
Power Windows (ANK-1049) – contains an error on "Emotion Detector"

> "Emotion Detector (Anthem Error Version)"
> Written by Neil Peart (words), Geddy Lee & Alex Lifeson (music)
> Appears on: Power Windows (ANK-1049)

It's unclear if this error appears on all pressings, a few or whether it was later corrected, but reports of this edition of the album containing a mastering error on this track exist. Apparently, the first note is cut off. Beware!

Note: the restoration of "What You're Doing" would indicate these releases occurred this year, as 80 minute long runtime CDs had begun to expand the medium.

(July 17)
Gowan releases his album *Lost Brotherhood*, featuring **Alex Lifeson** on guitar. Track listing as follows:

"All The Lovers In The World"
"Lost Brotherhood"
"Call It A Mission"
"The Dragon"
"Love Makes You Believe"
"Fire It Up"
"Out Of A Deeper Hunger"
"Tender Young Hero"
"Message From Heaven"
"Holding This Rage"

(Date Unknown)
Neil Peart privately publishes through Pottersfield Press (Canada) and Cumberland Press Ltd (US) his book *The Masked Rider: Cycling In West Africa*, limited to 50 copies made available to friends and family. This first edition is 169 pages.

(September 1 & 2)
Geddy Lee participates in *Music-Tennis*, a doubles tournament involving professional tennis players and musicians.

(September 4)
Anthem Records (Canada) and Mercury Records (US) release the **Rush** compilation *Chronicles* on 2xCD, 2xcassette and 3xLP formats. Track listing as follows:

CD 1 & cassette 1:
"Finding My Way"
"Working Man"
"Fly By Night"
"Anthem"
"Bastille Day"
"Lakeside Park"
"2112: I: Overture/II: The Temples Of Syrinx"
"What You're Doing (ATWAS - Chronicles Version)"
"A Farewell To Kings"
"Closer To The Heart" - LP 1 end
"The Trees" - LP 2 start
"La Villa Strangiato"
"Freewill"
"The Spirit Of Radio"

CD 2 & cassette 2:
"Tom Sawyer"
"Red Barchetta"
"Limelight"
"A Passage To Bangkok (Exit...Stage Left)" - LP 2 end
"Subdivisions" - LP 3 start
"New World Man"
"Distant Early Warning"
"Red Sector A"
"The Big Money"
"Manhattan Project"
"Force Ten"
"Time Stand Still"
"Mystic Rhythms (ASOH Chronicles Version)"
"Show Don't Tell"

The record companies also release a *Chronicles* video compilation on VHS and laserdisc. It comprises most (but not all) of the band's promotion material (aka videos) from 1977 to 1989.

"Closer To The Heart" - Seneca College
"The Trees (Live at the Hammersmith Odeon, 1979)"

"Limelight" – Le Studio
"Tom Sawyer (Exit...Stage Left – Video Version)"
"Red Barchetta (Exit...Stage Left – Video Version)"
"Subdivisions"
"Distant Early Warning"
"Red Sector A (Grace Under Pressure Tour – Video Version)"
"The Big Money" – standard edited version
"Mystic Rhythms"
"Time Stand Still"
"Lock And Key"

(Late Summer)
Neil Peart begins gathering his notes from the previous two years to assemble into lyrics, according to the *Roll The Bones* tour book.
"Dreamline" – in the *Roll The Bones Radio Special*, **Neil** says this was the first song he wrote during these writing sessions, spending three days on it.
"Face Up" – the line "turn it up, or turn that wild card down" **Neil** says started the exploration of the ideas and themes of chance in life.

(October)
Rush starts writing and rehearsing for their next album, at Chalet Studio, Claremount, Ontario, Canada (*Roll The Bones* sessions). In a WNEW 102.7 FM interview, **Geddy Lee** says these pre-production sessions last nine weeks.
"Bravado" – **Geddy Lee** suggests this song came together early in the sessions and was somewhat "spontaneous" (in a *Hit Parade* piece, March 1992). **Alex Lifeson** says on the *Roll The Bones Radio Special* that the guitar solo recorded for the pre-production demo was
"Roll The Bones" - On the *Roll The Bones Radio Special*, **Neil Peart** says he submitted the lyrics without the rap section and after **Geddy** and **Alex** liked those, he presented the rap.
"Where's My Thing? (Part IV, 'Gangster Of Boats' Trilogy)" – **Geddy Lee** says other tracks were developed as the instrumental intended for this album, but each time lyrics would find their why on those tracks. Finally, **Neil Peart** basically said, "No more lyrics until the instrumental is written," resulting in "Where's My Thing?"

(November)
Rush finishes their pre-production writing sessions, at Chalet Studio, Claremount, Ontario, Canada. **Neil Peart** tells *Powerkick* (June 1992) that these sessions finished early, allowing him time to work out his drum parts.

ROLL THE BONES

1991

(Early 1991)
Neil Peart later says he spent "four weeks" learning the drum parts before recording began on the album (*National Midnight Star*, April, 1992). In an October interview (*M.E.A.T.*, March 1992), **Alex Lifeson** says the band went right into the recording sessions rather than take a break. **Neil Peart** notes in the *Roll The Bones* tour book that the band cut its holidays short in order to begin recording.

(February)
Rush begins recording sessions for their fourteenth studio album, at Le Studio, Morin Heights, Quebec, Canada (*Roll The Bones* sessions). Co-produced and arrangements by *Rush* and Rupert Hine. Engineered by Stephan W. Tayler. In a WNEW 102.7 FM interview, **Geddy Lee** says these recording sessions lasted eight weeks. **Geddy** later says the bass and drum tracks were recorded "in four days" (December, 1991, *Guitar For A Practicing Musician*), whereas Alex later says "five days" (*Guitarist*, May, 1992). In an interview published in October (*Guitar Player*), **Geddy** says the guitar parts were recorded "in about eight days." Various interviews note that a good deal of guitar material also came straight from the demos in order to preserve the feel of the initial recording, rather than re-recording those parts at this stage, including:
"Ghost Of A Chance" – like "Bravado," this solo dates from the demo stage.
"Roll The Bones" – cited in the same context as "Bravado" and "Ghost Of A Chance," as examples of one-take and two-take guitar work on the album. In a 1992 *Guitarist* feature, **Alex** says the one-take solo from the demo recording is used in this song.

(March)
Rush finishes recording sessions for their fourteenth studio album, at Le Studio, Morin Heights, Quebec, and McClear Place Studios, Toronto, Ontario, Canada (*Roll The Bones* sessions). By all accounts, the sessions are finished a few months ahead of schedule. Rupert Hine provides additional keyboards and backing vocals.

(April 8)
Neil Peart participates in the *Buddy Rich Memorial Tribute Concert* at The Ritz Theatre, New York City, New York, US, performing on the piece "Cotton Tail."
"Bravado" – both a line from this song (the John Barth-inspired "We shall pay the price..." lyric) and the frustration **Peart** felt about lack of proper rehearsal and his overall performance prompts him to later call Rich's daughter, Cathy Rich, with the intention of organizing what will become the *Burning For Buddy* tribute album.

Neil says in a *Canadian Musician*, 1994, interview that the tribute concert took place at the end of the recording sessions and before the overdub sessions.

(Mid-April)
Rush begins mixing their album at Nomix Studios, London, England. These sessions last three weeks, according to a letter from **Alex Lifeson** to *Guitar For A Practicing Musician* magazine. **Alex** also notes in *Guitarist* magazine (May 1992) that the work in England was this month.
"Roll The Bones" – the band tried different things with the rap section, including female vocals, the idea of getting a real rapper, or John Cleese, but ultimately preferred **Geddy Lee**'s pitched-down vocals. In a December *Rockline* interview, **Neil Peart** says the rap vocals were recorded in England, along with the different experiments for that section.
"You Bet Your Life" – **Geddy** says in a 1992 *Hit Parader* interview that this track was hard to mix, having densely layered choruses.

(May)
Rush completes mixing their album at Nomix Studios, London, England.

Note: the letter from **Alex Lifeson** to *Guitar For A Practicing Musician* magazine says he returned home from England to find the May issue of the magazine waiting for him, placing the letter writing around this time.

(Spring)
Mixing begins for *Rush*'s album, by Bob Ludwig at Masterdisk, New York City, New York, US.

(Mid-June)
An interview with **Geddy Lee** (September, *Bass Player*) says the album is almost finished at this point and remains untitled.
"Where's My Thing? (Part IV, 'Gangster Of Boats' Trilogy)" – **Neil Peart** says in a December *Rockline* interview that "Gangster Of Boats" is what **Geddy** and **Alex** threaten to call the albums if he can't think of a proper title.

(June 18)

Neil Peart writes from Toronto, Ontario, Canada, for the October *Rush Backstage Club* newsletter that the band has just completed their album, titled *Roll The Bones*. In an October 1991 interview published in March 1992 (*M.E.A.T.* magazine), **Alex** confirms the album was completed two months ahead of schedule, moving it's release up from the originally planned January 1992.

(Summer)
Rush releases their promo CD singles for "Dreamline."

Canada CD promo single (PRO8):
"Dreamline"

US CD promo single (PRCD 4120-2):
"Dreamline"

(August 19)
Geddy Lee is interviewed for the *National Midnight Star*.

(August 29)
Alex Lifeson and **Geddy Lee** are interviewed for WNEW 102.7 FM (New York)'s album launch of *Roll The Bones*, at Q107.1 FM studios, Toronto, Ontario, Canada. Interviewer Dan Near notes that "Dreamline" has been getting radio attention lately.

(September)
Rush releases their "Where's My Thing? (Part IV, 'Gangster Of Boats' Trilogy)" single in the US.

US CD promo single (PRCD 4126-2)
"Where's My Thing? (Part IV, 'Gangster Of Boats' Trilogy)"

(September 2)
EastWest Records releases a promo sampler of *Roll The Bones* in the UK.

UK 12" promo sampler (SAM 869):
"Roll The Bones"
"Face Up"
"Dreamline"

(September 3)
Rush releases their album *Roll The Bones* in Canada (Anthem Records) and worldwide (Atlantic Records). Track listing as follows:

"Dreamline"
"Bravado"
"Roll The Bones"
"Face Up"
"Where's My Thing? (Part IV, 'Gangster Of Boats' Trilogy)"
"The Big Wheel"
"Heresy"
"Ghost Of A Chance"
"Neurotica"
"You Bet Your Life"

Around this time, Anthem Records releases the *Roll The Bones Radio Special* to radio stations in Canada to promote the album.

Roll The Bones Radio Special promo CD (PR10):
Track 1: "Roll The Bones Radio Special"
Track 2 – 22: "Interview Responses"

Note: the full Radio Special is an interview with the band by DJ John Derringer discussing the album. It also features tracks from the album. The Interview Responses are excerpts from the interview, basically the answers to Derringer's questions. The CD comes with a list of questions for radio DJs, for which they can play the corresponding answer excerpt on the air.

(September 30)
A *Maclean's* feature on *Rush* published on this date notes that "Dreamline" is the current single.

(Mid-October)
A *Rochester Times-Union* newspaper interview with **Neil Peart** notes *Rush* is currently rehearsing in Toronto, Ontario, Canada, for the upcoming tour.

(October 25)
Rush performs live at Copps Coliseum, Hamilton, Ontario, Canada. The opening act is Andy Curran & Soho 69.

(October 26)
Rush performs live at War Memorial, Rochester, New York, US. The opening act is Eric Johnson.

(October 28)
Rush performs live at Civic Arena, Pittsburgh, Pennsylvania, US. The opening act is Eric Johnson.

(October 29)
Rush performs live at Riverfront Coliseum, Cincinnati, Ohio, US. The opening act is Eric Johnson.

(October 31)
Rush performs live at Market Square Arena, Indianapolis, Indiana, US. The opening act is Eric Johnson.

(Autumn)
Rush releases their "Roll The Bones" singles in North America.

Canada cassette single (ANS 003):
"Roll The Bones"
"Face Up"

US CD promo singe (PRCD 4260-2):
"Roll The Bones"

Note: the US promo single lists the upcoming North American tour dates.

(November 1)
Rush performs live at Rosemont Horizon, Rosemont, Illinois, US. The opening act is Eric Johnson.

(November 3)
Rush performs live at Target Center, Minneapolis, Minnesota, US. The opening act is Eric Johnson.

(November 4)
Rush performs live at Civic Auditorium Arena, Omaha, Nebraska, US. The opening act is Eric Johnson.

(November 6)
Rush performs live at Expocenter, Topeka, Kansas, US. The opening act is Eric Johnson.

(November 7)
Rush performs live at The Arena, St. Louis, Missouri, US. The opening act is Eric Johnson.

(November 9)
Rush performs live at Redbird Arena, Normal, Illinois, US. The opening act is Eric Johnson.

(November 10)
Rush performs live at Bradley Center, Milwaukee, Wisconsin, US. The opening act is Eric Johnson.

(November 13 & 14)
Rush performs live at The Palace, Auburn Hills, Michigan, US. The opening act is Eric Johnson.

(November 16)
Rush performs live at John F. Savage Hall, University of Toledo, Toledo, Ohio, US. The opening act is Eric Johnson.

(November 17 & 18)
Rush performs live at Richfield Coliseum, Richfield, Ohio, US. The opening act is Eric Johnson.

(November 23)
An article on *Rush* in *Billboard* magazine published on this date notes that "Roll The Bones" is the second, current single off the album.

(November 26)
Rush performs live at Civic Center, Ottawa, Ontario, Canada. The opening act is Andy Curran & Soho 69.

(November 28)
Rush performs live at The Forum, Montreal, Quebec, Canada. The opening act is Andy Curran & Soho 69.

(November 29)

Rush performs live at Colisée de Québec, Quebec City, Quebec, Canada. The opening act is Andy Curran & Soho 69.

(December 1)
Rush performs live at Spectrum, Philadelphia, Pennsylvania, US. The opening act is Vinnie Moore.

(December 2)
Neil Peart appears on *Rockline*, from Philadelphia, Pennsylvania, US.

(December 3)
Rush performs live at Spectrum, Philadelphia, Pennsylvania, US. The opening act is Vinnie Moore.

(December 4)
Rush performs live at Capital Centre, Largo, Maryland, US. The opening act is Vinnie Moore.

(December 6 & 7)
Rush performs live at Madison Square Garden, New York City, New York, US. The opening act is Vinnie Moore.

(December 9)
Rush performs live at Civic Center, Providence, Rhode Island, US. The opening act is Vinnie Moore.

(December 10)
Rush performs live at The Centrum, Worcester, Massachusetts, US. The opening act is Vinnie Moore.

(December 12)
Rush performs live at Knickerbocker Arena, Albany, New York, US. The opening act is Vinnie Moore.

(December 13)
Rush performs live at Civic Center, Hartford, Connecticut, US. The opening act is Vinnie Moore.

(December 15)
Rush performs live at Memorial Auditorium, Buffalo, New York, US. The opening act is Vinnie Moore.

(December 16)
Rush performs live at Maple Leaf Gardens, Toronto, Ontario, Canada. The opening act is The Tragically Hip.

GANGSTER OF BOATS

1992

(January 17)
Rush rehearses at Pan American Center, Las Cruces, New Mexico, US.

(January 18)
Rush performs live at Pan American Center, Las Cruces, New Mexico, US. The opening act is Primus.

(January 20)
Rush performs live at Sports Arena, San Diego, California, US. The opening act is Primus.

(January 22 & 23)
Rush performs live at Great Western Forum, Los Angeles, California, US. The opening act is Primus.

(January 25)
Rush performs live at Selland Arena, Fresno, California, US. The opening act is Primus.

(January 27)
Rush performs live at Arco Arena, Sacramento, California, US. The opening act is Primus.

(January 29 & 30)
Rush performs live at Oakland Coliseum, Oakland, California, US. The opening act is Primus.

(February)
Rush releases their "Roll The Bones" singles In the UK and Europe

UK 7" single (A 7524):
"Roll The Bones"
"Show Don't Tell"

UK & Europe 7" Shaped Picture Disc (A 7524 TE):
"Roll The Bones"
"The Pass"
"It's A Rap (Part 1): Alex Lifeson Speaks"

UK & Europe CD single [hologram sleeve] (A 7524 CD):
"Roll The Bones"
"Anagram (for Mongo)"
"It's A Rap (Part 2): Geddy Lee Speaks"

UK & Europe CD single (A 7524 CDX):
"Roll The Bones"
"Where's My Thing? (Part IV, 'Gangster Of Boats' Trilogy)"
"Superconductor"
"It's A Rap (Part 3): Neil Peart Speaks"

German 7" single (7567-87588-7):
"Roll The Bones"
"Tom Sawyer (Exit...Stage Left)"

German 12" single (7567-85929-0):
"Roll The Bones"
"Tom Sawyer (Exit...Stage Left)"
"The Spirit Of Radio (Exit...Stage Left)"

Germany CD single (PM 1098)
"Roll The Bones (Radio Edit)"
"Neurotica"
"Heresy"

Europe 12" one-sided promo single (SAM 974):
"Roll The Bones (DJ Edit)"

"Roll The Bones (Radio Edit)" 3:37
Written by Neil Peart (words), Geddy Lee & Alex Lifeson (music)

Appears on: German CD promo single
I haven't heard this, but at nearly 2 minutes shorter than the album version, I can't imagine the "rap" section survived this. I'm guessing the edited material comes mostly out of the middle part of the song.

"Roll The Bones (DJ Edit)" 4:39
Written by Neil Peart (words), Geddy Lee & Alex Lifeson (music)
Appears on: Europe 12" one-sided promo single
Unfortunately, I have not heard this edit either. It cuts the track by 50 seconds, which could either be the "rap" section or various instrumental parts throughout.

"It's A Rap (Part 1): Alex Lifeson Speaks" 4:10
"It's A Rap (Part 2): Geddy Lee Speaks" 5:29
"It's A Rap (Part 3): Neil Peart Speaks" 5:56
Written by: N/A
Appears on: UK & Europe 7" Shaped Picture Disc (Alex), CD single [hologram sleeve] (Geddy), CD single (Neil)
These interview excerpt come from the Roll The Bones Radio Special, now mixed in with music from the song. They're interesting to listen to once or twice, though the full Radio Special is more rewarding, so don't expect to have these on repeat on your player. Still, nice to have.

Note: the singles featuring the various "It's A Rap" parts list the upcoming UK tour dates.

(February 2)
Rush performs live at Pacific Coliseum, Vancouver, British Columbia, US. The opening act is Primus.

(February 4)
Rush performs live at Seattle Center Coliseum, Seattle, Washington, US. The opening act is Primus.)

(February 5)
Rush performs live at Portland Memorial Coliseum, Portland, Oregon, US. The opening act is Primus.

(Mid-February)
Neil Peart records on the following for Rheostatics' album *Whale Music*, at Reaction Studios, Toronto, Ontario, Canada:
"Rain, Rain, Rain" - **Peart** records percussion on this track
"Palomar" – **Peart** records percussion on this track
"Guns" – **Peart** records drums and co-arranges this track

According to an article by Rheostatics' Dave Bidini, the sessions last an afternoon. Also present are Barenaked Ladies, who had recorded their vocals for "California Dreamline" earlier in the day (*Toronto Star* January 6, 2002).

Note: it is noted in several Barenaked Ladies-related articles that their Rheostatics recording session came about by invitation from producer Michael Phillip Wojewoda, as the Ladies were looking for a producer for their debut album (*Gordon*). The Ladies asked Wojewoda to work on their album immediately after their *Whale Music* recording session and their work on *Gordon* began in February (see the book *Have Not Been The Same: CanRock Renaissance 1985-1995* 2011, which details these sessions). All of this points to **Neil** recording his parts for Rheostatics during this hiatus in the tour.

(February 15)
Rush performs live at Convention Center Arena at HemisFair Park, San Antonio, Texas, US. The opening act is Primus.

(February 16)
Rush performs live at Reunion Arena, Dallas, Texas, US. The opening act is Primus.

(February 18)
Rush performs live at The Summit, Houston, Texas, US. The opening act is Primus.

(February 20)
Rush performs live at Erwin Special Events Center, Austin, Texas, US. The opening act is Primus.

(February 22)
Rush is scheduled to perform live at Shreveport, Louisiana, US, but the show is cancelled.

(February 23)
Rush performs live at Lakefront Arena, New Orleans, Louisiana, US. The opening act is Primus.

(February 25)
Rush performs live at Civic Center, Pensacola, Florida, US. The opening act is Primus.

(February 26)

Rush performs live at Memorial Coliseum, Jacksonville, Florida, US. The opening act is Primus.

(February 28)
Rush performs live at Miami Arena. Miami, Florida, US. The opening act is Primus.

(February 29)
Rush performs live at Suncoast Dome, St. Petersburg, Florida, US. The opening act is Primus.

(March)
Rush releases their "Ghost Of A Chance" singles in the US.

US cassette single (4-87498):
"Ghost Of A Chance"
"Where's My Thing? (Part IV, 'Gangster Of Boats' Trilogy)"
"An Interview With Rush"

US CD promo single (PRCD 4458-2):
"Ghost Of A Chance (Promo Edit)"
"Ghost Of A Chance"

> "Ghost Of A Chance (Promo Edit)" 4:25
> Written by Neil Peart (words), Geddy Lee & Alex Lifeson (music)
> Appears on: US CD promo single
> This edit of the song fades out early.
>
> "An Interview With Rush" 8:53
> Written by N/A
> Appears on: US cassette single
> This is an excerpt of the Roll The Bones Radio Special and like the "It's A Rap" segments, it's interesting to have, but not something you're likely to play over and over, though being on a cassette, your only other option was to fast forward through it to get to the end of the side and flip the tape again to listen to the actual music on Side One.

Note: this single is noted in M.E.A.T. magazine this month.

(March 2)
Rush performs live at Orlando Arena, Orlando, Florida, US. The opening act is Primus.

(March 4)
Rush performs live at The Omni, Atlanta, Georgia, US. The opening act is Primus.

(March 5)
Rush performs live at The Carolina Coliseum. Columbia, South Carolina, US. The opening act is Primus.

(March 7)
Rush performs live at Dean E. Smith Center, Chapel Hill, North Carolina, US. The opening act is Primus.

(March 8)
Rush performs live at Hampton Coliseum, Hampton, Virginia, US. The opening act is Primus.

(March 10)
Rush performs live at Richmond Coliseum, Richmond, Virginia, US. The opening act is Primus.

(March 12)
Rush performs live at Broome County Arena, Binghamton, New York, US. The opening act is Primus.

(March 14)
Rush performs live at Veterans Coliseum, New Haven, Connecticut, US. The opening act is Primus.

(March 15)
Rush performs live at Nassau Coliseum, Uniondale, New York, US. The opening act is Primus.

(April)
A *Lethbridge Herald* article this months notes that *Rush* is on a mid-tour break before the European leg of the tour.

(April 6)
Rush releases their "Ghost Of A Chance" singles in the UK and Europe.

7" single (A 7491):

"Ghost Of A Chance"
"Dreamline"

CD single (A 7491 CD):
"Ghost Of A Chance"
"Dreamline"
"Chain Lightning"
"Red Tide"

(April 10)
Rush performs live at Sheffield Arena, Sheffield, England. The opening act is Primus.

(April 12 & 13)
Rush performs live at National Exhibition Centre, Birmingham, England. The opening act is Primus.

(April 15)
Rush performs live at Scottish Exhibition Centre, Glasgow, Scotland. The opening act is Primus.

(April 17 & 18)
Rush performs live at Wembley Arena, London, England. The opening act is Primus.

(April 21)
Rush performs live at Music Hall, Hannover, Germany. The opening act is Primus.

(April 23)
Neil Peart does an interview with the *National Midnight Star* at Hotel Intercontinental, Koln, Germany.

Rush performs live at Sporthalle, Koln, Germany. The opening act is Primus.

(April 24)
Rush performs live at Festhalle, Frankfurt, Germany. The opening act is Primus.

(April 27)
Rush performs live at Eissporthalle, Berlin, Germany. The opening act is Primus.

(April 28)
Rush performs live at Frankenhalle, Nürnberg, Germany. The opening act is Primus.

(April 29)
Rush performs live at Hans-Martin-Schleyerhalle, Stuttgart, Germany. The opening act is Primus.

(Date Unknown)
Rush releases their "Bravado" promo single in the US.

US CD promo single (PRCD 4580-2):
"Bravado (Promo Edit)"

> "Bravado (Promo Edit)" 3:49
> Written by Neil Peart (words), Geddy Lee & Alex Lifeson (music)
> Appears on: US CD promo single
> This edit of the song fades out early.

(May 1)
Rush performs live at Le Zenith, Paris, France. The opening act is Primus.

(May 3)
Rush performs live at Ahoy Sportpaleis, Rotterdam, Holland. The opening act is Primus.

(May 21)
Rush performs live at Mid-South Coliseum, Memphis, Tennessee, US. The opening act is Mr. Big.

(May 23)
Rush performs live at Kemper Arena, Kansas City, Missouri, US. The opening act is Mr. Big.

(May 24)
Rush performs live at Kansas Coliseum, Wichita, Kansas, US. The opening act is Mr. Big.

(May 25)
Rush performs live at Myriad Arena, Oklahoma City, Oklahoma, US. The opening act is Mr. Big.

(May 27)
Rush performs live at Fiddler's Green Amphitheater, Englewood, Colorado, US. The opening act is Mr. Big.

(May 29)
Rush performs live at Delta Center, Salt Lake City, Utah, US. The opening act is Mr. Big.

(May 31)
Rush performs live at Shoreline Amphitheater, Mountain View, California, US. The opening act is Mr. Big.

(June)
Rheostatics release their album *Whale Music*, featuring "Rain, Rain, Rain," "Palomar" and "Guns" with **Neil Peart**.

> "Rain, Rain, Rain" 4:20
> Written by Martin Tielli
> Appears on: Whale Music
> Rheostatics were among the wave of quirky alternative bands coming out in the '90s, along side such artists as Barenaked Ladies (who also appear on the album). Neil's percussion parts on this decidedly odd (and par for the band) album track are noticeable throughout. Not one to dance around the room to, but fun in its way.
>
> "Palomar" 4:19
> Written by Tim Vesely
> Appears on: Whale Music
> This laid back acoustic number features a guitar, bass and percussion backing track, with Neil as one of three percussionists, so don't expect a Rush-style performance here. Still, it's a good song and an interesting guest appearance.
>
> "Guns" 1:50
> Written by Dave Clark, arr. by Neil Peart
> Appears on: Whale Music
> This is spoken word piece over Neil's drumming, which rips into a great solo at the end. Short, but sweet!

(June 1)
Rush performs live at Lawlor Events Center, Reno, Nevada, US. The opening act is Mr. Big.

(June 3 & 4)
Rush performs live at Irvine Meadows Amphitheater, Irvine, California, US. The opening act is Mr. Big.

(June 6)
Rush performs live at Thomas & Mack Center, University of Nevada Las Vegas, Las Vegas, Nevada, US. The opening act is Mr. Big.

(June 7)
Rush performs live at Desert Sky Pavilion, Phoenix, Arizona, US. The opening act is Mr. Big.

(June 9)
Rush performs live at Tingley Coliseum, Albuquerque, New Mexico, US. The opening act is Mr. Big.

(June 10)
Rush performs live at Lubbock Coliseum, Lubbock, Texas, US. The opening act is Mr. Big.

(June 12)
Rush performs live at Riverport Amphitheater, St. Louis, Missouri, US. The opening act is Mr. Big.

(June 13)
Rush performs live at Starwood Amphitheater, Nashville, Tennessee, US. The opening act is Mr. Big.

(June 14)
Rush performs live at Blockbuster Pavilion, Charlotte, North Carolina, US. The opening act is Mr. Big.

(June 16)
Rush performs live at Merriwether Post Pavilion, Columbia, Maryland, US. The opening act is Mr. Big.

(June 17)
Rush performs live at Great Woods Center, Mansfield, Massachusetts, US. The opening act is Mr. Big.

(June 19)
Rush performs live at Brendan Byrne Arena, East Rutherford, New Jersey, US. The opening act is Mr. Big.

(June 20)
Rush performs live at Jones Beach, Long Island, New York, US. The opening act is Mr. Big.

(June 21)
Rush performs live at Star Lake Amphitheater, Pittsburgh, Pennsylvania, US. The opening act is Mr. Big.

(June 23)
Rush performs live at Nutter Center, Dayton, Ohio, US. The opening act is Mr. Big.

(June 24)
Rush performs live at Deer Creek, Noblesville, Indiana, US. The opening act is Mr. Big.

(June 26)
Rush performs live at The New Pine Knob, Detroit, Michigan, US. The opening act is Mr. Big.

(June 27)
Rush performs live at Alpine Valley Music Theatre, East Troy, Wisconsin, US. The opening act is Mr. Big.

(June 28)
Rush performs live at World Music Theatre, Tinley Park, Illinois, US. The opening act is Mr. Big.

(Summer)
Following the tour, *Rush* takes a reported six months off before starting the next album.

(Date Unknown)
Geddy Lee records bass for the songs "I Nominate Dr. David" and "Some Dumb Machine," as part of Mendelson Joe's album *Women Are The Only Hope*. The album is not commercially released, though Joe makes it available to order directly from him on cassette (apparently, he has several such unreleased albums). Later in the digital age of 2012, *Women Are The Only Hope* are officially released by Joe via iTunes and Amazon for download.

> "Some Dumb Machine" 3:17
> Written by Mendelson Joe
> Appears on: Women Are The Only Hope
> If you're not familiar with the works of Mendelson Joe, you're missing out on some unique, catchy, original blues/folk. Seriously, check him out. You may not instantly love his work, but it'll grow on you and you'll be richer in spirit for it! This track features Geddy's bass prominently throughout.

> "I Nominate Dr. David" 3:44
> Written by Mendelson Joe
> Appears on: Women Are The Only Hope
> Bluesy-er than "Some Dumb Machine" and demonstrating Joe's social awareness, this song features Geddy's bass line sauntering along underneath, filling out the low end.

(October)
Neil Peart takes a cycling trip to Mali, Senegal and Gambia (he discusses the plan in a *National Midnight Star* interview, April 1992).

(November)
Mobile Fidelity Sound Labs releases their Ultradisc II 24KT gold CD edition of the *Rush* album *Moving Pictures*.

COUNTERPARTS

1993

(January)
Geddy Lee works for a month at his home studio in Toronto, Ontario, Canada, on musical ideas in advance of the next album's writing and rehearsing pre-production sessions. He says in a March 1994 *Guitar School* interview that he completes a couple of cassettes of ideas and a few complete songs worth of music.

(February)
Rush starts writing and rehearsing for their next album, at Chalet Studio, Claremont, Ontario, Canada. *Billboard* magazine (October 1993) notes the pre-production location. **Alex Lifeson** says in a November *Guitar* interview that the pre-production sessions lasted two months. In *Bass Player* magazine (December 1993), **Geddy Lee** says the writing stage went long, shortening the rehearsal time and putting **Neil Peart** under pressure to work out his drum parts before the band meets with producer Peter Collins. **Lee** also says after two months, they start recording. Songs worked on include:
"Between Sun & Moon" – Pye Dubois sent **Neil Peart** lyrics, including a poem titled "There Is A Lake Between Sun And Moon" and those were the lyrics the band responded to (*Counterparts* album premiere).
"Cold Fire" – went through various "permutations" in the writing and demoing stage, including a slow country version, none of which satisfied the band (*Counterparts* album premiere).
"Leave That Thing Alone" – In a *Guitar School* interview (quoted in *Merely Players*), **Alex Lifeson** notes the guitar solo comes from a *Roll The Bones* tour-era ADAT recording he made.
"Double Agent" – this is one of the last songs written for the album, according to **Geddy Lee** (*Counterparts* album premiere).

(March)
Rush "auditions" dozens of engineers for the new album (*Modern Drummer*, February 1994). Kevin "Caveman" Shirley is hired as sound engineer for the album. His employment starts in the winter, a month in advance of the sessions, as he tells *Solid-State-Logic.com* (March, 2011).

(Early Spring)
Neil Peart says after recording the demos, they worked with Peter Collins to refine them and then **Peart** went off for a week to learn the parts before recording them (*Modern Drummer*, February 1994).

(April to June)
Rush records their fifteenth studio album at Le Studio, Morin Heights, Quebec, and later McClear Pathé, Toronto, Ontario, Canada (*Counterparts* sessions). Co-produced and arrangements by Peter Collins and *Rush*. Engineered by Kevin "Caveman" Shirley. Mixed by Michael Letho. *Billboard* magazine (October 1993) notes that the recording takes place in the spring and mostly at Le Studio. In *Bass Player* magazine (December 1993), **Geddy Lee** says **Neil Peart** records his drum parts in two and a half days, mostly one take each, and that the bed tracks are completed in about a week. **Neil** (*Modern Drummer*, February 1994) says it is "one day and two afternoons" that he recorded his parts. That allows **Lee** time to work out vocals and for **Alex Lifeson** to overdub his guitars. **Alex** notes in *Spirit Of Rush* (July 1994) that the bass parts took **Geddy** five days to record, leaving him only about a week to work out his guitar parts before recording them.
John Webster records additional keyboards for the album.
Songs worked on include:
"Cold Fire" – Peter Collin's arrival helped sort this song out (*Counterparts* album premiere).
"Nobody's Hero" – it is Peter Collin's idea to bring in composer Michael Kamen for this song, **Alex Lifeson** says in a November *Guitar* interview. Kamen was working on the film *Last Action Hero* at the time in Los Angeles, California, US.
"Cut To The Chase" – the demo solo is retained for the album (*Guitar Player*, December 1993)
"The Speed Of Love" - the demo solo is retained for the album (*Guitar World*, February 1994)

> "Stick It Out (Work-In Progress Mix)" 4:47
> Written by Neil Peart (words), Geddy Lee & Alex Lifeson (music)
> Appears on: Unreleased
> This early mix features a number of notable differences to the final mix. The instruments have slightly different presence in places, such as the cymbal hits being higher in the mix, the guitars being mixed higher throughout and the synth flourishes are more noticeable. Just when you think the song is about to end, the dénouement repeats again before the final notes pound in. Certainly very interesting and a must for fans, as are all the work-in-progress mixes.
>
> "Cut To The Chase (Work-In Progress Mix)" 4:50
> Written by Neil Peart (words), Geddy Lee & Alex Lifeson (music)
> Appears on: Unreleased
> Right from the start, this mix has the bass more prominent. The backing guitar does not come in under the first "Can't stop moving," instead waiting until the final "Can't stop!" change. Geddy's vocals are echoed at the "It's the motor of the western world..." verse and don't seem to be double-tracks at the "Evil as a

murderer's dream" line. Overall all, the drums have a unique, "distant" quality, unlike the up-front clean sound of the album version.

"Double Agent (Work-In Progress Mix)" 4:52
Written by Neil Peart (words), Geddy Lee & Alex Lifeson (music)
Appears on: Unreleased
Geddy's opening vocals don't have the sonic depth of field as heard on the album version, instead being unadorned and upfront here. After the "narrator" vocals first passage, Geddy's "So tight!" is echoed. The first "Wilderness of mirrors chorus..." seems to have more vocal layers than the album cut. Just before the "narrator's" "...voices behind the door" passage, there's a loud, creepy guitar wail that may well give you a heart attack if you're not expecting it. Interestingly, after Geddy's "At war!" a similar wail comes in, just as loud, only this one you *can* here on the album version, only more quietly in the background. Geddy's "Was right!" is also echoed.

"Cold Fire (Work-In Progress Mix)" 4:28
Written by Neil Peart (words), Geddy Lee & Alex Lifeson (music)
Appears on: Unreleased
The opening lines ("It's a cold fire...fire...") are absent in places and Geddy's vocals are mixed slightly differently here and there throughout. The guitar solo sounds a bit hollow and distant. The most fascinating part of this mix is that it doesn't fade out, instead it continues to the end at full volume, ending in a nifty little percussion roll.

"Everyday Glory (Work-In Progress Mix)" 5:06
Written by Neil Peart (words), Geddy Lee & Alex Lifeson (music)
Appears on: Unreleased
This mix is not overly different from the album cut. It sounds somewhat thicker throughout and the guitars are mixed a little differently in places. The drums are mixed much for flatly, lacking the punch of the album mix. This is sort of true for all the "work-in-progress" mixes, but is more noticeable here. Geddy's chorus double-tracking is more pronounced here, too.

(July)
Rush's album is mastered by Bob Ludwig at Gateway Studios, Portland, Maine, US. **Alex Lifeson** says the album is finished this month (*M.E.A.T.* November, 1993). **Neil Peart** says in *Aquarian Weekly* (March 8, 1994) that the title, *Counterparts* (and unifying theme) came at the very end.

(July 13)
Geddy Lee performs "The Star-Spangled Banner" for the Major League Baseball All-Star Game, Oriole Park at Camden Yards, Baltimore, Maryland, US.

(Summer)
Alex Lifeson rehearses with Tom Cochrane and his band at Cochrane's house for the upcoming *Kumbaya Festival*. There he meets Cochrane's guitarist Bill Bell, with whom he will later collaborate on *Victor*.

(September 5)
Alex Lifeson performs with Tom Cochrane at the *Kumbaya Festival*, Ontario Place Forum, Toronto, Ontario, Canada.

(October)
Rush releases their "Stick It Out" promo singles in the US and UK.

US CD promo single (PRCD 5314-2):
"Stick It Out"

UK 12" promo sampler (SAM 1263):
"Stick It Out"
"Cold Fire"
"Nobody's Hero"
"Double Agent"

(October 13)
Album Network's world album premiere of **Rush**'s album *Counterparts* is broadcast on the radio.

(October 19)
Rush releases their album *Counterparts* in Canada (Anthem Records) and worldwide (Atlantic Records). Track listing as follows:

"Animate"
"Stick It Out"
"Cut To The Chase"
"Nobody's Hero"

"Between Sun & Moon"
"Alien Shore"
"The Speed Of Love"
"Double Agent"
"Leave That Thing Alone"
"Cold Fire"
"Everyday Glory"

(November)
In a *M.E.A.T.* magazine interview, **Alex Lifeson** says they plan to record as many shows as they can on this tour for a possible live album next.

Billboard magazine (October 1993) notes that *Rush* is in tour rehearsals this month.

(November)
Mobile Fidelity Sound Labs releases their Ultradisc II 24KT gold CD edition of the *Rush* album *2112*.

(November 4)
Neil Peart writes a Q&A for the *Rush Backstage Club* newsletter.

(December 13)
Geddy Lee writes his equipment list for the *Counterparts* tour book.

BURNING FOR BUDDY

1994

(January)
Geddy Lee and Nancy Young announce to the band that they are expecting another child, due in May. **Neil Peart** discusses the impact of this on the tour, which was originally blocked into June, but has to be cut back into early May to accommodate **Lee** being home for the birth. **Neil Peart** gets the idea to put together the Buddy Rich tribute album during the forthcoming summer hiatus after the *Counterparts* tour. He contacts Cathy Rich, Buddy's daughter, about putting plans together for the tribute album (Compuserve conference October, 1994). Liam Birt, **Rush**'s production manager, is also brought in to help coordinate the project (*Hamilton Spectator* October, 1994).

The process of organizing the recording sessions and selecting the featured drummers takes place via mailing charts (sheet music) and tapes (*Drum!* November, 1996).

(January 22)
Rush performs live at Civic Arena, Pensacola, Florida, US. The opening act is Candlebox.

(January 23)
Rush performs live at UNO Lakefront Arena, New Orleans, Louisiana, US. The opening act is Candlebox.

(January 24)
Geddy Lee and **Alex Lifeson** appear on *Rockline,* from Austin, Texas, US.

(January 25)
Rush performs live at Frank Erwin Center, Austin, Texas, US. The opening act is Candlebox.

(January 26)
Rush performs live at The Summit, Houston, Texas, US. The opening act is Candlebox.

(January 28)
Rush performs live at Reunion Arena, Dallas, Texas, US. The opening act is Candlebox.

(January 29)
Rush performs live at Convention Center Arena, San Antonio, Texas, US. The opening act is Candlebox.

(January 31)
Rush performs live at Pan American Center, Las Cruces, New Mexico, US. The opening act is Candlebox.

(February)
Rush releases its "Nobody's Hero" singles in the US.

US cassette single (4-87267):
"Nobody's Hero"
"Stick It Out"

US CD single (PRCD 5430-2):
"Nobody's Hero"

US CD promo single (PRCD 5497-2):
"Nobody's Hero (Master Edit Version)"

> "Nobody Hero (Master Edit Version)" 4:29
> Written by Neil Peart (words), Geddy Lee & Alex Lifeson (music)
> Appears on: US CD promo single
> This version fades out early, removing the last 25 seconds of the track, unfortunately, so you hear less of composer Michael Kamen's orchestrations. Kamen (1948 - 2003) was notable for his many film scores (X-Men, Robin Hood: Prince Of Thieves and Highlander, among many others) and worked with other rock bands, such as Queen and Metallica. This version is sometimes referred to as a "Work-In-Progress Mix," grouped with the earlier such mix from the Counterparts sessions and given the odd official name of this cut ("Master Edit Version"), that description may not be far from the truth.

Note: The date comes from 45worlds.com

(February)
Pocket Books publishes the anthology *Shock Rock II*, featuring the short story by Kevin J. Anderson and **Neil Peart** titled *Drumbeats*.

(February 1)
Rush performs live at Veterans Memorial Coliseum, Phoenix, Arizona, US. The opening act is Candlebox.

(February 3)
Rush performs live at Great Western Forum, Los Angeles, California, US. The opening act is Candlebox.

(February 5)
Rush performs live at Arrowhead Pond, Anaheim, California, US. The opening act is Candlebox.

(February 7)
Rush performs live at Sports Arena, San Diego, California, US. The opening act is Candlebox.

(February 8)
Rush performs live at Selland Arena, Fresno, California, US. The opening act is The Melvins.

(February 10)
Rush performs live at Arco Arena, Sacramento, California, US. The opening act is The Melvins.

(February 11)
Rush performs live at Cow Palace, San Francisco, California, US. The opening act is The Melvins.

(February 12)
Rush performs live at San Jose Arena, San Jose, California, US. The opening act is The Melvins.

(February 23)
Rush performs live at Murphy Athletic Center, Murfreesboro, Tennessee, US. The opening act is Candlebox.

(February 24)
Rush performs live at The Omni, Atlanta, Georgia, US. The opening act is Candlebox.

(February 25)
Rush performs live at Charlotte Coliseum, Charlotte, North Carolina, US. The opening act is Candlebox.

(February 27)
Rush performs live at Miami Arena, Miami, Florida, US. The opening act is Candlebox. This show is recorded for the later-aborted *Counterparts* tour live album. The following track appears on *Different Stages*:

"Show Don't Tell"

(March)
In an interview with *Guitar School* magazine published this month, **Geddy Lee** says following this tour, he will "toy with the idea of a solo project."

Rush releases its "Double Agent" single in the US.

US CD promo single (PRCD 5431-2):
"Double Agent"

(March 1)
Rush performs live at Orlando Arena, Orlando, Florida, US. The opening act is Candlebox.

(March 2)
Rush performs live at Veterans Memorial Coliseum, Jacksonville, Florida, US. The opening act is Candlebox.

(March 4)
Rush performs live at Thunderdome, St. Petersburg, Florida, US. The opening act is Candlebox.

(March 6)
Rush performs live at Dean Smith Center, Chapel Hill, North Carolina, US. The opening act is Candlebox.

(March 8)
Rush performs live at Madison Square Garden, New York City, New York, US. The opening act is Candlebox.

(March 9)
In an interview with *Aquarian Weekly* published on this date, **Neil Peart** says he wants to assemble a Buddy Rich tribute album.

Rush performs live at Madison Square Garden. New York City, New York, US. The opening act is Candlebox.

(March 11 & 12)
Rush performs live at Centrum. Worcester, Massachusetts, US. The opening act is Candlebox.

(March 22)
Rush performs live at The Palace, Auburn Hills, Michigan, US. The opening act is The Primus. This show is recorded for the later-aborted *Counterparts* tour live album. The following track appears on *Different Stages*:

"The Analog Kid"

(March 23 & 25)
Rush performs live at Richfield Coliseum, Richfield, Ohio, US. The opening act is The Primus.

(March 26)
Rush performs live at Market Square Arena, Indianapolis, Indiana, US. The opening act is The Primus.

(March 27)
Rush performs live at The Palace, Auburn Hills, Michigan, US. The opening act is The Primus. This show is recorded for the later-aborted *Counterparts* tour live album. The following footage appears on *Anatomy Of A Drum Solo*:

"Drum Solo"

> "Drum Solo (Live at The Palace of Auburn Hills, 1994)" 7:20
> Written by Neil Peart
> Appears on: Anatomy Of A Drum Solo
> It's great to have an official release of a drum solo from this tour. This tour just predates Neil's work with Freddie Gruber and his introduction of the "One O'clock Jump" segment, so what we get is the last vestige of his straight rock percussion gymnastics. It was after this period that Neil (jaw-dropping-ly) *wanted to get better*.

(March 29 & 30)
Rush performs live at Rosemont Horizon, Rosemont, Illinois, US. The opening act is The Primus.

(Spring)
In a *Guitar Shop* interview published in June, **Alex Lifeson** says the band's next project is a live album of the *Counterparts* tour, followed by 'An Evening With Rush' 20th Anniversary Tour. The set list will run chronologically from 1974 to 1994.

(April 1)
Rush performs live at Civic Center, Peoria, Illinois, US. The opening act is The Primus.

(April 2)
Rush performs live at Dane County Coliseum, Madison, Wisconsin, US. The opening act is The Primus.

(April 4)
Rush performs live at The Arena, St. Louis, Missouri, US. The opening act is The Primus.

(April 5)
Rush performs live at Kemper Arena, Kansas City, Missouri, US. The opening act is The Primus.

(April 7)
Rush performs live at Bradley Center, Milwaukee, Wisconsin, US. The opening act is The Primus.

(April 8)
Rush performs live at Target Center, Minneapolis, Minnesota, US. The opening act is The Primus.

(April 9)
Rush performs live at The Mark, Moline, Illinois, US. The opening act is The Primus.

(April 18)
Rush performs live at Memorial Auditorium, Buffalo, New York, US. The opening act is Candlebox.

(April 20)
Rush performs live at Civic Arena, Pittsburgh, Pennsylvania, US. The opening act is Candlebox.

(April 22)
Rush performs live at Brendan Byrne Arena, East Rutherford, New Jersey, US. The opening act is Candlebox.

(April 23)

Rush performs live at Nassau Coliseum. Uniondale, New York, US. The opening act is Candlebox.

(April 24)
Rush performs live at Civic Center, Hartford, Connecticut, US. The opening act is Candlebox.

(April 26)
Rush performs live at US Air Arena, Landover, Maryland, US. The opening act is Candlebox.

(April 27)
Rush is scheduled to perform live at Hampton Coliseum. Hampton, Virginia, US, but the show is cancelled because **Geddy Lee** loses his voice.

Note: it's unclear if the cancellation occurred prior to the show or during it. **Alex Lifeson** says in *Spirit Of Rush* (July, 1994) that **Lee**'s voice cracked three songs in.

(April 29 & 30)
Rush performs live at The Spectrum, Philadelphia, Pennsylvania, US. The opening act is Candlebox. The 30th show (and likely the 29th, as well) is recorded for the later-aborted *Counterparts* tour live album. The following track appears on *Different Stages*:

"Bravado"

(May 1)
Rush performs live at Civic Center, Providence, Rhode Island, US. The opening act is Candlebox.

(May 3)
Rush performs live at Knickerbocker Arena, Albany, New York, US. The opening act is Candlebox. Following this concert, **Alex Lifeson** gives an interview for *Spirit Of Rush* (July, 1994). He says he might be working on a solo album following the tour. He notes the tour was shortened due to **Geddy Lee** and Nancy Young expecting a child. **Alex** also notes that the band is considering bypassing the *Counterparts* live album idea and instead recording another studio album and following that with a live album.

(May 4)
Rush performs live at War Memorial, Rochester, New York, US. The opening act is Candlebox.

(May 6)
Rush performs live at The Forum, Montreal, Quebec, Canada. The opening act is The Doughboys.

(May 7)
Rush performs live at Maple Leaf Gardens, Toronto, Ontario, Canada. The opening act is I Mother Earth. **Alex Lifeson** meets some of the band (though not Edwin).

(May 15)
Kyla Avril Weinrib is born to **Geddy Lee** and Nancy Young, Toronto, Ontario, Canada.

(Mid-May)
Alex Lifeson notes in *Canadian Music* (June, 1995) that **Geddy** planned for a year off to spend time with his family and that later **Neil Peart** had plans for an additional 6 months off (18 months total). Around this time **Lifeson** contemplates a solo recording project (*Access* Jan/Feb 1996). **Alex** later says they recorded about 40 shows on the *Counterparts* tour (*A Show Of Fans*, December 21, 1995).

(Mid-May)
Neil Peart produces the Buddy Rich tribute album at The Power Station, New York City, New York, US. Engineered by Paul Northfield. The Buddy Rich Big Band and guest musicians are:

Chuck Bergeron	Bill Beaudoin	Chuck Loeb	John Hart
Jon Werking	Andy Fusco	Dave D'Angelo	Jack Stuckey
Steve Marcus	Walt Weiskopf	Gary Keller	George Gesslein
John Mosca	Rick Trager	Craig Johnson	Dan Collette
Dave Stahl	Greg Gisbert	Joe Magnarelli	Mike Ponella
Bob Milikan	Ross Konikoff	Tony Kadleck	Scott Wendholt

The drummers and percussionists who record their parts during the two weeks of sessions are:

Neil Peart	Simon Phillips	Dave Weckl	Steve Gadd
Matt Sorum	Steve Smith	Manu Katché	Mino Cinelu
Billy Cobham	Max Roach	Rod Morgenstein	Kenny Aronoff
Omar Hakim	Ed Shaughnessy	Joe Morello	Bill Bruford
Marvin "Mitty" Smith	Steve Ferrone		

During these sessions, **Neil** meets Freddie Gruber, the legendary drum teacher (*Modern Drummer*, November, 1995). The sessions are filmed by instructional video directors Paul Siegel and Rob Wallis, who again propose to **Neil** the idea of **Neil** doing an instructional video. The three eventually decide to film **Peart** recording a *Rush* album (*A Work In Progress* liner notes).

By the end of the sessions, **Neil Peart** has a reported 39 tracks recorded, prompting Atlantic Records to plan the release of multiple tribute albums (*Drum!* November, 1994, reports that three such albums are planned. However, ultimately only two are released, the second in 1997).

(June)
During the mixing sessions for the *Burning For Buddy* tribute album, **Neil Peart** and Kenny Arnoff record percussion overdubs for "Pick Up The Pieces," recorded previously with Steve Ferrone during the sessions in May. Mixing and overdubs take place at Le Studio, Morin Heights, Quebec, Canada (*Canadian Musician* December, 1994, and *Modern Drummer* February, 1996).

(Summer)
Neil Peart contacts Freddie Gruber to begin drum lessons with him. They meet for a week at Gruber's home. At the end of these lessons, Gruber imparts some technique exercises to work on in **Neil**'s own time (*Modern Drummer*, November, 1995).

(Date Unknown)
The audio recording of *Rush*'s February 20, 1979, Hammersmith Odeon concert is unexpectedly found by **Geddy Lee** in his basement (*Vancouver Sun* November 5, 1998). He and **Alex Lifeson** listen to the recording, ultimately deciding that despite the performance issues (**Geddy**'s vocals) it is of sufficient quality and historical significance to consider using as part of a future release (*Big-O* October, 1998).

(September)
Alex Lifeson says the *Burning For Buddy* album is complete by this date (*Rock N' Roll Reporter* February, 1996).

(September 4)
Alex Lifeson performs at the *Kumbaya Festival*, Ontario Place Forum, Toronto, Ontario, Canada. Other artists on the bill include Tom Cochrane, Lawrence Gowan, Barenaked Ladies and Jane Siberry.

> "All Along The Watch Tower (Kumbaya Festival, 1994)" 6:53
> Written by Bob Dylan
> Appears on: The Kumbaya Album 1995
> Lifeson, Cochrane, Gowan and everyone let rip on this performance of Jimi Hendrix' cover of Dylan's famous song. The concert footage shows Alex and guitarist Bill Bell (with whom he'd later work on Victor) having a blast rocking out.

(October)
Mobile Fidelity Sound Labs releases their Ultradisc II 24KT gold CD edition of the *Rush* album *Signals*. This edition features "The Weapon (Alternate Album Master Version)" instead of the standard album version.

(October 4)
Atlantic Records releases *Burning For Buddy: A Tribute To The Music Of Buddy Rich* worldwide, produced by and featuring **Neil Peart** on the tracks "Cotton Tail" and "Pick Up The Pieces."

> "Cotton Tail" 4:36
> Written by Duke Ellington
> Appears on: Burning For Buddy: A Tribute To The Music Of Buddy Rich
> This Duke Ellington number became a favourite of jazz musicians over the years and Buddy Rich's performances are among the many by famous acts, such as Ella Fitzgerald. Listen to any of Rich's solos and you'll hear why he had such an impact on Neil (if you thought a Neil Peart drum solo is staggering, Buddy Rich might well cause your head to explode). Neil and Rich's band give it their all on this album and this track is no exception.

> "Pick Up The Pieces" 5:40
> Written by Average White Band (Roger Ball & Hamish Stuart), arr. Arif Mardin
> Appears on: Burning For Buddy: A Tribute To The Music Of Buddy Rich
> Steve Ferrone brought this piece to the project (it was never performed by Buddy Rich, but instead dated from Ferrone's time in Average White Band) and played on the track with precision, but very little flash. Around the 5 minute mark is a drum break where Ferrone, reportedly disliking solos, basically marks time. Afterwards, slightly unhappy with that section, Neil and Kevin Arnoff overdub a few extra percussion bits to liven it up. Neil's contribution to the recording is small, but it does help. Surprisingly, this track goes mostly undocumented on Rush fan sites.

(October 5)

Neil Peart participates in an online conference interview via Compuserve promoting the launch of *Burning For Buddy: A Tribute To The Music Of Buddy Rich*.

(Autumn)
Alex Lifeson and Bill Bell work on the following at Lerxst Sound (his home studio), Toronto, Ontario, Canada, for a forthcoming *Guitar World* compilation *The Guitars That Rule The World, Part II: Smell The Fuzz*.
"Strip And Go Naked" – **Alex** says in both an *Access* magazine and *Rockline* (1996) interview that this piece came quickly and was written and recorded in a day.

Alex later notes in a *Canadian Musician* (June, 1996) interview that following the recording of this track, he and Bell continued writing, a process that would evolve into the *Victor* sessions. In the same interview, **Lifeson** says this was after a lengthy summer break after the tour.

(October)
The Orbit Room, a bar owned by Tim Notter and **Alex Lifeson**, opens this month.

Note: since its opening, **Alex Lifeson** occasionally plays with the house band, The Dexters, as **'Big Al' Dexter**.

(Late October)
Alex Lifeson begins work with Bill Bell on his solo album at Lerxst Sound, Toronto, Ontario, Canada (*Victor* sessions). The time of the month comes from a June 1996 *Canadian Musician* interview.

(December)
Sebastian Bach records vocals for the following for **Alex Lifeson**'s solo album, at Lerxst Sound, Toronto, Ontario, Canada (*Victor* sessions):
"Promise" – in a January, 1995, *Rockline* interview, **Alex** says Bach was in town for Christmas and recorded his vocals then. Bach's vocal take is not used for the album and is later replaced by Edwin's.

Alex says in the *Rockline* interview that not all the material was written by this point.

VICTOR

1995

(Winter)
Bill Bell has to leave **Alex Lifeson**'s solo album project in order to work on Tom Cochrane's album (*Ragged Ass Road* sessions) around this time. **Lifeson** later notes that this allows him to record demo material by himself (*The Spirit Of Rush* February, 1996).

Six months after the initial lessons with Freddie Gruber, **Neil Peart** contacts him for a follow-up. They meet again at Peart's home, Wentworth-Nord, Quebec, Canada. Following these few days of lessons, Gruber leaves **Peart** with more advanced exercises to practice (*Modern Drummer*, November, 1995).

Note: It would seem that about this time is when **Neil Peart** requests an additional six months off (noted by **Alex Lifeson**, *Access* Jan/Feb 1996). **Peart** says at a *Rush* band meeting that he won't be ready to start work on a new album for "maybe after a year" because he wants to pursue the exercises Freddie Gruber set down for him (*Modern Drummer*, November, 1995), which extends the band's hiatus to the 18 month mark. In the *Access* interview, **Alex** explains this additional six months opens the window for him to plan to complete his solo album.

(Date Unknown)
Alex Lifeson records guitar on the tracks "Just Scream," "Crawl" and "Will Of The Gun" for Tom Cochrane's *Ragged Ass Road* album, at MetalWorks Studios, Mississauga, Ontario, Canada.

(March)
Alex Lifeson approaches Les Claypool of Primus to record bass guitar on his solo album (*Victor* sessions, noted in *Rock N' Roll Reporter* (February, 1996).

(Spring)
In an interview given around this time for *Canadian Musician* (published in June), **Alex Lifeson** notes the Tom Cochrane worked on **Lifeson**'s solo album.
"Promise" – **Alex** notes that Sebastian Bach recorded vocals for a song.

Note: in various interviews, **Alex** says he had "local" people record the demo vocals for the album to hear what the songs sounded like, which is likely Cochrane's role here.

In *A Show Of Fans* interview (Winter, 1996), **Alex Lifeson** says the last three months of the Victor sessions saw him working practically every day on the album. Prior to this, it was nearly every day. He also explains that demos tracks for all the songs were recorded first for the album, before proper overdubs are started.

Alex Lifeson participates in a celebrity golf tournament with Tom Cochrane at Islington Golf Club, Toronto, Ontario, Canada.

(Dates Unknown)
Geddy Lee records bass guitar on demos for k.d. lang songs worked on by Ben Mink. Mink discusses this in a *Rolandca.com* interview (August, 2000).

Note: Ben Mink doesn't say which album sessions or date this work was for, but this year would coincide with *Rush*'s hiatus. **Geddy** repeatedly says he was living the domestic life at this time, but that doesn't preclude behind the scenes work with his friend Mink.

(Mid-May)
This month, according to *The Spirit Of Rush* interview (February, 1996), **Alex Lifeson** enlists Edwin, of I Mother Earth, to record vocals for his solo album after listening to the band's album during the *Victor* sessions. Edwin simultaneously records vocals for I Mother Earth's *Scenery And Fish* album. His *Victor* sessions last a week and a half (*Rock N' Roll Reporter* February, 1996).
"Promise" – it is at this point that **Lifeson** decides to replace Sebastian Bach's vocals, so that there is a singular male lead singer on the album.

(June)
Neil Peart and his friend 'Brutus' embark on a two week motorcycle trip to Yellowknife, Northwest Territories, Canada (*Cycle Canada* April, 1996).
"Test For Echo" – the phrase comes to mind when **Neil** sees the inuksuk overlooking the city. He purchases a winter scene postcard of it, which later forms the basis for the album cover artwork. **Neil** explains that the song title came from lyrics given to him by Pye Dubois (*Modern Drummer* November, 1996).

(July)

Alex Lifeson completes recording work on his solo album at Lerxst Sound, Toronto, Ontario, Canada (*Victor* sessions). Tracks worked on since October include:
"Mr. X" - Peter Cardinali plays bass.
"At The End" – Adrian Živojinović does programming.
"Shut Up Shuttin' Up" - Peter Cardinali plays bass. Charlene Živojinović and Esther provide vocals.
"The Big Dance" - Adrian Živojinović co-wrote and does programming. Les Claypool plays bass.
"Victor" – **Alex Lifeson** later says he wrote the track before deciding to use W.H. Auden's poem over it (*Rockline*, 1996). Peter Cardinali plays bass. Colleen Allen plays horns.

(Summer)
Alex Lifeson mixes *Victor* at McClear Pathé, Toronto, Ontario, Canada. **Alex** says it was during these sessions that Bill Bell was able to return to the project (*The Spirit Of Rush*, February 1996). Tracks worked on since October include:
"Start Today" – Dalbello records her vocals for this song after **Alex** asks her, following her completion of her album *whore* at the same studio where he is mixing his solo album (*rockreunion.com*, 2001). **Alex** says ran into her at the studio early in the mixing sessions and that he had planned for this track to use a female singer. Dalbello agrees and returns a week later, after her sessions are complete, and recorded her parts (*A Show Of Fans*, December 21, 1995). Her session took place in a day (*The Spirit Of Rush* February, 1996).
"Unknown 'Tom Jones' Song" – In *The Spirit Of Rush* interview (February, 1996), **Alex Lifeson** says there is one song, partially completed, that was left off the album because it didn't hold up to the rest of the material. **Alex** had the idea of getting singer Tom Jones to do the vocals, before dropping the song altogether. The song was demoed (including demo vocals) and the backing guitar, bass and drum bed track are completed, with lead guitar and vocal not recorded.

Alex later notes in a *Billboard* interview (December 2, 1995) that as the solo album progresses, it becomes a band project. At this point the band, **Victor**, is essentially: **Alex Lifeson**, Bill Bell, Blake Manning and Edwin.

Note: this line-up appears as "the band" in promotional material.

Bob Ludwig masters **Victor**'s album at Gateway Mastering Studios, Portland, Maine, US. **Alex Lifeson** is present at these sessions.

Around this time, **Neil Peart** prepares lyrics and notes in advance of the upcoming **Rush** writing and rehearsing sessions for their next album (*Jam* October 16, 1996).

(Date Unknown)
Neil Peart records his drum lessons for John Xepoleas' forthcoming instructional Book+CD *Drum Lessons With The Greats 2*.

(September 5)
Alex Lifeson performs live at Kumbaya Festival, at Ontario Place Forum, Toronto, Ontario, Canada. Also on the bill is Barenaked Ladies, Blue Rodeo, Sarah MacLauchlan and others. **Lifeson** performs with The Boomers (with Ian Thomas).

(September 10)
Alex Lifeson says **Victor**'s album is completed by this date (*Access* Jan/Feb 1996). He also says that work on the new **Rush** album starts a few weeks after this date. **Alex** confirms in several interviews (including *Rock N' Roll Reporter* February, 1996) that he doesn't have a record deal to release *Victor* at this point and that upon its completion there is no guarantee of its release.

(October)
Rush begins writing and rehearsing material for their sixteenth studio album at Chalet Studios, Claremont, Ontario, Canada (*Test For Echo* sessions, noted in the tour book). In a *The Spirit Of Rush* interview (February, 1996), **Alex Lifeson** says that by the end of the first week, he and **Geddy Lee** had recorded a good deal of material and ideas. **Neil** notes in the tour book that after several weeks, he hears the initial demos by **Alex** and **Geddy**.

Tom Cochrane releases his *Ragged Ass Road* album this month. It includes "Just Scream," "Crawl" and "Will Of The Gun" featuring **Alex Lifeson**.

> "Just Scream" 4:54
> Written by Tom Cochrane
> Appears on: Ragged Ass Road
> Ragged Ass Road was Cochrane's follow-up to his hugely successful Mad, Mad World album and its single "Life Is A Highway." "Just Scream" is louder, heavier and angrier, a good mid-tempo rock song. Alex's guitar work on this track seems to reflect the aggressive playing he was employing around this time (Counterparts and Victor). Good stuff here.
> And while we're on the subject of Tom Cochrane, Alex's son Justin has a photography credit on Tom's next album, Songs Of A Circling Spirit.
>
> "Crawl" 4:15
> Written by Tom Cochrane

Appears on: Ragged Ass Road
Alex employs his approach of adding colour and support throughout this track, filling out the song without overpowering it. This is a nice bit of heartland rock.

"Will Of The Gun" 4:46
Written by Annette Ducharme
Appears on: Ragged Ass Road
A drum-driven groove keeps this track chugging along. Alex pops up throughout, beefing up the song, another good heartland rocker.

(October 1)
DCI Music Video releases the 2xVHS set *The Making Of Burning For Buddy* documentary, filmed during the May 1994 sessions for the **Neil Peart**-produced Buddy Rich tribute albums. The documentary is later re-issued on DVD.

(Autumn)
Rush pre-production sessions continue for the new album, at Chalet Studios, Claremont, Ontario, Canada. An *Access* interview with **Alex Lifeson** (Jan/Feb 1996) given at this time says the sessions will move to Bearsville, New York, US, to record the basic tracks, followed by sessions in Toronto, Ontario, Canada, from January to April.
"Totem" – **Neil Peart** comes across the Freud book "Totem And Taboo" at the studio and the title inspires him.
"Resist" – the working title is "Taboo," following the "Totem And Taboo" inspiration (*Jam* October 16, 1996).

(November 1)
Rush begins the pre-production "refining" of the songs, at Chalet Studios, Claremont, Ontario, Canada (*Test For Echo* tour book).

(November)
Alex Lifeson does an interview with *The Spirit Of Rush* (February, 1996) and notes that the band is five weeks into their writing and rehearsal sessions (at Chalet Studios, Claremont, Ontario, Canada). He says he recently recorded with I Mother Earth (on the track "Like A Girl," *Scenery And Fish*) and that *Rush* is scheduled to return to work after these sessions, on January 8th, 1996. *Guitar* magazine reports that the band has seven songs at this point (November, 1996).
"Limbo" - In the interview for the *Test For Echo* world premiere, **Alex Lifeson** says the instrumental came late in these sessions, at the end of the writing stage and after pre-production has begun, where **Neil Peart** is already working out his drum parts.

Note: The date comes from *The Spirit Of Rush* article, that notes this interview comes 18 months after the previous May, 1994, interview. Upcoming December releases (the "Don't Care" and "Promise" singles) are also discussed.

(Late Autumn)
Alex Lifeson gives an interview at Atlantic Records, New York City, New York, US, for *Guitar* magazine (published February, 1996). He is there to present **Victor**'s self-titled album to Atlantic Records with the first playback. The article notes that by this point, *Rush* is in pre-production for their next album.

(December 2)
A *Billboard* magazine interview with **Alex Lifeson** notes that the following forthcoming **Victor** singles are aimed at specific markets:
"Don't Care" – directed at heavy metal outlets
"Promise" – directed at mainstream outlets

(December 4)
Victor releases their singles for "Don't Care" and "Promise" in the US.

US CD promo single (PRCD 6550):
"Don't Care"

US CD promo single (PRCD 6551):
"Promise (Radio Edit)"

> "Promise (Radio Edit)" 4:30
> Written by Alex Lifeson (words & music) & Bill Bell (music)
> Appears on: US CD promo single
> This edit removes about 1:15 or so audible seconds of music from the track throughout, similar to the video version (see below).
>
> "Promise (Video Version)" 5:00
> Written by Alex Lifeson (words & music) & Bill Bell (music)
> Appears on: N/A
> Cutting the track down by about 40 seconds to make the video more time friendly for MuchMusic and MTV, the missing bits are instrumental passages from here and there. Both edits kind of help tighten the song up somewhat.

(Early December)
Most of the songs for *Rush*'s next album are written and arranged by this point, at Chalet Studios, Claremont, Ontario, Canada (*Test For Echo* sessions, via tour book). Producer Peter Collins joins the sessions.
"Resist" – **Geddy Lee** says this is one of the song Peter Collins had a hand in improving the arrangement for upon his arrival (*A Show Of Fans* September 23, 1996).
"Totem" – **Geddy Lee** says this is one of the song Peter Collins had a hand in improving the arrangement for upon his arrival (*A Show Of Fans* September 23, 1996).

(Mid-December)
In an interview given around this time (*A Show Of Fans*, Winter 1996), **Alex Lifeson** notes that *Rush* just finished their sessions after ten weeks. He also says the songs are in the writing stage and the band plans to record shows on the next tour for a live album. Tracks worked on since October include:
"Test For Echo" – **Neil Peart** uses lyrics by Pye Dubois for this song.

Note: The interview takes place a few weeks after the "Promise" single's release and before Christmas (**Alex** still has shopping to do).

Note: In a *Billboard* interview (August 3, 1996), **Alex** says during the *Test For Echo* sessions, the band discusses plans for the next album.

TEST FOR ECHO

1996

(January)
Victor releases their singles for "I Am The Spirit" in the US.

US CD promo single (PRCD 6686):

"I Am The Spirit (Radio Edit)" 4:46
Written by Alex Lifeson (words & music) & Bill Bell (music)
Appears on: US CD promo single
Similar to the "Promise" radio edit, this cuts out about 45 seconds of bits and pieces throughout to shorten the track.

John Xepoleas releases his instructional Book+CD *Drum Lessons with the Greats 2*, featuring **Neil Peart**. The book features three lessons from **Neil** and the accompanying CD features those lessons performed by him, covering his drum solo material and how to develop drum fills.

"Leave That Thing Alone (Drums-only Version)" 4:16
Written by Geddy Lee & Alex Lifeson
Appears on: Drum Lessons with the Greats 2
The track starts with John X's intro, before going into Neil performing Leave That Thing Alone. Presumably he's playing to the Rush recording of Alex and Geddy (similar to how he does on his own instructional video A Work In Progress), but we get to here the isolated drums and it's a pretty neat listen, as there's a lot going on and you may hear things you didn't quite notice before.

"The Drum Also Waltzes" 2:08
Written by Neil Peart
Appears on: Drum Lessons with the Greats 2
The track starts with John X's intro, before going into Neil performing the waltz section of his live drum solo. It's great to get this isolated performance recorded clean in the studio.

Note: The other tracks for **Neil Peart**'s portion are short examples of his fills, breaks and other pieces, each clip being introduced by John Xepoleas and lasting only a few seconds, making it pointless to try to describe. Bits that **Neil** plays include "Show Don't Tell" (introduced by Xepoleas as "Show And Tell"), "YYZ" (mispronounced by Xepoleas as "YY-Zee") and "Roll The Bones."

(January 8)
Rush begins recording the basic tracks for their sixteenth studio album, at Bearsville Studio, Bearsville, New York, US. Co-produced and arrangements by *Rush* and Peter Collins. Engineered by Clif Norrell. **Alex Lifeson** says, in a 1996 *Scene* (Eastern Ohio) interview, that the drum parts were recorded during the Bearsville sessions.

Note: The date comes indirectly from a *Detroit Free Press* interview published Friday, Jan. 12th, which says the band started work on Monday, placing it on the 8th. This aligns with **Alex Lifeson**'s November interview where his gives this date.

(January 9)
Victor releases their self-titled album, *Victor*, in Canada (Anthem Records) and worldwide (Atlantic Records). Track listing as follows:

"Don't Care"
"Promise"
"Start Today"
"Mr. X"
"At The End"
"Sending Out A Warning"
"Shut Up Shuttin' Up"
"Strip And Go Naked"
"The Big Dance"
"Victor"
"I Am The Spirit"

(January 10)
Alex Lifeson gives an interview to the *Detroit Free Press* during the sessions at Bearsville Studio, Bearsville, New York, US.

(January 15)
Rush continues their recording sessions for their sixteenth studio album, at Reaction Studios, Toronto, Ontario, Canada (*Test For Echo* sessions).

Alex Lifeson gives an interview on *Rockline* from Toronto, Ontario, Canada. He says there is no album title at this point (and confirms recording began the previous week).

(March)
Rush completes recording sessions for their album, at Reaction Studios, Toronto, Ontario, Canada (*Test For Echo* sessions). Tracks worked on since January include:
"Limbo" – features samples from 1962 Bobby "Boris" Pickett And The Crypt-Kickers song "Monster Mash." *Rush* had to pay licensing fees to use the recording.

(April)
Rush mixes their album at McClear Pathé, Toronto, Ontario, Canada. Engineered by Andy Wallace.
"Driven" – the first track mixed on the album (*Guitar* November, 1996).

Geddy Lee later says that naming the album *Test For Echo* came quite late in the process and that it came from the song of the same name (*Test For Echo* world premiere, September 5, 1996).

(April 23)
I Mother Earth releases their album *Scenery And Fish* in Canada. It includes the song "Like A Girl," featuring **Alex Lifeson**.

> "Like A Girl" 4:39
> Written by I Mother Earth (Jagori Tanna & Christian Tanna)
> Appears on: Scenery And Fish
> The mid-'90s was the height of post-grunge alternative rock and it's interesting to note that Toronto stations like CFNY ("the spirit of radio!"), who had previously helped get Rush on the airwaves, were at this point leaving them behind as classic rock staples and embracing bands like I Mother Earth. The song is standard fare of the genre and Alex's guitar work is noticeable, but not flashy. I Mother Earth having opened for Rush and Edwin doing vocals for Victor makes it no surprise that Alex would return the favour and appear on their album.
> It's also interesting to note that the album was partly recorded at Le Studio and co-produced by Paul Northfield.

(May)
Neil Peart says in a *Detroit Free Press* interview (October 25, 1996) that following the completion of recording for *Test For Echo* and just before his "One O'clock Jump" sessions, he shoots his forthcoming instructional video. The *A Work In Progress* sessions recreate the recording sessions at Bearsville Studio, Bearsville, New York, US (*Modern Drummer* November, 1996)

(May 20)
Neil Peart records the following for the forthcoming *Burning For Buddy: A Tribute To The Music Of Buddy Rich II* tribute album, at Electric Lady Studios, New York City, New York, US:
"One O'clock Jump" – a rendition of the 1937 Count Basie number.

(August 3)
A *Billboard* interview with **Alex Lifeson** published on this date says *Rush* will work on the next live album during the early 1997 tour hiatus. It also announces that it will feature "unreleased tracks" from the February 20, 1978, Hammersmith Odeon concert, and will also include *Counterparts* tour tracks.

(Summer)
Neil Peart says in an interview (*Jam*, October 16, 1996) that *Rush* is working on a CD-ROM release about the band. **Geddy Lee** discusses it, as well, in an interview given in the summer (*A Show Of Fans* September 23, 1996). **Neil** says they "have people digging through stuff" in the *Rush* archive for material to include. The plan as he describes it is to include videos, information, trivia, bits of **Neil**'s writings and a host of other things.

Note: the date of the **Geddy Lee** interview comes from his statements in the interview about the then-current release of the *Working Man: A Tribute To Rush* album (Magna Carta Records) in August.

Note: The CD-ROM project would eventually be put on hold following the summer of 1997.

(September 6)
Rush releases their singles for "Test For Echo" in the US.

US CD promo single (PRCD 6853):
"Test For Echo"

US CD promo single (PRCD 6853-2):
"Test For Echo"
"Test For Echo (Radio Edit)"

> "Test For Echo (Radio Edit)" 5:01
> Written by Neil Peart & Pye Dubois (words), Geddy Lee & Alex Lifeson (music)
> Appears on: US CD promo single
> This edit removes nearly a minute of the track throughout. You're best to stick with the album cut.

Note: The date comes from *Billboard* (August 3, 1996)

(September 10)
Rush releases their album *Test For Echo* in Canada (Anthem Records) and worldwide (Atlantic Records). Track listing as follows:

"Test For Echo"
"Driven"
"Half A World"
"The Color Of Right"
"Time And Motion"
"Totem"
"Dog Years"
"Virtuality"
"Resist"
"Limbo"
"Care Away The Stone"

(October)
Pottersfield Press releases an expanded edition, the first commercially available, of **Neil Peart**'s book *The Masked Rider: Cycling In West Africa*. This edition is 286 pages.

Note: The release date comes from the interview published in *Jam*, October 16, 1996.

(October 19)
Rush performs live at Knickerbocker Arena. Albany, New York, US.

(October 20)
Rush performs live at Marine Midland Arena, Buffalo, New York, US.

(October 22)
Rush performs live at Nutter Center, Dayton, Ohio, US.

(October 23)
Rush performs live at Van Andel Arena, Grand Rapids, Michigan, US.

(October 25)
Rush performs live at The Palace. Auburn Hills, Michigan, US.

(October 26)
Rush performs live at Rockford MetroCentre, Rockford, Illinois, US.

(October 28)
Rush performs live at United Center, Chicago, Illinois, US.

(October 29)
Rush performs live at Target Center, Minneapolis, Minnesota, US.

(October 31)
Rush performs live at Kiel Center, St. Louis, Missouri, US.

(November 1)
Rush performs live at Bradley Center, Milwaukee, Wisconsin, US.

(November 3)
Rush performs live at Civic Arena, Pittsburgh, Pennsylvania, US.

(November 4)
Rush performs live at Gund Arena, Cleveland, Ohio, US.

(November 6)
Rush performs live at CoreStates Center, Philadelphia, Pennsylvania, US.

(November 7)
Rush performs live at USAir Arena, Landover, Maryland, US.

(November 8)
A *Connecticut Post* article published on this date notes **Neil Peart** has finished his instructional video *A Work In Progress* by this point.

(November 9)
Rush performs live at The FleetCenter, Boston, Massachusetts, US.

(November 10)
Rush performs live at Hartford Civic Center, Hartford, Connecticut, US.

(November 15)
Alex Lifeson performs live (as **"Big Al" Dexter**) with **The Dexters**, at The Orbit Room, Toronto, Ontario, Canada. The show is recorded and later issued as a limited edition, cassette-only live album by **The Dexters**, *Second Anniversary At The Orbit Room*. **"Big Al"** performs on the following tracks:

"Born Under A Bad Sign" – a cover of the 1967 song by Albert King
"All Along The Watch Tower" – a cover of the 1967 song by Bob Dylan
"For What It's Worth / White Rabbit" – covers of the 1967 song by Buffalo Springfield and the 1967 song by Jefferson Airplane

(November 20)
Rush performs live at San Jose Arena, San Jose, California, US.

(November 21)
Rush performs live at Arco Arena, Sacramento, California, US.

(November 23)
Rush performs live at Sports Arena, San Diego, California, US.

(November 24)
Rush performs live at Thomas & Mack Arena, UNLV, Las Vegas, Nevada, US.

(November 26 & 27)
Rush performs live at Great Western Forum, Los Angeles, California, US.

(November 29)
Rush performs live at America West Arena, Phoenix, Arizona, US.

(November 30)
Rush performs live at UTEP Special Events Center, El Paso, Texas, US.

(Date Unknown)
Rush releases their singles for "Half The World" in North America.

Canada CD promo single (PRCD 17):
"Half The World"

US CD promo single (PRCD 6930):
"Half The World"

(December 2)
Rush performs live at The Alamodome, San Antonio, Texas, US.

(December 3)
Rush performs live at Reunion Arena, Dallas, Texas, US.

(December 5)
Rush performs live at The Summit, Houston, Texas, US.

(December 6)
Rush performs live at UNO Lakefront Arena, New Orleans, Louisiana, US.

(December 8)

Rush performs live at Coral Sky Amphitheater, West Palm Beach, Florida, US.

(December 9)
Rush performs live at Ice Palace Arena, Tampa, Florida, US.

(December 11)
Rush performs live at The Omni, Atlanta, Georgia, US.

(December 12)
Rush performs live at Charlotte Coliseum, Charlotte, North Carolina, US.

(December 14)
Rush performs live at Nassau Coliseum, Uniondale, New York, US.

(December 15)
Rush performs live at Continental Arena, East Rutherford, New Jersey, US.

(December 18)
Rush performs live at The Phoenix Concert Theatre, Toronto, Ontario, Canada, as part of the *Molson Canadian Blind Date* concert series. The *Blind Date* series, which previously included bands such as Metallica, is made up of unannounced shows and the 800 contest winners do not know who they were going to see until they arrived (hence the *Blind Date* angle). As such, the band didn't advertise this show in advance.

RETROSPECTIVE I + II

1997

(Early 1997)
During the hiatus in touring, **Geddy Lee** and engineer Paul Northfield begin work on mixing material for the next live album (*Different Stages* sessions), including the 1978 Hammersmith Odeon recording.

Note: in a 1998 *Big-O* interview, **Alex Lifeson** let **Geddy** take lead on the production of the live album, keeping his own involvement minimal. He also says production on the album took 18 months, starting with the mixing during this hiatus.

Rush releases their "Driven" single in the US.

US CD promo single (PRCD 8009):
"Driven"

Note: the liner notes promote the upcoming spring 2nd leg of the *Test For Echo* tour, which places the release during this hiatus.

(February 25)
An article published on this date in the *Ottawa Sun* says **Rush** is planning to re-issue their "early albums" remastered.

(February 26)
Geddy Lee, **Neil Peart** and **Alex Lifeson** receive the Order of Canada at a ceremony held at Rideau Hall, Ottawa, Ontario, Canada. Governor General Romeo LeBlanc presides. Following the ceremony, the band members can use the letters "OC" after their name.

(Date Unknown)
Neil Peart works on the *Retrospective* compilations (*A Show Of Fans* June 21, 1997).

(Spring)
Rush releases their "Virtuality" single in the US.

US CD promo single (PRCD 8139):
"Virtuality (Promo Edit)"
"Virtuality"

> "Virtuality (Promo Edit)" 4:50
> Written by Neil Peart (words), Geddy Lee & Alex Lifeson (music)
> Appears on: US CD promo single
> I have not heard this edit. I'd be curious to know what in that 53 seconds was removed from the song. I'm guessing a verse and possibly a chorus somewhere.

Note: This promo single says Rush is currently on tour and a sticker on the case lists all the US *Test For Echo* tour dates for this leg, placing its release as just before the tour, in order to promo it.

(May 6)
Mercury Records and Anthem Records release the first of the *Rush Remasters* series. The remasters of *Rush*'s Mercury-era albums are done by Bob Ludwig at Gateway Mastering, Portland, Maine, US.

Rush
Fly By Night – this edition contains "By-Tor And The Snow Dog (Standard CD Edition)"
Caress Of Steel
2112
All The World's A Stage – this edition restores "What You're Doing"
A Farewell To Kings
Hemispheres
Permanent Waves

Mercury Records and Anthem Records release the **Rush** compilation *Retrospective I: 1974-1980*. Track listing as follows:

"The Spirit Of Radio"
"The Trees"
"Something For Nothing"

"Freewill"
"Xanadu"
"Bastille Day"
"By-Tor And The Snow Dog (Standard CD Edition)"
"Anthem"
"Closer To The Heart"
"2112: I: Overture"
"2112: II: The Temples Of Syrinx"
"La Villa Strangiato"
"Fly By Night"
"Finding My Way"

> "2112: I: Overture" 4:32
> Written by Neil Peart (words), Geddy Lee & Alex Lifeson (music)
> Appears on: Retrospective I: 1974-1980, Gold
> This is the album version as a standalone cut, ending right after "And the meek shall inherit the Earth" where "The Temples Of Syrinx" would come in (and is the next track on the CD, previously released on its own on various singles [see May, 1977]). By itself, the ending seems to leave itself hanging as you wait for "Syrinx" to start, but as a Rush fan, you're not likely to listen to one without the other, so for the sake of Retrospective and Gold, splitting the pieces up into separate tracks works.

(May 7)
Rush performs live at Hospitality Point, San Diego, California, US.

(May 8)
Rush performs live at Desert Sky Pavilion, Phoenix, Arizona, US.

(May 10)
Rush performs live at Glen Helen Blockbuster Pavilion, Devore, California, US.

(May 11)
Rush performs live at Shoreline Amphitheater, Mountain View, California, US.

(May 14)
Rush performs live at Rose Garden, Portland, Oregon, US.

(May 15)
Geddy Lee meets with Ben Mink at Mink's home studio in Vancouver, British Columbia, Canada The two jam and decide to attempt writing a song together by the end of the year (*WMMR* December 18, 2000).

(May 16)
Rush performs live at GM Place, Vancouver, British Columbia, Canada.

(May 17)
Rush performs live at The Gorge, George, Washington, US.

(May 19)
Rush performs live at BSU Pavilion, Boise, Idaho, US

(May 20)
Rush performs live at Delta Center, Salt Lake City, Utah, US.

(May 22)
Rush performs live at Fiddler's Green Amphitheater, Englewood, Colorado, US.

(May 24)
Rush performs live at Coca-Cola Starplex Amphitheater, Dallas, Texas, US. The show is recorded and the following track appears in the live album *Different Stages*:

"The Trees"

(May 25)
Rush performs live at Woodlands Pavilion, Woodlands, Texas, US.

(Late May to Early June)
During the tour hiatus, **Neil Peart** takes a cycling trip through Colorado, US.

(June 3)

Mercury Records and Anthem Records release the second of the *Rush Remasters* series. The remasters of *Rush*'s Mercury-era albums are done by Bob Ludwig at Gateway Mastering, Portland, Maine, US.

Moving Pictures
Exit...Stage Left – this edition includes "A Passage To Bangkok"
Signal
Grace Under Pressure
Power Window
Hold Your Fire
A Show Of Hands

Mercury Records and Anthem Records release the *Rush* compilation *Retrospective II: 1981-1987*. Track listing as follows:

"The Big Money"
"Red Barchetta"
"Subdivisions"
"Time Stands Still"
"Mystic Rhythms"
"The Analog Kid"
"Distant Early Warning"
"Marathon"
"The Body Electric"
"Mission"
"Limelight"
"Red Sector A"
"New World Man"
"Tom Sawyer"
"Force Ten"

(June 4)
Rush performs live at Riverbend Music Center, Cincinnati, Ohio, US. The show is recorded and the following track appears on the live album *Different Stages* (Japan Edition only):

"Force Ten"

> "Force Ten (Different Stages – Japan Bonus Track)" 4:55
> Written by Neil Peart & Pye Dubois (words), Geddy Lee & Alex Lifeson (music)
> Appears on: Different Stages (Japan Edition)
> The Japanese branch of Atlantic Records chose to include this extra song on the release of Different Stages in that territory. Hunting that edition down can get pricey. This performance of the song is excellent, though.

(June 5)
Rush performs live at Starwood Amphitheater, Nashville, Tennessee, US.

(June 7)
Rush performs live at Sandstone Amphitheater, Bonner Springs, Kansas, US.

(June 8)
Rush performs live at Riverport Amphitheater, St. Louis, Missouri, US.

(June 10)
Rush performs live at Deer Creek Music Center, Noblesville, Indiana, US.

(June 11)
Rush performs live at Star Lake Amphitheater, Burgettstown, Pennsylvania, US.

(June 13)
Rush performs live at Marcus Amphitheater, Milwaukee, Wisconsin, US.

(June 14)
Rush performs live at World Music Theater, Tinley Park, Illinois, US. The show is recorded and makes up most of the live album *Different Stages*. The following track has been released individually:

"The Spirit Of Radio

> "The Spirit Of Radio (Different Stages – Single Version)" 5:00
> Written by Neil Peart (words), Geddy Lee & Alex Lifeson (music)
> Appears on: "The Spirit Of Radio / 2112" US promo CD single

This cut of the song starts with the guitar intro and ends with a fade out over the crowd noise at the end.

(June 16)
Rush performs live at Polaris Amphitheater, Columbus, Ohio, US.

(June 17)
Rush performs live at Pine Knob Music Theater, Detroit, Michiga, US.

(June 19)
Rush performs live at PNC Bank Arts Center, Holmdel, New Jersey, US.

(June 20)
Rush performs live at Nissan Pavilion, Bristow, Virginia, US.

(June 22)
Rush performs live at Blockbuster-Sony E-Centre, Camden, New Jersey, US.

(June 23)
Rush performs live at Great Woods Center, Mansfield, Massachusetts, US. The show is recorded and the following tracks appear in the live album *Different Stages*:

"Leave That Thing Alone"
"2112"

> "2112 (Different Stages – Single Version)" 21:25
> Written by Neil Peart (words), Geddy Lee (music, except "Discovery" & "Presentation") & Alex Lifeson (music)
> Appears on: "The Spirit Of Radio / 2112" US promo CD single
> Starting with a quick fade in over the crowd, the entire "2112" epic is performed lived here. The Test For Echo Tour would be the only time the song would be played unabridged. The track ends with a fade out.

(June 25)
Rush performs live at Jones Beach, Wantagh, New York, US.

(June 26)
Rush performs live at Performing Arts Center, Darien Center, New York, US.

(June 28)
Rush performs live at Molson Centre, Montreal, Quebec, Canada.

(June 30)
Rush performs live at Molson Amphitheatre, Toronto, Ontario, Canada. The show is recorded and the following footage has been released:

"Closer To The Heart (Live at the Molson Amphitheatre – Video Version)"

R40 Bonus DVD:
"Limelight"
"Half The World"
"Limbo"
"Virtuality"
"Nobody's Hero"
"Test For Echo"
"Leave That Thing Alone"
"2112"

R40 Completist DVD/Blu-ray:
"Animate"
"Resist"
"Natural Science"

> "Closer To The Heart (Live At The Molson Amphitheatre – Video Version)" 4:54
> Written by Neil Peart & Peter Talbot (words), Geddy Lee & Alex Lifeson (music)
> Appears on: N/A
> At the time this video was released, Rush fans were hopeful for a full concert video from the Test For Echo tour. The concert video was discussed in interviews, but ultimately never saw the light of day. Eventually, footage would appear on the R40 boxed set, with 12 of the 25 songs (including this video) now available. This video hitting the airwave was bittersweet at the time, as Neil with in the midst of his time away from the band and fans weren't certain what the future had in store for Rush. It was great to the trio rocking out to

one of their signature songs (and the extended jam takes the performance to a whole new level), but for all we knew, this might be it for new material from the band. Since Neil's return and continued work by Rush, it's become much more enjoyable to watch this video. The audio starts with a fade-in over the crowd just before the opening guitar and fades out at the end after the last note.
Play it loud!

Note: In a 2014 *Rolling Stone* interview, **Geddy Lee** says the band had "forgotten about" the filming of the concert because of the "dark period" which followed; however, they were aware of it shortly after the tour (discussing it in period interviews) and even released the aforementioned promo video of the "Closer To The Heart" Molson Amphitheatre performance in 1999.

(July 2)
Rush performs live at Molson Amphitheatre, Toronto, Ontario, Canada. The show is recorded and the following track appears in the live album *Different Stages*:

"Resist"

Note: **Neil Peart** says in his book *Roadshow* this Toronto date was attended by his wife Jackie Taylor and their daughter Selena.

(July 3)
Rush performs live at Colisée de Québec, Quebec City, Quebec, Canada.

(July 4)
Rush performs live at Corel Centre, Ottawa, Ontario, Canada.

Note: In a 1998 *Big-O* interview, **Alex Lifeson** says 40-50 concerts are recorded during the *Test For Echo* tour. The *Different Stages* press release says all the shows on the *Test For Echo* tour are recorded

(July 20)
Atlantic Records releases *Burning For Buddy II: A Tribute To The Music Of Buddy Rich* worldwide, produced by and featuring **Neil Peart** on the track "One O'clock Jump."

> "One O'clock Jump" 7:46
> Written by Count Basie
> Appears on: Burning For Buddy II: A Tribute To The Music Of Buddy Rich
> This Count Basie standard will sound familiar to Rush fans, as Neil has used it to close out his drum solos in concerts. It's the piece he played originally in 1991 at the Buddy Rich Memorial Scholarship concert, where he was ultimately unhappy with his performance due to lack of proper rehearsal time and less-than-ideal show conditions. Had that performance been better, the Burning For Buddy project might never have happened. Here, Neil gives himself a second crack at it and the results are superb.

(Summer)
Following the tour, **Neil Peart** begins writing a book about the *Test For Echo* tour and his motorcycling between tour dates. In a *Drums Etc.* (September, 1997) interview given around this time, **Neil** suggests the title for the book could be *Landscape With Drums* (in his book *Roadshow*, he says the full title would have been *American Echoes: Landscape With Drums*).

(Date Unknown)
Alex Lifeson records the following for the forthcoming Christmas compilation *Merry Axemas: A Guitar Christmas*, likely at Lerxst Sound, Toronto, Ontario, Canada:
"The Little Drummer Boy" – a version of the traditional carol first recorded by The Trapp Family Singers (yes, *that* Trapp Family, ala *The Sound Of Music*) in 1955 as its original title "Carol of the Drums."

(Date Unknown)
Prior to **Geddy Lee** beginning to work on the *Test For Echo* tour concert recordings, engineer Robert Scovill filters out from the shows those which have "technical glitches" or were sub-par performances, narrowing the list to a dozen shows. Scovill does this work at his home studio in Arizona, US (*Guitar World* January, 1999).

(August 10)
Selena Peart Taylor, daughter of Jackie Taylor and **Neil Peart**, dies in a single-vehicle accident in her Jeep on Hwy 401, west of Brighton, Ontario, Canada.

(Mid-August)
At Selena's funeral, **Neil Peart** tells **Geddy Lee** and **Alex Lifeson** to consider him retired (*Ghost Rider*).

In a 2002 *Guitar Player* interview, **Alex** says he doesn't play guitar for about a year following Selena's death.

(September)

Several weeks following Selena's death, **Neil Peart** and Jackie Taylor travel to London, England, and there pursue grief counselling. They stay in London for six months (*Ghost Rider* and *Roadshow*).

(October 9)
Warner Music releases **Neil Peart**'s instructional VHS *A Work In Progress*, which examines the drumming on *Rush*'s *Test For Echo* album.

> "Momo's Dance Party (A Work In Progress Edit)" 3:05
> Written by Neil Peart
> Appears on: A Work In Progess VHS & DVD
> This percussion piece first appeared on Neil's A Work In Progress VHS and it was for a while the only version fans heard. It is an edit, though, fading in about 40 seconds into the music. Some of the melody sounds similar to "Pieces Of Eight" (which was written first, in 1985). The title takes it name from an African tribesman whom Neil met and performed with in a village on one of his cycling trips through Togo. The titular dance party happened in the village around them as they played. The instrumental here layers African rhythms and percussion into an energetic work that is definitely worth tracking down (though I'd recommend the full version found on Anatomy Of A Drum Solo). This edit is heard over the closing credits of A Work In Progress.

(Late 1997)
Geddy Lee says work on what would become *My Favorite Headache* began with Ben Mink at this time (*WMMR* interview, December 18, 2000). In a *Bass Frontiers* article, **Geddy** says his desire to work on solo material came during *Rush*'s "long hiatus" (September, 2000). **Lee** says the writing sessions took place in Vancouver, British Columbia and Toronto, Ontario, Canada (*Jam* January 18, 2000). The *My Favourite Headache* press release says **Lee** and Mink record "a number of times" this year. **Geddy** says in a *Global Bass* interview that the writing and demoing sessions take place over years, where the two would work together at one of their home studios for seven to ten day, then they "wouldn't do anything for two or three months," then do another seven to ten day session and break again for several months, and so on (December, 2000).
"My Favourite Headache" – **Geddy** says the skeleton of this song pre-dated these sessions, though it was one of the last worked on for the album.
"Slipping" – **Geddy** says this song was written early in the process and was the song that prompted him and Mink to continue working.
"Still" - **Geddy** says in a January 2001 issue of *Bass Player* that this song was among the earliest written for the album.

(November)
Epic Records releases the Christmas compilation *Merry Axemas: A Guitar Christmas*, featuring **Alex Lifeson**'s version of "The Little Drummer Boy."

> "The Little Drummer Boy" 3:25
> Written by Katherine Kennicott Davis (arr. by Alex Lifeson, based on add. arr. by Harry Simeone & Henry Onorati)
> Appears on: Merry Axemas: A Guitar Christmas
> The album's title might lead you think this would be a heavy arrangement, but what Alex gives us is a thoughtful, gentle performance, perfect for a quiet winter eve by the fireplace with some egg nog. He closes his performance with a little phrase from "Deck The Halls."

(December 27)
In a *Toronto Sun* interview published on this date promoting the *Retrospective I: 1974-1980* compilation, **Alex Lifeson** says "Rush has put itself on hold" in the wake of Selena Taylor's death.

DIFFERENT STAGES

1998

(January 7)
From London, England, **Neil Peart** writes a letter to Freddie Gruber thanking him for his support.

(Mid-January)
Jackie Taylor, common-law wife of **Neil Peart**, is diagnosed with terminal cancer while in London, England. The following day, **Neil** and Jackie take their scheduled flight back to Toronto, Ontario, Canada. **Neil** later reflects that his January 7th letter to Freddie Gruber was written a week or two before Jackie's diagnosis (*NeilPeart.net* January, 2012)

(March)
Neil Peart and Jackie Taylor travel to Barbados. In his book *Ghost Rider*, **Neil** says this was two months after the couple's return to Toronto.

(June 20)
Jacqueline "Jackie" Taylor, common-law wife of **Neil Peart**, dies of cancer in Barbados.

(July 7)
DreamWorks Records releases the soundtrack album *Small Soldiers: Music From The Motion Picture*, featuring the "DJ Z-Trip Remix" of **Rush**'s "Tom Sawyer."

Also, released is a promo CD sampler for the soundtrack album.

Small Soldiers: Music From The Motion Picture Sampler (PRO-CD-5101):
"Love Removal Machine (Brick Bazooka Mix)" The Cult
"Tom Sawyer (Alternative/Punchit and Scratchit Mix)" Rush
"Tom Sawyer (Rock/Slamfist Mix)" Rush

> "Tom Sawyer (DJ Z-Trip Remix)" aka "(Small Soldiers Remix)" 6:36
> Written by Neil Peart & Pye Dubois (words), Geddy Lee & Alex Lifeson (music); remixed by DJ Z-Trip
> Appears on: Small Soldiers: Music From The Motion Picture soundtrack album
> Opinions will be divided on these remixes. Some fans will believe that any additional production or remixing to any Rush song (let alone one of the band's signature songs) is nothing short of sacrilege. Other fans (like me) take DJ remixes for what they are, another artist's take on the track, one that is neither disrespectful nor harmful to the original. Alex Lifeson certainly likes this remix, as noted in period interviews. As remixes go, this one of pretty good, though you may miss Neil's drums, which seem to be replaced. Parts are repeated to good effect and bits are moved around, so there's a lot to keep you interested. Most of the power of the original is still there, so as with the other remixes on this soundtrack album, this one puts a different spin on an old favourite.
>
> "Tom Sawyer (Alternative/Punchit and Scratchit Mix)" 4:21
> Written by Neil Peart & Pye Dubois (words), Geddy Lee & Alex Lifeson (music); remixed by DJ Z-Trip
> Appears on: Small Soldiers: Music From The Motion Picture promo sampler
> Similar to the original "DJ Z-Trip Remix," this version removes some of the extended moments to create an overall tighter version that gets more to the point.
>
> "Tom Sawyer (Rock/Slamfist Mix)" 3:40
> Written by Neil Peart & Pye Dubois (words), Geddy Lee & Alex Lifeson (music); remixed by DJ Z-Trip
> Appears on: Small Soldiers: Music From The Motion Picture promo sampler
> This mix seems to pare down the original "DJ Z-Trip Remix" even further, with a more noticeable fade out at the end. Not as good as the "Alternative/Punchit and Scratchit Mix."

(July 4)
Geddy Lee and **Alex Lifeson** attend a concert by Jimmy Page & Robert Plant at the Molson Amphitheatre, Toronto, Ontario, Canada.

(August 20)
Neil Peart embarks from his home in Wentworth-Nord, Quebec, Canada, on what would become a 14-month-long motorcycle "journey" throughout North America. **Peart** later documents this time in his book *Ghost Rider: Travels On The Healing Road*.

(Late Summer)
Alex Lifeson gives an interview with *Big-O* (October 1998), saying *Different Stages* is going into production for release after 18 months working on it. He says that the album was remixed several different times and two weeks prior it was decided to include additional songs ("The Analog Kid" and "Show Don't Tell"). In a *Long Island Entertainment* piece

(October 1998), it is noted that this addition pushes the live album's release back from October 6 to November. **Geddy Lee** says "The Analog Kid" slipped through the cracks, but he caught it in time to include it and decides to put "Show Don't Tell" on while he is at it.

(Autumn)
In a *Long Island Entertainment* interview (October 1998), **Geddy Lee** says he has been recording with friends, but has no plans to record a solo album.

Geddy says *Rush* may consider a live video concert release of a *Test For Echo* show filmed during the tour. **Alex Lifeson** says a similar thing in an interview with *Big-O* (October 1998). In a January 1999 *Rockline* interview, they confirm the footage is from the June 30, 1997, Molson Amphitheatre concert.

Around this time, *Rush* releases its promo single for "The Spirit Of Radio" and "2112."

US CD promo single (PRCD 8693):
"The Spirit Of Radio (Different Stages – Single Version)"
"2112 (Different Stages – Single Version)"

Note: The single sleeve says it is from the forthcoming live album.

(November 10)
Rush releases their fourth live album *Different Stages* in Canada (Anthem Records) and worldwide (Atlantic Records). The show is mostly made up of the June 14, 1997, Tinley Park, Illinois, US, *Test For Echo* tour, with additional songs from Dallas, Texas (May 24, 1997), Mansfield, Massachusetts, US (June 23, 1997), Toronto, Ontario, Canada (July 2, 1997) and from the *Counterparts* tour: Philadelphia, Pennsylvania (April 30, 1994), Miami, Florida (February 27, 1994), Auburn Hills, Michigan (March 22, 1994), The Japan release features the bonus track "Force Ten" from the June 4, 1997, Cincinnati, Ohio, US, concert. Disc 1 features enhanced CD-ROM material in the form of lightshow animation that can be played with the music on the CD.

(November 15)
Geddy Lee and **Alex Lifeson** participate in a webcast from Atlantic Records, New York City, New York, US. They say they're still looking at the possibility of a releasing a concert film of the tour.

GHOST RIDER

1999

(January 20)
Geddy Lee and **Alex Lifeson** appear on *Rockline*. They say a video excerpt from the June 30, 1997, Molson Amphitheatre was recently released.

Note: The description of the live video matches the "Closer To The Heart" live video promoting *Different Stages*.

(Date Unknown)
Geddy Lee records bass and keyboards for the track "The Road" by Euphoria, for their debut album, venue unknown.

(Date Unknown)
Geddy Lee records bass on the I Mother Earth song "Good For Sule," for the band's album *Blue Green Orange*, at either Stigsound or Le Studio, Morin Heights, Quebec, Canada.

(Date Unknown)
Geddy Lee receives a call from Matt Stone (co-creator of the TV series *South Park*) asking he and **Alex Lifeson** to record a version of "O Canada" for the forthcoming *South Park* film. The call comes while he is at Ben Mink's home studio in Vancouver, British Columbia, Canada (*Global Bass* December, 2000). **Alex** says in an *AT&T Worldnet* chat that the call came late in the film's production.

(Date Unknown)
Geddy Lee and **Alex Lifeson** record the following over two days at Lerxst Sound, Toronto, Ontario, Canada (*Global Bass* December, 2000):
"O Canada" - this rendition of the Canadian national anthem is done for the film *South Park: Bigger, Longer And Uncut*.

(Date Unknown)
Alex Lifeson co-mixes No. 9's self-titled album.

Note: No. 9 is a project formed by former Platinum Blond members Mark Holmes and Sascha Tukatsch, as well as David Barrett. It is independently released on CD and through CDBaby.com

(Date Unknown)
After recording five demo tracks, **Geddy Lee** and Ben Mink decide to send the material out to a close circle of colleagues to get some input. Val Azoli (formerly of SRO Productions and currently of Atlantic Records) encourages them to put an album together (*My Favourite Headache* world premiere). In a *Jam* interview, **Geddy** says this was about halfway through the writing process (November, 2000).

(June 20)
South Park: Bigger, Longer And Uncut soundtrack album, featuring "O Canada" by **Geddy Lee and Alex Lifeson of Rush featuring Terrence and Phillip.**

> "O Canada" 1:10
> Written by Calixa Lavellée (music) & Robert Stanley (words), arr. by Alex Lifeson & Geddy Lee
> Appears on: *South Park: Bigger, Longer And Uncut* soundtrack album
> There's nothing too flashy or wild in this version and even the characters of Terrence and Phillip sing the song straight (until the end, when they start laughing). This was recorded and released without Neil Peart, who was traveling North America in the wake of his personal tragedies, and at the time fans wondered if this was the shape of things to come, at least for the foreseeable future. It was nice to know that Geddy and Alex were still recording, though

(Date Unknown)
In a *Jam* interview (January 16, 2000), it's noted **Geddy Lee** does pre-production work for the band Rocket Science at his home studio and at other small studios in Toronto, Ontario, Canada. **Lee**'s nephew, Rob Higgins, is a member of Rocket Science. Higgins says in a *Chart Attack* article (June 28, 2001) that songs are recorded as written and the sessions occur "every few months" for their eventual album, *Foolscap* (released in 2001).

(July 13)
Euphoria releases their self-titled debut album, featuring **Geddy Lee** on the track "The Road," on Six Degrees Records.

> "The Road" 6:20
> Written by Ken Ramm & Geddy Lee
> Appears on: Euphoria
> The piece starts with rambling guitar work (strangely, only in the left channel at first), before the music rolls in with an organic, trance-y flavour which really does evoke an unhurried journey down a country road,

before picking up the pace a little bit. The acoustic guitar and rhythmic harmonicas decorate the light keyboards (by Geddy) that underscore the entire piece. Geddy's bass is also noticeable throughout. This is really a wonderful piece with lots of subtle shades and upfront, colourful performances.

I Mother Earth releases their *Blue Green Orange* album, featuring **Geddy Lee** on the track "Good For Sule."

> "Good For Sule" 5:35
> Written by I Mother Earth (Jagori Tanna & Christian Tanna)
> Appears on: Blue Green Orange
> It's interesting that both this and the Euphoria Geddy Lee guest appearances were released on the same day, because despite being otherwise unrelated tracks, both share certain spirit in their gently arranged reflection (or maybe it's just me). This track is definitely an alt-rock acoustic number, moody, but not weighed down too much by its own introspection. This is also a bit different I Mother Earth from the days Alex recorded with them and with Edwin on Victor. By now, Edwin has been replaced by Brian Byrne and this album, the successor to Scenery And Fish, has been described as more mellow than the earlier album was. This is a good song and Geddy's bass stands out nicely.

(July 29)
Neil Peart pens a letter to his friend 'Brutus,' from his home in Wentworth-Nord, Quebec, Canada.

Note: The letter, written during a break in **Neil's** 14-month healing journey, serves as an example of some of the themes, ideas and phrases which would later surface in his lyrics for the *Vapor Trails* album, such as:
"Ghost Riding" – **Neil** felt hollow and apart from the world during his travels, as if he was a ghost atop his motorcycle.
"Little victories" – small accomplishments that are achieved in a given day.

(Date Unknown)
Rocket Science releases their demo EP, featuring **Geddy Lee** (co-producer) on the track "Space Suit." The recording later appears on their album *Foolscap*.

> "Space Suit" 3:31
> Written by Rob Higgins
> Appears on: Rocket Science EP, Foolscap
> This is a groovin' rock song and Geddy's backing vocals are noticeable throughout.

(October)
On his journeys on "the healing road," **Neil Peart** climbs Telescope Peak, Death Valley. The following day, he is introduced to photographer Carrie Nuttall by friend and **Rush** photographer Andrew MacNaughtan, in Los Angeles, California, US.
"Telescope Peak" – meeting Carrie effectively ended **Neil's** 14-month motorcycle journey. He later writes lyrics to this song thematically marking the change.

MY FAVOURITE HEADACHE

2000

(January)
A *Mackietone News* article published this month notes *Rush* is planning to returned to studio work in October. It also notes that **Alex Lifeson** has been working at Lerxst Sound, Toronto, Ontario, Canada, with his son Adrian on Adrian's own material.

(January 6)
Alex Lifeson appears on *Off The Record* on TSN, Canada.

(Early 2000)
Geddy Lee and Ben Mink step up work on the material they've been writing and recording. The take a reported "few weeks" to finish the demo stage, now with the plan to properly record the album (*Global Bass* December, 2000). **Lee** says in a *LiveDaily* interview (November 7, 2000) that some of the demo material ends up in the finished versions of some tracks.

(Spring)
Geddy Lee and Ben Mink begin recording material for **Lee**'s solo album (*My Favourite Headache* sessions). Co-produced by **Geddy Lee**, Ben Mink and David Leonard. Engineered by David Leonard. The sessions between spring and summer take place at The Peasant's Tent, East and West, Toronto, Ontario, and Vancouver, British Columbia, and Factory Studios, Vancouver, British Columbia, Canada. **Geddy** says in a January 2001 issue of *Bass Player* that despite being a genuine collaboration, Ben Mink preferred to remain in a "low profile" role, so the project would be put out under **Geddy Lee**'s name.

Alex Lifeson produces and mixes the tracks "Wasted Me" (also plays guitar), "Dangerous Game" (possibly plays guitar, as well) and "Dead Love" (unconfirmed if he plays guitar on this track) for 3 Doors Down, at American Sectors Studio, New Orleans, Louisiana, US. These sessions last three weeks (*MemphisFlyer.com* November 11, 2014).

Note: "Dead Love" remains unreleased. A version of "Dangerous Game" appears in the follow-up album *Away From The Sun*, but **Alex Lifeson** is not credited anywhere on the sleeve, nor is the session info, suggesting this is a re-recording and that **Alex**'s version remains unreleased.

Alex Lifeson performs live with 3 Doors Down at their album launch party, Biloxi, Mississippi, US. He plays on the song "Dangerous Game."

Note: though not identified by name one of the three tracks **Alex** plays on for the band, that he performed it live here suggests it was at least the second of two (possibly three) tracks.

(May)
In a 2000 *Bass Frontiers* article, **Geddy Lee** says drummer Matt Cameron was recruited after the songs were written and demoed with a temp drum track. Matt records his parts in the three-week window before Pearl Jam's European Tour, taking two weeks to record his drums (*My Favourite Headache* world premiere). Cameron's sessions take place at Studio X, Seattle, Washington, US (*LiveDaily* November 7, 2000). **Geddy** notes in a WMMR interview that Cameron recorded on eleven tracks, but one didn't make it on the album (December 18, 2000).

(May 27)
Geddy Lee and **Alex Lifeson** attend the ceremony for *Rush*'s induction onto Canada's Walk Of Fame.

(Date Unknown)
Alex Lifeson records the following (likely at Lerxst Sound, Toronto, Ontario, Canada):
"March Of The High Guard" – recorded for the forthcoming sci-fi TV series *Gene Roddenberry's Andromeda*.

(July 29 & 30)
This weekend (coincidentally, **Geddy Lee**'s 47th birthday), **Lee** and Ben Mink write and recorded the following at **Geddy**'s home studio, Toronto, Ontario, Canada (*My Favorite Headache* sessions):
"Home On The Strange"

On the 30th, **Lee** contacts drummer Jeremy Taggart (Our Lady Peace) about recording drums for the track.

(July 31)
Jeremy Taggart records drums for **Geddy Lee**'s solo project (*My Favourite Headache* sessions). Taggerts sessions take place at Reaction Studios, Toronto, Ontario, Canada (*LiveDaily* November 7, 2000).
"Home On The Strange" – Taggart plays drums on this track. **Geddy** says this is the last song worked on for the album (*Metal Edge* May, 2001).

An *MTV.com* (August 15, 2000) article notes that **Alex Lifeson** did the theme music for the forthcoming TV series *Gene Roddenberry's Andromeda*, has been performing with The Dexters at the Orbit Room, Toronto, Ontario, Canada (as Big Al Dexter), and produced three tracks for 3 Doors Down.

VH1.com reports on August 16th that **Lee** completes work on the album around this time ("last week"). The album liner notes simply say recording finished in the "summer."

"Window To The World" - In a *WMMR* interview, **Geddy Lee** confirms there are unused versions of the song with different tempos.

(Mid-2000)
Alex Lifeson says in a May 13, 2002, *Mobile Entertainment* interview that it is around this time that **Neil Peart** lets the band know he is ready to return to work with **Rush**. He says this conversation happened as **Geddy Lee** is finishing up *My Favourite Headache*.

(Summer)
Geddy Lee's album *My Favourite Headache* is edited (by Roger Lian) and mixed (by Howie Weinberg) at Masterdisk, New York City, New York, US.

After **Geddy Lee** finishes work on his solo album, **Alex Lifeson** starts production work with Lifer on their second album, *Lifer* (*Guitar Player* August, 2002). In an April 15, 2002, *Launch.com* interview, **Alex Lifeson** says around this time he is producing a band recording at Lerxst Sound, Toronto, Ontario, Canada (note: this is very likely Lifer).

(September 9)
Neil Peart marries Carrie Nuttall, in Montecito, California, US. **Geddy Lee** is in attendance (note it's not mentioned in reports whether **Alex Lifeson** attended).

(Date Unknown)
3 Doors Down release "Kryptonite" singles in Europe and Australasia. One of the B-side tracks is "Wasted Me," produced and mixed by **Alex Lifeson**.

> "Wasted Me" 3:11
> Written by Brad Arnold, Chris Henderson, Matt Roberts and Todd Harrell
> Appears on: "Kryptonite" Europe CD single, "Kryptonite" Australasia CD single
> While there's no quest Alex worked on the production side of this track (he fully credited on the single sleeve), it's uncertain whether he plays on the song. The guitar solo could be his, it's hard to tell (Alex is so adept at fitting seamlessly into a song). Listen for yourself and decide.

Note: these singles appear to have been issued later in the year, compared to the North American singles released in January which don't feature this track (seemingly because it didn't exist yet).

(October 2)
The TV series *Gene Roddenberry's Andromeda* premieres, featuring theme music by **Alex Lifeson**.

> "March Of The High Guard" :50
> Written by Alex Lifeson
> Appears on: N/A
> This sci-fi theme by Alex is suitably space-y, with layered guitars creating a synth-like tone.

(October 5)
Geddy Lee attends a Pearl Jam concert at the Air Canada Centre, Toronto, Ontario, Canada.

(October 8)
Neil Peart and Carrie Nuttall hold a wedding reception in Southern California, US.

(November 10)
The Dexters (with **Alex Lifeson** as 'Big Al' Dexter) perform live at the Capitol Event Theatre, Toronto, Ontario, Canada, as part of The Orbit Room's 6th anniversary event, *Soul In The City 2000*. The concert has a limited CD release as, featuring 'Big Al' on the track "Red Beans And Rice," a cover of the 1965 instrumental by Booker T & The McG's.

> "Red Beans And Rice (Live at the Capitol Theatre, 2000)" 4:20
> Written by Steve Cropper, Donald Dunn, Al Jackson Jr. & Booker T Jones
> Appears on: Soul In The City 2000
> A blistering version of the piece, this performance is worth the effort to hunt down. Alex provides his reliable chord support and then the solo comes in halfway, shredding up the joint as only he can, before dropping back to a support role for the other solos. Hearing him called "'Big Al' Dexter!" just before his solo is amusing, too.

Note: **Alex** reportedly played on several songs during the show, including the closing jam session.

(November 13)
Geddy Lee participates in an online chat with fans via *BarnesAndNoble.com* promoting *My Favorite Headache*.

Geddy Lee does a phone interview with *Global Bass*.

(November 14)
Geddy Lee releases his album *My Favourite Headache* on Atlantic Records worldwide. The CD-ROM component accesses a full interview with **Geddy** on the making of the album. Track listing as follows:

"My Favourite Headache"
"The Present Tense"
"Window To The World"
"Working At Perfekt"
"Runaway Train"
"The Angel's Share"
"Moving To Bohemia"
"Home On The Strange"
"Slipping"
"Still"
"Grace To Grace"

Note: The Canadian and British release of the album has the title spelt "Favourite," whereas the US and international editions spell it "Favorite."

Around this time, **Geddy Lee** releases his "My Favorite Headache" single in the US.

US CD promo single (PRCD 300343):
"My Favorite Headache (Promo Edit)"

> "My Favorite Headache (Promo Edit)" 4:09
> Written by Geddy Lee & Ben Mink
> Appears on: US CD promo single
> This version removes bits of instrumental from throughout the track.

Geddy Lee does an album signing at Compact Disc World, Edison, New Jersey, US.

(November 15)
Geddy Lee does an album signing at Desirable Disc, Dearborn, Michigan, US.

(November 16)
Geddy Lee does an album signing at Best Buy, Brooklyn, Ohio, US.

(November 17)
Geddy Lee does an album signing at Rolling Stones, Norridge, Illinois, US.

(November 24)
Geddy Lee does an album signing at Sunrise Records, St. Catharines, Ontario, Canada.

(November 27)
Geddy Lee does a radio interview at KISW 99.9FM , Seattle, Washington, US.

(Late November)
Geddy Lee's *My Favorite Headache* promotional tour continues in San Jose, Los Angeles (a *Rockline* interview) and Orange County (for a CD signing), California, US.

(December 18)
Geddy Lee does an interview with WMMR 93.5 FM at their studio in Philadelphia, Pennsylvania, US. He says he's been working with Rocket Science on their recording more material (*Foolscap* sessions).

(December 20)
Geddy Lee does an online chat via MSN, promoting *My Favorite Headache*.

GRACE TO GRACE

2001

(January 3)
Rush and their equipment personnel begin setting up gear at Reaction Studios, Toronto, Ontario, Canada, in advance of the band's writing sessions (noted in a January 12, *Jam!Showbiz*, article as occurring on the previous Wednesday).

In a KLBJ 93.7 FM interview (April 10, 2002), **Alex Lifeson** says the band took the approach of writing thirteen songs and selecting the best ten or eleven for the album (only to later change their mind and release all the songs).

(January 5)
Geddy Lee gives an interview to *Jam!Showbiz* (January 12, 2001), reportedly during the set-up stage for the writing sessions *Rush*'s next album.

(January 8)
Rush begins writing and demoing their seventeenth studio album at Reaction Studios, Toronto, Ontario, Canada. **Neil Peart** says in the *Vapor Trails* tour book that work began on "a cold Monday" this month. In a *Jam!Showbiz* article (May 7, 2002), **Alex Lifeson** says the first two weeks are spent talking and not playing much.

(January 13)
Geddy Lee releases his "Grace To Grace" single in the US.

US CD promo single (PRCD 300391):
"Grace To Grace"

Note: *Billboard* single review on this date

(Mid-January)
Neil Peart says in the *Vapor Trails* tour book that after "a couple of weeks" he has assembled some lyrics, however **Alex Lifeson** and **Geddy Lee** are still putting down musical ideas. When he has written "a half dozen" song lyrics, **Neil** takes a break (as **Alex** and **Geddy** are still not ready to start fitting lyrics to music) and starts his book (what will become *Ghost Rider: Travels On The Healing Road*).
"Telescope Peak" – the "best" lyrics from this song would eventually be repurposed into other songs for *Vapor Trails* album, such as "Ghost Rider" and "How It Is."

(February)
In a *Jam!Showbiz* article (October 23, 2000), it's noted the band are scheduled up to this month for writing sessions for their album. In a *Jam!Showbiz* article (May 7, 2002), **Alex Lifeson** describes what was recorded during the first few months as "junk" and that they took a break following these initial sessions. He tells the *North York Post* (June, 2002) that the break was for a few weeks.

(March)
Alex Lifeson says in *Brave Words & Bloody Knuckles* (July, 2002) that it was three months before they had anything written. In a *Jam!Showbiz* article (May 7, 2002), he says that at the three-month point, the album "took on a life of its own." Following the break, **Geddy Lee** and **Alex Lifeson** jam a lot and produce "a lot of out-there things," including:
"One Little Victory"
"Ceiling Unlimited"
"Nocturne"
"Earthshine" – noted in the *BW&BK* article being the first song completed (though later heavily revised)
"Peaceable Kingdom" – planned as an instrumental. **Geddy** notes that most of the finished backing track comes from a jam by him and **Alex** (*Contents Under Pressure*).

Note: From *Vapor Trails* tour book and *Bass Player* July, 2002.

(Date Unknown)
Lifer releases their self-titled second album, produced by **Alex Lifeson**.

(April 28)
Geddy Lee releases his "Home On The Strange" single in the US:

US CD promo single (PRCD 300520):
"Home On The Strange"
CD-ROM Interview

Note: *Billboard* single review on this date.

(May 30)
Geddy Lee posts a message to fans on his official website *GeddyLee.net* noting the progress of *Rush*'s sessions for the new album. He notes that "a collection of songs is starting to take shape."

(June)
Six months into their writing sessions, *Rush* reportedly have the following demos in various states of completion:
"Sweet Miracle" – the first song written for the album (*Rockline*, 2002)
"Earthshine" – the music is re-written fully during these sessions
"Out Of The Cradle" – one of the earliest songs written during these sessions
"The Stars Look Down" - one of the earliest songs completed (*Snakes & Arrows* liner notes)
"Vapor Trail"
"Secret Touch"
"How It Is" – much of the finished version features the original demo recordings from this period, as later attempts to re-record the song fall short (*Bass Player* July, 2002).

In a KLBJ 93.7 FM interview (April 10, 2002), **Alex Lifeson** says a lot of the album was written by this point. In a CNN interview (June 3, 2002), **Geddy Lee** says the band took a break for a month in June.

(July)
In a CNN interview (June 3, 2002), **Geddy Lee** says the band reconvened this month to continue work on the new album (Reaction Studios, Toronto, Ontario, Canada). Around this time, Producer/engineer Paul Northfield joins *Rush*'s sessions for their album. Songs developed after the arrival of Northfield include:
"Freeze" – Part IV of the 'Fear' Trilogy
"Peaceable Kingdom"
"Ghost Rider" – reportedly a nearly abandoned song that Northfield's input saved.

(Mid-August)
Rush begins recording for their seventeenth studio album, Reaction Studios, Toronto, Ontario, Canada (*Vapor Trails* sessions). **Neil Peart** describes in the *Vapor Trails* tour book the sessions from this point on as an overlapping process of writing, demoing and recording (where previously these stages were mostly separate). Engineered by Paul Northfield, **Geddy Lee** and **Alex Lifeson**.

Note: The date comes from a September 16, 2001, *Vancouver Province* article.

(September)
In a *Guitar Center* magazine published this month, **Geddy Lee** says he's currently writing with *Rush*.

(September 11)
The coordinated terrorist suicide attack on New York City, New York, US, and Washington D.C., US, via the hijacking of four airline flights (including United Airlines Flight 93, which crashed in Pennsylvania), occurs on this date.
"Peaceable Kingdom" – in a *Jam!Showbiz* article (May 7, 2002), **Alex Lifeson** says this track was intended as an instrumental, but co-producer Paul Northfield suggested it be given lyrics. The week following 9/11, **Neil Peart** penned lyrics for the song. In the *Vapor Trails* tour book, **Neil** describes this song as "a chilling reflection of the events" of this date.

Alex Lifeson also says in the *Jam!Showbiz* article that the album's songs were otherwise all written by this point.

(September 25)
Anthem Music Video and Mercury Records releases the *Rush* video compilation *Chronicles* on DVD in North America.

"Closer To The Heart" – Seneca College
"The Trees (Live at the Hammersmith Odeon, 1979)"
"Limelight" – Le Studio
"Tom Sawyer" – Le Studio
"Red Barchetta (Exit...Stage Left – Video Version)"
"Subdivisions"
"Distant Early Warning"
"Red Sector A (Grace Under Pressure Tour – Video Version)"
"The Big Money" – standard edited version
"Mystic Rhythms"
"Time Stand Still"
"Lock And Key"
"The Enemy Within" – Hidden Easter egg video
"Afterimage" – Hidden Easter egg video

Note: Date from September 16, 2001, *Vancouver Province* article.

(November)

Rush completes their recording sessions for their album, at Reaction Studios, Toronto, Ontario, Canada (*Vapor Trails* sessions).

(November 26)
Geddy Lee attends the Hard Rock Café re-launch, Toronto, Ontario, Canada.

(December)
Rush begins work on mixing the tracks of their album, at Metalworks, Mississauga, Ontario, Canada. **Neil Peart** says in the *Vapor Trails* tour book that the initial mixing sessions are difficult and there are several "unsatisfying" mixes done before engineer David Leonard joins the project.

Neil Peart is in the revision stage of his book *Ghost Rider* during the mixing sessions for the album (*Classic Rock* October, 2004).

VAPOR TRAILS

2002

(February)
Rush completes mixing work on its album, at Metalworks, Mississauga, Ontario, Canada (*Vapor Trails* sessions).

Rush's album *Vapor Trails* is mastered by Howie Weinberg, with additional mastering and sequencing by Roger Lian, at Masterdisk, New York City, New York, US. In a *Jam!Showbiz* article (May 7, 2002), **Alex Lifeson** says **Geddy Lee** supervised the mastering process and details problems that were discovered with digital distortion on the album, requiring additional re-mixing of tracks.

Note: This would seem to be the root of the well-documented problem which befell *Vapor Trails* as it fell victim to the Loudness War of the time (*ProRec.com* August 31, 2002). The overall poor quality of the commercial release would lead to **Rush** eventually doing a full re-mix of the album years later in an attempt to fix it.

(March 29)
Rush release their "One Little Victory" singles in North America.

US CD promo single (PRCD 300749):
"One Little Victory"

US CD promo single (PRCD 300857):
"One Little Victory"
"Earthshine"

Note: Dates come from *ChartAttack.com* March 18, 2002.

(April 10)
Alex Lifeson gives an interview with KLBJ 93.7 FM. He says **Rush** have spent the last couple of weeks putting the concert production together.

(April 14)
Geddy Lee posts a message to fans on his official website *GeddyLee.net* discussing the recording of *Vapor Trails* and the upcoming tour.

(April 23)
Warner Music re-issues **Neil Peart**'s instructional video *A Work In Progress* on DVD.

(May 14)
Rush releases their seventeenth studio album, *Vapor Trails*, in Canada (Anthem Records) and worldwide (Atlantic Records). Track listing as follows:

"One Little Victory"
"Ceiling Unlimited"
"Ghost Rider"
"Peaceable Kingdom"
"The Stars Look Down"
"How It Is"
"Vapor Trail"
"Secret Touch"
"Earthshine"
"Sweet Miracle"
"Nocturne"
"Freeze (Part IV of 'Fear')"
"Out Of The Cradle"

(Mid-May)
Rush starts their rehearsals for their upcoming tour, at the Civic Center, Glens Falls, New York, US. In a *Bass Guitar* interview (January, 2003), **Geddy Lee** says the tour rehearsals last six weeks.
"Resist" – **Geddy Lee** and **Alex Lifeson** develop the acoustic version of the song during rehearsals for the tour.

(June 3)
In a CNN interview broadcast on this date, **Alex Lifeson** says he's been recording with his son Adrian at Lerxst Sound, Toronto, Ontario, Canada.

(Late June)

Rush starts their production rehearsals for the upcoming tour.

(June 28)
Rush performs live at Meadows Music Centre, Hartford, Connecticut, US.

> "Between Sun & Moon (Live At Hartford, 2002)" 4:48
> Written by Neil Peart & Pye Dubois (words), Geddy Lee & Alex Lifeson (music)
> Appears on: Rush: Beyond The Lighted Stage DVD & Blu-ray
> This performance appears as an extra feature on the DVD and Blu-ray of the *Beyond The Lighted Stage* documentary. Interestingly, it would appear that this footage mixes bootleg audio recorded from the audience with the production camera footage shot on the night for the video projections. This combination was likely necessary because a professional camera crew wasn't on hand to shoot the concert. It does serve to elevate the bootleg audio to a somewhat official status by it appearing on a legitimate release. This also marks the first live performance of the song and it's a good rendition (one can hardly complain about anything, given the importance of this concert, the return of Rush to the stage).

(June 29)
Rush performs live at Montage Mountain Amphitheatre, Scranton, Pennsylvania, US.

(July 1)
Rush performs live at Verizon Wireless Amphitheatre, Charlotte, North Carolina, US.

(July 3)
Rush performs live at Verizon Wireless Amphitheatre, Virginia Beach, Virginia, US.

(July 4)
Rush performs live at Alltel Pavilion @ Walnut Creek, Raleigh, North Carolina, US.

(July 5)
ECW Press and Pottersfield Press releases **Neil Peart**'s book *Ghost Rider: Travels On The Healing Road*, which documents **Neil**'s 14-month motorcycle journey between 1998 and 1999.

(July 6)
Rush performs live at Saratoga Performing Arts Center, Saratoga Springs, New York, US.

(July 7)
Rush performs live at Darien Lake Performing Arts Center, Darien Center, New York, US.

(July 9)
Rush performs live at Nissan Pavilion, Bristow, Virginia, US.

(July 10)
Rush releases their "Secret Touch" single in the US.

US CD promo single (PRCD 300863):
"Secret Touch (Radio Edit)"
"Secret Touch"

> "Secret Touch (Radio Edit)" 4:47
> Written by Neil Peart (words), Geddy Lee & Alex Lifeson (music)
> Appears on: US CD promo single
> This version removes nearly two minutes of the track throughout.

(July 11)
Rush performs live at PNC Bank Arts Center, Holmdel, New Jersey, US.

(July 12)
Rush performs live at Tweeter Center, Mansfield, Massachusetts, US.

(July 14)
Rush performs live at Tweeter Center, Camden, New Jersey, US.

(July 15)
Rush performs live at Jones Beach, Wantagh, New York, US.

(July 17)
Rush performs live at Molson Amphitheatre, Toronto, Ontario, Canada.

(July 19)

Rush performs live at Marcus Amphitheatre, Milwaukee, Wisconsin, US.

(July 20)
Rush performs live at Tweeter Center, Tinley Park, Illinois, US.

(Late July)
Alex Lifeson shoots his scenes for an episode of *Trailer Park Boys*, Halifax, Nova Scotia, Canada (*Canada.com* July 28, 2002).

(August 1)
Rush performs live at Sandstone Amphitheatre, Bonner Springs, Kansas, US.

(August 2)
Rush performs live at UMB Bank Pavilion, Maryland Heights, Missouri, US.

(August 4)
Rush performs live at Riverbend Music Center, Cincinnati, Ohio, US.

(August 6)
Rush performs live at Post-Gazette Pavilion, Burgettstown, Pennsylvania, US.

(August 8)
Rush performs live at Polaris Amphitheatre, Columbus, Ohio, US.

(August 9)
Rush performs live at Verizon Wireless Music Center. Noblesville, Indiana, US.

(August 11 & 12)
Rush performs live at DTE Energy Music Theatre, Clarkston, Michigan, US.

(August 14)
Rush performs live at AmSouth Amphitheatre, Nashville, Tennessee, US.

(August 16)
Rush performs live at C.W. Mitchell Pavilion, The Woodlands, Texas, US.

(August 17)
Rush performs live at Verizon Wireless Amphitheatre, San Antonio, Texas, US.

(August 19)
Rush performs live at Smirnoff Music Center, Dallas, Texas, US.

(August 21)
Rush performs live at Journal Pavilion, Albuquerque, New Mexico, US.

(August 23)
Rush performs live at Delta Center, Salt Lake City, Utah, US.

(August 24)
Rush performs live at Fiddler's Green Amphitheatre, Englewood, Colorado, US.

(September 8)
Rush performs live at GM Place, Vancouver, British Columbia, Canada.

(September 10)
Rush performs live at Skyreach Centre, Edmonton, Alberta, Canada.

(September 12)
Rush performs live at Pengrowth Saddledome, Calgary, Alberta, Canada.

(September 14)
Rush performs live at The Gorge, Seattle, Washington, US.

(September 15)
Rush performs live at Rose Garden, Portland, Oregon, US.

(September 17)
Rush performs live at Chronicle Pavilion, Concord, California, US.

(September 18)
Rush performs live at Autowest Amphitheater, Sacramento, California, US.

(September 20)
Rush performs live at Shoreline Amphitheater, Mountain View, California, US.

(September 21)
Rush performs live at MGM Grand Garden Arena, Las Vegas, Nevada, US.

(September 23_
Rush performs live at Staples Center Arena, Los Angeles, California, US.

(September 25)
Rush performs live at Coors Amphitheater, San Diego, California, US.

(September 27)
Rush performs live at Cricket Pavilion, Phoenix, Arizona, US. This concert is filmed and the following song later appears as a bonus track on the *Rush In Rio* CD:

"Between Sun & Moon"

> "Between Sun & Moon (Live in Phoenix, 2002)" 4:47
> Written by Neil Peart & Pye Dubois (words), Geddy Lee & Alex Lifeson (music)
> Appears on: Rush In Rio CD
> Not a bad live version and a lot of great energy. The track fades in over the count-in

(September 28)
Rush performs live at Verizon Wireless Amphitheater, Irvine, California, US.

(September 30)
Electronic Arts releases their video game *Need For Speed: Hot Pursuit 2* for the GameCube console. The in-game soundtrack features an instrumental edit of *Rush*'s "One Little Victory."

> "One Little Victory (NFS:HP2 Instrumental Edit)" 4:07
> Written by Neil Peart (words), Geddy Lee & Alex Lifeson (music)
> Appears on: Need For Speed: Hot Pursuit 2 video game
> This is an edit of the original Rush backing, with none of Geddy's vocals, making for an awesome alternative to the standard version. The distortion throughout which plagued the original album is still present, but don't let that stop you from turning it up loud. The missing bits are removed here and there throughout the track, but it's not all that noticeable unless you're singing, air drumming or playing air guitar along with it.

(October 5)
Rush performs live at Foro Sol, Mexico City, Mexico.

(October 10)
Rush performs live at St. Pete Times Forum, Tampa, Florida, US.

(October 11)
Rush performs live at Mars Music Amphitheatre, West Palm Beach, Florida, US.

(October 13)
Rush performs live at Phillips Arena, Atlanta, Georgia, US.

(October 15)
Rush performs live at Baltimore Arena, Baltimore, Maryland, US.

(October 16)
Rush performs live at Blue Cross Arena, Rochester, New York, US.

(October 18)
Rush performs live at Bell Center, Montreal, Quebec, Canada.

(October 19)
Rush performs live at Colisée Pepsi, Quebec City, Quebec, Canada. This concert is filmed and the following song later appears as a bonus track on the *Rush In Rio* CD:

"Vital Signs"

> "Vital Signs (Live In Quebec City, 2002)" 4:57

Written by Neil Peart (words), Geddy Lee & Alex Lifeson (music)
Appears on: Rush In Rio CD
A great stand-alone live version this, that rivals the Montreal, 1981, "New World Man" B-side recording of the song.

(October 22)
Rush performs live at the Air Canada Centre, Toronto, Ontario, Canada. **Alex Lifeson** finishes shooting his scenes with the cast of *Trailer Park Boys* during this show (*Fireworks* October, 2004).

(October 24)
Rush performs live at Madison Square Garden, New York City, New York, US.

(October 25)
Rush performs live at Giant Center, Hershey, Pennsylvania, US.

(October 27)
Rush performs live at First Union Center, Philadelphia, Pennsylvania, US.

(October 28)
Rush performs live at Fleet Center, Boston, Massachusetts, US.

(October 30)
Rush performs live at The United Center, Chicago, Illinois, US.

(November 1)
Rush performs live at Hilton Coliseum, Ames, Iowa, US.

(November 2)
Rush performs live at Target Center. Minneapolis, Minnesota, US.

(November 4)
Rush performs live at Gund Arena, Cleveland, Ohio, US.

(November 6)
Rush performs live at Continental Airlines Arena, East Rutherford, New Jersey, US.

(November 8)
Rush performs live at Mohegan Sun Casino, Uncasville, Connecticut, US.

(November 10)
Rush performs live at Verizon Arena, Manchester, New Hampshire, US.

(November 20)
Rush performs live at Olympic Stadium, Porto Alegre, Brazil.

(November 22)
Rush performs live at Estadio Morumbi, São Paulo, Brazil.

(November 23)
Rush performs live at Maracana Stadium, Rio de Janeiro, Brazil. The concert is filmed and released in 2003 on CD and DVD as *Rush In Rio*. The following tracks have been released individually:

"YYZ (Rush In Rio – MX Multiangle Version)" 4:52
Written by Geddy Lee & Neil Peart
Appears on: Rush In Rio DVD
This version starts abruptly during the last notes of "Earthshine" and fades out at the end. The multiangle feature on the DVD allows the viewer to jump back and forth between four different angles as the track plays, which is interesting and gives the viewer different ways to watch the songs.

"YYZ (Rush In Rio – Sampler Version)" 4:40
Written by Geddy Lee & Neil Peart
Appears on: US CD promo sampler
This version fades in at the start and fades out before Geddy thanks the audience at the end.

"YYZ (Rush In Rio – Working Men CD Version)" 4:50
Written by Geddy Lee & Neil Peart
Appears on: Working Men CD
This version fades in at the start and fades out after Geddy thanks the audience at the end.

"YYZ (Rush In Rio – Working Men DVD Version)" 4:39
Written by Geddy Lee & Neil Peart
Appears on: Working Men DVD
This version fades in at the start and fades out at the end before Geddy thanks the audience.

"Closer To The Heart (Rush In Rio – Working Men CD Version)" 3:21
Written by Neil Peart & Peter Talbot (words), Geddy Lee & Alex Lifeson (music)
Appears on: Working Men CD
This version starts with Geddy's full intro and fades in out at the end.

"Closer To The Heart (Rush In Rio – Working Men DVD Version)" 3:15
Written by Neil Peart & Peter Talbot (words), Geddy Lee & Alex Lifeson (music)
Appears on: Working Men DVD
This version edits the first part of Geddy's intro (it starts with "Somebody told...Somebody told me...") and fades in out at the end.

"One Little Victory (Rush In Rio – Sampler Version)" 5:25
Written by Neil Peart (words), Geddy Lee & Alex Lifeson (music)
Appears on: US CD promo sampler
This version fades out at the end.

"Dreamline (Rush In Rio – Sampler Version)" 5:11
Written by Neil Peart (words), Geddy Lee & Alex Lifeson (music)
Appears on: US CD promo sampler
This version fades at the beginning and fades out at the end.

"O Baterista (Rush In Rio – MX Multiangle Version)" 8:21
Written by Geddy Lee & Neil Peart
Appears on: Rush In Rio DVD
This version starts abruptly at the end of "Leave That Thing Alone" and fades out just after the solo ends, shaving off the 40 seconds of crowd noise and Geddy and Alex coming onstage to perform "Resist."

"O Baterista (Rush In Rio – AOADS Version)" 8:14
Written by Neil Peart (Count Basie: "One O'clock Jump," arr. by Peart)
Appears on: Anatomy Of A Drum Solo DVD
This version fades in over the last few notes of "Leave That Thing Along" and fades out just after the solo ends.

"Resist (Rush In Rio – Live Acoustic Version)" 4:40
Written by Neil Peart (words), Geddy Lee & Alex Lifeson (music)
Appears on: US CD promo sampler, US CD promo single
This version fades in over the crowd noise (which can be heard after "O Baterista" on the album) and fades out quickly at the end.

"2112: I: Overture / II: The Temples Of Syrinx (Rush In Rio – Sampler Version)" 6:51
Written by Neil Peart (words), Geddy Lee & Alex Lifeson (music)
Appears on: US CD promo sampler, Working Men CD
This version fades in quickly at the start and fades out over the crowd noise at the end. Of note is the fact that this edit previously appeared Rush In Rio promo sampler prior to its inclusion on the Working Men CD.

"2112: I: Overture / II: The Temples Of Syrinx (Rush In Rio – Working Men DVD Version)" 6:49
Written by Neil Peart (words), Geddy Lee & Alex Lifeson (music)
Appears on: Working Men DVD
The clip's audio is virtually identical to the Sampler Version (see above). The extra seconds of runtime come from a longer silence at the end.

"La Villa Strangiato (Rush In Rio - MX Multiangle Version)" 7:14
Written by Geddy Lee, Alex Lifeson & Neil Peart ("Powerhouse" by Raymond Scott, arr. by Lee/Lifeson/Peart)
Appears on: Rush In Rio DVD
This starts abruptly with the crowd noise before the band starts the piece and fades out during the "Monsters (Reprise)" part, cutting off the last few minutes.

"Working Man (Rush In Rio – Sampler Version)" 5:13
Written by Geddy Lee & Alex Lifeson
Appears on: US CD promo sampler
This version fades in quickly and fades out earlier than the album version.

THE SPIRIT OF RADIO: GREATEST HITS 1974 – 1987 & RUSH IN RIO

2003

(Early 2003)
Rush releases their "Sweet Miracles" single in the US.

US CD promo single (PRCD 300930):
"Sweet Miracle"

Note: *Billboard* January 31, 2003 (released after this date)

(Date Unknown)
Alex Lifeson remixes the All Systems Go! track "Fascination Unknown," likely at Lerxst Sound, Toronto, Ontario, Canada.

(February 1)
Space shuttle *Columbia (OV-102)* disintegrates upon re-entry of Earth's atmosphere, over Texas and Louisiana, US. All hands are lost.
"Countdown" – **Rush** had previously attended *Columbia*'s maiden voyage in 1981 and written this song about the experience.

(February 10)
Alex Lifeson participates in a live online chat via *AT&T Worldnet*.

(February 11)
Mercury Records, Anthem Records and Atlantic Records release the **Rush** compilation *The Spirit Of Radio: Greatest Hits 1974-1987* in their respective territories. The 100,000 copies include a bonus DVD of videos.

CD:
"Working Man"
"Fly By Night"
"2112: I: Overture / II: The Temples Of Syrinx"
"Closer To The Heart"
"The Trees"
"The Spirit Of Radio"
"Freewill"
"Limelight"
"Tom Sawyer"
"Red Barchetta"
"New World Man"
"Subdivisions"
"Distant Early Warning"
"The Big Money"
"Force Ten"
"Time Stand Still"

Limited Edition Bonus DVD:
"Closer To The Heart" – Seneca College
"Tom Sawyer" – Le Studio
"Subdivisions"
"The Big Money" – standard edited version
"Mystic Rhythms"

Note: **Geddy Lee** says in a *USAToday.com* chat that **Rush** didn't have much input on this collection, but did give their opinion on its cover artwork.

(February 23)
All Systems Go! release their "Fascination Unknown" single, featuring a remix of the track by **Alex Lifeson**.

    "Fascination Unknown (Remix by Alex Lifeson)" 3:10
    Written by Greg Dulli & All Systems Go!
    Appears on: CD single

Not radically different from the standard version, this remix by Alex is beefier, with more prominent guitars and bass and some other differently mixed bits and pieces throughout.

(Mid-March)
While Carrie Nuttall is vacationing at a surf camp in Mexico, **Neil Peart** takes a road trip by car from Los Angeles, California, US, to Big Bend National Park, Texas, US. This trip later forms the basis for his book *Traveling Music*.

(May 6)
Geddy Lee posts a message on his official website, GeddyLee.net, discussing the recent tour and the forthcoming *Rush In Rio* DVD, which he says he hopes they'll have finished soon.

(Date Unknown)
During production of the *Rush In Rio* DVD, it is suggested to the band by Ray Danniels that **Rush** also release the concert on CD (*Rush In Rio* liner notes).

(July 3)
In the press release for **Rush**'s involvement in the forthcoming *Molson Canadian Rocks For Toronto* SARS benefit concert in Toronto, Ontario, Canada, **Neil Peart** notes that **Alex Lifeson** is working on *Rush In Rio* and **Geddy Lee** is with his family, in France. **Alex** says in 2003 *Classic Rock* interview that he is "down south" taking a break from the *Rio* mixing when the invitation to do the benefit show comes in.

(July 29)
In an article published on the date, **Alex Lifeson** says the band has been working on *Rush In Rio* for the last seven weeks (**Lifeson** on mixing the audio, **Geddy Lee** on the visuals and **Neil Peart** on early stage assembly of the material).

(July 30)
Rush performs live at Downsview Park, Toronto, Ontario, Canada, as part of *Molson Canadian Rocks For Toronto*. Also on the bill are The Rolling Stones, AC/DC, Justin Timberlake, The Guess Who, Sam Roberts, The Flaming Lips, Kathleen Edwards, The Isley Brothers, Sass Jordan, La Chicane, Dan Ackroyd and Jim Belushi (as the Blues Brothers).

(Date Unknown)
Alex Lifeson records guitar for the track "Hey Bop A-Rebop," a cover of the 1945 Lionel Hampton song, for The Stickmen album *Side Two*. The Stickmen was formed by Bernie LaBarge, of The Dexters, hence the connection to **Alex**.

(October)
Atlantic Records releases a CD promo sampler for **Rush**'s live album *Rush In Rio*.

US CD promo sampler (PRCD 301227):
"Working Man (Rush In Rio – Sampler Version)"
"One Little Victory (Rush In Rio – Sampler Version)"
"2112: I: Overture / II: The Temples Of Syrinx (Rush In Rio – Sampler Version)"
"Dreamline (Rush In Rio – Sampler Version)"
"YYZ (Rush In Rio – Sampler Version)"
"Resist (Rush In Rio – Live Acoustic Version)"

(October 17)
In a *ClassicRockRadio.eu* interview posted on this date, **Alex Lifeson** notes that **Geddy Lee** and Nancy Young are vacationing in Vietnam.

The Dexters (with **Alex Lifeson** as 'Big Al' Dexter), perform live at The Capitol Theatre, Toronto, Ontario, Canada, for their 9th anniversary festivities, *Soul In The City 3*. 'Big Al' performs on "The Letter," a cover of the 1967 song by The Box Tops.

(October 21)
Rush releases their concert film and live album, *Rush In Rio*, in Canada (Anthem Records) and worldwide (Atlantic Records), both on 2xDVD and 3xCD. The concert is from the November 23, 2002, Rio de Janeiro, Brazil, date of the *Vapor Trails* tour. The DVD and CD editions differ in the following way:

Rush In Rio 2xDVD
DVD 1: Rio de Janeiro concert

DVD 2:
The Boys In Brazil Documentary
MX Multiangle Songs:
    1. "YYZ"
    2. "O Baterista"
    3. "La Villa Strangiato"
Easter Eggs:
    "By-Tor And The Snow Dog" Animation

"Anthem" – Castle Session video

Rush In Rio 3xCD
CD 1: Rio de Janeiro concert (Set 1)

CD 2: Rio de Janeiro concert (Set 2)

CD 3: Rio de Janeiro concert (Set 2 con't + Encore)
Bonus track: "Between Sun & Moon (Live in Phoenix, 2002)"
Bonus track: "Vital Signs (Live in Quebec City, 2002)"

Around this time, **Rush** releases its "Resist" single in the US.

US CD promo single (P1ZOE1279P):
"Resist (Rush In Rio – Live Acoustic Version)"

(December 13)
The Stickmen release their album *Side Two*, featuring **Alex Lifeson** on the track "Hey Bop A-Rebop."

> "Hey Bop A-Rebop" 5:45
> Written by Curley Hamney & Lionel Hampton
> Appears on: Side Two
> A funk rock cover of the old jazz standard by Lionel Hampton and His Orchestra, this track is a lot of fun and Alex gets into the groove with some panache. Recommended!

(December 31)
Alex Lifeson, his wife Charlene, their son Justin and Justin's wife Michelle attend a New Year's Eve event at the Ritz-Carlton hotel, Naples, Florida, US. Shortly before midnight, **Alex**, Justin and Michelle are arrested at the hotel. The six arresting charges include assault on a police officer, resisting arrest and disorderly intoxication. In his book *Roadshow*, **Neil Peart** gives a detailed account of the events which led to the arrests. Published court records go into more detail of the incident which, in short, plays out thusly:

Justin twice got on stage during the festivities to address the crowd. Hotel security then attempted to escort Justin off the property. **Alex** intervened and sheriff's deputies were called. The deputies assaulted Justin and **Alex** in the hotel's stairwell (including being beaten, tasered and **Alex** having his nose broken). The two were then cuffed, processed at the local jail.

Note: An employee of the hotel witnessed the assault and would come forward in 2005.

FEEDBACK & R30

2004

(January 1)
Alex Lifeson's son Justin and daughter-in-law Michelle are released from jail, Naples, Florida, US.

(January 2)
Alex Lifeson is released from jail, Naples, Florida, US.

(Early 2005)
Paul Siegel and Rob Wallis suggest to **Neil Peart** that he do another instructional drum video.

(March 22)
The Florida State Attorney's Office formally files two charges of battery on a police officer against **Alex Lifeson** for the incident on New Year's Eve, 2003.

Note: Under terms of the bond, **Lifeson** is permitted to travel outside US, which allows for the forthcoming tour to proceed as planned.

(Late-March)
Alex Lifeson says the idea to do some cover songs came from a friend of the band's. The original plan was to do "a few" songs. They ended up with five songs in advance of going into the studio to record. (*Birmingham Evening Mail* August 28, 2004). **Geddy Lee** and **Alex Lifeson** work at **Lee**'s home studio, Toronto, Ontario, Canada, communicating with **Neil Peart** about the project.

Rush begins recording their covers project at Phase One Studios, Toronto, Ontario, Canada (*Feedback* sessions). Co-produced by David Leonard and **Rush**. Engineered by David Leonard. The band adds three more songs to project after recording sessions begin (*Birmingham Evening Mail* August 28, 2004).

(April)
Rush completes work on their covers project at Phase One Studios, Toronto, Ontario, Canada (*Feedback* sessions). **Geddy Lee** says in a *Toronto Sun* interview that the sessions took three weeks (August 22, 2004). Since the start of the sessions in March, the band works on the following:
"Manic Depression" – a cover of the 1967 Jimi Hendrix. The band records a "rough version" of the song, but feels it's not up to their standards (*Rocky Mountain News* June 24, 2004).

Alex Lifeson notes that the band "ran out of time" before being able to record more material for the covers project, having other things scheduled.

(May)
Rush's *Feedback* EP is mixed at Phase One Studios, Toronto, Ontario, Canada, by David Leonard.

Rush's *Feedback* EP is mastered at Marcussen Mastering, Hollywood, California, US, by Stephen Marcussen.

(May 26)
Rush performs live at Starwood Amphitheatre, Antioch, Tennessee, US.

Note: **Neil Peart** documents the R30 tour for a planned book about the subject, what would become *Roadshow*.

(May 28)
Rush performs live at Verizon Wireless Amphitheater, Charlotte, North Carolina, US.

(May 29)
Rush performs live at Verizon Wireless Amphitheater, Virginia Beach, Virginia, US. During **Neil Peart**'s drum solo in this show, his sample of "One O'clock Jump" for the finale doesn't trigger, so he plays on without it.

(May 31)
Rush performs live at Post Gazette Pavilion, Burgettstown, Pennsylvania, US.

(Date Unknown)
Rush releases their single "Summertime Blues" in the US and Europe.

US CD promo single (PRCD301512):
"Summertime Blues" – a cover of the 1958 Eddie Cochran song (Blue Cheer arrangement)

Europe CD promo single (PRO4967):

"Summertime Blues" – a cover of the 1958 Eddie Cochran song (Blue Cheer arrangement)

(June 2)
Rush performs live at Germain Amphitheater, Columbus, Ohio, US.

(June 4)
Rush performs live at Verizon Wireless Amphitheater, Noblesville, Indiana, US.

(June 5)
Rush performs live at Tweeter Center, Tinley Park, Illinois, US.

(June 7)
Rush performs live at Marcus Amphitheater, Milwaukee, Wisconsin, US.

(June 8)
Rush performs live at DTE Energy Music Theatre, Clarkston, Michigan, US.

(June 10)
Rush performs live at Blossom Music Center, Cuyahoga Falls, Ohio, US.

(June 12)
Rush performs live at UMB Bank Pavilion, Maryland Heights, Missouri, US.

(June 13)
Rush performs live at Verizon Wireless Amphitheater, Bonner Springs, Kansas, US.

(June 23)
Rush performs live at Smirnoff Music Center, Dallas, Texas, US.

(June 25)
Rush performs live at Verizon Wireless Amphitheater, San Antonio, Texas, US.

(June 26)
Rush performs live at C.W. Mitchell Pavilion, Woodlands, Texas, US.

(Date Unknown)
Director Pierre Lamoureux says that partway into the tour, *Rush* decides to film one of the shows for future commercial release. He says the Red Rocks Amphitheater and Radio City Music Hall shows are considered, but logistically don't work out. The Montreal date is also considered before Frankfurt, Germany is decided upon.

(June 28)
Warner Music Vision releases the 2xDVD concert film *Toronto Rocks*, shot during the *Molson Canadian Rocks For Toronto* SARS benefit concert July 3, 2003, Toronto, Ontario, Canada. It features *Rush*'s performances of "Limelight," "Freewill," "Paint It Black" and "The Spirit Of Radio."

(June 29)
Rush releases their eighteenth studio project, the covers EP, *Feedback*, in Canada (Anthem Records) and worldwide (Atlantic Records). Track listing as follows:

"Summertime Blues" – a cover of the 1958 Eddie Cochran song (Blue Cheer arrangement)
"Heart Full Of Soul" – a cover of the 1965 song by The Yardbirds
"For What It's Worth" - a cover of the 1967 Buffalo Springfield song
"The Seeker" – a cover of the 1970 song by The Who
"Mr. Soul" – a cover of the 1967 Buffalo Springfield song
"Seven And Seven Is" – a cover of the 1966 Love song
"Shape Of Things" – a cover of the 1966 song by The Yardbirds
"Crossroads" – a cover of the 1937 Robert Johnson song "Cross Road Blues" (Cream arrangement)

Note: there is some inconsistency about whether *Feedback* is considered a proper studio album or merely an EP, an Extended Play single. The official documentary *The Game Of Snakes & Arrows* refers to *Snakes & Arrows* as the band's nineteenth studio album, which would suggest *Feedback* is the eighteenth. Both **Neil Peart** and **Geddy Lee** refer to *Feedback* as an EP in various interviews, such as **Neil** in *Modern Drummer* (August, 2007) and to *Snakes & Arrows* as the nineteenth studio album (in the same article, no less). The later *Retrospective III* collection's cover art sets *Feedback* apart from the other releases, which would suggest the band views it as part of their catalogue, but not on par with the bona fide albums (and no songs from *Feedback* appear on the compilation CD). The 2013 boxed set *The Studio Albums 1989-2007* includes *Feedback*. For the purpose of this Chronology, it is listed as their nineteenth studio release, with the caveat that its length and lack of original songs separates it from the other eighteen studio works.

Rush performs live at Red Rocks Amphitheater, Morrison, Colorado, US. A photo taken during this show by Andrew MacNaughtan (and later touched up by Hugh Syme) is used for the cover of **Neil Peart**'s book *Roadshow*.

(June 30)
Rush performs live at USANA Amphitheater, West Valley City, Utah, US.

(July 2)
Rush performs live at White River Amphitheater, Auburn, Washington, US.

(July 3)
Rush performs live at Clark County Amphitheater, Ridgefield, Washington, US.

(July 6)
Rush performs live at Hollywood Bowl, Hollywood, California, US.

(July 7)
Rush performs live at Coors Amphitheater, Chula Vista, California, US.

(July 9)
Rush performs live at Shoreline Amphitheater, Mountain View, California, US.

(July 10)
Rush performs live at Chronicle Pavilion, Concord, California, US.

(July 12)
Rush performs live at Sleep Train Amphitheater, Marysville, California, US.

(July 14)
Rush performs live at Verizon Wireless Amphitheater, Irvine, California, US. Actor Jack Black attends this concert and is the guest dryer operator for the concert. During "2112," Black does an impromptu piece of "performance art" onstage in praise of the band, as described in **Neil Peart**'s book *Roadshow*.

(July 16)
Rush performs live at Cricket Pavilion, Phoenix, Arizona, US.

(July 17)
Rush performs live at MGM Grand Garden Arena, Las Vegas, Nevada, US.

(July 29)
Rush performs live at Sound Advice Amphitheater, West Palm Beach, Florida, US.

(July 30)
Rush performs live at Tampa Bay Amphitheater, Tampa, Florida, US.

(August 1)
Rush performs live at Hi-Fi Buys Amphitheater, Atlanta, Georgia, US.

(August 3)
Rush performs live at Nissan Pavilion, Bristow, Virginia, US.

(August 4)
Rush performs live at Tweeter Center, Camden, New Jersey, US.

(August 6)
Rush performs live at Meadows Music Theater, Hartford, Connecticut, US.

(August 7)
Rush performs live at Montage Mountain, Scranton, Pennsylvania, US.

(August 9)
Rush performs live at Saratoga PAC, Saratoga Springs, New York, US.

(August 11)
Rush performs live at Jones Beach, Wantagh, New York, US.

(August 12)
Rush performs live at Tweeter Center, Mansfield, Massachusetts, US.

(August 14)

Rush performs live at PNC Bank Arts Center, Holmdel, New Jersey, US.

(August 15)
Rush performs live at Darien Lake, Buffalo, New York, US.

(August 18 & 19)
Rush performs live at Radio City Music Hall, New York City, New York, US.

(August 21)
Rush performs live at Bell Centre, Montreal, Quebec, Canada.

(August 22)
Rush performs live at Molson Amphitheater, Toronto, Ontario, Canada.

(September 1)
ECW Press publishes **Neil Peart**'s book *Traveling Music: The Soundtrack to My Life and Times* worldwide.
"Traveling Music" – the verse which opens the book appears to go by this title and would later be adapted into "Workin' Them Angels" for the *Snakes & Arrows* album.

(September 8 & 9)
Rush performs live at Wembley Arena, London, England.

(September 11)
Rush performs live at NEC Arena, Birmingham, England.

(September 12)
Rush performs live at Evening News Arena, Manchester, England.

(September 14)
Rush performs live at SECC Arena, Glasgow, Scotland.

(September 15)
Rush performs live at NEC Arena, Birmingham, England.

(September 17)
Rush performs live at Konig-Pilsner Arena, Oberhausen, Germany.

(September 19)
Rush performs live at Schleyerhalle, Stuttgart, Germany.

(September 21)
Rush performs live at Mazda Palace, Milan, Italy.

(September 22)
Rush is scheduled to perform live at Olympiahalle, Munich, Germany, but the show is cancelled reportedly because the tour trucks are unable to reach Munich from Milan in time, due to restrictions on travel through a connecting tunnel under the Alps.

(September 24)
Rush performs live at Festhalle, Frankfurt, Germany. This show is recorded and later released as *R30: 30th Anniversary World Tour* (DVD and Deluxe DVD+CD Editions, and later Blu-ray). The following tracks are released individually:

> "The Spirit Of Radio (R30 – Working Men CD Version)" 5:06
> Written by Neil Peart (words), Geddy Lee & Alex Lifeson (music)
> Appears on: Working Men CD
> This version fades in over the segue from the "R30 Overture" and fades out at the end.
>
> "The Spirit Of Radio (R30 – Working Men DVD Version)" 5:02
> Written by Neil Peart (words), Geddy Lee & Alex Lifeson (music)
> Appears on: Working Men DVD
> On the Working Men DVD, the song fades in longer over the segue from the "R30 Overture" and fades out earlier.
>
> "Subdivisions (R30 – AOADS Version)" 5:38
> Written by Neil Peart (words), Geddy Lee & Alex Lifeson (music)
> Appears on: Anatomy Of A Drum Solo DVD
> Beginning with Geddy saying "This is one you might remember from Signals..." and fading out at the end, this version is shorter than the cut that appears on Working Men. The video is also unique compared to the R30 concert film in that it's only Neil's drum cameras rather than the whole band.

"Subdivisions (R30 – Working Men CD Version)" 5:57
Written by Neil Peart (words), Geddy Lee & Alex Lifeson (music)
Appears on: Working Men CD
This cut fades in just before Geddy's intro to the song (which finishes the "Animate" track on the original album) and fades out at the end before Geddy continues to address the crowd in German.

"Subdivisions (R30 – Working Men DVD Version)" 5:36
Written by Neil Peart (words), Geddy Lee & Alex Lifeson (music)
Appears on: Working Men DVD
The audio is nearly identical to the edit that appears on Anatomy Of A Drum Solo, though the footage is obviously straight off the R30 DVD

"Bravado (R30 – R:BTLS Version)" 6:09
Written by Neil Peart (words), Geddy Lee & Alex Lifeson (music)
Appears on: Rush: Beyond The Lighted Stage DVD & Blu-ray
This cut fades in quickly over the crowd and fades out at the end.

"YYZ (R30 – R:BTLS Version)" 4:38
Written by Geddy Lee & Neil Peart
Appears on: Rush: Beyond The Lighted Stage DVD & Blu-ray
This cut fades in quickly over the crowd and fades out at the end.

"One Little Victory (R30 – Working Men CD Version)" 5:25
Written by Neil Peart (words), Geddy Lee & Alex Lifeson (music)
Appears on: Working Men CD
This version was previously unreleased at the time Working Men came out. The later R30 Blu-ray would restore this track to the concert film (and it would also be included in the R40 boxed set). The concert would only appear (incomplete) on CD on the original 2005 Deluxe DVD+CD Edition, without this track, meaning the Working Men CD is the only way to purchase the audio recording of the song. The track fades in quickly on the sound of the dragon breathing fire and fades out as Geddy says "Danke Schoen!"

"One Little Victory (R30 – Working Men DVD Version)" 5:25
Written by Neil Peart (words), Geddy Lee & Alex Lifeson (music)
Appears on: Working Men DVD
This version starts with the complete dragon video. The track fades out after Geddy says "Danke Schoen!"

"The Seeker (R30 – Retrospective III Version)" 3:45
Written by Pete Townsend
Appears on: Retrospective III: 1989-2008 DVD
This version fades in quickly as Geddy introduces the song and fades out at the end.

"Tom Sawyer (R30 – AOADS Version)" 5:03
Written by Neil Peart & Pye Dubois (words), Geddy Lee & Alex Lifeson (music)
Appears on: Anatomy Of A Drum Solo DVD
This isolated version fades in quickly at the beginning and end. The video is an interesting alternate cut, being only the drum cameras.

"Dreamline (R30 – Working Men CD Version)" 5:13
Written by Neil Peart (words), Geddy Lee & Alex Lifeson (music)
Appears on: Working Men CD
This version fades in over the crowd noise (which finishes the "Tom Sawyer" track on the original album) and fades out earlier at the end.

"Dreamline (R30 – Working Men DVD Version)" 5:13
Written by Neil Peart (words), Geddy Lee & Alex Lifeson (music)
Appears on: Working Men DVD
The audio appears to be identical to the Working Men CD. The footage is straight off the R30 concert film, of course.

"Secret Touch (R30 – Retrospective III Version)" 7:14
Written by Neil Peart (words), Geddy Lee & Alex Lifeson (music)
Appears on: Retrospective III: 1989-2008 DVD
This version fades in on Geddy's intro and banter with the audience, then fades out at the end.

"Red Sector A (R30 – S&AL DVD Bonus Version)" 5:13
Written by Neil Peart (words), Geddy Lee & Alex Lifeson (music)
Appears on: Snakes & Arrows Live DVD and Blu-ray

Having an R30 song on Snakes & Arrows Live is something of a curiosity, though the track was previously unreleased at the time Snakes & Arrows Live DVD and Blu-ray came out. The later R30 Blu-ray would restore this track to the concert film (and it would also be included in the R40 boxed set). This version fades in on the crowd noise and fades out over it at the end.

"Resist (R30 – Retrospective III Version)" 7:14
Written by Neil Peart (words), Geddy Lee & Alex Lifeson (music)
Appears on: Retrospective III: 1989-2008 DVD
This version fades in as Alex and Geddy take to their stools to perform and fades out after Geddy thanks the audience.

"Working Man (R30 – Working Men CD Version)" 5:37
Written by Geddy Lee & Alex Lifeson
Appears on: Working Men CD
This version fades in over crowd noise which actually replaces the segue from "Xanadu" (I suppose they wanted a cleaner start to the song here) and fades out at the end, after Geddy thanks the crowd.

"Working Man (R30 – Working Men DVD Version)" 5:25
Written by Geddy Lee & Alex Lifeson
Appears on: Working Men CD
Here the track fades in over the segue from "Xanadu" (no re-editing, as heard on the Working Men CD). It fades out after the song, before Geddy thanks the crowd.

Neil Peart's drum solo from this show, "Der Trommler," forms the basis for **Neil**'s second instructional video, *Anatomy Of A Drum Solo*.

(September 25)
Rush performs live at T-Mobile Arena, Prague, Czech Republic.

(September 27)
Rush performs live at Sporthalle, Hamburg, Germany.

"Ich Bin Ein Hamburger" – While the show itself is not professionally filmed for commercial release, **Neil Peart** includes a rough cut of the drum solo from this show on the "Sidebar 1" portion of his *Anatomy Of A Drum Solo* DVD. The footage is taken from the production cameras and the audio is a rough mix from the house sound board.

(September 29)
Rush performs live at Globe Arena, Stockholm, Sweden.

(October 1)
Rush performs live at Ahoy Sportpaleis, Rotterdam, Holland.

(Dates Unknown)
Alex Lifeson works on 5.1 surround sound mixes for the following concert films:

Exit...Stage Left
Grace Under Pressure Tour
A Show Of Hands

Note: In an October 12, 2005 *Billboard* article **Geddy Lee** says **Alex Lifeson** spent "a good chunk of last year" at work on these mixes.

CANADA FOR ASIA

2005

(Mid-January)
Rush, Ed Robertson (of Barenaked Ladies) and Mike Smith (in character as Bubbles, from *Trailer Park Boys*) perform "Closer To The Heart" for the *Canada For Asia* tsunami relief concert, which airs January 13th.

(Early 2005)
Neil Peart, Paul Siegel and Rob Wallis organize the studio filming of **Peart**'s second instructional video (*Anatomy Of A Drum Solo*).

(Date Unknown)
Neil Peart records voice-over work for *Aqua Teen Hunger Force Colon Movie Film For Theatre* as 'Neil.'

(April)
Geddy Lee does an interview with *Q Classics* (July, 2005), wherein he notes that after seven months off, **Rush** plans to start writing again.

(April 10)
Naples Florida News reports John Cannivet's eye-witness account of the incident at the Ritz-Carlton, Naples, Florida, US, which led to the arrest of **Alex Lifeson** and his son and daughter-in-law. He account supports the **Lifeson** family's version of events on New Year's Eve, 2003, including detailing the violence against **Alex** and Justin by police.

(April 13)
The misdemeanour charges against **Alex Lifeson**'s daughter-in-law Michelle are dropped by the Florida State Attorney's Office, in the incident on New Year's Eve, 2003.

(April 18)
Alex Lifeson and his family attend the scheduled trail start date of Justin (Živojinović) Zivojinovich's case, Naples, Florida, US. The start date is pushed back to April 19th to allow for the defence to motion the court to dismiss the resisting arrest charge.

(April 19)
Alex Lifeson and his family attend court with his son Justin, in Naples, Florida, US. The defence motions the court to dismiss the resisting arrest charge. Retired Senior Circuit Judge Charles T. Carlton delays ruling until a later date. Jury selection takes place.

(April 20)
Alex Lifeson and his family attend the trail of his son Justin, in Naples, Florida, US. Opening arguments take place. Judge Carlton reduces the charge to a misdemeanour.

(April 21)
A plea agreement is reached in the cases of **Alex Lifeson** and his son Justin, where both plea no-contest to misdemeanour charges of resisting arrest with violence and agree to pay fines, various court-related costs and restitution to the Ritz-Carlton hotel. Adjudication in the cases is withheld pending completion of one-year probation, resulting in no conviction on either man's record.

Note: A conviction in **Alex Lifeson**'s case would have made it extremely difficult (if impossible) to live and work in the US.

(June 3)
It is reported on this date (*Naples Florida News*) that **Alex Lifeson**, his son Justin and daughter-in-law Michelle have filed a lawsuit against the Ritz-Carlton hotel, its security director and three Collier County Sheriff's Deputies involved in the New Year's Eve, 2003, incident.

(June 7)
Alex Lifeson performs live at the Phoenix Concert Theatre, Toronto, Ontario, Canada, as part of the White Ribbon Concert, with Jim Cuddy and John Kastner. Also on the bill are Barenaked Ladies and Bruce Cockburn.

(June 10)
Alex Lifeson issues a statement to fans via *Rush.com* thanking them for their support. **Lifeson** simultaneously issues press release about the lawsuit filed against the Ritz-Carlton hotel, its security director and three Collier County Sheriff's Deputies involved in the New Year's Eve, 2003, incident.

(July)

Corporal Amy Stanford files a lawsuit against **Alex Lifeson**, citing permanent and progressive injuries resulting from the New Year's Eve, 2003, incident.

(Mid-July)
Neil Peart, Paul Siegel and Rob Wallis shoot the studio segments of **Peart**'s instructional video, at Allaire Studio, Shokan, New York, US (*Anatomy Of A Drum Solo* sessions). The sessions last three days (*Modern Drummer* April 2006).

(Summer)
A few weeks after shooting the studio segments for *Anatomy Of A Drum Solo*, **Neil Peart** is shown the first edit of the video (*Modern Drummer* April 2006).

(October 2)
It is reported on this date (*Naples Florida News*) that two of the three Collier County Sheriff's Deputies involved in the New Year's Eve, 2003, incident with **Alex Lifeson** and his family have filed a countersuit against **Lifeson** and his family, alleging they acted properly in discharging their duties.

(October 12)
In an *All Headline News* interview published on this date with Pierre Lamoureux (producer and director of the *R30* concert film), Lamoureux talks about **Rush**'s catalogue of released and unreleased material in their archive, saying over the last year, work has gone into the archive with the band in preparation for future releases.
Grace Under Pressure Tour – Pierre says footage has been found which wasn't on the original VHS and Laserdisc releases.

(November 12)
Geddy Lee and **Neil Peart** apparently join the **Lifeson** family lawsuit against the Ritz-Carlton hotel, its security director and three Collier County Sheriff's Deputies involved in the New Year's Eve, 2003, incident, alleging the injuries **Alex** suffered that morning "caused a reduction in the band's touring performances and recording sessions," resulting in a loss of revenue (*Naples Florida News*)

Note: The article published on the day says the other band members *could* join the suit, but doesn't clarify if they did. However, in August, 2006, the judge rules against **Lee** and **Peart**'s claim, so at some point they did formally join the suit.

(November 22)
Rush releases their live concert film *R30: 30th Anniversary World Tour* in Canada (Anthem Records) and worldwide (Atlantic Records). There are two editions of the concert released, the standard DVD edition and the Deluxe DVD+CD Edition.

Standard DVD edition:
DVD 1: Frankfurt concert [edited]

Deluxe DVD+CD Edition:
DVD 1: Frankfurt concert [edited]

DVD 2: DVD Extras:
    August 24, 1979 Geddy Lee Interview at Ivor Wynne Stadium, Hamilton
    1980 Rush interview at Le Studio (incorrectly listed as 1981 Moving Pictures era)
    1990 Artist of the Decade interviews
    1994 Juno Awards CBC news report
    2002 Geddy Lee & Alex Lifeson Vapor Trails interview
    "Finding My Way (Mpeg 1)" – Don Kirshner's Rock Concert
    "In The Mood (Mpeg 1)" – Don Kirshner's Rock Concert
    "Fly By Night" – Church Sessions video
    "A Farewell To Kings" – Seneca College
    "Xanadu" – Seneca College
    "Circumstances (Live at the Hammersmith Odeon, 1979)"
    "La Villa Strangiato (Live at the Hammersmith Odeon, 1979)"
    "The Spirit Of Radio" – Soundcheck at Ivor Wynne Stadium, Hamilton
    "Freewill" - *Molson Canadian Rocks For Toronto* 2003
    "Closer To The Heart" - *Canada For Asia* 2005
    Bonus Easter Egg: Rush Hits St. John's
    Bonus Easter Egg: 1990 Alex Lifeson Artist of the Decade interview

CD 1: Frankfurt concert [edited] (Disc 1)

CD 2: Frankfurt concert [edited] (Disc 2)

Note: "Frankfurt concert [edited]" refers to the fact that this is not the complete concert. The complete concert would see a home video release on the Blu-ray re-issue.

In an interview for the *R30* press release, **Neil Peart** says he's currently working on his next book, about the *R30* tour, titled *Roadshow: Landscape With Drums, A Concert Tour by Motorcycle,* and on his *Anatomy Of A Drum Solo* instructional DVD.

(Late 2005)
Neil Peart co-writes the following with Matt Scannell of Vertical Horizon (*NeilPeart.net* June 17, 2006):
"Even Now"

Note: at some point either around this time or later, the two co-write the following (*NeilPeart.net* June, 2012):
"A Promise Or A Threat" – a country song
"Untitled Cartoon Theme"

(December 12)
Neil Peart releases his 2xDVD instructional video *Anatomy Of A Drum Solo* via Hudson Music, worldwide. The featured drum solo is "Der Trommler," from the 2004, Frankfurt, Germany, concert (*R30 - 30th Anniversary World Tour*).

DVD 1: *Anatomy Of A Drum Solo*
Preamble - includes "Der Trommler" (*R30 - 30th Anniversary World Tour*)
Element 1 - includes "Momo's Dance Party"
Element 2
Element 3
Element 4 - includes "Pieces Of Eight"
Sidebar 1 - includes "Ich Bin Ein Hamburger" from the September 27, 2004 Hamburg, Germany concert
Sidebar 2
Special Features:
       - Bonus Audio Clips
           - "Momo's Dance Party" [isolated]
           - "Pieces Of Eight" [isolated]
Full Screen Examples
"Der Trommler" Multi-Angle Drum-Cam
"The Rhythm Method (ASOH – AOADS Version)"
The Making Of Paragon

DVD 2: Bonus Features
Bonus Performances:
       - Exploration #2
       - "Tom Sawyer (R30 – AOADS Version)"
       - "Subdivisions (R30 – AOADS Version)"
       - "Drum Solo (Live at The Palace of Auburn Hills, 1994)"
       - "O Baterista (Rush In Rio – AOADS Version)"
Photo Gallery
Interview with Paul Northfield & Lorne Wheaton
The Neighbourhood: Setting up Neil's drums with Lorne Wheaton
DVD-ROM

      "Momo's Dance Party" 3:45
      Written by Neil Peart
      Appears on: Anatomy Of A Drum Solo DVD
      This is the complete recording in all its percussive glory, with the full opening of the piece not heard on A Work In Progress.

GOLD

2006

(January)
Rush begins discussing getting to work on new material. **Neil Peart** works on the final draft of his book *Roadshow*. (*MikeDolbear.com* January 2006). *MTV News* December 12, 2005, reports that **Rush** is scheduled to start writing sessions this month.

(February)
From his home in Los Angeles, California, US, **Neil Peart** sends lyrics to **Geddy Lee** and **Alex Lifeson**, who are working at **Lee**'s home studio, Toronto, Ontario, Canada. The two assemble the lyrics and music into work-in-progress demos (*Snakes & Arrows* writing sessions). These sessions last about five weeks (*Canadian Musician* April 2007).

Steven Wilson of Porcupine Tree contacts **Alex Lifeson**. Wilson sends **Lifeson** in-progress material for Porcupine Tree's next album (*Fear Of A Blank Planet* session). **Alex** requests to play on the entire album, but ultimately records a guitar solo for the track "Anesthetize" (*Classic Rock* July, 2007).

Note: The *Fear Of A Blank Planet* liner notes indicate the writing sessions were between January and July this year and in the *Classic Rock* interview, **Alex Lifeson** says he was contacted by Steven Wilson during the **Rush** writing sessions following an published interview from this month.

(February 8)
Alex Lifeson records guitar work for the songs "Everybody's Broken" and "Testify All Over Me," for John Kastner's album *Have You Seen Lucky*. Among the earliest reports of this sessions is from *ChartAttack.com* on this date.

(March)
Rush convenes at **Neil Peart**'s home in Wentworth-Nord, Quebec, Canada. **Alex Lifeson** and **Geddy Lee** play demo recordings of material they have assembled for the next album (*Snakes & Arrows* writing sessions) (*Billboard* September 14, 2006). They have five songs at this point (*The Game Of Snakes & Arrows* documentary). Songs assembled by this point include:
"Bravest Face"
"The Way The Winds Blows"

(April 9)
On this date, *Billboard* reports that **Rush** is in the early stages of work on their next studio album.

(April 25)
Mercury Records and Anthem Records release the **Rush** 2xCD compilation *Gold* in North America and Europe.

CD 1:
"The Spirit Of Radio"
"The Trees"
 "Freewill"
"Xanadu"
"Bastille Day"
"By-Tor And The Snow Dog (Standard CD Edition)"
"Anthem"
"Closer To The Heart"
"2112: I: Overture"
"2112: II: The Temples Of Syrinx"
"La Villa Strangiato"
"Fly By Night"
"Finding My Way"
"Working Man"

CD 2:
"The Big Money"
"Red Barchetta"
"Subdivisions"
"Time Stands Still"
"Mystic Rhythms"
"The Analog Kid"
"Distant Early Warning"
"Marathon"
"The Body Electric"
"Mission"

"Limelight"
"Red Sector A"
"New World Man"
"Tom Sawyer"
"Force Ten"

Note: the track listing is nearly identical to the earlier *Retrospective I* and *II* compilations, with "Working Man" replacing "Something For Nothing."

(May)
Rush spends this month working on the songs developed during the winter/spring sessions for their nineteenth studio album at Cherry Beach Studios, Toronto, Ontario, Canada (*Snakes & Arrows* tour book). During these sessions, the band hires engineer Rich Chycki and producer Nick Raskulinecz for the next pre-production sessions.

Simultaneous to these *Snakes & Arrows* sessions, **Neil Peart** develops drum parts for Vertical Horizon's tracks "Welcome To The Bottom" and "Save Me From Myself," as well as **Neil**'s co-written song "Even Now" (*NeilPeart.net* June 17, 2006).

(May 11)
John Kastner releases his album *Have You Seen Lucky*, featuring **Alex Lifeson** on the tracks "Everybody's Broken" and "Testify All Over Me."

> "Everybody's Broken" 3:30
> Written by John Kastner
> Appears on: Have You Seen Lucky
> This is an upbeat little modern rock number, with dependable guitar work from Alex (not flashy or getting in the way of the song).

> "Testify All Over Me" 2:43
> Written by John Kastner
> Appears on: Have You Seen Lucky
> A contemporary mid-tempo rock love ballad, this song features Alex's guitars filling out the backing track, again not doing too much and sitting neatly in the song.

(Early June)
Rush finishes its initial writing and recording pre-production sessions at Cherry Beach Studios, Toronto, Ontario, Canada (*Snakes & Arrows* tour book). At this point, the band has eight songs with which they are happy.

(June 13)
Rush releases their concert film DVD+CD boxed set *Replay x3* in Canada (Anthem Records) and worldwide (Atlantic Records).

Replay x3 Standard Edition:
DVD 1: *Exit...Stage Left*

DVD 2: *Grace Under Pressure Tour*
- This version does not include the complete "The Big Money" promo video

DVD 3: *A Show Of Hands*
- This version does not include "Lock And Key"

CD: *Grace Under Pressure Tour* Soundtrack
- This is the audio from the concert film

Replay x3 Best Buy Edition:
DVD 1: *Exit...Stage Left*

DVD 2: *Grace Under Pressure Tour*
- This version does not include the complete "The Big Money" promo video

DVD 3: *A Show Of Hands*
- This version does not include "Lock And Key"

CD: *Grace Under Pressure Tour* Soundtrack
- This is the audio from the concert film and also contains the following unlisted bonus tracks:
    "Limelight (Replay GUP Tour - Best Buy CD Version)"
    "Closer To The Heart (Replay GUP Tour - Best Buy CD Version)"
    "The Spirit Of Radio (Replay GUP Tour - Best Buy CD Version)"
    "Tom Sawyer (Replay GUP Tour Best - Buy CD Version)"

(June 14)
Neil Peart records his drum parts for the Vertical Horizon songs "Even Now" (co-written by Matt Scannell), "Welcome To The Bottom" and Save Me From Myself" at Capitol Records Studio B, Hollywood, California, US (*Burning The Days* sessions) (*NeilPeart.net* June 17, 2006).

(Summer)
Alex Lifeson travels to Greece (*Guitar Player* September, 2007).
"Workin' Them Angels" – while there he buys a bouzouki, and while playing it decides to use it on the album's upcoming recording sessions. Ultimately, it appears on this track.

(Date Unknown)
Alex Lifeson films his role in *Trailer Park Boys: The Movie*, playing a police officer, along with Gord Downey (of The Tragically Hip).

(Date Unknown)
Alex Lifeson records guitar parts for "Eyes Of A Child" and "Light Reflects" at Lerxst Sound, Toronto, Ontario, Canada, for Edwin's forthcoming album *Better Days*.

(August)
Alex Lifeson and **Geddy Lee** record the following at Lerxst Sound, Toronto, Ontario, Canada. Produced by **Alex Lifeson**. Mixed by Richard Chycki at Mixland Music & DVD, Toronto, Ontario, Canada.
"I Fought The Law" – a cover of the 1960 song by The Crickets. Recorded as **The Big Dirty Band** (**Alex Lifeson**, **Geddy Lee**, Adam Gontier, Care Failure, Ian Thomley and Jeff Burrow), for the film *Trailer Park Boys: The Movie*.
"Liquor & Whores" – penned by Mike Smith. Recorded as **Bubbles & The Shit Rockers** (Mike Smith, **Alex Lifeson**, Andy Curran and Tom Wilson), for the film *Trailer Park Boys: The Movie*.

A *Windsor Star* article (September 8) notes that **Neil Peart** is unavailable to work on "I Fought The Law," hence Jeff Burrow's recruitment.

(August 9)
US District Court Judge John E. Steele rules that **Geddy Lee** and **Neil Peart** don't have legal standing for their loss-of-revenue claim in the **Lifeson** family lawsuit against the Ritz-Carlton hotel, its security director and three Collier County Sheriff's Deputies involved in the New Year's Eve, 2003, incident.

(September)
Rush resumes their pre-production sessions at Cherry Beach Studios, Toronto, Ontario, Canada (*Snakes & Arrows* tour book). These sessions last "about six weeks" (*Arizona Republic* July 24, 2007).
"Far Cry" – this song develops musically from an early jam between **Geddy Lee** and **Alex Lifeson**, then is married the following day with lyrics written by **Neil Peart** (which are delivered around the same time). **Lee** says it was written in about a day, early in these session, though one of the last written for the album during the pre-production sessions (*The Game Of Snakes & Arrows* documentary and *Guitar Player* September, 2007).

(October)
Rush concludes their pre-production sessions at Cherry Beach Studios, Toronto, Ontario, Canada (*Snakes & Arrows* tour book). By this point they have "rough" versions of eleven songs, including:
"Bravest Face"
"The Way The Winds Blows"
"Far Cry"
"Armor and Sword"
"Faithless"
"Spin Drift"
"Good News First"
"We Hold On"
"The Larger Bowl" – the title takes its name from the dysentery-induced dream **Neil Peart** experienced in his 1988 bicycle tour of Cameroon.
"Workin' Them Angels" – adapted from the opening lyric to "Traveling Music," from **Neil**'s book of the same name. Apparently, the idea to use them was **Geddy Lee**'s.

Co-producer Nick Raskulinecz is present for a week during these sessions (*Canadian Musician* April 2007).

(October 3)
Anthem Entertainment releases *Trailer Park Boys: The Movie Soundtrack*, featuring **The Big Dirty Band**'s cover of "I Fought The Law" and **Bubbles & The Shit Rockers**' "Liquor & Whores."

>"I Fought The Law" 3:51
>Written by Sonny Curtis
>Appears on: Trailer Park Boys: The Movie Soundtrack

This version starts with a quit refrain of the title chorus before exploding into a modern hard rock cover of the classic song. The outro guitar is vintage Alex. Definitely seek this one out! The video was directed by long-time Rush photographer Andrew MacNaughtan and features the Trailer Park Boys, Geddy, Alex and the rest of The Big Dirty Band.

"Liquor & Whores" 3:00
Written by Mike Smith
Appears on: Trailer Park Boys: The Movie Soundtrack
Ostensibly "Take 2," this hilarious country number is sung by Smith in character as 'Bubbles.' NSWF and awesome!

Edwin releases his album *Better Days*, featuring **Alex Lifeson** on the songs "Light Reflects" and "Eyes Of A Child."

"Light Reflects" 4:48
Written by Bill Bell
Appears on: Better Days
Alex once again works with Edwin, with whom Alex recorded previously with I Mother Earth and Victor. This is an ethereal number, with light, float-y guitar work. Very cool.

"Eyes Of A Child" 3:38
Written by David Martin, Denis Tougas & Jeff Dalzeil
Appears on: Better Days
This is a sombre, mournful song about losing someone. It has some subtle guitar work by Alex and some nice piano.

Jakalope releases their album *Born 4*, featuring **Alex Lifeson** on the song "24 Star (No Apologies)."

"24 Star (No Apologies)" 3:00
Written by Katie B, Philip Caivano & Dave Olgilvie
Appears on: Born 4
Jakalope's music is an interesting mix of pop and industrial, which you'd expect from the production work of Dave "Rave" Olgivie and Trent Reznor. This song is a good example of their work. Alex's guitar work is heavy and grinding, but not overly distinctive (which isn't bad, as it works for the song, but unless you knew it was him, you may not be able to tell from the song alone).

(Mid-November)
Three weeks after the October sessions **Rush** begins recording sessions for their nineteenth studio album, at Allaire Studios, Shokan, New York, US (*Canadian Musician* April 2007). Engineered by Rich Chycki. Co-produced and arrangements by **Rush** and Nick Raskulinecz. The original intention is to record the drum tracks and possibly half the bass tracks at Allaire Studios over twelve days, followed by sessions at Lerxst Sound, Toronto, Ontario, Canada, for guitars until the end of January, 2007, followed by vocals in February, 2007. Instead, the band works at Allaire Studios for five weeks (*The Game Of Snakes & Arrows* documentary). **Geddy Lee** says in *Revolver* (April, 2007) that it was five and a half weeks. **Alex Lifeson** later tells *Guitar Player* magazine (September, 2007) that since he was planning to record his guitar overdubs in Toronto, he did not bring a lot of his gear to Allaire, so when the decision was made to stay, he didn't have the gear he planned to use, so made due with what was there.
"The Main Monkey Business" – the last track recorded during the main sessions (after which **Neil Peart** has his primary drum kit shipped off), done live in the studio with all three band members together (*The Game Of Snakes & Arrows* documentary). This is the most re-written track during the sessions (*Drumhead* September, 2007).

The Allaire Studios sessions are filmed by Andrew MacNaughtan for *The Game Of Snakes & Arrows* documentary.

(November 23)
On this date, **Rush** and production and support crew have Thanksgiving dinner and screen the film *Team America: World Police* for co-producer Nick Raskulinecz, at Allaire Studio, Shokan, New York, US (*Jam!Showbiz* April 27, 2007).

(Early December)
Rush completes recording sessions for their nineteenth studio album, at Allaire Studio, Shokan, New York, US. According to **Neil Peart**, the band finishes ahead of their anticipated completion estimate. Songs worked on between November and December include:
"Spindrift" – during the sessions, "radical changes" are made to this track (*Guitar World*, August, 2007).
"Faithless" – Ben Mink records strings for this track.
"Hope" – **Alex Lifeson** writes and performs this piece solo. The album cut is the first take and it was mixed immediately after it was recorded.
"Malignant Narcissism" – this number comes spontaneously from **Geddy Lee** noodling on bass between vocal takes. The drums and bass are recorded near the end of the sessions in a day (*Modern Drummer* August, 2007). **Alex Lifeson** was away during the initial creation of the piece and **Neil Peart** did not have his primary drum kit, so his parts are recorded on his practice kit. When **Alex** returns and develops his parts, the track is done in a couple of days (*Bass Player* August, 2007). The instrumental takes its title from the Matt Stone/Trey Parker film *Team America: World Police*.

Two song's vocal tracks remain incomplete at this point (*The Game Of Snakes & Arrows* documentary).

(December 14)
Neil Peart And Cathy Rich release the 2xDVD set *The Making Of Burning For Buddy* documentary, via Alfred Music.

SNAKES & ARROWS

2007

(January)
Rush begins mixing sessions for their nineteenth studio album at Ocean Way Recording, Hollywood, California, US, with Rich Chycki. According to Nick Raskulinecz, mixing takes "nearly four weeks" (*EQ* September, 2007).

About this time, **Geddy Lee** and **Alex Lifeson** meet screenwriters Derek Haas and Michael Brandt and **Alex** discusses the possibility of doing music for a film someday.

(Date Unknown)
Director/Producers Sam Dunn and Scot McFadyen begin work on an in-depth *Rush* documentary, what will later become *Beyond The Lighted Stage*.

(Early 2007)
Alex Lifeson and Rich Chycki mix *Snakes & Arrows* in 5.1 surround sound at Mixland Music & DVD and Lerxst Sound, Toronto, Ontario, Canada.

(March)
Geddy Lee appears in the **Iron Diamond** ESPN fantasy baseball ads.

Alex Lifeson records guitar on the song "Sacred & Mundane" for Tiles' album *Fly Paper*, at Blister Factory, Distillery District, Toronto, Ontario, Canada. Produced, Mixed, Engineered and Recorded by Terry Brown. Hugh Syme plays keyboards on the track.

(March 12)
Rush release their "Far Cry" singles in the US.

US CD promo single (133692):
"Far Cry (Radio Edit)"
"Far Cry"

> "Far Cry (Radio Edit)" 4:34
> Written by Neil Peart (words), Geddy Lee & Alex Lifeson (music)
> Appears on: US CD promo single
> This edit pares down the track by removing bits of instrumental throughout, as well as the part of the first chorus ("It's a far cry from the way we thought we'd share it"). There's probably more absent here than you'd notice without a side-by-side comparison, but as edits go, it's pretty good.

(Spring)
Rush rehearse for the upcoming *Snakes & Arrows* tour. The schedule, described by **Geddy Lee** in the *Toronto Sun* (May 6, 2007), is the band rehearsing individually for several weeks, then four weeks together at a Toronto venue, then two weeks in an arena with the production team.

(April 11)
US District Judge Paul A. Magnuson rules against the civil claim brought by the **Lifeson** family against the Ritz-Carlton hotel, its security director and three Collier County Sheriff's Deputies involved in the New Year's Eve, 2003, incident. **Alex Lifeson** says the plan is to appeal the ruling.

(April 16)
Porcupine Tree releases their album *Fear Of A Blank Planet*, featuring **Alex Lifeson** on the song "Anesthesize."

> "Anesthesize" 17:43
> Written by Steven Wilson
> Appears on: Fear Of A Blank Planet
> Fear Of A Blank Planet is composed in the vein of '70s prog-rock concept albums and takes its inspiration from the Bret Easton Ellis book Lunar Park and deals with themes of alienation, social disconnection and the modern world. At nearly 18 minutes, this track changes styles fluidly, drifting between Pink Floyd-like ethereal soundscapes, nigh-Industrial distorted guitars and various other moods. Its easy to see why Alex was drawn to the band's works and while his contribution to this track is short (his solo comes in around the 4 minute mark), it adds to the over texture of the piece.

(May 1)

Rush releases their nineteenth studio album, *Snakes & Arrows*, in Canada (Anthem Records) and worldwide (Atlantic Records). Track listing as follows:

"Far Cry"
"Armor and Sword"
"Workin' Them Angels"
"The Larger Bowl"
"Spindrift"
"The Main Monkey Business"
"The Way The Wind Blows"
"Hope"
"Faithless"
"Bravest Face"
"Good News First"
"Malignant Narcissism"
"We Hold On"

Note: This is the last studio album released on Atlantic Records.

Mercury Records and Anthem Entertainment release the following concert films individually, all of which were previously released on DVD in the *Replay x3* DVD boxed set:

Exit...Stage Left DVD

Grace Under Pressure Tour DVD
- does not contain the complete "The Big Money" promo video

A Show Of Hands DVD
- does not contain "Lock And Key" from the Laserdisc 1st Pressing

(May 28)
Porcupine Tree performs live at Danforth Music Hall, Toronto, Ontario, Canada. **Alex Lifeson** attends the concert.

(June 1)
Rush releases their "Spindrift" single in the US.

US CD promo single (PRCD 260476):
"Spindrift (Radio Edit)"
"Spindrift"

> "Spindrift (Radio Edit)" 3:42
> Written by Neil Peart (words), Geddy Lee & Alex Lifeson (music)
> Appears on: US CD promo single
> I haven't heard this edit, but suspect the 30 second quiet intro and the reprise outro would be the first parts to go, which would bring the track down to around 4 minutes, after which bits on instrumental throughout could account for the 1:40 reduction in the track length.

Note: This promo single appears to have been released primarily to harder rock radio stations

(June 6)
Neil Peart posts a drums-only mix of "The Main Monkey Business" on his official website.

> "The Main Monkey Business (Drums-only Mix)" 6:04
> Written by Geddy Lee & Alex Lifeson
> Appears on: N/A
> This is Neil's isolated rum track from the Snakes & Arrows instrumental. It certainly makes for interesting listening, even without Geddy and Alex's parts. The track was previously available to stream off Neil's site, but has since been taken down. You can still find it floating around the internet, though, so seek it out if you haven't heard it.

(June 9)
Geddy Lee and his family attend the wedding of his son Julian Weinrib to Lauren McGuire (*Toronto Sun* May 6, 2007).

(June 13)
Rush performs live at HiFi Buys Amphitheater, Atlanta, Georgia, US.

(June 15)
Rush performs live at Sound Advice Amphitheater, West Palm Beach, Florida, US.

(June 16)
Rush performs live at Ford Amphitheater at Florida State Fairgrounds, Tampa, Florida, US.

(June 18)
Rush performs live at Verizon Wireless Amphitheater, Charlotte, North Carolina, US.

(June 20)
Rush performs live at Walnut Creek, Raleigh, North Carolina, US.

(June 22)
Rush performs live at Verizon Wireless Amphitheatre, Virginia Beach, Virginia, US.

(June 23)
Rush performs live at Nissan Pavilion, Bristow, Virginia, US.

(June 25)
Rush performs live at Post Gazette Pavilion, Pittsburgh, Pennsylvania, US.

(June 26)
Rush releases their *Snakes & Arrows* MVI DVD in Canada (Anthem Records) and the US (Atlantic Records).

Snakes & Arrows MVI DVD
DVD content:
- *Snakes & Arrows* album (Hi-rez stereo audio)
- *Snakes & Arrows* album (5.1 surround sound)
- *A Game Of Snakes & Arrows* documentary
- Lyrics
- *A Game Of Snakes & Arrows* bio (note: this is the same essay as appears in the tour book)
- Photo Gallery
- Credits

CD-ROM content:
- *Snakes & Arrows* album (Hi-rez stereo audio)
- *A Game Of Snakes & Arrows* documentary
- Photo Gallery
- *A Game Of Snakes & Arrows* bio (note: this is the same essay as appears in the tour book)
- Lyrics
- Wallpaper
- IM Icons
- Ringtones
- Poster (when buyers register their copy online, they are sent an exclusive poster)

(June 27)
Rush performs live at Tweeter Center, Mansfield, Massachusetts, US.

(June 29)
Rush performs live at Montage Mountain, Scranton Pennsylvania, US.

(June 30)
Rush performs live at Saratoga Performing Arts Center. Saratoga Springs, New York, US.

(July 2)
Rush performs live at Jones Beach Amphitheater, Wantagh, New York, US.

(July 4)
Rush performs live at Six Flags, Darien Lake, New York, US.

(July 6)
Rush performs live at Tweeter Center, Camden, New Jersey, US.

(July 8)
Rush performs live at PNC Arts Center, Homdel, New Jersey, US.

(July 9)
Rush performs live at Mohegan Sun Arena, Uncasville, Connecticut, US.

(July 18)
Rush performs live at Pengrowth Saddledome, Calgary, Alberta, Canada.

(July 20)

Rush performs live at White River Amphitheater, Seattle, Washington, US.

(July 21)
Rush performs live at The Amphitheater at Clark County, Portland, Oregon, US.

(July 23)
Rush performs live at Hollywood Bowl, Los Angeles, California, US.

(July 25)
Rush releases their single for "The Larger Bowl" in the US.

US CD promo single (PRCD 294844):
"The Larger Bowl"

Note: this promo single appears to have been released primarily to adult rock-oriented radio stations.

Rush performs live at Verizon Wireless Amphitheater, Irvine, California, US.

(July 27)
Rush performs live at Cricket Pavilion, Phoenix, Arizona, US.

(July 28)
Rush performs live at MGM Grand Garden Arena, Las Vegas, Nevada, US.

(July 30)
Rush performs live at Coors Amphitheatre, San Diego, California, US.

(August 1)
Rush performs live at Shoreline Amphitheater, Mountain View, California, US.

(August 3)
Rush performs live at Sleep Train Pavilion, Concord, California, US.

(August 4)
Rush performs live at Sleep Train Amphitheater, Marysville, California, US.

(August 6)
Rush performs live at USANA Amphitheater, Salt Lake City, Utah, US.

(August 8)
Rush performs live at Red Rocks Amphitheatre, Morrison, Colorado, US

(August 11)
Rush performs live at Smirnoff Music Center, Dallas, Texas, US.

(August 12)
Rush performs live at Verizon Wireless Amphitheater, Selma, Texas, US.

(August 14)
Rush performs live at Cynthia Woods Mitchell Pavilion, Houston, Texas, US.

(August 23)
Rush performs live at Verizon Wireless Amphitheater, Bonner Springs, Kansas, US.

(August 24)
Rush performs live at Verizon Wireless Amphitheater, St. Louis, Missouri, US.

(August 26)
Rush performs live at Verizon Wireless Amphitheater, Noblesville, Indiana, US.

(August 28)
Rush performs live at DTE Energy Music Theater, Detroit, Michigan, US.

(August 30)
Rush performs live at Blossom Music Center, Cuyahoga Falls, Ohio, US.

(September 1)
Rush performs live at Riverbend Music Center, Cincinnati, Ohio, US.

(September 2)
Rush performs live at Germain Amphitheater, Columbus, Ohio, US.

(September 3)
Rush releases *Snakes & Arrows* Special 2007 UK Tour Edition CD+MVI DVD in the UK.

Disc 1: *Snakes & Arrows* CD

Disc 2: *Snakes & Arrows* MVI DVD

Note: the MVI content is the same as the North American edition.

(September 6)
Rush performs live at Marcus Amphitheater, Milwaukee, Wisconsin, US.

(September 8)
Rush performs live at Midwest Bank Amphitheater, Chicago, Illinois, US.

(September 9)
Rush performs live at Xcel Energy Center, St. Paul, Minnesota, US.

(September 12)
Rush performs live at John Labatt Centre, London, Ontario, Canada.

(September 14)
Rush performs live at Colisée de Québec, Quebec City, Quebec, Canada.

(September 15)
Rush performs live at Bell Centre, Montreal, Quebec, Canada.

(September 17)
Rush performs live at Madison Square Garden, New York, New York, US.

(September 19)
Rush performs live at Air Canada Centre, Toronto, Ontario, Canada.

(September 21)
Rush performs live at Scotiabank Place, Ottawa, Ontario, Canada.

(September 22)
Rush performs live at Air Canada Centre, Toronto, Ontario, Canada.

(October 3)
Rush performs live at SECC Arena, Glasgow, Scotland.

(October 5)
Rush performs live at Metro Radio Arena, Newcastle, England.

(October 6)
Rush performs live at Hallam FM Arena, Sheffield, England.

(October 9 & 10)
Rush performs live at Wembley Arena, London, England.

(October 12)
Rush performs live at NEC Arena, Birmingham, England.

(October 14)
Rush performs live at MEN Arena, Manchester, England.

(October 16 & 17)
Rush performs live at Ahoy Rotterdam, Rotterdam, Netherlands. Both shows are recorded and later released as the live album and concert film *Snakes & Arrows Live*. The following tracks are released individually:

> "Limelight (S&A Live – Working Men CD Version)" 4:51
> Written by Neil Peart (words), Geddy Lee & Alex Lifeson (music)
> Appears on: Working Men CD
> Somewhat by necessity, the live album version of the concert removes things like the video intros to the songs, such as the 'Harry Satchel,' Great White North and South Park clips, whereas the concert film DVD

retains them. So the audio on the CD is not always identical between tracks as the DVD. To cover the absent video intros, some extra crowd noise is sometimes employed. The Nightmare intro to the concert doesn't appear on the live album CD, instead fading in over extended crowd noise. This version off Working Men starts identically to the live album and fades out over the crowd noise before "Digital Man" starts.

"Limelight (S&A Live – Working Men DVD Version)" 4:46
Written by Neil Peart (words), Geddy Lee & Alex Lifeson (music)
Appears on: Working Men DVD
The DVD version of the song fades in quickly over the crowd as we see the end of the Nightmare intro video behind Alex, making the audio here shorter than the Working Men CD. It fades out at the end.

"Digital Man (S&A Live – TCS Version)" 6:45
Written by Neil Peart (words), Geddy Lee & Alex Lifeson (music)
Appears on: Taking Center Stage: A Lifetime Of Live Performance (Guitar Center Bonus Content)
This mix has everything but the drums low in the mix, so unless you're a drum student, you're not likely to get a whole lot out of this on repeat viewings. The footage is exclusively Neil's production drum camera angles.

"Entre Nous (S&A Live – R:BTLS Version)" 4:58
Written by Neil Peart (words), Geddy Lee & Alex Lifeson (music)
Appears on: Rush: Beyond The Lighted Stage DVD & Blu-ray
This version fades in on the count-in and fades out at the end.

"Freewill (S&A Live – Working Men CD Version)" 5:44
Written by Neil Peart (words), Geddy Lee & Alex Lifeson (music)
Appears on: Working Men CD
This version fades in over the crowd noise between it and the preceding song ("Mission") and fades out at the end as Geddy thanks the audience.

"Freewill (S&A Live – Working Men DVD Version)" 5:44
Written by Neil Peart (words), Geddy Lee & Alex Lifeson (music)
Appears on: Working Men DVD
The Working Men DVD version has more crowd noise at the start and less at the end, compared to the CD cut.

"The Main Monkey Business (S&A Live – TCS Version)" 6:10
Written by Geddy Lee & Alex Lifeson
Appears on: Taking Center Stage: A Lifetime Of Live Performance DVD
This mix has everything but the drums low in the mix. The footage is exclusively Neil's production drum camera angles.

"Far Cry (S&A Live – Working Men CD Version)" 5:22
Written by Neil Peart (words), Geddy Lee & Alex Lifeson (music)
Appears on: Working Men CD
This version fades in over the crowd noise between it and the preceding song ("Dreamline") and fades out at the end before "Workin' Them Angels" starts. Both the live album and this cut are another example of the necessary changes made to the CD. "Far Cry" opens the second set of the show, but preceding it is a funny video clip of a snakes and arrows game board with Alex demonstrating the various levels of cosmic enlightenment. When the 'Birth Of Man' game square opens, there's an unearthly screech just before the band jumps in with the song. On the live album and here, the intro video and screech are replaced with crowd noise.

"Far Cry (S&A Live – Alternative Cut)" 5:20
Written by Neil Peart (words), Geddy Lee & Alex Lifeson (music)
Appears on: Snakes & Arrows Live DVD & Blu-ray
This "Alternative Cut" of the song from the concert features the complete rear screen animation. The track starts with the screech and fades out quickly (faster than the later Working Men cut).

"Far Cry (S&A Live – Working Men DVD Version)" 5:23
Written by Neil Peart (words), Geddy Lee & Alex Lifeson (music)
Appears on: Working Men DVD
The Working Men DVD version starts with the screech and fades out at the end.

"Far Cry (S&A Live – R:BTLS Version)" 5:24
Written by Neil Peart (words), Geddy Lee & Alex Lifeson (music)
Appears on: Rush: Beyond The Lighted Stage DVD & Blu-ray
This cut starts with end of the intro video, where the camera pans over the snakes and arrows game board to the 'Birth Of Man' square and the door opens. The footage ends on a fade out.

"Workin' Them Angels (S&A Live – Promo Version)" 5:03

Written by Neil Peart (words), Geddy Lee & Alex Lifeson (music)
Appears on: US CD promo single
This version fades in over the crowd noise between it and the preceding song ("Far Cry") and fades out at the end before "Armor and Sword" starts.

"The Way The Wind Blows (S&A Live – Alternative Cut)" 6:28
Written by Neil Peart (words), Geddy Lee & Alex Lifeson (music)
Appears on: Snakes & Arrows Live DVD & Blu-ray
This "Alternative Cut" of the song from the concert features the complete rear screen animation. The track fades quickly on Geddy's intro and fades out at the end.

"Natural Science (S&A Live – TCS Version)" 8:32
Written by Neil Peart (words), Geddy Lee & Alex Lifeson (music)
Appears on: Taking Center Stage: A Lifetime Of Live Performance DVD
This mix has everything but the drums low in the mix. The footage is exclusively Neil's production drum camera angles.

"Tom Sawyer (S&A Live – Working Men CD Version)" 5:33
Written by Neil Peart & Pye Dubois (words), Geddy Lee & Alex Lifeson (music)
Appears on: Working Men CD
This version fades in over the crowd noise before Geddy's banter with the audience. This banter, however, is from a different point in the concert. It comes from his opening greeting to Rotterdam, made after "Entre Nous." Here, it is also edited down before "Tom Sawyer" starts. In the original concert, the South Park 'L'il Rush' intro leads into "Tom Sawyer." I guess someone felt "Tom Sawyer" needed some kind of Geddy intro rather than the song just starting, so some editing was done? It's kind of strange and, given Working Men is a collection of highlights from three concert releases, it's kind of pointless that one venue gets an intro near the end of the CD. The resulting edit isn't bad, just rather odd. The track fades out at the end.

"Tom Sawyer (S&A Live – Working Men DVD Version)" 5:28
Written by Neil Peart & Pye Dubois (words), Geddy Lee & Alex Lifeson (music)
Appears on: Working Men DVD
This cut starts with the South Park intro and Eric Cartman's count-in. It fades out quickly as Geddy thanks Rotterdam (as "Tom Sawyer" closed the second set before the encore). No re-editing here.

(October 19)
Rush performs live at Oberhausen, Germany, Oberhausen, Germany.

(October 21)
Rush performs live at SAP-Arena, Mannheim, Germany.

(October 23)
Rush performs live at Forum Arena, Milan, Italy.

(October 26)
Rush performs live at Spektrum, Oslo, Norway.

(October 27)
Rush performs live at Globe Arena, Stockholm, Sweden.

(October 29)
Rush performs live at Hartwall Arena, Helsinki, Finland.

(November – December)
During the recording sessions these months for Barenaked Ladies' children's album *Snacktime!*, **Geddy Lee** records his vocal part for the title track, over the phone.

SNAKES & ARROWS LIVE

2008

(January 8)
Mobile Fidelity Sound Labs releases their Ultradisc II 24KT gold CD edition of the **Rush** album *Permanent Waves*.

(January 25)
Tile releases its album *Fly Paper*, featuring **Alex Lifeson** on the track "Scared & Mundane."

> "Sacred & Mundane" 5:26
> Written by Tiles
> Appears on: Fly Paper
> A solid rocker with some different textures and movements, this song has some great guitar work by Alex.

(Date Unknown)
Alex Lifeson shoots his instructional videos for "The Spirit Of Radio," "Limelight" and "Tom Sawyer," for iVideosongs.com.

(Date Unknown)
Neil Peart films his scene for the film *Adventures Of Power*, performing as himself.

(March)
Alex Lifeson settles the lawsuit brought against him by Cpl. Amy Stanford.

(March 10)
Rush releases their "Workin' Them Angels" single in the US.

US CD promo single :
"Workin' Them Angels (Radio Edit)"
"Workin' Them Angels (S&A Live – Promo Version)"
"Workin' Them Angels"

> "Workin' Them Angels (Radio Edit)" 4:19
> Written by Neil Peart (words), Geddy Lee & Alex Lifeson (music)
> Appears on: US CD promo single
> This version only cuts out about 25 seconds of audible run time

Note: The date comes from a February *Marketwire.com* post about the forthcoming single and live album, *Snakes & Arrows Live*.

(March 12)
iVideosongs.com posts **Alex Lifeson**'s instructional videos for the "The Spirit Of Radio," "Limelight" and "Tom Sawyer" on their website.

(March 22)
Geddy Lee and **Alex Lifeson** perform as special guests on "YYZ" with Foo Fighters at their concert at the Air Canada Centre, Toronto, Ontario, Canada.

(March 27)
MTV Games release the video game *Rock Band 2* on various home consoles. Among the downloadable content is "Working Man (Vault Edition)" by **Rush**.

(Early April)
Rush rehearses for the second leg of the *Snakes & Arrows* tour (AKA *Snakes & Arrows Live* tour), in Toronto, Ontario, Canada. Rehearsals last for a week and a half (*New Orleans Times-Picayune* April 19, 2008).

(April 11)
Rush performs live at Coliseo de Puerto Rico, San Juan, Puerto Rico.

(April 13)
Rush performs live at Bank Atlantic Center, Ft. Lauderdale, Florida, US.

(April 14 & 15)
Rush releases its 2xCD live album *Snakes & Arrows Live* in the UK and North America respectively on Anthem Records (Canada) and Atlantic Records (UK and US). The concert is from the Rotterdam, Netherlands, show (October 16 & 17, 2007).

On April 15th, **Rush** performs live at Amway Center, Orlando, Florida, US.

(April 17)
Rush performs live at Jacksonville Veterans Memorial Arena, Jacksonville, Florida, US.

(April 19)
Rush is scheduled to perform live at New Orleans Arena, New Orleans, Louisiana, US, but the show has to be rescheduled to April 20th (via a straight swapping of dates with Woodlands Pavillion, Houston, Texas, show originally scheduled for the 20th) when National Basketball Association team New Orleans Hornets schedules its opening play-off game for the same day, necessitating the move.

Rush performs live at Woodlands Pavilion, Houston, Texas, US.

(April 20)
Rush performs live at New Orleans Arena, New Orleans, Louisiana, US.

(April 23)
In the **Lifeson** family lawsuit appeal (re: the New Year's Eve, 2003, incident), the US Court of Appeals for the 11th Circuit rules that it is up to a jury to decide on the issue of whether "lies and embellishments" by Ritz-Carlton hotel security and staff knowingly put Justin Zivojinoch at risk of physical injury, thereby re-instating that portion of the lawsuit (*Naples Florida News*).

Rush performs live at Frank Erwin Center, Austin, Texas, US.

(April 25)
Rush performs live at The Music Center at Fair Park, Dallas, Texas, US.

(April 26)
Rush performs live at Ford Center, Oklahoma City, Oklahoma, US.

(April 29)
Rush performs live at Journal Pavilion, Albuquerque, New Mexico, US.

(May)
Rich Chycki begins work on mixing material for what will be the *Snakes & Arrows Live* concert film, at Mixland Music & DVD, Toronto, Ontario, Canada. During the course of the tour, he sends the material to **Alex Lifeson**, who works on the material himself on his weeks off, at Lerxst Sound, Toronto, Ontario, Canada (*Sound&Vision.com* July 22, 2009).

(May 1)
Rush performs live at Cricket Pavilion, Phoenix, Arizona, US.

(May 3)
Rush performs live at Reno Events Center, Reno, Nevada, US.

(May 4)
Rush performs live at Sleep Train Pavilion, Concord, California, US.

(May 6)
Barenaked Ladies release their studio album *Snacktime!*, featuring **Geddy Lee** on the track "The Canadian Snacktime Trilogy I: Snacktime."

> "The Canadian Snacktime Trilogy I: Snacktime" 3:30
> Written by Kevin Hearn
> Appears on: Snacktime!
> This very Gordon-Lightfoot-esque song celebrates the simple joy of snacktime. Geddy's part comes in amongst various recordings of people (including Lightfoot himself) saying their favourite snacks. Geddy's is barbecue potato chips.

Rush performs live at Nokia Theatre, Los Angeles, California, US.

(May 8)
Rush performs live at Nokia Theatre, Los Angeles, California, US.

(Date Unknown)
Rush film their scene for the movie *I Love You, Man* at Avalon, Hollywood, California, US. The footage is shot on a day off mid-tour (*Entertainment Weekly* March 20, 2009).

(May 10)

Rush performs live at Mandalay Bay Events Center, Las Vegas, Nevada, US.

(May 11)
John Howard Rutsey dies. The family's obituary says his death was the result of "complications from his lifelong affliction with diatetes."

Rush performs live at Verizon Wireless Amphitheatre, Irvine, California, US.

(Mid-May)
Alex Lifeson and **Geddy Lee** issue a statement in memoriam of **John Rutsey**.

(Date Unknown)
Producer Rupert Hine contacts *Rush* about contributing to the planned benefit collection *Songs For Tibet: The Art Of Peace*.

(May 20)
Rush performs live at iWireless Center, Moline, Illinois, US.

(May 22)
Rush performs live at Xcel Energy Center, St Paul, Minnesota, US.

(May 24)
Rush performs live at MTS Center, Winnipeg, Manitoba, Canada. The band donates $100,000 from the proceeds of this show to the Canadian Museum of Human Rights, which is established this year and to be located in Winnipeg. The Museum later opens in 2014.

(May 25)
Rush performs live at Brandt Center, Regina, Saskatchewan, Canada. The band records the following for inclusion on the *Songs For Tibet: The Art Of Peace* collection:

"Hope"

> "Hope (Live for The Art Of Peace)" 2:23
> Written by Alex Lifeson
> Appears on: Songs For Tibet: The Art Of Peace
> This is an excellent live version of Alex's acoustic instrumental piece and a nice alternative to the Rotterdam recording from Snakes & Arrows Live.

(May 27)
Rush performs live at Rexall Place, Edmonton, Alberta, Canada.

(May 29)
Rush performs live at GM Place, Vancouver, British Columbia, Canada.

(May 31)
Rush performs live at The Gorge Amphitheatre, Seattle, Washington, US.

(June 1)
Rush performs live at Clark County Amphitheatre, Portland, Oregon, US.

(June 3)
Rush performs live at Idaho Center, Boise, Idaho, US.

(June 5)
Rush is scheduled to perform at Red Rocks Amphitheater, Morrison, Colorado, US, but the show is rescheduled to June 25 due to rain.

(June 7)
Rush performs live at Starlight Theatre. Kansas City, Missouri, US.

(June 9)
Rush performs live at United Center, Chicago, Illinois, US.

(June 10)
Rush performs live at Joe Louis Arena, Detroit, Michigan, US.

(June 12)
Rush performs live at Bell Center, Montreal, Quebec, Canada.

(June 14)
Rush performs live at Wachovia Center, Philadelphia, Pennsylvania, US.

(June 15)
Rush performs live at Tweeter Center, Mansfield, Massachusetts, US. Donna Halper visits with the band backstage at the concert.

(June 25)
Rush is scheduled to perform live at Verizon Amphitheatre, Indianapolis, Indiana, US, but the show is rescheduled to July 24.

Rush performs live at Red Rocks Amphitheater, Morrison, Colorado, US. This show replaces the rain cancellation of June 5.

(June 27)
Rush performs live at Summerfest, Marcus Amphitheater, Milwaukee, Wisconsin, US.

(June 28)
Rush performs live at Verizon Wireless Amphitheatre, St Louis, Missouri, US.

(June 30)
Rush performs live at Riverbend Music Center, Cincinnati, Ohio, US.

(July 2)
Rush performs live at Post Gazette Amphitheatre, Pittsburgh, Pennsylvania, US.

(July 4)
Rush performs live at Marc Etess Arena, Atlantic City, New Jersey, US.

(July 5)
Rush performs live at SPAC, Saratoga Springs, New York, US.

(July 7)
Rush performs live at Mohegan Sun, Uncasville, Connecticut, US.

(July 9)
Rush performs live at the Molson Amphitheatre, Toronto, Ontario, Canada. TSN director Eric Neuschwander attends the concert and **Neil Peart**'s drum solo inspires him to ask **Peart** to record a version of "The Hockey Theme." Neuschwander later contacts Andy Curran at SRO Productions with the proposal.

(July 11)
Rush performs live at Verizon Arena, Manchester, New Hampshire, US.

(July 12)
Rush performs live at PNC Bank Arts Center, Holmdel, New Jersey, US.

(July 14)
Rush performs live at Jones Beach, Wantagh, New York, US.

(July 16)
Rush shoots their appearance on *The Colbert Report*, NEP Studio 54, New York City, New York, US. They are interviewed and performed "Tom Sawyer."

(July 17)
Rush performs live at Hershey Stadium, Hershey, Pennsylvania, US.

(July 19)
Rush performs live at Nissan Pavilion, Washington, DC, US.

(July 20)
Rush performs live at Charlotte Amphitheatre, Charlotte, North Carolina, US.

(July 21)
Rush releases on iTunes the downloadable track "Working Man (Vault Edition)."

iTunes Download:
"Working Man (Vault Edition)

(July 22)

Rush performs live at Verizon Wireless Amphitheatre at Encore Park, Alpharetta, Georgia, US. The concert is filmed and the following songs appear as bonus footage on the *Snakes & Arrows Live* DVD and Blu-ray:

"Ghost Of A Chance"
"Red Barchetta"
"The Trees"
"2112: I: Overture / II: The Temples Of Syrinx"

> "Ghost Of A Chance (Live in Alpharetta, 2008)" 5:50
> Written by Neil Peart (words), Geddy Lee & Alex Lifeson (music)
> Appears on: Retrospective III 1989-2008
> This is the same performance as appears on the Oh, Atlanta! bonus footage from Snakes & Arrows Live, though it fades in and out at slightly different points, this cut has the music come in a bit sooner.

> "The Trees (Live in Alpharetta, 2008 – TCS Version)" 5:50
> Written by Neil Peart (words), Geddy Lee & Alex Lifeson (music)
> Appears on: Taking Center Stage: A Lifetime Of Live Performance DVD
> This mix has everything but the drums low in the mix. The footage is exclusively Neil's production drum camera angles.

Note: the footage is titled *Oh, Atlanta! The Authorized Bootlegs*, though Alpharetta, Georgia, is its own city north of Atlanta.

(July 24)
Rush performs live at Verizon Amphitheatre, Indianapolis, Indiana, US. This show replaces the previously scheduled concert from June 25.

(August 5 & 12)
The Art Of Peace Foundation releases the *Songs For Tibet: The Art Of Peace* 2xCD collection on iTunes and CD respectively. It contains **Rush**'s performance of "Hope" from May 25th, Regina, Saskatchewan, Canada.

(August 22)
US District Judge John E. Steele dismisses the **Lifeson** family lawsuit (re: the New Year's Eve, 2003, incident), Fort Myers, Florida, US. The parties involved reach a confidential agreement to settle the case (*Naples Florida News*)

(Late 2008)
Alex Lifeson films his parts for the film *Suck*, in Toronto, Ontario, Canada, as a border guard.

(November 25)
Rush releases their concert film *Snakes & Arrows Live* on DVD and Blu-ray via Zoë Vision & Anthem Entertainment. The main concert footage is from the Rotterdam, Netherlands, show (October 16 & 17, 2007). Addition footage dates from the July 22, 2008, Alpharetta, Georgia, and Frankfurt, Germany (September 24, 2004).

Snakes & Arrows Live DVD Edition
DVD 1: Rotterdam concert set 1
Bonus Features:
- 'What's That Smell'
- 2007 Tour Outtakes
- 'What's That Smell' Outtakes
- "Far Cry (S&A Live – Alternative Cut)"
- "The Way The Wind Blows (S&A Live – Alternative Cut)"
- "Red Sector A (R30 – S&AL DVD Bonus Version)"

DVD 2: Rotterdam concert set 2

DVD 3: *Oh, Atlanta! The Authorized Bootlegs*
"Ghost Of A Chance"
"Red Barchetta"
"The Trees"
"2112: I: Overture / II: The Temples Of Syrinx"

Snakes & Arrows Live Blu-ray Edition
Blu-ray: Rotterdam concert
Bonus Features:
- 'What's That Smell'
- 2007 Tour Outtakes
- 'What's That Smell' Outtakes
- "Far Cry (S&A Live – Alternative Cut)"
- "The Way The Wind Blows (S&A Live – Alternative Cut)"

- "Red Sector A (R30 – S&AL DVD Bonus Version)"
- *Oh, Atlanta! The Authorized Bootlegs*

(Autumn)
In a *UGO.com* interview (December 11, 2008) with **Alex Lifeson** published on this date, **Alex** says *Rush* is taking a break before resuming work in the autumn of 2009.

WORKING MEN

2009

(January 23)
In a *GuitarInternational.com* interview published on this date, **Alex Lifeson** says Rich Chycki has just re-mixed the following for the forthcoming *Retrospective III* compilation:
"One Little Victory"
"Earthshine"

(January 24)
Alex Lifeson performs "Closer To The Heart" with the Trailer Park Boys at their live show, Massey Hall, Toronto, Ontario, Canada. This is also the last day of shooting for the movie *Trailer Park Boys: Countdown to Liquor Day*, in which **Lifeson** previously shot his role as 'Undercover Prostitute #1.'

(March 3)
Rush releases their compilation album R*etrospective III: 1989-2008* in Canada (Anthem Records) and worldwide (Atlantic Records). Two editions are released, a CD-only version and a CD+DVD version. The DVD contains the related promo videos and bonus material. Track listing as follows:

CD:
"One Little Victory (2009 Retrospective III Remix)"
"Dreamline"
"Workin' Them Angels"
"Presto"
"Bravado"
"Driven"
"The Pass"
"Animate"
"Roll The Bones"
"Ghost Of A Chance (Live in Alpharetta, 2008)"
"Nobody's Hero"
"Leave That Thing Alone"
"Earthshine (2009 Retrospective III Remix)"
"Far Cry"

DVD:
"Stick It Out"
"Nobody's Hero"
"Half The World"
"Driven"
"Roll The Bones"
"Show Don't Tell"
"The Pass"
"Superconductor"
"Far Cry"
"Malignant Narcissism"
"The Seeker (R30 – Retrospective III Version)"
"Secret Touch (R30 – Retrospective III Version)"
"Resist (R30 – Retrospective III Version)"

>"One Little Victory (2009 Retrospective III Remix)" 5:10
>Written by Neil Peart (words), Geddy Lee & Alex Lifeson (music)
>Appears on: Retrospective III 1989-2008
>Done mainly as an experiment to see if the original recordings could be salvaged from the wreckage of the Loudness War, Rich Chycki re-mixed both this and "Earthshine" from scratch and the results are impressive! This mix differs significantly from the later *Vapor Trails Remixed* album version (by Dave Botrill), with clearer drums and not sounding as densely mixed. This mix breathes a lot more throughout.

>"Earthshine (2009 Retrospective III Remix)" 5:37
>Written by Neil Peart (words), Geddy Lee & Alex Lifeson (music)
>Appears on: Retrospective III 1989-2008
>Similarly to the "One Little Victory" remix, this mix differs from the later *Vapor Trails Remixed* album version (by Dave Botrill) and again, it seems to have a lot more breathing room and the drums are punchier. Honestly, I prefer this remix to the 2013 album remix.

Note: Based on various interview statements, it would seem that the band had a lot of input into the track selection for this compilation. It's also noteworthy that by not including "Show Don't Tell," *Retrospective III* does not overlap with the previous collection *Chronicles*, nor obviously *Retrospective I* and *II* or *Gold*.

(March 21)
Alex Lifeson says in an interview published on this date (*MusicRadar.com*) that **Rush** is currently on a break and is looking at autumn to return to work. He also says the next project is not planned as a concept album.

(May)
Around this time, **Alex Lifeson** and Rich Chycki renovate Lerxst Sound, Toronto, Ontario, Canada. This month Chycki "moves in" to the studio (*Sound&Vision.com* July 22, 2009).

(August 11)
Rush releases their live album *Grace Under Pressure Tour* Soundtrack as a standalone CD in Canada (Anthem Records) and worldwide (Mercury Records). This CD was previously only available with the *Replay x3* DVD boxed set. It does not contain the Best Buy-only bonus tracks.

(August 12)
Olivia Louise Peart is born to **Neil Peart** and Carrie Nuttall, Los Angeles, California, US.

(Autumn)
Neil Peart is asked to record "The Hockey Theme."

(September 22)
Vertical Horizon releases their album *Burning The Days*, featuring **Neil Peart** on the songs "Save Me From Myself," "Welcome To The Bottom" and "Even Now," the latter co-written by **Peart** and Matt Scannell.

> "Save Me From Myself" 4:18
> Written by Matt Scannell
> Appears on: Burning The Days
> A typical alt-rocker, heavy on guitars and angst, this track features a fairly reserved Neil, who pounds out the backbeat and not much else. It serves the song just fine, but don't expect Rush-levels of percussive showmanship.
>
> "Welcome To The Bottom" 5:48
> Written by Matt Scannell
> Appears on: Burning The Days
> A more dynamic track than "Save Me From Myself," this has some flashier drum work from Neil.
>
> "Even Now" 6:44
> Written by Matt Scannell & Neil Peart
> Appears on: Burning The Days
> You'll immediately notice this song is wordier than the other tracks on this album, which is likely Neil's contribution. It's fascinating to hear someone else sing his words besides Geddy (or even going back to the JR Flood days). The drum work is heavy and intense, suiting the song, and demonstrating how this track is truly a collaboration, rather than simply a guest appearance.

(October 21)
Neil Peart meets with Drum Workshop and the talk results in **Peart** commissioning a new drum kit for "The Hockey Theme" recording.

(November 13 & 17)
Rush releases their live compilation *Working Men* in Europe and North America respectively, on both CD and DVD.

CD Edition:
"Limelight (S&A Live – Working Men CD Version)"
"The Spirit Of Radio (R30 – Working Men CD Version)"
"2112: I: Overture / II: The Temples Of Syrinx (Rush In Rio – Sampler Version)"
"Freewill (S&A Live – Working Men CD Version)"
"Dreamline (R30 – Working Men CD Version)"
"Far Cry (S&A Live – Working Men CD Version)"
"Subdivisions (R30 – Working Men CD Version)"
"One Little Victory (R30 – Working Men CD Version)"
"Closer To The Heart (Rush In Rio – Working Men CD Version)"
"Tom Sawyer (S&A Live – Working Men CD Version)"
"Working Man (R30 – Working Men CD Version)"
"YYZ (Rush In Rio – Working Men CD Version)"

DVD Edition:

"Limelight (S&A Live – Working Men DVD Version)"
"The Spirit Of Radio (R30 – Working Men DVD Version)"
"2112: I: Overture / II: The Temples Of Syrinx (Working Men DVD Version)"
"Freewill (S&A Live – Working Men DVD Version)"
"Dreamline (R30 – Working Men DVD Version)"
"Far Cry (S&A Live – Working Men DVD Version)"
"Subdivisions (R30 – Working Men DVD Version)"
"One Little Victory (R30 – Working Men DVD Version)"
"Closer To The Heart (Rush In Rio – Working Men DVD Version)"
"Tom Sawyer (S&A Live – Working Men DVD Version)"
"Working Man (R30 – Working Men DVD Version)"
"YYZ (Rush In Rio – Working Men DVD Version)"

(December)
Rush meets with Nick Raskulinecz in Los Angeles, California, US, to discuss ideas for the next project. **Geddy Lee** suggests releasing a collection of the band's instrumentals and writing a new, long form instrumental for it. **Neil Peart** suggests writing a few songs to tell a "steampunk" story. Following the meeting, **Neil** begins writing the lyrics and outlining the story (*Time Machine* tour book). He comes up with the chapter titles "Caravan," Carnival" and "Caravel" (*Classic Rock – Clockwork Angels Fan Pack* June 11, 2012).

(December 7)
Neil Peart records his parts for "The Hockey Theme" at Ocean Way Studios, Oxnard, California, US (*Fire On Ice* sessions). He then shoots the performance footage at Drum Channel's studio, Oxnard, California, US.

(December 8)
Rush re-issues their concert film *R30: The 30th Anniversary World Tour* on Blu-ray via Zoë Vision & Anthem Entertainment. This release features the complete concert (the original 2005 DVD releases feature an edited version of the concert), but lacks all of the original bonus material.

CARAVAN + BU2B

2010

(Early January)
Neil Peart (in Los Angeles, California, US) sends his steampunk story lyrics to **Geddy Lee** and **Alex Lifeson** (in Toronto, Ontario, Canada). **Lee** and **Lifeson** work on the material while jamming at **Lee**'s home studio (*Clockwork Angels* sessions) (*Time Machine* tour book).
"Clockwork Angels" – **Alex** had previously recorded a "pretty length piece" at Lerxst Sound, Toronto, Ontario, Canada, and he and **Geddy** work it into what will become this song (*MusicRadar.com* May 25, 2012).
"Caravan" – this is the first song of the project "written from scratch" (*Classic Rock - Clockwork Angels Fan Pack* June 11, 2012).
"BU2B" – the music comes to **Geddy** one night when he can't sleep.

(January 10)
David Barrett meets with **Alex Lifeson** at Lerxst Sound, Toronto, Ontario, Canada, and following a listen of Barrett's solo album, **Lifeson** discusses ideas for Barrett's next project (what will come The David Barrett Trio's debut album) (*GuitarPlayyer* January 10, 2011).

(January 22)
Neil Peart posts his performance of "The Hockey Theme" on his YouTube VEVO Channel.

> "The Hockey Theme" 1:01
> Written by Dolores Claman
> Appears on: N/A
> Commonly referred to as CBC's *Hockey Night In Canada* theme (because the CBC broadcast of hockey games in Canada used it from 1968 to 2008, before losing it to CTV after not being able to renegotiate for its use). Neil has said this piece is his "One Hot Minute" and that's probably the best way to describe it.

(Early March)
Rush convenes at **Geddy Lee**'s house in Toronto, Ontario, Canada, and listens to the five completed song demos for the steampunk story project (*Clockwork Angels* sessions) (*Time Machine* tour book).
"Caravan" - It is decided to concentrate on this track to complete for the upcoming tour.
"BU2B" – the original title is "Brought Up To Believe," but it's decided to shorten it. It is also decided to concentrate on this track to complete for the upcoming tour.
"Clockwork Angels"
"The Anarchist" – this is one of the first songs written for the project (*MusicRadar.com* May 25, 2012), it comes from a **Lee** and **Lifeson** jam (*Classic Rock - Clockwork Angels Fan Pack* June 11, 2012).
"The Garden" – this is one of the first songs written for the project (*MusicRadar.com* May 25, 2012). **Geddy** is the primary music writer on this piece (*Corus Radio* June 15, 2012).

(March 23)
Universal Records releases the **Rush** compilation *Time Stand Still: The Collection* in Europe. Track listing as follows:

"The Sprit Of Radio"
"Tom Sawyer"
"Freewill"
"Fly By Night"
"The Big Money"
"Time Stand Still"
"Limelight"
"Finding My Way"
"By-Tor And The Snow Dog (Standard CD Edition)"
"A Passage To Bangkok"
"Distant Early Warning"
"The Trees"
"Closer To The Heart"

(March 28)
Rush is inducted into the Canadian Songwriters Hall Of Fame, along with their songs "Closer To The Heart," "Limelight," "The Spirit Of Radio," "Subdivisions" and "Tom Sawyer." The ceremony takes place at the Toronto Centre for the Arts, Toronto, Ontario, Canada.

(Date Unknown)

Geddy Lee, **Alex Lifeson** and **Neil Peart** record their voice-over parts for the forthcoming videogame *Guitar Hero: Warriors of Rock*.

(Early April)
Rush rehearses and arranges the following track over two weeks in Toronto, Ontario, Canada (*Time Machine* tour book):
"Caravan"
"BU2B"

(April 13)
Rush begins work on the following at Blackbird Studios, Nashville, Tennessee, US. Engineered by Rich Chycki. Produced by Nick Raskulinecz and *Rush*. The first two days sessions are spent recording bass and drum parts, followed by ten days of overdubs and mixing (*Time Machine* tour book).
"Caravan"
"BU2B"

The band has six songs written by this point, including "Caravan" and "BU2B" (*Classic Rock Presents Prog* May 2010):
"Clockwork Angels" – one of the four other songs written by this point (*MusicRadar.com* August 31, 2010)
"The Garden" – one of the other songs written by this point (*Clockwork Angels* tour book)

(Late-April)
The following tracks are mixed by Nick Raskulincz at Sound Kitchen, Franklin, Tennessee, US:
"Caravan (Single Mix"
"BU2B (Single Mix)"

(Date Unknown)
The following tracks are mastered by Ted Jensen at Sterling Sound, New York City, New York, US:
"Caravan (Single Mix)"
"BU2B (Single Mix)"

(Mid-April)
Neil Peart begins pre-rehearsal warm-up sessions for the upcoming *Time Machine* tour Drum Channel, Oxnard, California, US. During the rehearsals, he shoots instructional and interview segments for his forthcoming DVD *Taking Center Stage*, which documents a drummer's work on tour. Shooting takes place "a week or so" before the full band tour rehearsals (*Taking Center Stage* Guitar Centre Bonus Interview and *MusicRadar.com* November 7, 2011).

(June 1)
Rush releases their "Caravan" + "BU2B" singles worldwide, including on Amazon and iTunes.

Digital download single:
"Caravan (Single Mix)"
"BU2B (Single Mix)"

Canada CD promo single (PRCD 19):
"Caravan (Single Mix)"
"BU2B (Single Mix)"

> "Caravan (Single Mix)" 5:40
> Written by Neil Peart (words), Geddy Lee & Alex Lifeson (music)
> Appears on: Digital download single, Canada CD promo single, 2011 Record Store Day 7" single
> Don't expect the differences here to leap out at you, but a side-by-side comparison shows this mix is drier throughout, meaning there isn't a lot of sonic "blending" of the different tracks, each one standing more on its own. The result is that the drums have clearer punch and Geddy's vocals are louder and more distinct.

> "BU2B (Single Mix)" 4:21
> Written by Neil Peart (words), Geddy Lee & Alex Lifeson (music)
> Appears on: Digital download single, Canada CD promo single, 2011 Record Store Day 7" single
> This original release of the track does not feature the opening ambient 50 second intro, as it was recorded for the album after the single's release. The rest of the track, like with "Caravan," is a bit drier, with the drums being punchier and Geddy's vocals being a bit louder.

(June 10)
Banger Films, D&E Entertainment & Alliance Films release the *Rush* documentary *Rush: Beyond The Lighted Stage* in a select theatre run.

(June 25)
Rush are given a star on the Hollywood Walk of Fame, Hollywood, California, US. **Geddy Lee** and **Alex Lifeson** attend, along with Donna Halper.

(June 29)
Banger Films, D&E Entertainment & Alliance Films release the **Rush** documentary *Rush: Beyond The Lighted Stage* on DVD and Blu-ray.

DVD 1: *Rush: Beyond The Lighted Stage* documentary

DVD 2: Special Features
- Being Bullied And The Search For The First Gig
- Reflections On *Hemispheres*
- Presto And Roll The Bones Rap
- The Rush Fashion
- Hobbies On The Road
- Rush Trekkies
- Pre-Gig Warm-Up
- "Best I Can (Live at Laura Secord Secondary School, 1974)"
- "Working Man (Live at Laura Secord Secondary School, 1974)"
- "La Villa Strangiato" Pinkpop Festival, 1979
- "Between Sun & Moon (Live At Hartford, 2002)"
- Dinner With Rush at a Hunting Lodge
- "Far Cry (S&A Live – R:BTLS Version)"
- "Entre Nous (S&A Live – R:BTLS Version)"
- "Bravado (R30 – R:BTLS Version)"
- "YYZ (R30 – R:BTLS Version)"

Blu-ray:
Rush: Beyond The Lighted Stage documentary
Special Features (same as above)

Rush performs live at Hard Rock Casino Pavilion, Albuquerque, New Mexico, US.

(July 1)
Rush performs live at Starlight Theatre, Kansas City, Missouri, US.

(July 3)
Rush performs live at Summerfest, Milwaukee, Wisconsin, US.

(July 5)
Rush performs live at Charter One Pavilion, Chicago, Illinois, US.

(July 7)
Rush is scheduled to perform live at Charter One Pavilion. Chicago, Illinois, US, but the show is rained out and rescheduled to August 23rd.

(July 9)
Rush performs live at Bayfest, Sarnia, Ontario, Canada.

(July 11)
Rush performs live at Ottawa Bluesfest, Ottawa, Ontario, Canada.

(July 13)
Rush performs live at Molson Canadian Amphitheatre, Toronto, Ontario, Canada.

(July 15)
Rush performs live at Festival d'ete de Quebec, Quebec City, Quebec, Canada.

(July 17)
Rush performs live at Air Canada Centre. Toronto, Ontario, Canada.

(July 19)
Rush performs live at Mohegan Sun. Uncasville, Connecticut, US.

(July 21)
Rush performs live at Susquehanna Bank Center, Camden, New Jersey, US.

(July 23)
Rush performs live at SPAC, Saratoga Springs, New York, US. Hudson Music specially shoots footage of **Neil Peart** at his drum kit for the entire concert, for the *Taking Center Stage* drum instructional DVD project. The pre-show warm-up and interviews are also shot at this show.

(July 24)
Rush performs live at Nikon at Jones Beach, Wantagh, New York, US.

(August 5)
Rush performs live at USANA Amphitheatre, Salt Lake City, Utah, US.

(August 7)
Rush performs live at White River Amphitheatre, Seattle, Washington, US.

(August 9)
Rush performs live at Shoreline Amphitheatre, San Francisco, California, US.

(August 11)
Rush performs live at Gibson Amphitheatre, Los Angeles, California, US.

(August 13)
Rush performs live at Verizon Wireless Amphitheater, Irvine, California, US.

(August 14)
Rush performs live at MGM Grand Garden Arena, Las Vegas, Nevada, US.

(August 16)
Rush performs live at Red Rocks Amphitheater, Morrison, Colorado, US.

(August 17)
Neil Peart visits with his friend, writer Kevin J. Anderson, and they hike up Mount Evans, Colorado, US. It is here that they "workshop" a book version of the *Clockwork Angels* story.

(August 18)
Rush performs live at Red Rocks Amphitheater, Morrison, Colorado, US.

(August 20)
Rush performs live at Intrust Bank Arena, Wichita, Kansas, US.

(August 22)
Rush performs live at Verizon Wireless Amphitheater, St. Louis, Missouri, US.

(August 23)
Rush performs live at Charter One Pavilion, Chicago, Illinois, US. This show replaces the rained out July 7th concert.

(August 25)
Rush performs live at Qwest Center, Omaha, Nebraska, US.

(August 27)
Rush performs live at Minnesota State Fair, St. Paul, Minnesota, US.

(August 29)
Rush performs live at Nationwide Arena, Columbus, Ohio, US.

(August 31)
Mercury Records releases the *Rush* compilation *Icon*, as part of their *Icon* series, in North America. Track listing as follows:

"Working Man"
"Fly By Night"
"The Necromancer"
"The Twilight Zone"
"Closer To The Heart"
"Circumstances"
"Freewill"
"Limelight"
"The Analog Kid"
"Red Sector A"
"Marathon"
"Force Ten"

Rush performs live at Allentown Fair, Allentown, Pennsylvania, US.

(September 2)

Rush performs live at New York State Fair, Syracuse, New York, US.

(September 3)
Rush performs live at PNC Bank Arts Center, Holmdel, New Jersey, US.

(September 14)
Rush performs live at TD Garden, Boston, Massachusetts, US.

(September 16)
Rush performs live at Consol Energy Center, Pittsburgh, Pennsylvania, US.

(September 18)
Rush performs live at Jiffy Lube Live Amphitheater, Bristow, Virginia, US.

(September 21)
Rush performs live at BOK Center. Tulsa, Oklahoma, US.

(September 23)
Rush performs live at AT&T Center, San Antonio, Texas, US.

(September 25)
Rush performs live at Cynthia Woods Mitchell Pavilion, Houston, Texas, US.

(September 28)
Eagle Rock Entertainment releases the *Rush Classic Albums* episode *2112 - Moving Pictures* on DVD and Blu-ray. Special features include additional and extended interviews and performances of "2112: I: Overture" and "YYZ."

(September 26)
Rush performs live at Superpages.com Center, Dallas, Texas, US.

(September 29)
Rush performs live at Verizon Wireless Amphitheatre @ Encore Park, Atlanta, Georgia, US.

(October 1)
Rush performs live at Ford Amphitheatre, Tampa, Florida, US.

(October 2)
Rush performs live at Cruzan Amphitheatre, West Palm Beach, Florida, US.

(October 8)
Rush performs live at Estadio Morumbi, São Paulo, Brazil.

(October 10)
Rush performs live at Praca da Apoteose, Rio de Janeiro, Brazil.

(October 15)
Rush performs live at G.E.B.A., Buenos Aires, Argentina.

(October 17)
Rush performs live at Estadio Nacional, Santiago, Chile.

(Late 2010)
Following the *Time Machine* tour's 1st leg, **Alex Lifeson** begins production work at Lerxst Sound, Toronto, Ontario, Canada, for The David Barrett Trio's self-titled debut album (*GuitarPlayyer* Jannuary 10, 2011).

TIME MACHINE

2011

(January)
Scenes for the film *Irvine Welsh's Ecstasy* are filmed in Sault Ste. Marie, Ontario, Canada. **Alex Lifeson** shoots his scenes as 'Dr. Figg.' On set, **Lifeson** meets actor/musician Keram Malicki-Sanchez, with whom he later works on Malicki-Sanchez's album *Come To Life*.

Rich Chycki work on the 5.1 mix of **Rush**'s album *Moving Pictures*, planned for the 30th anniversary (*Gibson* February 18, 2011). Mixing takes place at Mixland, Ontario, Canada.

Neil Peart shoots additional instructional and interview footage over two days in Death Valley, California, US, for the *Taking Center Stage* project.

(January 12)
Drum Channel releases **Neil Peart**'s *Fire On Ice: The Making of the Hockey* on DVD.

(Date Unknown)
Geddy Lee records bass and vocals for the tracks "When I Close My Eyes" and "March Of The Shikker," for The Black Sea Station album *Transylvania Avenue*. Ben Mink recruits **Lee** for the project.

(February 3)
Rich Chycki finishes mixing work on "Red Barchetta," as part of the 5.1 mix project for **Rush**'s *Moving Pictures* album.

(February 4)
Rich Chycki posts on his website that he has spent the last month working on the 5.1 mix of **Rush**'s album *Moving Pictures*.

(Early 2011)
Geddy Lee and **Alex Lifeson** write new material for the next album (*Clockwork Angels* sessions) (*Gibson* February 18, 2011).
"Carnies" – the jams later form the foundation of this song
"Take That Lampshade Off Yo Head" - the jams later form the foundation of this instrumental.

A few months after shooting *Ecstasy*, **Alex Lifeson** calls Keram Malicki-Sanchez to follow up with the album Keram is recording, offering to play on several tracks. **Lifeson** ultimately records on "Mary Magdalene," "Moving Dark Circles" and "The Devil Knows Me Well," venue unknown, possible Lerxst Sound, Toronto, Ontario, Canada.

Screenwriters Derek Haas and Michael Brandt (also the director) contact **Alex Lifeson** about recording music for their film *The Double* (TheRushForum.com August 15, 2011). **Alex** agrees and discusses the project with the film composer John Debney. Ultimately, **Alex** records guitar for the soundtrack music and writes the following (likely at Lerxst Sound, Toronto, Ontario, Canada):
"Don't Look Back" – Engineered by Rich Chycki.

(March)
Rush continues work on their next studio album (*Clockwork Angels* sessions) (*Mojo* March 2011). At this point it is reported that they have four unrecorded songs written and two more in-progress.

(March 29)
The Black Sea Station releases their album *Transylvania Avenue*, featuring **Geddy Lee** on the tracks "When I Close My Eyes" and "March Of The Shikker."

> "When I Close My Eyes" 4:49
> Written by The Black Sea Station
> Appears on: Transylvania Avenue
> Klezmer is basically Eastern European Jewish folk music, with all the rich cultural flavour you'd expect. Geddy previously dabbled in klezmer by way of his Finjan collaboration (also done through Ben Mink). This instrumental is haunting, beautiful and evocative of a small country village and its inhabitants. Geddy's bass work keeps the lower end nice and solid.

> "March Of The Shikker" 3:32
> Written by The Black Sea Station
> Appears on: Transylvania Avenue
> "Shikker" is a pejorative Yiddish word for "a drunk," just to give the title some context. Geddy speaks Yiddish throughout the track, which is a jaunty number that bounces along in a fun way, like a drunk stumbling home in a jovial mood.

(March 30)
Rush performs live at Bank Atlantic Center, Ft. Lauderdale, Florida, US.

(April)
Audio Fidelity releases the 24KT gold Hybrid SACD/DSD edition of the *Rush* album *Roll The Bones*.

(April 1)
Rush is scheduled to perform live at Greensboro Coliseum, Greensboro, North Carolina, US, but the show is moved to the following day.

(April 2)
Rush performs live at Greensboro Coliseum, Greensboro, North Carolina, US, replacing the show cancelled the previous day.

(April 3)
Rush performs live at Bridgestone Arena, Nashville, Tennessee, US.

(April 5)
Rush re-issues *Moving Pictures* in the following formats, in Canada (Anthem Records) and worldwide (Mercury Records):

Moving Pictures CD+DVD Deluxe Edition:
CD: *Moving Pictures* (2011 Remaster)

DVD: *Moving Pictures* 5.1 Surround Sound Mix
Bonus Videos:
- "Tom Sawyer" – Le Studio
- "Limelight" – Le Studio
- "Vital Signs" – Le Studio

Moving Pictures CD+Bly-ray Deluxe Edition:
CD: *Moving Pictures* (2011 Remaster)

Blu-ray: *Moving Pictures* 5.1 Surround Sound Mix
Bonus Videos:
- "Tom Sawyer" – Le Studio
- "Limelight" – Le Studio
- "Vital Signs" – Le Studio

Note: The stereo remaster is by Andy VanDette. The sleeve indicates that the "Vital Signs" video is previously unreleased, but it did previously appear on the *Through The Camera Eye* VHS and Laserdisc video collection.

Rush performs live at KFC Yum! Center, Louisville, Kentucky, US.

(April 6)
Rush is scheduled to perform live at Huntington Center, Toledo, Ohio, US, but the show is moved to April 13th.

(April 8)
Rush performs live at Giant Center, Hershey, Pennsylvania, US.

(April 10)
Rush performs live at Madison Square Garden, New York, New York, US.

(April 12)
Rush performs live at United Center, Chicago, Illinois, US.

(April 13)
Rush performs live at Huntington Center, Toledo, Ohio, US.

(April 15)
Rush performs live at Quicken Loans Arena, Cleveland, Ohio, US. This concert is recorded and later released as *Time Machine 2011: Live In Cleveland* and, as an excerpt, *Moving Pictures: Live 2011*.

"Tom Sawyer (Time Machine – LP Version)" 4:53
Written by Neil Peart & Pye Dubois (words), Geddy Lee & Alex Lifeson (music)
Appears on: Moving Pictures: Live 2011 LP & iTunes download
Because the band played Moving Pictures in its entirety at each concert during this tour, they were in the position of having the live version of the album to release on its own. Doing so necessitated fading in at the beginning, over the crowd noise on this song (the start of Side 1).

"Vital Signs (Time Machine – LP Version)" 4:53
Written by Neil Peart (words), Geddy Lee & Alex Lifeson (music)
Appears on: Moving Pictures: Live 2011 LP & iTunes download
This version fades out over the crowd noise at the end.

(April 16)
Rush releases their "Caravan" + "BU2B" single in North America and Europe as part of Record Store Day.

North America 7" single [white] (527398-7):
"Caravan (Single Mix)"
"BU2B (Single Mix)"

North America 7" single [red] (527398-7):
"Caravan (Single Mix)"
"BU2B (Single Mix)"

Europe 7" single [white] (7567-88268-5):
"Caravan (Single Mix)"
"BU2B (Single Mix)"

Europe 7" single [red] (7567-88268-5):
"Caravan (Single Mix)"
"BU2B (Single Mix)"

(April 17)
Rush performs live at The Palace, Auburn Hills, Michigan, US.

(April 19)
Rush performs live at Copps Coliseum, Hamilton, Ontario, Canada. **Geddy Lee** performs despite having strep throat (*Rolling Stone* September 23, 2013).

(April 20)
On this date, **Geddy Lee** awakens with an ear infection and has to visit a doctor.

Rush performs live at Bell Centre, Montreal, Quebec, Canada.

(April 22)
Rush performs live at 1st Mariner Arena, Baltimore, Maryland, US.

(May 4)
Rush performs live at Hartwall Arena, Helsinki, Finland.

(May 6)
Rush performs live at Globe, Stockholm, Sweden.

(May 8)
Rush performs live at Malmo Arena, Malmo, Sweden.

(May 12)
Rush performs live at O2, Dublin, Ireland.

(May 14)
Rush performs live at SECC Arena, Glasgow, Scotland.

(May 16)
Rush performs live at Motorpoint Arena, Sheffield, England.

(May 19)
Rush performs live at MEN Arena, Manchester, England.

(May 21)
Rush performs live at Metro Radio Arena, Newcastle, England.

(May 22)
Rush performs live at LG Arena, Birmingham, England.

(May 25)
Rush performs live at O2, London, England.

(May 27)
Rush performs live at Ahoy Arena, Rotterdam, Holland.

(May 29)
Rush performs live at Festhalle, Frankfurt, Germany.

(June 8)
Rush performs live at BI-LO Center, Greenville, South Carolina, US.

(June 9)
Neil Peart appears on *The Late Show with David Letterman* to perform a drum solo for Drum Solo Week on the show, at Ed Sullivan Theater, New York City, New York, US.

(June 10)
Rush performs live at New Orleans Arena, New Orleans, Louisiana, US.

(June 12)
Rush performs live at Frank Erwin Center, Austin, Texas, US.

(June 140)
Rush performs live at Don Haskins Center, El Paso, Texas, US.

(June 16)
Rush performs live at US Airways Center, Phoenix, Arizona, US.

(June 18)
Rush performs live at Cricket Wireless Amphitheatre, San Diego, California, US.

(June 20 & 22)
Rush performs live at Gibson Ampitheatre, Los Angeles, California, US.

(June 24)
Rush performs live at MGM Grand Garden Arena, Las Vegas, Nevada, US.

(June 26)
Rush performs live at Sleep Train Pavilion, Concord, California, US.

(June 28)
Rush performs live at Sleep Country Amphitheater, Portland, Oregon, US.

(June 30)
Rush performs live at Rogers Arena, Vancouver, British Columbia, US.

(July 2)
Rush performs live at The Gorge, Seattle, Washington, US.

(July 19)
Mercury Records releases the *Rush* 2xCD compilation *Icon 2*, as part of their *Icon* series, in North America. Track listing as follows:

CD 1:
"Working Man"
"Fly By Night"
"The Necromancer"
"The Twilight Zone"
"Closer To The Heart"
"Circumstances"
"Freewill"
"Limelight"
"The Analog Kid"
"Red Sector A"
"Marathon"
"Force Ten"

CD 2:
"Bastille Day (ATWAS – Icon 2 Version)"
"2112 (ATWAS – Icon 2 Version)"
"The Spirit Of Radio (Exit...Stage Left – Icon 2 Version)"

"Tom Sawyer (Exit...Stage Left)"
"La Villa Strangiato (Exit...Stage Left)"
"Closer To The Heart (Exit...Stage Left)"
"New World Man (GUP Tour – Icon 2 Version)"
"Closer To The Heart (GUP Tour – Icon 2 Version)"
"Vital Signs (GUP Tour – Icon 2 Version)"
"The Big Money (ASOH - Icon 2 Version)"
"Mystic Rhythms (ASOH Icon 2 Version)"
"Time Stand Still (ASOH Icon 2 Version)"

(July 31)
The 26th Annual KoSA International Percussion Workshop, Camp & Festival takes place (July 26 – 31) at Castleton State College, Castleton, Vermont, US. **Neil Peart** participates on the closing day.

(Date Unknown)
Alex Lifeson records guitar work for the song "Shift" by The Wilderness Of Manitoba, for their album *Between Colours*, at Revolution Recording, Toronto, Ontario, Canada.

(Date Unknown)
Geddy Lee films his scenes for the short TV movie *Sunshine Sketches Of A Little Town*, in the role of "Fred."

(August 31)
Roadrunner Records issues their press release announcing their signing of **Rush**, to release their future material worldwide (excluding Canada, which is still under Anthem Records).

(September 1)
Rush is scheduled to start their recording sessions (and to complete their writing sessions) this month, but decide to postpone work for another month (*Classic Rock - Clockwork Angels Fan Pack* June 11, 2012).

ECW Press publishes **Neil Peart**'s book *Far And Away: A Prize Every Time* worldwide.

(September 16)
The Wilderness Of Manitoba release their album *Between Colours*, featuring **Alex Lifeson** on the track "Shift."

> "Shift" 4:20
> Written by The Wilderness Of Manitoba
> Appears on: Between Colours
> Canadian indie folk rock at it's finest (emphasis on rock on this one), this is Wilderness's fourth album. The track pounds along and doesn't let up for a moment and Alex's guitar solo soars through it. Get this one!

(September 21)
Alex Lifeson records guitar work for the song "Losin'" by Jason Plumb And The Willing, for their album *All Is More Than Both*.

(Late September to Early October)
Geddy Lee and **Alex Lifeson** work on reviewing the existing material and writing some new pieces, at **Lee**'s home studio, Toronto, Ontario, Canada, in advance of the band's upcoming studio sessions (*Classic Rock - Clockwork Angels Fan Pack* June 11, 2012).
"Seven Cities Of Gold" – the music develops out of this pre-studio period (*MusicRadar.com* May 25, 2012).

(Mid-October)
Rush resumes work writing and recording material for *Clockwork Angels*, at Revolution Recording, Toronto, Ontario, Canada. The first week is spent in discussions, followed by writing new material. **Geddy Lee** says the resumption started off "sluggish" before becoming "fruitful" (*Rolling Stone* October 28, 2011). Nick Raskulinecz says the new music is written in about two weeks by **Alex Lifeson** and **Geddy Lee**, while he and **Neil Peart** work on drum parts for the earlier completed songs (*MusicRadar.com* May 8, 2012).
 "Take That Lampshade Off Yo Head" - this instrumental is one of the first of the new batch of material worked on. The writing of this instrumental "kick starts" the writing process of these sessions (*Corus Radio* June 15, 2012).
"Seven Cities Of Gold" – "The next day" after assembling "Take That Lampshade Off Yo Head," **Neil Peart** sends the lyrics to this song and it is written and arranged in a few hours (*Corus Radio* June 15, 2012).
"The Wreckers" – Due to technical difficulties in their smaller studio, **Alex Lifeson** and **Geddy Lee** move to the larger studio with **Neil Peart** and Nick Raskulinecz (who are working on drum parts. **Geddy** worked out a guitar part on one of **Alex**'s acoustic guitars and put **Neil**'s lyrics to it. Later, back in the smaller studio, **Geddy** played guitar and **Alex** played bass for the demo. For the album recording, they played their respective instruments.
"Carnies" – this song's music is based on the early 2011 jam sessions. **Geddy** assembles the song from the jam and **Neil**'s lyrics (*Classic Rock - Clockwork Angels Fan Pack* June 11, 2012).

(Early-Autumn)

In a *Guitar World* interview, **Alex Lifeson** notes that the *Clockwork Angels* story is made up of five songs (including "Caravan" and "BU2B") and that overall the band has eight songs completed (January, 2012):
"Wish Them Well" – apparently this song was written, "scrapped" and re-written. At the time of the interview, this song is shelved (*Guitar World* January, 2012 and *Clockwork Angels* tour book).

(October 11)
Freddie Gruber, drummer and drum teacher (of **Neil Peart**, among others), dies in Los Angeles, California, US. His obituary notes his death comes after "a long illness."
"Headlong Flight" – the lyrics are inspired by something Freddie said to Carrie Nuttall in his last days, about wishing he could live it all again.

(October 12)
Neil Peart issues a Memoriam to Freddie Gruber, posted on HudsonMusic.com and FreddieGruber.com.

Hudson Music releases **Neil Peart**'s instructional film *Taking Center Stage: A Lifetime Of Live Performance* on a 3xDVD set. The film centers on the July 23, 2010, Saratoga Springs, New York, concert, but features some clips from the Rotterdam *Snakes & Arrows* concert and in-studio clips. Purchasing the DVD allows buyers to download exclusive content from GuitarCenter.com.

Disc 1:
Opening Titles
Introduction
Preparation For The Tour
Show Day
The Show (Saratoga Springs concert part 1)

Disc 2:
The Show (Saratoga Springs concert part 2)
Closing Remarks And Credits

Disc 3:
The Story Of "Caravan"
"Bravado" Discussion And Performances
"Natural Science (S&A Live – TCS Version)"
"The Trees (Live in Alpharetta, 2008 – TCS Version)"
Interview with Lorne "Gump" Wheaton
Interview with Louie From DW
Photo Gallery
pdf eBook
About Hudson Music's Teacher Integration Program
About Hudson Music
Public Service Information

GuitarCenter.com Bonus Content:
- "Digital Man (S&A Live – TCS Version)"
- "Far Cry" In-Studio Performance
- Neil Peart Interview
- "Subdivisions In-Studio Performance
- "The Main Monkey Business (S&A Live – TCS Version)"

(October 28)
The film *The Double* is released, featuring **Alex Lifeson** on both the soundtrack music and the closing credit song "Don't Look Back."

> "Don't Look Back" 3:17
> Written by Alex Lifeson
> Appears on: The Double motion picture
> This song by Alex plays over most of the end credits of the film, followed by a reprise of some score music (by John Debney, but also featuring Alex on guitar). The track itself is very Alex, with bizarre, rhythmic guitar orchestrations, layered thick in some places and allowing for solos in others. While not entirely Rush-sounding, it's not too far afield from some of the band's work on Snakes & Arrows.

(November)
Rush continues work writing and recording material for *Clockwork Angels*, at Revolution Recording, Toronto, Ontario, Canada (*Corus Radio* June 15, 2012). Nick Raskulinecz says that it was around this time that the *Clockwork Angels* theme overtook the entire project (previously it was planned as a suite, separate from how the rest of the album might develop) (*MusicRadar.com* May 8, 2012).
"Halo Effect" – **Alex** and **Geddy** write the music in the studio (*MusicRadar.com* May 25, 2012).

"BU2B2" - Nick Raskulinecz specifically says it was one of the tracks to come of out of these sessions. **Alex** develops the arrangement himself.

"Headlong Flight" – this song develops from the instrumental "Take That Lampshade Off Yo Head." The lyrics are the last **Neil Peart** writes, inspired by Freddie Gruber (see above). **Geddy Lee** puts the lyrics to the instrumental, creating this song. Nick says this song came the day after **Neil** presented his vision of the entire concept album.

(November 1)
Left Field Media releases the concert recording of **Rush**'s live Cleveland, Ohio, 1974, show as *Rush ABC (Agora Ballroom, Cleveland, Ohio, August 6, 1974)*. The show was originally broadcast on WMMS 100.7 FM. Three additional tracks from the April, 1975, Cleveland concert also appear on the album.

(November 8)
Rush release their live album and concert film *Time Machine 2011: Live In Cleveland* and their live album *Moving Pictures: Live 2011* via Anthem Records, Roadrunner Records and Zoë Records worldwide. The concert material comes primarily from the April 14, 2011, Cleveland, Ohio, concert, with bonus footage from the 1974 Laura Secord Secondary School concert and the 1976 Passaic, New Jersey, concert.

Time Machine 2011: Live In Cleveland CD Edition
CD 1: Cleveland concert part 1
CD 2: Cleveland concert part 2

Time Machine 2011: Live In Cleveland DVD Edition
DVD: Cleveland concert
Bonus Material:
- Outtakes from 'History of Rush, Episodes 2 & 17'
- "Tom Sawyer" featuring the cast of 'History of Rush, Episode 17'
- "Need Some Love (Live at Laura Secord Secondary School, 1974)"
- "Anthem (Live in Passaic, 1976)"
- 12 Page Collectable Booklet

Time Machine 2011: Live In Cleveland Blu-ray Edition
Blu-ray: Cleveland concert
Bonus Material:
- Outtakes from 'History of Rush, Episodes 2 & 17'
- "Tom Sawyer" featuring the cast of 'History of Rush, Episode 17'
- "Need Some Love (Live at Laura Secord Secondary School, 1974)"
- "Anthem (Live in Passaic, 1976)"
- 12 Page Collectable Booklet

Moving Pictures: Live 2011 LP & Download Editions
"Tom Sawyer (Time Machine – LP Version)"
"Red Barchetta"
"YYZ"
"Limelight"
"The Camera Eye"
"Witch Hunt" – part III of 'Fear'
"Vital Signs (Time Machine – LP Version)"

(November 13)
Neil Peart attends and speaks at the Freddie Gruber Memorial, at Sportsman's Lodge, Sherman Oaks, California, US.

(November 21)
Mercury Records and Anthem Records release the **Rush** boxed sets *Sectors 1*, *Sectors 2* and *Sectors 3*, containing their first twelve studio albums and first three live albums, plus three of the studio albums in 5.1 Surround Sound. The albums come in mini vinyl replica sleeves. The stereo remasters are by Andy VanDette.

Sectors 1 boxed set
CD 1: *Rush* (2011 Remaster)

CD 2: *Fly By Night* (2011 Remaster)
- contains "By-Tor And The Snow Dog (Standard CD Version)"

DVD: *Fly By Night* 5.1 Surround Sound

CD 3: *Caress Of Steel* (2011 Remaster)

CD 4: *2112* (2011 Remaster)

CD 5: *All The World's A Stage* (2011 Remaster)

Sectors 2 boxed set
CD 1: *A Farewell To Kings* (2011 Remaster)

DVD: *A Farewell To Kings* 5.1 Surround Sound

CD 2: *Hemispheres* (2011 Remaster)

CD 3: *Permanent Waves* (2011 Remaster)

CD 4: *Moving Pictures* (2011 Remaster)

CD 5: *Exit...Stage Left* (2011 Remaster)

Sectors 3 boxed set
CD 1: *Signals* (2011 Remaster)

DVD: *Signals* 5.1 Surround Sound

CD 2: *Grace Under Pressure* (2011 Remaster)

CD 3: *Power Windows* (2011 Remaster)

CD 4: *Hold Your Fire* (2011 Remaster)

CD 5: *A Show Of Hands* (2011 Remaster)

(Early December)
Rush completes recording work on their *Clockwork Angels* album, at Revolution Recording, Toronto, Ontario, Canada. Tracks worked on since October include (*Clockwork Angels* tour book):
"Wish Them Well" – after all the rewrites, the song is completed. **Neil** is in Los Angeles, California, US, when **Geddy** records his vocal parts.
"The Garden" – Jason Sniderman plays piano on this track

(December 2)
Crier Records releases the Andrew Cole/Tom Cochrane *Voices* project single, featuring **Alex Lifeson** on the track "Voices At 4 AM."

CLOCKWORK ANGELS

2012

(January)
Rush begins mixing sessions for *Clockwork Angels*, at Henson Studios, Los Angeles, California, US. Mixed by Nick Raskulinecz.

(January 18)
The string parts for the following songs are recorded for *Rush*'s *Clockwork Angels* album, at Ocean Way Studios, Los Angeles, California, US. **Neil Peart** is present at the sessions.
"Halo Effect"
"The Anarchist"
"The Wreckers"
"BU2B2"
"The Garden"

The strings players are conducted by David Campbell (who write their arrangements) and are later known as the Clockwork Angels String Ensemble:

Audrey Solomon	Jonathon Dinklage	Entcho Todorov	Adele Stein
Jacob Szekely	Joel Derouin	Gerry Hilera	Mario DeLeon
Hiroko Taguchi			

Note: I'm 100% certain who was involved in the album recording sessions from this group, but the names are all listed as part of the tour Ensemble on *Rush.com*.

(January 24)
Rush have a photo shoot with photographer Andrew MacNaughtan, in Los Angeles, California, US.

(January 25)
Andrew MacNaughtan (friend and photographer of *Rush*) dies of a heart attack in Los Angeles, California, US.

(Date Unknown)
Rush records the following at Lerxst Mobile, West Hollywood, California, US:
"BU2B" – the extended intro is recorded by **Alex Lifeson** and **Geddy Lee** at **Alex**'s hotel room and is added to track for the album (*MusicRadar.com* May 25, 2012).

(February)
Production work starts for *Rush*'s forthcoming tour (*Metal Express Radio* May 21, 2012), simultaneous to post-production work on the album.

(February 9)
Writer Kevin J. Anderson announces on his Facebook page that he is currently penning the novel version of the *Rush* album *Clockwork Angels*.

(Mid-March)
Rush completes mixing work on their *Clockwork Angels* album, at Henson Studios, Los Angeles, California, US. Songs worked on include:
"Caravan" – this song is remixed from the original single version, to bring it in line with the rest of the album (*Metal Express Radio* May 21 and *MusicRadar.com* May 25, 2012).
"BU2B" – in addition to the extended intro, this song is remixed from the original single version, to bring it in line with the rest of the album (*Metal Express Radio* May 21 and *MusicRadar.com* May 25, 2012).

Neil Peart works with Vertical Horizon on a demo for the band's songs "Instamatic" at Henson Studios, Los Angeles, California, US.

(March 27)
Jason Plumb And The Willing release their album *All Is More Than Both*, featuring **Alex Lifeson** on the track "Losin'."

> "Losin'" 4:28
> Written by Jason Plumb
> Appears on: All Is More Than Both
> This track features a few variations in tone, moving through soft and hard sections. Ed Robertson of Barenaked Ladies appears on this track, too, and Alex lays down a ripping guitar solo that tears through a minute and a half of the song.

(April 11)
Neil Peart and Carrie Nuttall move to a larger house in Los Angeles, California, US (*NeilPeart.net* June, 2012).

Neil Peart accepts *Revolver* magazine's Golden Gods Lifetime Achievement Award on behalf of *Rush*, at the Golden Gods awards ceremony, at Club Nokia, Los Angeles, California, US. Tenacious D presents the award. It is reported that Geddy Lee is currently in Japan and Alex Lifeson is in Toronto, Ontario, Canada (Alex was previously slated to accept the award, but a personal matter at home prevented him from making the trip).

(April 16)
Neil Peart records drum parts for Vertical Horizon's song "Instamatic" and "South For The Winter," at Henson Studios, Los Angeles, California, US (*NeilPeart.net* June, 2012).

(April 19 & 20)
Rush releases their "Headlong Flight" single in worldwide.

iTunes single:
"Headlong Flight"

UK CD promo single (PRO16867):
"Headlong Flight (Radio Edit)"
"Headlong Flight"

Europe CD promo single (RR 16967):
"Headlong Flight (Radio Edit)"
"Headlong Flight"

> "Headlong Flight (Radio Edit)" 5:07
> Written by Neil Peart (words), Geddy Lee & Alex Lifeson (music)
> Appears on: UK CD promo single, Europe CD promo single
> Of course at over 7 minutes, the original track would have to be cut down for most radio stations, so 2 minutes are taken out to create this "Radio Edit." The intro is pared down about 30 seconds, other bits of instrumental are removed and the verses "...It didn't always feel that way, I don't regret it – I don't forget it..." are cut out, as are from the second refrain the lines "...Some nights were bright, I wish that I cold live it all again." The narrated part before the drum and guitar solos ("*The days were dark and the nights were bright...*") is entirely removed, as is the extended refrain that follows it ("All the highlights of that headlong flight..."). Despite all that, the edit holds together nicely and makes for a decent alternative to the full album version.

(May 3)
Rush attends a House of Commons question session, Parliament, Ottawa, Ontario, Canada, in advance of their receiving the Governor General's Performing Arts Award on May 5th.

(May 4)
Rush attends a ceremony at Rideau Hall, Ottawa, Ontario, Canada, as part of the Governor General's Performing Arts Award festivities.

(May 5)
Geddy Lee, Alex Lifeson and Neil Peart receive the Governor General's Performing Arts Award at a ceremony at the National Arts Centre, Ottawa, Ontario, Canada.

(May 21)
In a *Metal Express Radio* interview published on this date, Alex Lifeson says a good deal of the original multitrack recordings of older *Rush* studio material is missing, including:
"Working Man" – the original album multi-tracks are entirely missing, but a second alternate set of multi-tracks exist, which formed the basis for the previously released "Vault Edition."
2112 – multi-track parts of this album are apparently missing.
Permanent Waves – the entire album's multi-tracks are missing, having been stored at Trident Studios, London, England (possibly lost around the time of the studio's initial sale in 1981).

Other tapes are too brittle or otherwise unplayable, not having aged well.

(June)
In an interview published on this date in *Prog* magazine, Geddy Lee says the idea of re-mixing *Vapor Trails* is in flux and *Rush* is considering having different people remix tracks from various albums for fun.

Neil Peart starts his warm-up rehearsals in advance of the band tour rehearsals, Los Angeles, California, US (*Classic Rock – Clockwork Angels Fan Pack* June 11, 2012).

(June 8, 12 & 13)

Rush releases their twentieth studio album, *Clockwork Angels*, worldwide (on Anthem Records in Canada [June 12th] and on Roadrunner Records [Australia on June 8th, US on June 12th and Europe on June 13th]). Two editions are released. Track listing as follows:

Clockwork Angels CD:
"Caravan"
"BU2B"
"Clockwork Angels"
"The Anarchist"
"Carnies"
"Halo Effect"
"Seven Cities Of Gold"
"The Wreckers"
"Headlong Flight"
"BU2B2"
"Wish Them Well"
"The Garden"

Classic Rock Fanpack Edition
Clockwork Angels CD
Classic Rock presents Clockwork Angels magazine

Note: The CD sleeve lists all the track times as 0:00. Clever.

(June 16)
Billboard reports on this date that **Neil Peart** recently recorded the audio book *Clockwork Angels: The Novel*, by Kevin J. Anderson.

(July)
Rush begins rehearsals for seven to eight weeks for the forthcoming tour (*M Music & Musicians* June, and *Classic Rock - Clockwork Angels Fan Pack* June 11, 2012).

(July 24)
Rush releases their single for "The Wreckers" in the US and Europe.

US CD promo single:
"The Wreckers (Radio Edit)"
"The Wreckers"

Europe CD promo single (PRO16978):
"The Wreckers (Radio Edit)"
"The Wreckers"

> "The Wreckers (Radio Edit)" 4:21
> Written by Neil Peart (words), Geddy Lee & Alex Lifeson (music)
> Appears on: US CD promo single, Europe CD promo single
> Sadly, I have not heard this edit, but given only 40 seconds is cut, it's probably not that drastic.

(September 1)
ECW Press publishes *Clockwork Angels: The Novel* by Kevin J. Anderson (from a story and lyrics by **Neil Peart**). The book is also released as an audiobook read by **Neil Peart** (BrillianceAudio) on CD and downloadable. The audio book is later released in a boxed set as The Watchmaker's Edition.

(September 7)
Rush performs live at Verizon Wireless Arena, Manchester, New Hampshire, US. Several fans record the following:

"The Joke" – shot from different angles in the audience, presumably on cell phones, this is **Alex Lifeson** telling a joke. It's later cut together from the fan footage and used as an Easter Egg on the *Clockwork Angels Tour* DVD and Blu-ray.

Note: The *Clockwork Angels* tour features the Clockwork Angels String Ensemble during the second set.

(September 9)
Rush performs live at Jiffy Lube Live Amphitheater, Bristow, Virginia, US.

(September 11)
Rush performs live at Consol Energy Center, Pittsburgh, Pennsylvania, US.

(September 13)
Rush performs live at Banker's Life Fieldhouse, Indianapolis, Indiana, US.

(September 15)
Rush performs live at United Center, Chicago, Illinois, US.

(September 18)
Rush performs live at The Palace, Auburn Hills, Michigan, US.

(September 20)
Rush performs live at Nationwide Arena, Columbus, Ohio, US.

(September 22)
Rush performs live at Scottrade Center, St. Louis, Missouri, US.

(September 24)
Rush performs live at Target Center, Minneapolis, Minnesota, US.

(September 26)
Rush performs live at MTS Center, Winnipeg, Manitoba, Canada.

(September 28)
Rush performs live at Credit Union Center, Saskatoon, Saskatchewan, Canada.

(September 30)
Rush performs live at Rexall Place, Edmonton, Alberta, Canada.

(October 10)
Rush performs live at Webster Bank Arena, Bridgeport, Connecticut, US.

(October 12)
Rush performs live at Wells Fargo Center, Philadelphia, Pennsylvania, US.

(October 14 & 16)
Rush performs live at Air Canada Center, Toronto, Ontario, Canada.

(October 18)
Rush performs live at Bell Centre, Montreal, Quebec, Canada.

(October 20)
Rush performs live at Prudential Center, Newark, New Jersey, US.

(October 22)
Rush performs live at Barclays Center, Brooklyn, New York, US.

(October 24)
Rich Chycki posters on Twitter that he has been working on a 5.1 surround sound mix of *Rush*'s *2112* album "for months."

Rush performs live at TD Garden, Boston, Massachusetts, US.

(October 26)
Rush performs live at First Niagara Center, Buffalo, New York, US.

(October 28)
Rush performs live at Quicken Loans Arena, Cleveland, Ohio, US. *Rush* fan Karl Sloman (a teacher from London, Ontario) is the subject of an episode of Global TV's *Walk The Walk*, wherein he meets the band and **Neil Peart** in particular backstage prior to this concert.

(October 30)
Rush performs live at Time Warner Cable Arena, Charlotte, North Carolina, US.

(November 1)
Rush performs live at Verizon Wireless Ampitheater, Atlanta, Georgia, US.

(November 3)
Rush performs live at 1-800-ASK-GARY Ampitheater, Tampa, Florida, US.

(November 13)
Rush performs live at Key Arena, Seattle, Washington, US.

(November 15)
Rush performs live at HP Pavilion, San Jose, California, US.

(November 17)
Rush performs live at Honda Center, Anaheim, California, US.

(November 19)
Rush performs live at Gibson Ampitheater, Los Angeles, California, US.

(November 21)
Rush performs live at Valley View Casino Center, San Diego, California, US.

(November 23)
Rush performs live at MGM Grand Garden Arena, Las Vegas, Nevada, US.

(November 25)
Rush performs live at US Airways Center, Phoenix, Arizona, US. This concert is recorded and the following tracks appear on the *Clockwork Angels Tour* live album and concert film:

"Middletown Dreams"
"The Pass"
"Manhattan Project"

(November 28)
Rush performs live at American Airlines Center, Dallas, Texas, US. This concert is recorded for the *Clockwork Angels Tour* live album and concert film. The following track is also released individually:

"The Garden"

> "The Garden (CA Tour – Single Version)" 7:14
> Written by Neil Peart (words), Geddy Lee & Alex Lifeson (music)
> Appears on: Canada 10" single, US 10" single, Europe 10" single
> This version starts cleanly on the music, no crowd noise, and fades out the same as the CD version. This is one of the best songs on Clockwork Angels and hearing the Ensemble perform it live is very moving. It's interesting to note that Ensemble member Jonathon Dinklage is the brother of actor Peter Dinkage, who later appeared in the tour video clip for the "Roll The Bones" rap on the R40 Tour.

(November 30)
Rush performs live at AT&T Center, San Antonio, Texas, US. This concert is listed in the credits of the *Clockwork Angels Tour* live album and concert film, suggesting it was recorded and material from it appears on the releases.

(December 2)
Rush performs live at Toyota Center, Houston, Texas, US.

(December 18)
Rush re-issues *2112* in the following formats worldwide:

2112 CD+DVD Deluxe Edition
CD: *2112* (2011 Remaster)
Bonus Tracks:
- "2112: I: Overture (Live in Edmonton, 1981)"
- "2112: II: The Temples Of Syrinx (Live in Edmonton, 1981)"
- "A Passage To Bangkok (Live in Manchester, 1980)"

DVD: *2112* 5.1 Surround Sound
Digital Comic Book
Lyrics
Liner Notes
Photo Gallery

2112 CD+Blu-ray Deluxe Edition
CD: *2112* (2011 Remaster)
Bonus Tracks:
- "2112: I: Overture (Live in Edmonton, 1981)"
- "2112: II: The Temples Of Syrinx (Live in Edmonton, 1981)"
- "A Passage To Bangkok (Live in Manchester, 1980)"

Blu-ray: *2112* 5.1 Surround Sound
Digital Comic Book

Lyrics
Liner Notes
Photo Gallery

2112 Hardcase Edition
Hardcase:
Liner Notes
Lyrics
Comic Book

CD: *2112* (2011 Remaster)
Bonus Tracks:
- "2112: I: Overture (Live in Edmonton, 1981)"
- "2112: II: The Temples Of Syrinx (Live in Edmonton, 1981)"
- "A Passage To Bangkok (Live in Manchester, 1980)"

Blu-ray: *2112* 5.1 Surround Sound
Digital Comic Book
Lyrics
Liner Notes
Photo Gallery

CLOCKWORK ANGELS TOUR

2013

(February 20)
Rush releases their single for "The Anarchist" in the UK.

US CD promo single:
"The Anarchist (Radio Edit)"
"The Anarchist"

> "The Anarchist (Radio Edit)" 4:18
> Written by Neil Peart (words), Geddy Lee & Alex Lifeson (music)
> Appears on: UK CD promo single
> This is a rather difficult to find single and I haven't heard this edit. Some accounts note the opening is altered, with lyrics removed. At two and a half minutes, it would seem a good chunk of the piece has been cut.

(February 26)
The David Barrett Trio releases their self-titled debut album, produced by **Alex Lifeson**.

(March 5)
Audio Fidelity releases the 24KT gold Hybrid SACD/DSD edition of the ***Rush*** album *Counterparts*.

(April 2)
Geddy Lee throws out the ceremonial first pitch of the Toronto Blue Jays vs Cleveland Indians Major League Baseball home opener game, at Rogers Centre, Toronto, Ontario, Canada.

(April 17)
Rush rehearses at the Nokia Theatre, Los Angeles, California, US, for their performance at the Rock And Roll Hall Of Fame induction ceremony.

(April 18)
Rush performs live at the Nokia Theatre, Los Angeles, California, US, as part of their induction into the Rock And Roll Hall Of Fame.

(April 20)
Back On Black releases on the ***Rush*** concert recording *Rush ABC (Agora Ballroom, Cleveland, Ohio, August 6, 1974)* on LP, for Record Store Day, worldwide.

(April 23)
Rush performs live at Frank Erwin Center, Austin, Texas, US.

(April 26)
Rush performs live at BB&T Center, Ft. Lauderdale, Florida, US.

(April 28)
Rush performs live at Amway Center, Orlando, Florida, US.

(May 1)
Rush performs live at Bridgestone Arena, Nashville, Tennessee, US.

(May 3)
Rush performs live at PNC Arena, Raleigh, North Carolina, US.

(May 5)
Rush performs live at Farm Bureau Live At Virginia Beach, Virginia Beach, Virginia, US.

(May 7)
Rush performs live at 1st Mariner Arena, Baltimore, Maryland, US.

(May 9)
Rush performs live at Mohegan Sun, Uncasville, Connecticut, US.

(May 11)
Rush performs live at Etess Arena, Atlantic City, New Jersey, US.

(May 15)
Rush releases their Mastered For iTunes Editions of their catalogue on iTunes. The albums can be purchased individually or in bundled sets.

Set 1: *The Complete Mercury Years*
Rush (Mastered For iTunes)

"Working Man (Vault Edition)" (Mastered For iTunes)

Fly By Night (Mastered For iTunes)
- contains "By-Tor And The Snow Dog (Standard CD Edition)" (Mastered For iTunes)

Caress Of Steel (Mastered For iTunes)

2112 Deluxe Edition (Mastered For iTunes)
Bonus Tracks:
- "2112: I: Overture (Live in Edmonton, 1981)" (Mastered For iTunes)
- "2112: II: The Temples Of Syrinx (Live in Edmonton, 1981)" (Mastered For iTunes)
- "A Passage To Bangkok (Live in Manchester, 1980)" (Mastered For iTunes)

All The World's A Stage (Mastered For iTunes)

A Farewell To Kings (Mastered For iTunes)

Hemispheres (Mastered For iTunes)

Permanent Waves (Mastered For iTunes)

Moving Pictures (Mastered For iTunes)

Exit...Stage Left (Mastered For iTunes)

Signals (Mastered For iTunes)

Grace Under Pressure (Mastered For iTunes)

Power Windows (Mastered For iTunes)

Hold Your Fire (Mastered For iTunes)

A Show Of Hands (Mastered For iTunes)

Set 2: *The Studio Albums 1989-2007*
Presto (Mastered For iTunes)

Roll The Bones (Mastered For iTunes)

Counterparts (Mastered For iTunes)

Test For Echo (Mastered For iTunes)

Vapor Trails (Mastered For iTunes)

Feedback (Mastered For iTunes)

Snakes & Arrows (Mastered For iTunes)

Note: The Mastered For iTunes Edition of *Vapor Trails* is later replaced by *Vapor Trails Remixed*, though it is unclear whether the *Remixed* version is a Mastered For iTunes Edition.

(Mid-May)
Alex Lifeson and **Geddy Lee** enlist producer David Bottrill to remix their *Vapor Trails* album for a future release. The remixing process takes place while **Rush** in on the European leg of their tour, with **Lee** and **Lifeson**'s input made "long distance" (*Classic Rock* September 18, 2013).

(May 22)
Rush performs live at Manchester Arena, Manchester, England.

(May 24)

Rush performs live at O2 Arena, London, England.

(May 26)
Rush performs live at LG Arena, Birmingham, England.

(May 28)
Rush performs live at Motorpoint Arena, Sheffield, England.

(May 30)
Rush performs live at SECC Arena, Glasgow, Scotland.

(June 2)
Rush performs live at Ziggo Dome, Amsterdam, Holland.

(June 4)
Rush performs live at Lanxess Arena, Cologne, Germany.

(June 6)
Rush performs live at O2 World Arena, Berlin, Germany.

(June 8)
Rush performs live at Sweden Rock Festival, Solvesborg, Sweden.

(June 10)
Rush performs live at Hartwell Arena, Helsinki, Finland.

(June 21)
Rush performs live at Giant Center, Hershey, Pennsylvania, US.

(June 23)
Rush performs live at Nikon at Jones Beach, Wantagh, New York, US.

(June 25)
Rush performs live at the Performing Arts Center, Saratoga Springs, New York, US.

(June 28)
Rush performs live at First Midwest Bank Amphitheatre, Chicago, Illinois, US.

(June 30)
Rush performs live at Van Andel Arena, Grand Rapids, Michigan, US.

(July 2)
Rush performs live at Riverbend Music Center, Cincinnati, Ohio, US.

(July 4)
Rush performs live at Summerfest, Milwaukee, Wisconsin, US.

(July 6)
Rush performs live at Copps Coliseum, Hamilton, Ontario, Canada.

(July 8)
Rush performs live at Ottawa Bluesfest, Ottawa, Ontario, Canada.

(July 10)
Rush performs live at Festival d'ete, Quebec City, Quebec, Canada. Rain forces this concert to be halted before it's finished.

(July 12 & 14)
Rush performs live at Metro Centre, Halifax, Nova Scotia, Canada.

(July 24)
Rush are scheduled to perform at the Scotiabank Saddledome, Calgary, Alberta, Canada, but recent flooding in and around the city leaves the Saddledome partially under water, forcing the concert to be relocated.

Rush performs live at Enmax Centrium, Red Deer, Alberta, Canada, replacing the Saddledome concert.

(July 26)
Rush performs live at Rogers Arena, Vancouver, British Columbia, Canada.

(July 28)
Rush performs live at Sleep Country Amphitheater, Portland, Oregon, US.

(July 31)
Rush performs live at USANA Amphitheatre, Salt Lake City, Utah, US.

(August 2)
Rush performs live at Pepsi Center, Denver, Colorado, US.

(August 4)
Rush performs live at Sprint Center, Kansas City, Missouri, US.

Note: *Rush* agrees to not discuss work for at least a year following the conclusion of the tour (*NeilPeart.net* November, 2013).

(August 12)
Alex Lifeson performs live with Keram Malicki-Sanchez at the *Come To Life* record release party, at the Supermarket, Toronto, Ontario, Canada.

(Late August)
A few weeks following the *Clockwork Angels* tour (*Prog* April 2014), **Alex Lifeson** records his solo for John Wesley's track "Once A Warrior" (*Disconnected* sessions), at Lerxst Sound, Toronto, Ontario, Canada.

(September 30)
Rush releases their *Vapor Trails Remixed* album in Canada (Anthem Records) and worldwide (Atlantic Records). The remix is by David Bottrill. Track listing as follows:

"One Little Victory (2013 Remix)"
"Ceiling Unlimited (2013 Remix)"
"Ghost Rider (2013 Remix)"
"Peaceable Kingdom (2013 Remix)"
"The Stars Look Down (2013 Remix)"
"How It Is (2013 Remix)"
"Vapor Trail (2013 Remix)"
"Secret Touch (2013 Remix)"
"Earthshine (2013 Remix)"
"Sweet Miracle (2013 Remix)"
"Nocturne (2013 Remix)"
"Freeze (Part IV of 'Fear') (2013 Remix)"
"Out Of The Cradle (2013 Remix)"

Rhino Records releases the *Rush* 7xCD boxed set *The Studio Albums 1989-2007*. This set covers the Atlantic Records-era studio albums (but not the live albums). The albums are remastered by Andy VanDette, except for *Vapor Trails Remix* by David Bottrill.

CD 1: *Presto*

CD 2: *Roll The Bones*

CD 3: *Counterparts*

CD 4: *Test For Echo*

CD 5: *Vapor Trails Remixed*

CD 6: *Feedback*

CD 7: *Snakes & Arrows*

Note: the release of *Vapor Trails Remixed* would seem to replace commercial availability of the original mix of the album, which goes out of print around this time.

(October 1)
Audio Fidelity releases the 24KT gold Hybrid SACD/DSD edition of the *Rush* album *Hemispheres*.

(October 8)
Vertical Horizon releases its album *Echoes From The Underground*, featuring **Neil Peart** on the tracks "Instamatic" an "South For The Winter."

"Instamatic" 4:46
Written by Matt Scannell
Appears on: Echoes From The Underground
Neil's drums are hard hitting and punctuate this mid-tempo alt-rocker, his forth with Vertical Horizon. Not too shabby.

"South For The Winter" 7:10
Written by Matt Scannell
Appears on: Echoes From The Underground
This slow number features minimal drum work from Neil until the very end, when climax rolls in.

(October 16)
Neil Peart climbs Angel's Landing, South-western Utah, US.

(November 19)
Rush releases their *Clockwork Angels Tour* live album and concert film in Canada (Anthem Records) and worldwide (Roadrunners Records). Various formats are released, as follows:

Clockwork Angels Tour CD Edition
CD 1: Dallas concert set 1

CD 2: Dallas concert set 2 *Clockwork Angels*

CD 3: Dallas concert set 2 cont + encore
Bonus Tracks:
- "Limelight (Soundcheck – Dallas, 2013)"
- "Middletown Dreams (Live in Phoenix, 2013)"
- "The Pass (Live in Phoenix, 2013)"
- "Manhattan Project (Live in Phoenix, 2013)"

Clockwork Angels Tour DVD Edition
DVD 1: Dallas concert

DVD 2: Special Features
- "Limelight (Soundcheck – Dallas, 2013)"
- "Middletown Dreams (Live in Phoenix, 2013)"
- "The Pass (Live in Phoenix, 2013)"
- "Manhattan Project (Live in Phoenix, 2013)"
- Can't Stop Thinking Big
- Behind The Scenes Featuring Jay Baruchel
- Outtakes
- Interview With Dwush
- Family Goy
- Family Sawyer
- The Watchmaker (Intermission Film)
- Office Of The Watchmaker (Closing Film)
Easter Egg: 'The Joke'

Clockwork Angels Tour Blu-ray Edition
Blu-ray: Dallas concert
Special Features:
- "Limelight (Soundcheck – Dallas, 2013)"
- "Middletown Dreams (Live in Phoenix, 2013)"
- "The Pass (Live in Phoenix, 2013)"
- "Manhattan Project (Live in Phoenix, 2013)"
- Can't Stop Thinking Big
- Behind The Scenes Featuring Jay Baruchel
- Outtakes
- Interview With Dwush
- Family Goy
- Family Sawyer
- The Watchmaker (Intermission Film)
- Office Of The Watchmaker (Closing Film)
Easter Egg: 'The Joke'

North American *Clockwork Angels Tour* Boxed Set Edition
DVD 1: Dallas concert
DVD 2: Special Features
Exclusive 'Blah Blah Blah' T-shirt

Canada *Clockwork Angels Tour* Blu-ray+DVD+CD Deluxe Edition
Blu-ray: Dallas concert
Special Features
DVD 1: Dallas concert
DVD 2: Special Features
CD 1: Dallas concert set 1
CD 2: Dallas concert set 2 *Clockwork Angels*
CD 3: Dallas concert set 2 cont + encore
Bonus Tracks

Note: The *Clockwork Angels Tour* Press Release says the concert is from the Dallas, Texas, date, but in a *VH1.com* interview, **Geddy Lee** says the "bulk" of the show is from Dallas, but that they also shot the Phoenix, Arizona, concert and used the best shots and the best angles from both nights. Which material comes from which night is not specified exactly. Sources say the Special Features tracks come from Phoenix, but I'm not 100% certain.

(November 29)
Rush releases their single "The Garden" as part of Black Friday in North America and Europe.

Canada 10" single (Picture Disc) (1686-135427):
"The Garden"
"The Garden (CA Tour – Single Version)"

US 10" single (Picture Disc) (1686-135427):
"The Garden"
"The Garden (CA Tour – Single Version)"

Europe 10" single (Picture Disc) (RR3542-7):
"The Garden"
"The Garden (CA Tour – Single Version)"

R40

2014

(February)
Neil Peart spends this month at his home in Wentworth-Nord, Quebec, Canada.

(March 16)
Boom! Studios begins its six-issue run of the comic series *Clockwork Angels*, co-written by Kevin J. Anderson and **Neil Peart**, based upon their novel (itself based upon the *Rush* album) of the same name.

(March 20)
In a *RollingStone.com* interview with **Alex Lifeson** posted on this date, it is noted that the band met recently to discuss a 40th Anniversary Tour.

Note: In a *RollingStone.com* interview, **Neil Peart** says prior to committing to a tour, *Rush* considers a follow-up covers album project ala *Feedback*, but interest in the idea is apparently low.

(March 31 & April 1)
John Wesley (of Porcupine Tree) releases his solo album *Disconnected* worldwide, featuring **Alex Lifeson** on the track "Once A Warrior."

> "Once A Warrior" 6:51
> Written by John Wesley
> Appears on: Disconnected
> This prog rocker suits Alex well and being as sensitive to the needs of the song as he is, Alex constructs his solo perfectly. One is reminded of such performances as "La Villa Strangiato," starting quietly and building in intensity. Great work!

(April)
Neil Peart travels to Telescope Peak, Death Valley National Park, California, US.

(April 15)
Rush re-releases its album *Rush - ReDISCovered* LP boxed set on Universal Music.

Rush - ReDISCovered LP boxed set
LP: *Rush* (Direct Metal Mastering) (Moon Records edition replica)
Rush Poster replica
3x Band member lithographs
Rush Family Tree poster
Digit download card

Keram (Malicki-Sanchez) releases his album *Come To Life*, which is executive produced by **Alex Lifeson**, who also plays on the tracks "Mary Magdalene" (mixed by Rich Chycki), "Moving Dark Circles" and "The Devil Knows Me Well." The album is mastered Andy VanDette.

> "Mary Magdalene" 6:15
> Written by Keram Malicki-Sanchez
> Appears on: Come To Life
> Alex plays lead guitar on this track and his performance really soars. The song rocks and I highly recommend it.

> "Moving Dark Circles" 6:37
> Written by Keram Malicki-Sanchez
> Appears on: Come To Life
> This rocker shifts tempos and moods effectively and Alex's guitar work really shines in the solo work. Also recommended.

> "The Devil Knows Me Well" 11:11
> Written by Keram Malicki-Sanchez
> Appears on: Come To Life
> This blues rocker takes on epic proportions, with some stellar playing from Alex throughout! Very highly recommended!

(June 10)
Geddy Lee and **Alex Lifeson** travel from Toronto, Ontario, to Jack Garland Airport, North Bay, Ontario, Canada, to attend Nipissing University's convocation ceremony (to receive honorary doctorate degrees; **Neil Peart** also receives

one, but does not attend from Los Angeles, California, US). Their plane is unable to land due to bad weather and they miss the ceremony, having to return to Toronto.

(Summer)
Geddy Lee and his family spend their summer in Toronto, Ontario, Canada, in support of the recent birth of his grandchild to his son, Julian Weinrib and Julian's wife (*RollingStone.com* November 11, 2014). He also notes he spent much of the previous year travelling with his wife, Nancy Young, and their daughter Kyla.

Neil Peart visits the dilapidated remains of Le Studio, Morin Heights, Quebec, for a Banger Films' project. Some reports say it is related to a documentary on the studio itself, while other say the subject is **Geddy Lee**.

(July 15)
Audio Fidelity releases the 24KT gold Hybrid SACD/DSD edition of the *Rush* album *Presto*.

(November 11)
Rush releases its *R40* boxed set on Zoë Records worldwide. The set contains the concert films *Rock In Rio*, *R30 - 30th Anniversary World Tour*, *Snakes & Arrows Live*, *Time Machine 2011: Live In Cleveland* and *Clockwork Angels Tour*, as well as bonus material. Several editions are issued.

R40 DVD boxed set
DVD 1: *Rock In Rio*
 Rio de Janeiro concert

DVD 2: *Rock In Rio* Bonus Material
The Boys In Brazil Documentary
MX Multiangle Songs:
    1. "YYZ"
    2. "O Baterista"
    3. "La Villa Strangiato"
Easter Eggs:
    "By-Tor And The Snow Dog" Animation
    "Anthem" - Castle Session video

DVD 3: *R30 - 30th Anniversary World Tour* Frankfurt concert (edited)

DVD 4: *R30 - 30th Anniversary World Tour* DVD Extras:
    August 24, 1979 Geddy Lee Interview at Ivor Wynne Stadium, Hamilton
    1980 Rush interview at Le Studio (incorrectly listed as 1981 Moving Pictures era)
    1990 Artist of the Decade interviews
    1994 Juno Awards CBC news report
    2002 Geddy Lee & Alex Lifeson Vapor Trails interview
    "Finding My Way (Mpeg 1)" - Don Kirshner's Rock Concert
    "In The Mood (Mpeg 1)" - Don Kirshner's Rock Concert
    "Fly By Night" - Church Sessions video
    "A Farewell To Kings" - Seneca College
    "Xanadu" - Seneca College
    "Circumstances (Live at the Hammersmith Odeon, 1979)"
    "La Villa Strangiato (Live at the Hammersmith Odeon, 1979)"
    "The Spirit Of Radio" - Soundcheck at Ivor Wynne Stadium, Hamilton
    "Freewill" - *Molson Canadian Rocks For Toronto* 2003
    "Closer To The Heart" - *Canada For Asia* 2005
    Bonus Easter Egg: Rush Hits St. John's
    Bonus Easter Egg: 1990 Alex Lifeson Artist of the Decade interview

DVD 5: *Snakes & Arrows Live* Rotterdam concert set 1
Bonus Features:
    - 'What's That Smell'
    - 2007 Tour Outtakes
    - 'What's That Smell' Outtakes
    - "Far Cry (S&A Live - Alternative Cut)"
    - "The Way The Wind Blows (S&A Live - Alternative Cut)"
    - "Red Sector A (R30 - S&AL DVD Bonus Version)"

DVD 6: *Snakes & Arrows Live* Rotterdam concert set 2
Oh, Atlanta! The Authorized Bootlegs
    "Ghost Of A Chance"
    "Red Barchetta"
    "The Trees"
    "2112: I: Overture / II: The Temples Of Syrinx"

DVD 7: *Time Machine 2011: Live In Cleveland* concert
Bonus Material:
- Outtakes from 'History of Rush, Episodes 2 & 17'
- "Tom Sawyer" featuring the cast of 'History of Rush, Episode 17'
- "Need Some Love (Live at Laura Secord Secondary School, 1974)"
- "Anthem (Live in Passaic, 1976)"

DVD 8: *Clockwork Angels Tour* Dallas concert

DVD 9: *Clockwork Angels Tour* Special Features
- "Limelight (Soundcheck – Dallas, 2013)"
- "Middletown Dreams (Live in Phoenix, 2013)"
- "The Pass (Live in Phoenix, 2013)"
- "Manhattan Project (Live in Phoenix, 2013)"
- Can't Stop Thinking Big
- Behind The Scenes Featuring Jay Baruchel
- Outtakes
- Interview With Dwush
- Family Goy
- Family Sawyer
- The Watchmaker (Intermission Film)
- Office Of The Watchmaker (Closing Film)
Easter Egg: 'The Joke'

DVD 10: *R40 Bonus*
1974: Laura Secord Secondary School Performance [April 1974, St. Catharines, Ontario]:
- "Need Some Love"
- "Before And After"
- "Best I Can"
- "I've Been Runnin'"
- "Bad Boy" – a cover of the Larry Williams song
- "The Loser"
- "Working Man"
- "In The Mood (edited)"
1976: Capitol Theatre [December 10, 1976, Passaic, New Jersey]:
- "Bastille Day"
- "Anthem"
- "Lakeside Park"
- "2112"
- "Fly By Night / In The Mood"
1988: [*A Show Of Hands*]
- "Lock And Key (ASOH – R40 Version)"
1997: Molson Amphitheatre [June 30, 1997, Toronto, Ontario]:
- "Limelight"
- "Half The World"
- "Limbo"
- "Virtuality"
- "Nobody's Hero"
- "Test For Echo"
- "Leave That Thing Alone / Drum Solo"
- "2112"
2011: I Still Love You Man
2013: Rock And Roll Hall Of Fame Induction

Rush: Backstage Club & Best Buy *R40* DVD Editions
DVD 1: *Rock In Rio*
DVD 2: *Rock In Rio* Bonus Material
DVD 3: *R30 – 30th Anniversary World Tour* Frankfurt concert (edited)
DVD 4: *R30 – 30th Anniversary World Tour* DVD Extras
DVD 5: *Snakes & Arrows Live* Rotterdam concert set 1
Bonus Features
DVD 6: *Snakes & Arrows Live* Rotterdam concert set 2
Oh, Atlanta! The Authorized Bootlegs
DVD 7: *Time Machine 2011: Live In Cleveland* concert
Bonus Material
DVD 8: *Clockwork Angels Tour* Dallas concert
DVD 9: *Clockwork Angels Tour* Special Features
DVD 10: *R40 Bonus*

DVD 11: *R40 Completist* [Rush: Backstage Club & Best Buy DVD Exclusive disc]
R30 - 30th Anniversary World Tour [extra tracks]:
- "Bravado"
- "YYZ"
- "The Trees"
- "One Little Victory"
- "Secret Touch"
- "Red Sector A"
- "La Villa Strangiato"
- "By-Tor And The Snow Dog"

Anthem Vault:
- "Anthem" – Castle Session

Molson Amphitheatre, June 30, 1997, Toronto:
- "Animate"
- "Resist"
- "Natural Science"

R40 Blu-ray Edition
Blu-ray 1: *Rock In Rio*
Rio de Janeiro concert
The Boys In Brazil Documentary

Blu-ray 2: *R30 - 30th Anniversary World Tour* Frankfurt concert (complete)

Blu-ray 3: *Snakes & Arrows Live* Rotterdam concert
Bonus Features:
'What's That Smell'
2007 Tour Outtakes
'What's That Smell' Outtakes
"Far Cry (S&A Live – Alternative Cut)"
"The Way The Wind Blows (S&A Live – Alternative Cut)"
"Red Sector A (R30 – S&AL DVD Bonus Version)"
Oh, Atlanta! The Authorized Bootlegs
- "Ghost Of A Chance"
- "Red Barchetta"
- "The Trees"
- "2112: I: Overture / II: The Temples Of Syrinx"

Blu-ray 4: *Time Machine 2011: Live In Cleveland* concert
Bonus Material:
Outtakes from 'History of Rush, Episodes 2 & 17'
"Tom Sawyer" featuring the cast of 'History of Rush, Episode 17'
"Need Some Love (Live at Laura Secord Secondary School, 1974)"
"Anthem (Live in Passaic, 1976)"

Blu-ray 5: *Clockwork Angels Tour* Dallas concert
Special Features:
"Limelight (Soundcheck – Dallas, 2013)"
"Middletown Dreams (Live in Phoenix, 2013)"
"The Pass (Live in Phoenix, 2013)"
"Manhattan Project (Live in Phoenix, 2013)"
Can't Stop Thinking Big
Behind The Scenes Featuring Jay Baruchel
Outtakes
Interview With Dwush
Family Goy
Family Sawyer
The Watchmaker (Intermission Film)
Office Of The Watchmaker (Closing Film)
Easter Egg: 'The Joke'

Blu-ray 6: *R40 Bonus*
1974: Laura Secord Secondary School Performance [April 1974, St. Catharines, Ontario]:
- "Need Some Love"
- "Before And After"
- "Best I Can"
- "I've Been Runnin'"
- "Bad Boy" – a cover of the Larry Williams song

- "The Loser"
- "Working Man"
- "In The Mood (edited)"

1976: Capitol Theatre [December 10, 1976, Passaic, New Jersey]:
- "Bastille Day"
- "Anthem"
- "Lakeside Park"
- "2112"
- "Fly By Night / In The Mood"

1988: [A Show Of Hands]
"Lock And Key (ASOH – R40 Version)"

1997: Molson Amphitheatre [June 30, 1997, Toronto, Ontario]:
- "Limelight"
- "Half The World"
- "Limbo"
- "Virtuality"
- "Nobody's Hero"
- "Test For Echo"
- "Leave That Thing Alone / Drum Solo"
- "2112"

2011: I Still Love You Man
2013: Rock And Roll Hall Of Fame Induction

Rush: Backstage Club & Best Buy *R40* Blu-ray Editions
Blu-ray 1: *Rock In Rio*
Blu-ray 2: *R30 – 30th Anniversary World Tour* Frankfurt concert (complete)
Blu-ray 3: *Snakes & Arrows Live* Rotterdam concert
Bonus Features
Blu-ray 4: *Time Machine 2011: Live In Cleveland* concert
Bonus Material
Blu-ray 5: *Clockwork Angels Tour* Dallas concert
Special Features
Blu-ray 6: *R40 Bonus*

DVD: *R40 Completist* [Rush: Backstage Club & Best Buy Blu-ray Exclusive disc]
Interviews:
 August 24, 1979 Geddy Lee Interview at Ivor Wynne Stadium, Hamilton
 1980 Rush interview at Le Studio (incorrectly listed as 1981 Moving Pictures era)
 1990 Artist of the Decade interviews
 1994 Juno Awards CBC news report
 2002 Geddy Lee & Alex Lifeson Vapor Trails interview

The Anthem Vault:
 "Anthem" – Castle Sessions
 "Fly By Night" – Castle Sessions
 "Finding My Way (Mpeg 1)" – Don Kirshner's Rock Concert
 "In The Mood (Mpeg 1)" – Don Kirshner's Rock Concert
 "Circumstances (Live at the Hammersmith Odeon, 1979)"
 "La Villa Strangiato (Live at the Hammersmith Odeon, 1979)"
 "A Farewell To Kings" – Seneca College
 "Xanadu" – Seneca College
 "The Spirit Of Radio" – Soundcheck at Ivor Wynne Stadium, Hamilton
 "Freewill" - *Molson Canadian Rocks For Toronto* 2003
 "Closer To The Heart" - *Canada For Asia* 2005

Molson Amphitheatre, June 30, 1997, Toronto:
- "Animate"
- "Resist"
- "Natural Science"

Note: to summarize:
 Rush In Rio DVDs are identical to original 2003 release.
 Rush In Rio Blu-ray removes the MX multi-angles and Easter Eggs (though the "Anthem" Castle Session promo video is on the Backstage Club and Best Buy Editions).
 R30 – 30th Anniversary World Tour DVDs are identical to the original Deluxe Edition 2005 release (but you don't get the bonus CDs)
 R30 – 30th Anniversary World Tour Blu-ray is the complete concert, but no bonus material at all, same as the 2009 Blu-ray re-issue.
 Snakes & Arrows Live DVD and Blu-ray are both the same as their 2008 releases (meaning the *R30* version of "Red Sector A" appears on *R40* DVD boxed set here only, unless you have the Backstage Club and Best Buy

Edition, where you'll have it twice; if you have the *R40* Blu-ray boxed set, you'll have it twice, regardless, as its on the full *R30* Blu-ray disc and not the Backstage Club and Best Buy Edition *Completist* disc).

Time Machine 2011: Live In Cleveland DVDs and Blu-ray are both the same as their 2011 release, meaning you'll have "Anthem" from the Passaic, New Jersey, show twice, as it's part of the complete concert on the *R40 Bonus* disc.

Clockwork Angels Tour DVDs and Blu-ray are both the same as their 2013 releases.

R40 Bonus disc is identical between DVD and Blu-ray.

R40 Completist disc differs between DVD and Blu-ray:

> *R40 Completist* DVD Edition disc contains the leftover tracks from the *R30 - 30th Anniversary World Tour* concert, so you'll have the entire concert, just not all in one place.
>
> *R40 Completist* Blu-ray Edition disc contains the Interviews and Anthem Vault material missing from the *R30 - 30th Anniversary World Tour* Blu-ray.

Conclusion: The DVD and Blu-ray editions are nearly identical in content if you get the Backstage Club / Best Buy Editions. The Blu-ray Edition has the complete *R30* concert in one place, but loses entirely the *Rush In Rio* MX multi-angles and the "By-Tor And The Snow Dog" animation Easter Egg content. The DVD Edition has *everything*, but the *R30* concert is broken up between two discs. If you don't get either of the DVD or Blu-ray Backstage Club / Best Buy Editions (so no *R40 Completist* disc):

> DVD has all the *R30* Bonus Material (Interviews and Anthem Vault) and the *Rush In Rio* MX multi-angles and the "By-Tor And The Snow Dog" animation Easter Egg content, but not the complete *R30* concert itself.
>
> Blu-ray has the complete *R30* concert, but lacks the *R30* Bonus Material (Interviews and Anthem Vault) and the *Rush In Rio* MX multi-angles and the "By-Tor And The Snow Dog" animation Easter Egg content.

In an interview with *RollingStone.com* published on this date, **Geddy Lee** says the band is in discussion about the forthcoming tour and how to proceed.

(November 20)
ECW Press publishes Neil Peart's book *Far And Near: On Days Like These* worldwide.

R40 TOUR

2015

(January)
In preparation for the upcoming tour, **Alex Lifeson** begins a regimen of playing guitar more regularly, at Lerxst Sound, Toronto, Ontario, Canada.

(January 27)
Universal Music releases **Rush**'s album *Fly By Night* as part of the 12 Months of Rush.

Fly By Night (Direct Metal Mastering) LP
- contains "By-Tor And The Snow Dog (Extended Ending Version)"
    - Digit download card (320kbps MP4 vinyl ripped Digital Audio)

Fly By Night Digital Audio Edition
- DSD (2.8mHz), 192khz / 24-bit, 96kHz / 24-bit
- contains "By-Tor And The Snow Dog (Extended Ending Version)"

Fly By Night Pure Audio Blu-ray
- 5.1 surround sound version seems identical to the *Sectors 1* DVD

   "By-Tor And The Snow Dog (Extended Ending Version)" 9:32
   Written by Neil Peart (words), Geddy Lee & Alex Lifeson (music)
   Appears on: Fly By Night (Direct Metal Mastering) LP, *Fly By Night* Digital Audio Edition
   This track has had quite a release history. To recap, the original 1975 LP pressing employed the gimmick wherein the closing chimes ran into the run-out groove, allowing them to chime continuously until the listener lifted the needle from the vinyl. The label gives the track length as 8:57, but really it's as long as you leave the record playing. Then, the Archives and Mercury and Anthem re-issues did away with the run-out groove gimmick and the track ended at the appointed 8:57 mark. Then along comes the CD format and for whatever reason, the song is pared down to 8:37 and this is the version familiar to a lot of fans. 2015 rolls around and we're presented with this version, which when compared to photos of the album master tapes, suggests this is the complete, unedited recording, featuring 50 audible seconds of the chimes. So there you have it! This is the version you probably want to own in order to have the full experience of "By-Tor And The Snow Dog." The mastering sounds really good, it's full and clear. Highly Recommended.

(February 24)
Universal Music releases **Rush**'s album *Caress Of Steel* as part of the 12 Months of Rush.

Caress Of Steel (Direct Metal Mastering) LP
       - Digit download card (320kbps MP4 vinyl ripped Digital Audio)

Caress Of Steel Digital Audio Edition
- DSD (2.8mHz), 192khz / 24-bit, 96kHz / 24-bit

(March)
Rush begins band rehearsals for the *R40* tour (*Classic Rock* July, 2015).

(March 7)
Rush attends the Juno gala dinner and awards ceremony at the Hamilton Convention Centre, Hamilton, Ontario, Canada. There they receive the 2015 Allan Waters Humanitarian Award.

(March 17)
Universal Music releases **Rush**'s album *2112* and *All The World's A Stage* as part of the 12 Months of Rush.

2112 (Direct Metal Mastering) LP Hologram Edition
         - Digit download card (320kbps MP4 vinyl ripped Digital Audio)

2112 Digital Audio Edition
- DSD (2.8mHz), 192khz / 24-bit, 96kHz / 24-bit

All The World's A Stage (Direct Metal Mastering) LP
         - Digit download card (320kbps MP4 vinyl ripped Digital Audio)

All The World's A Stage Digital Audio Edition
- DSD (2.8mHz), 192khz / 24-bit, 96kHz / 24-bit

(April 21)
Universal Music releases *Rush*'s album *A Farewell To Kings* as part of the 12 Months of Rush.

A Farewell To Kings (Direct Metal Mastering) LP
       - Digit download card (320kbps MP4 vinyl ripped Digital Audio)

A Farewell To Kings Digital Audio Edition
- DSD (2.8mHz), 192khz / 24-bit, 96kHz / 24-bit

A Farewell To Kings Pure Audio Blu-ray
- 5.1 surround sound version seems identical to the *Sectors 2* DVD

(May 1)
MMCXII Books publishes Hugh Symes book *The Art Of Rush: Serving A Life Sentence*. **Neil Peart** writes the introduction. Three editions are released: Classic Edition, Special Edition (signed and numbered) and Roadcase Deluxe Limited Edition.

(May 8)
Rush performs live at BOK Center, Tulsa, Oklahoma, US.

(May 10)
Rush performs live at Pinnacle Bank Arena, Lincoln, Nebraska, US.

(May 12)
Rush performs live at Xcel Energy Center, St. Paul, Minnesota, US.

(May 14)
Rush performs live at Scottrade Center, St. Louis, Missouri, US.

(May 16)
Rush performs live at Austin360 Amphitheater, Austin, Texas, US.

(May 18)
Universal Music releases *Rush*'s album *Hemispheres* as part of the 12 Months of Rush.

Hemispheres (Direct Metal Mastering) LP
       - Digit download card (320kbps MP4 vinyl ripped Digital Audio)

Hemispheres Digital Audio Edition
- DSD (2.8mHz), 192khz / 24-bit, 96kHz / 24-bit

Rush performs live at American Airlines Center, Dallas, Texas, US.

(May 20)
Rush performs live at Toyota Center, Houston, Texas, US.

(May 22)
Rush performs live at Smoothie King Center, New Orleans, Louisiana, US.

(May 24)
Rush performs live at Amalie Arena, Tampa, Florida, US.

(May 26)
Rush performs live at Verizon Wireless Ampitheater, Atlanta, Georgia, US.

(May 28)
Rush performs live at Greensboro Coliseum, Greensboro, North Carolina, US.

(May 30)
Rush performs live at Jiffy Lube Live Amphitheater, Bristow, Virginia, US.

(June 8)
Rush performs live at Nationwide Arena. Columbus, Ohio, US.

(June 10)
Rush performs live at First Niagara Center, Buffalo, New York, US.

(June 12)
Rush performs live at United Center, Chicago, Illinois, US.

(June 14)
Rush performs live at The Palace, Auburn Hills, Michigan, US.

(June 16)
Universal Music releases ***Rush***'s album *Permanent Waves* as part of the 12 Months of Rush.

Permanent Waves (Direct Metal Mastering) LP
        - Digit download card (320kbps MP4 vinyl ripped Digital Audio)

Permanent Waves Digital Audio Edition
- DSD (2.8mHz), 192khz / 24-bit, 96kHz / 24-bit

(June 17 & 19)
Rush performs live at Air Canada Centre, Toronto, Ontario, Canada. Both concerts are recorded for a future *R40* concert film and live album release.

(June 21)
Rush performs live at Bell Centre, Montreal, Quebec, Canada.

(June 23)
Rush performs live at TD Garden, Boston, Massachusetts, US.

(June 25)
Rush performs live at Wells Fargo Center, Philadelphia, Pennsylvania, US.

(June 27)
Rush performs live at Prudential Center. Newark, New Jersey, US.

(June 29)
Rush performs live at Madison Square Garden, New York City, New York, US.

(July 9)
Rush performs live at Sprint Center, Kansas City, Missouri, US.

(July 11)
Rush performs live at Pepsi Center, Denver, Colorado, US.

(July 13)
Rush performs live at Maverik Center, Salt Lake City, Utah, US.

(July 15)
Rush performs live at Scotiabank Saddledome, Calgary, Alberta, Canada.

(July 17)
Rush performs live at Rogers Arena, Vancouver, British Columbia, Canada.

(July 19)
Rush performs live at Key Arena, Seattle, Washington, US.

(July 21)
Rush performs live at Moda Center, Portland, Oregon, US.

(July 23)
Rush performs live at SAP Center, San Jose, California, US.

(July 24)
Universal Music releases ***Rush***'s album *Moving Pictures* as part of the 12 Months of Rush.

Moving Pictures (Direct Metal Mastering) LP Boxed Set
        - Digit download card (320kbps MP4 vinyl ripped Digital Audio)
    - *Moving Pictures* T-shirt
        - note: both a Large and X-Large T-Shirt Boxed Set are released

Moving Pictures Digital Audio Edition
- DSD (2.8mHz), 192khz / 24-bit, 96kHz / 24-bit

(July 25)
Rush performs live at MGM Grand Garden Arena, Las Vegas, Nevada, US.

(July 27)
Rush performs live at US Airways Center, Phoenix, Arizona, US.

(July 30)
Rush performs live at Verizon Wireless Amphitheater, Irvine, California, US.

(August 1)
Rush performs live at The Forum, Los Angeles, California, US.

(September 15)
ECW Press publishes the Kevin J. Anderson and **Neil Peart** book *Clockwork Lives*. There are two editions: hardcover and, via the *Rush Backstage Club*, limited edition hardcover.

(September 25)
Universal Music releases *Rush*'s album *Exit...Stage Left* as part of the 12 Months of Rush.

Exit...Stage Left (Direct Metal Mastering) LP
       - Digit download card (320kbps MP4 vinyl ripped Digital Audio)

Exit...Stage Left Digital Audio Edition
- DSD (2.8mHz), 192khz / 24-bit, 96kHz / 24-bit

Many thanks to the following people:

Mom & Dad, for everything. Forever.
Tim, Mel, Emmet, Jill, Dave, Jack, Mark & Liv, and a special 'see you soon' to my future niece.
Tom (for introducing me to Rush's music) and Laura, Charlie & Jamie (part of my Bowmanville family).
Michael, Elyn & Willow, it's never too far a walk to your house.
Adam, Suzy & Grayson, someday we'll meet in person.
Ashley & Roger, general badassery.
Mary-Margaret, for coffee and hanging with me.
Perch Creek, for making me smile.

About The Author

Patrick Lemieux is a Canadian artist and writer who makes his home in Toronto, Ontario. He has exhibited his artwork in galleries and venues around North America. He is co-author of the book *The Queen Chronology*, author of *The Mike Oldfield Chronology* and *The Barenaked Ladies Chronology*, and author & illustrator of *Revenge Of The Dark Witch Of Oz: The Illustrated Screenplay* and *Play Of Light: The Art Of Patrick Lemieux*. You can follow him on Twitter @MadTheDJ and visit his blog: *http://madthedj.wordpress.com/*

Bibliography

Books:
Kurt Gooch, Jess Suhs, *KISS Alive Forever: The Complete Touring History* (Billboard Book, 2002)
Bill Banasiewiscz, *Rush: Visions (The Official Biography)* (Omnibus Press, 1988)
Martin Popoff, *Contents Under Pressure* (Voyageur Press, 2013)
Michael Barclay, Ian A.D. Jack, Jason Schneider, *Have Not Been The Same: CanRock Renaissance 1985-1995* (ECW Press, 2011)
Neil Peart, *The Masked Rider: Cycling In West Africa* (Pottersfield Press, 2003 Reprint)
Neil Peart, *Ghost Rider: Travels At The Healing Road* (ECW Press, 2002)
Neil Peart, *Travelling Music: The Soundtrack To My Life And Times* (ECW Press, 2004)
Neil Peart, *Roadshow: Landscape With Drums - A Concert Tour By Motorcycle* (Rounder, 2006)
Rush, tour books (Anthem Entertainment 1976 - 2015)
Patrick Lemieux, Adam Unger, *The Queen Chronology: The Recording And Release History Of The Band* (Across The Board Books, 2013)
Patrick Lemieux, *The Barenaked Ladies Chronology: The Recording And Release History Of The Band* (Across The Board Books, 2014)

Videos:
Rush: Exit...Stage Left (1981)
Rush: Through The Camera Eye (1985)
Rush: Grace Under Pressure Tour (1986)
Rush: A Show Of Hands (1988)
Rush: Chronicles (1990 & 2001)
Neil Peart: A Work In Progress (1997 & 2002)
Rush In Rio (2003)
Rush: R30 - 30th Anniversary World Tour (2005)
Neil Peart: Anatomy Of A Drum (2005)
Rush: Replay x3 (2006)
Rush: Snakes & Arrows MVI (2007)
Rush: Snakes & Arrows Live (2008)
Rush: Working Men (2009)
Neil Peart: Fire On Ice: The Making Of "The Hockey Theme" (2010)
Rush: Beyond The Lighted Stage (2010)
Classic Albums: Rush: 2112 & Moving Pictures (2010)
Rush: Time Machine 2011: Live In Cleveland (2011)
Neil Peart: Taking Centre Stage - A Lifetime Of Performance (2011)
Rush: Clockwork Angels Tour (2013)
Rush: R40 (2014)

Websites:
Setlist.fm
Rush.Wikia.com
RushTime.de
NeilPeart.net
991.com
Spotify
RollingStone.com
www.genvager.nu
MusicByMailCanada.com

Discogs.com
RushIsABand.com
By-Tor.com
2112.net
WowHD.co.uk
CBC.ca
Radio.com
ResistMusic.com

45Cat.com
RushChronicles.com
Nimitz.net
MaxWebster.ca
en.wikipedia.org
Music.cbc.ca
JunoAwards.ca
45Worlds.com

RushVault.com
TheRushForum.com
Cygnus-x1.net
Siddalls.com
YouTube.com
RaymondScott.com
CDBaby.com
Mofi.com

Copyright © 2015, Patrick Lemieux

Also From Patrick Lemieux and Across The Board Books™

THE QUEEN CHRONOLOGY
By Patrick Lemieux & Adam Unger

192 Pages
Non-Fiction
$24.99 US

The Queen Chronology is a comprehensive account of the studio recording and release history of Freddie Mercury, Brian May, John Deacon and Roger Taylor, who joined forces in 1971 as the classic line-up of the rock band Queen.

Years of extensive research have gone into the creation of the Chronology which covers the very beginnings of the band members' careers, their earliest songwriting efforts and recording sessions through the recording and releasing of Queen's 15 original studio albums with their classic line-up, to the present-day solo careers of Brian May and Roger Taylor.

Available at Lulu.com, Amazon and BarnesAndNoble.com

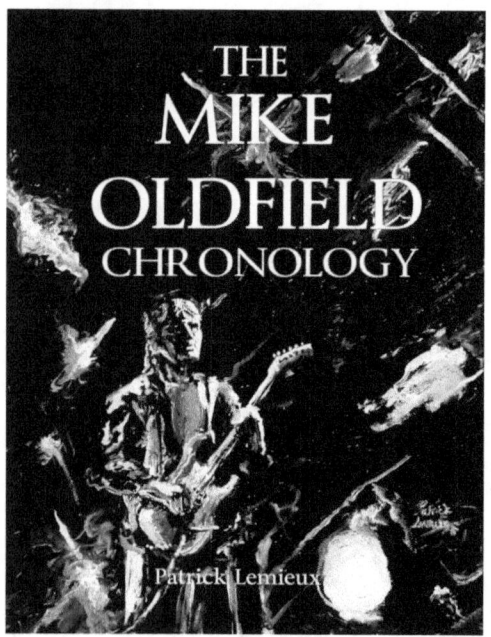

THE MIKE OLDFIELD CHRONOLOGY
By Patrick Lemieux

222 Pages
Non-Fiction
$24.99 US

The Mike Oldfield Chronology is a comprehensive look at the recording and release history of the man who, for over 40 years, has created some of the world's most innovative and groundbreaking music.

In 1973, Mike Oldfield released his debut album, *Tubular Bells*, which captured the world's imagination. The chart successes followed with such hit singles as "In Dulci Jubilo," "Portsmouth," "Guilty" and "Moonlight Shadow," and the albums *Hergest Ridge*, *Ommadawn*, *Five Miles Out* and *Crises*, to name only a few. In 2012, Oldfield rocked the world stage again at the Summer Olympic Games' Opening Ceremony in London and in 2014, released his 25th studio album, *Man On The Rocks*.

Available at Lulu.com, Amazon, BarnesAndNoble.com

THE BARENAKED LADIES CHRONOLOGY
By Patrick Lemieux

214 Pages
Non-Fiction
$24.99 US

The Barenaked Ladies Chronology is a comprehensive look at the recording and release history of Ed Robertson, Steven Page, Jim Creeggan, Andy Creeggan, Tyler Stewart and Kevin Hearn, the past and present members of a band which continues to captivate audience the world over after more than 20 years.

This Chronology covers every aspect of the band's recording careers both as Barenaked Ladies and beyond. It looks at the band's indie releases, studio and live albums, singles and collections. In 1991, the band released The Yellow Tapes, the first indie demo release to go platinum in Canada. This was followed by a string of hits from their albums, which include *Gordon*, *Rock Spectacle* and *Stunt*.

Available at Lulu.com, Amazon and BarnesAndNoble.com

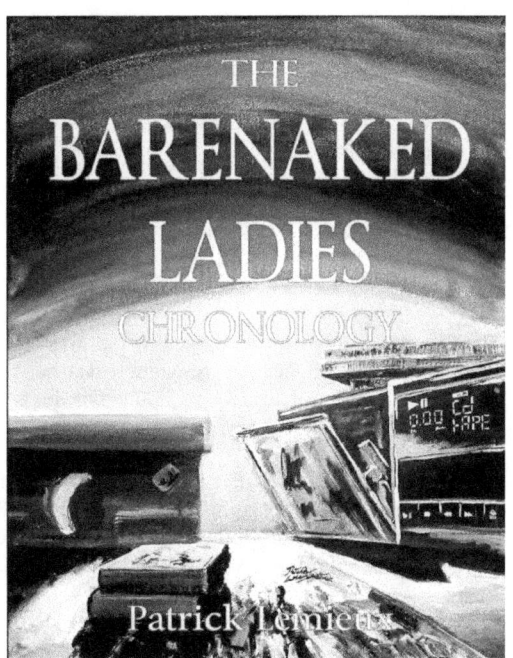

HORIZON LINE
Book One
By Patrick Lemieux

140 Pages
Black & Whte
Fiction
$19.99 US

At last, the first collected volume of the independent Canadian comic book series *Horizon Line*.

Two young lives are turned upside down as mysterious events unfold around them.

Secrets are reveal as a game of life and death plays out.

"The dominoes are starting to fall."

Available at Lulu.com, Amazon and BarnesAndNoble.com

REVENGE OF THE DARK WITCH OF OZ
The Illustrated Screenplay
By Patrick Lemieux

115 Pages
Fiction
$19.99 US

Dorothy Gale finds herself trapped in the mysterious land of Oz and her presence threatens to re-ignite a war between magic and machines. The secret to getting home lies in the lost City of Emerald Light.

Revenge Of The Dark Witch Of Oz is a science fiction/fantasy adaptation of L. Frank Baum's The Wonderful Wizard Of Oz. The tale is told in an illustrated screenplay format, complete with paintings, detailed images, sketches and storyboards.

Available at Lulu.com, Amazon and BarnesAndNoble.com

Play Of Light: The Art Of Patrick Lemieux
By Patrick Lemieux

100 Pages
Full Colour
Non-Fiction
$39.99 US

Journey through the theatre-inspired and story-driven work of Canadian artist and illustrator Patrick Lemieux. It is an exploration backstage, of the fantastical and of reality-based pieces, collected here for the first time, complete with notes, photos, sketches and paintings in full colour documenting his process.
Experience the play of light!

Available at Lulu.com, Amazon and BarnesAndNoble.com

www.ingramcontent.com/pod-product-compliance
Lightning Source LLC
Chambersburg PA
CBHW080546230426
43663CB00015B/2733